The Family & Change

CONSULTING EDITOR:

Charles H. Page

THE UNIVERSITY OF MASSACHUSETTS

The Family & Change

EDITED BY

John N. Edwards

THE UNIVERSITY OF KENTUCKY

ALFRED · A · KNOPF : NEW YORK

THIS IS A BORZOI BOOK
PUBLISHED BY ALFRED A. KNOPF, INC.

First Printing
Copyright © 1969 by Alfred A. Knopf, Inc.

All rights reserved under International and Pan-American Copyright Conventions. Published in the United States by Alfred A. Knopf, Inc., New York, and simultaneously in Canada by Random House of Canada Limited, Toronto. Distributed by Random House, Inc., New York.

Library of Congress Catalog Card Number: 69–11386

Manufactured in the United States of America

Preface

This book focuses on the family in a context of change. The reason for this focus is primarily twofold. Of the rather large number of texts on the family, comparatively few provide an extensive treatment of the changing character of this institution. As a consequence, the student sometimes obtains a static view of the family group. This volume is intended, therefore, to provide some balance to this predominant depiction by giving major consideration to the dynamic nature of this sociologically important unit. Second, the reader will note that throughout this volume there is a thread of concern with the theoretical implications of the included studies on familial change. Extant theories of change, on the whole, neither explain current alterations nor predict with any degree of specificity what may be expected in the future. If any attempts at social planning with respect to the family are to meet with even moderate success, they must be based on sound theory and sound, theoretically-derived research. To this end, I have pointed out some of the deficiencies in our present conceptualizations of the family and change and have suggested a few basic considerations for future theory construction. It is hoped that in so doing there will be an intensified interest taken in developing "good" theory pertaining to the family and change.

It almost goes without saying, I believe, that the origins and conception of a book are generally obscure and represent the culmination of many ideas, class discussions, and, not least, interaction with one's colleagues and friends. This being the case, there are many individual contributions to any book, and it becomes most difficult to trace and acknowledge each of their origins. There are, however, two individuals whose advice and constructive criticism have been most valuable and who have made significant suggestions in the course of completing this manuscript. Nicholas Babchuk, particularly, has offered sage advice throughout the duration of this project. From time to time, he also has given welcomed encouragement. Charles H. Page has contributed a number of quite sound and practically feasible suggestions about various parts of the book. However, I have not, I fear, always had the sagacity to accept their counsel in full. Any shortcomings in the manuscript are, as a result, peculiarly my own.

Of course my greatest debt of gratitude is due those scholars and their publishers who have permitted me to include their works. Obviously, without their contributions, this volume would have lacked the depth as well as the weight they provide.

Finally, I wish to acknowledge a contribution of another sort by dedicating this book to Jess and Mary, legatees and innovators of change in the family.

J.N.E.

Contents

Part II · Changes in Family Structure and Functions

The Family & Change

Introduction: An Overview of Familial Change

The Family in History

However else the twentieth century may be characterized in subsequent epochs, it will undoubtedly be identified as a period of accelerated social change. It is evident to professional observers of change and laymen alike that rapid flux in this century is pandemic and for many, a way of life. With the increased emphasis on planned change, it is particularly fitting that social scientists reexamine the family in the context of alteration. The often repeated but debatable assertion that the family is the "cornerstone of society" makes such an investigation even more paramount. It is also clearly evident that to date our theoretical knowledge of family change is incomplete and lacks codification. The family as an area of study has been dominated for centuries by philosophers, theologians, and, above all, ideologues who have fervently promoted pet notions of dubious validity. Social scientific interest in this historical context is comparatively recent, and one that has developed mainly since the 1930s.

But present societal conditions suggest an even more intensified interest than now exists, for at no other time in man's history has the ubiquity of change been so obvious or have alterations been as intensive and rapid. There are a sizable number of individuals living today who, in spite of their aging memories, can vividly recall the vanishing frontiers, the aftermath of the Civil War, the demise of horsedrawn transportation, and the mass exodus from rural areas. These same individuals are now witnessing the small but significant beginning of what may be one solution to a growing population—the exploration and perhaps eventual mass migration to outer space. All of these changes have had and will continue to have a dramatic impact on the family.

In longer perspective, however, alterations of various sorts have always been manifest in human society. Change is neither recent nor local. It is not too improbable that the second generation "family" of *Homo sapiens* was at least dimly aware of its differences with the first. Most certainly familial changes occupied the attention of such philosophers as Plato more than two thousand years ago. There is even evidence that a very major if not the first crisis in Occidental family life occurred immediately after the Peloponnesian War. Again, in 90 A.D., Plutarch remarked upon the severe decline in moral virtues that were considered an inextricable part of the good society and family life. In reading the works of still later philosophers and other writers, one is repeatedly struck by their concern with the effects of social change on the family.

Not until the nineteenth century was this concern shared by those with a more dispassionate and scientific view. Even then, most observers of the family were not valuefree or *wertfrei* in the broader meaning of the term. Their main interest lay in promulgating and promoting specific theories and particular points of view. In so doing, various kinds of evidence regarding alterations were readily accepted while other pertinent but contradictory data were rejected. Some students of behavior thus contended that the human family had historically changed from an essentially matrilineal institution to one that was patrilineal in character; other writers during this period, such as Sir Henry Maine, marshalled equally cogent and considerable evidence to support the idea that patriarchy existed in the earliest forms of the family.[1]

A similar controversy but with different protagonists raged with respect to the type of marriage found among the earliest families. Lewis Morgan and Friedrich Engels, for example, found evidence of the existence of group marriage.[2] Edward Westermarck, on the other hand, amassed and produced data which led him to conclude that primitive families were primarily monogamous in nature.[3] Regardless of their conclusions, one thing is certain: Familial change has been and continues to be an inextricable part of human history. Due to increasing structural differentiation, such alterations have become especially intensive in such industrialized societies as the United States.

The Changing American Family

Change in familial relationships is a basic sociological datum. But to speak of the changing American family as if it were a uniform entity (or any family system, for that matter) can be somewhat misleading. Even in the earliest historical moments of American society, the cultural base of its population was diverse and varied.[4] Except for the first English immigrant family that found a strange, indigenous population, the families in the South, in Manhattan, and in New England in general differed considerably from one another. Each family, as a culture-bearing group, imported the beliefs, attitudes, and behavior patterns of its native society. Transplanted on American shores, these patterns eventually were intermixed and commingled but left their distinctive marks on family composition and relationships.

Within the matrix of a predominantly Christian heritage and the quest for equalitarian individualism, in certain regions there existed a ban on clergy involvement in marriage and a strong patriarchy. The Puritan ethos, still embodied in some of our current sexual mores, was unevenly embraced, and in some areas, as in the South, it was almost nonexistent. Women, especially those who became the wives of plantation owners, were held in high esteem; at the same time, their roles were usually subordinate, though varying considerably in their content from one geographical region to another. Coinciding with the escape from oppression and search for individualism, there flourished the southern feudal manor with its aristocratic spirit and denial of individual rights. Still later, on the frontier, just as in Puritan New England, premarital sex was not unknown. It was more than an isolated case in which a man and woman lived together and had several children before the nuptial rites were performed. Unlike the situation in the East, marriages on the isolated, sparsely populated frontier could not be arranged by the family of orientation. Even within given regions, such as the South, sharp contrasts in the family existed. The white southern family, approximating the middle-class ideal of the family today, resided alongside a Negro system lacking the husband-father role, a position eliminated through the trading and selling of male slaves and widespread illegitimacy.

Despite the diversity that comprised family life in historical America, one of the more significant changes has been the assimilation of various and quite different cultural heritages. Yet, even today, a certain obscurity and vagueness result in applying the term "American family" to those that comprise our population. Differences in social class, racial, ethnic, and religious background are manifest, each influencing family composition and role relationships to some degree. Still, in one sense, the concept is appropriate, for in this diversity there is a unity that belies heterogenous origins.

In discussing changes in the family, moreover, it is sometimes desirable (though as indicated above, somewhat limiting in certain cases), to speak of an all-inclusive entity lacking in distinctive characteristics. Frequently, this is not only desirable but necessary in order to comprehend the enormity and complexity of societal alterations, because, patently, there are large numbers of factors influencing change in any social group. That some of these factors may be difficult to separate from others and their impact difficult to measure makes the task even more complicated. In addition, positing the concept of the American family points up the fact that the differential characteristics among families are relative rather than absolute differences. This suggests that while it may ultimately be desirable to make generalizations about the variations in families, there are sufficient generic qualities that exist which allow us to discuss the American family as a whole and as a changing institution.

As in other areas in the study of the family, social scientists interested in change traditionally have concentrated their efforts on the pragmatic aspects of the subject. Throughout the early decades of this century, family sociologists in particular voiced their concern over the increase in divorce rates, the release of women from the boundaries of the home, the decline in births, and the presumed potential for increased illegitimacy. Each of these factors was interpreted by most as an indication of family "individuation," a trend that was perceived as threatening to the solidarity and continued existence of the family in the United States. Especially during the depression years and those following World War II, many writers forecast the ultimate disintegration of the American family. In 1941, for instance, Pitirim Sorokin stated: "As it has become more and more contractual, the family of the last few decades has grown ever more unstable, until it has reached the point of actual disintegration." [5] Other writers pointed to the radical shift or loss of family functions, a phenomenon widely interpreted as a trend toward the decline of family groups.[6] Calmer assessments such as that by Ernest Burgess,[7] who lauded the lack of rigidity in the family and saw the changes in family relations as a closer approximation of democratic ideals, were somewhat less heralded even though they represented the majority view.

Although there was increased empirical emphasis during this era, the major focus and impact of many of these studies was their emotional appeal, promoted by the writer's personal insight and his ability to evoke a response. Subsequent empirical investigations often failed to support the arguments set forth by these writers. However, their sharp focus on individuation and the adjustment of the individual continues to influence and guide the direction of research in the field. A sizable proportion of current research still reflects a pragmatic interest in its focus on the individual and the adjustment of individual family members. Along with other factors, this practical and applied focus has had a decided effect on the effort to develop theories of familial change.

The Modern Study of Familial Change

A great many of the analyses of change, including those in this volume, view the family as the dependent variable in the context of altering relationships. Comparatively little attention, on the other hand, has been given to the consideration of the family as an agent of change. In conceptualizing change in the former manner, many social scientists, particularly sociologists, have sought the antecedent or precipitating factors that contribute to the changing structure and functions of the familial group. The search for contributing or causative factors, therefore, has centered on such external sources as the processes of industrialization and urbanization.

Still other analyses, perhaps fewer in number, take a less macroscopic view of the changing family in concentrating on the immediate sources of alterations, for example, type of occupation. Viewed overall, many of these sources are actually operational definitions of more global factors (for instance, social differentiation) or intervening variables in the chain of cause-and-effect relationships.

As illustrated in Table 1, these two types of analyses merely begin at different points. But they also generally differ in the resulting levels of analysis; one is fairly abstract and global, and the other is more specific and microscopic.

TABLE 1

Typical Conceptualizations of Change and the Family

SOURCES OF CHANGE	INTERVENING STRUCTURES	UNITS OF CHANGE
Industrialization	Occupational types	Number of family members
Urbanization	Place of residence	Role relationships
Social value orientations and norms	Size of residence	Familial functions and types
Differentiation and expansion of other institutional functions	System of stratification	Extent and types of kinship ties

Each type largely ignores the influence of the family and the reciprocal effect it may have on other social relationships or even on those
which are seen as changing the family. Most studies of change, in
other words, are limited to an analysis of a unidirectional process.

Sometimes the emphasis on unidirectionality has been an outgrowth
of the analyst's theoretical orientation. The evolutionary approach to
change is an outstanding example of this. Especially prevalent during
the nineteenth century, this approach was promulgated by what Ralph
Linton referred to as "calm ethnocentrism." [8] Nineteenth-century Europeans in particular assumed that their own social orders and institutions represented the apex of social development. In view of their
monogamous marital institutions and preoccupation with sexual matters, it was an easy but erroneous jump to order monogamy, polygyny,
polyandry, and group marriage (including the attendant sexual promiscuity) in a descending series on the evolutionary scale. Their fallacy
stemmed from the assumption that institutions with widely differing
characteristics, separated in space, constituted different stages in the
evolutionary spiral, some equivalent to a "primitive" state and others
to a more "civilized" nature. With the dawn of the twentieth century,
increased recognition of the interdependent nature of behavioral and
cultural items and the questioning of previously held assumptions
marked the demise of this theory's additional elaboration.

However, as sociological interest in social change has expanded recently, discussions of evolutionary theory have been renewed.[9] But
the clearest expression of this interpretation as it pertains to the study
of the family today emerges from the optimistic overtones of the
majority of analyses concerning familial change. Only in rare instances
is the evolutionary approach embraced in a consistent and explicit
manner.

Another theoretical approach positing the unidirectionality of change
is the Marxist framework. In the extreme Marxist conception (not
espoused by Marx himself), social institutions such as the family are
almost totally dependent on economic relationships. Any alterations
in the economy therefore affect the family with little or no reciprocal
effects on the evolution of economic relationships. On this basis,
Engels contended that monogamy, as a marriage form and foundation for family formation, far from being the highest form as suggested by evolutionary theorists, represented the victory of private
property over economic collectivism.[10] Group marriage and polyg-
ynous arrangements, conversely, were the results of "natural" communism, and any change in the direction of monogamous mating was

to be viewed with extreme pessimism. From Engels' point of view, the principal impact of the monogamous family institution was to promulgate various social ills—prostitution, female subjugation, and the indissolubility of marriage.

Although the focus on a single direction of alterations sometimes stems from an analyst's theoretical stance, it is more commonly a consequence of the necessity to marshal data in an orderly and succinct manner. It is not so much that reciprocity between units of change is unrecognized but that the complexity of the phenomena imposes severe limitations on any given analysis. Even those adopting the institutional approach to change, while recognizing numerous variations, deal mainly with the affects of other institutions on the family.[11] Yet it appears that this emphasis on unidirectionality stands as one of the most singular deficiencies in the social-scientific endeavor to understand sequential change. It is only of late, as certain of the articles included here point out, that a greater effort has been made to specify reciprocal interchanges. But if the study of familial change is to be more fruitful in the formation of precise hypotheses than formerly, an increased focus on exchanges between social systems will be imperative.

The modern study of the family and change is at a crossroad of development. With the cries of woe concerning family changes from the beginnings of recorded history to the passioned polemics of the nineteenth-century social philosophers, it is indeed remarkable that the analysis of change has advanced to this juncture. With this dubious history of observation and thought, social scientists have encountered numerous difficulties in applying the same objectivity to familial change as that employed in other areas of investigation.

Still, far more remains in the development of adequate methodological and theoretical tools for this study. The revised interest in comparative and longitudinal research along with the continued search for interrelated empirical laws can only be interpreted as optimistic signs of fruition. In actuality, the attempt to understand familial change other than for itself is quite strategic. The family, from a sociological point of view, occupies a central position in any social structure, even if one cannot agree that it is the "cornerstone of society." Regardless of its specific structure and varying functions in different societies, the family is everywhere an empirical reality. Some maintain, furthermore, that a form of family structure is requisite to the persistence of societies themselves.[12]

Without provisions for the maintenance of cognitive and affective interaction between adults and infants such as that found in families, stable adults could not be produced on a large enough scale to insure the ongoing operation of societies. It follows, therefore, that a basic knowledge of the dynamics of change as it affects and emanates from the family is essential to an understanding of societal change in general.

The Family and Change

This collection of readings presents a sampling of works that deal specifically with family change. The focus on change is intended to acquaint the student of the family with this often neglected but crucial area of study. For the general student of social change, the articles contained in this volume offer a representative cross section of the literature pertaining to familial alterations. As such, the materials included can serve as the basis for a case study in a specific area of social behavior and change.

Strictly speaking, the desired end of developing general propositions about the family and change necessitates comparative analysis, drawing on comparable research of family systems in several cultures. For instance, to test fully the relationship between modernization and the emergence of a conjugal family structure, it is imperative to examine the process of modernization in various societies. In this way, intervening and historically unique conditions may be controlled and accounted for.

Due to limitations of space and availability of comparable, cross-cultural materials, the articles and excerpts presented here focus almost exclusively on the American family. Uppermost is the fact that the bulk of sociological research pertaining to social change and familial alterations is not comparative in design. However, at various points throughout the book, we shall make reference to selected comparative cases which the serious student will wish to pursue. The bibliography at the end of the collection provides several additional references to material on the changing family in other societies.

While the focus on the American case imposes certain restrictions, as indicated above, it does permit a more intensive and thorough investigation of change relationships. Specifically, this approach allows us the opportunity to examine in greater detail some of the presumed causes of change, the types of alterations occurring, and some of the issues regarding future short-term changes. In adopting this focus, we are also able to analyze at greater length some of the theoretical implications for the study of the family in modern industrialized society, implications that pertain to change in other such societies. It is, then, only for the sake of brevity that the term "the family" is used, even when the reference is solely to the American family.

The volume is comprised of four parts. The first part of the collection is concerned with the impact of industrialization and urbanization on the modern family. Most of the studies contained in this section directly assess the evidence regarding familial isolation in urban society and evaluate the roles that industrialization and urbanization play as sources of change. Part II explores in more specific detail the structure and functions of the modern family and points up some of the far-ranging ramifications of social change as it impinges upon family members. The third part of the volume is addressed to the family of the future. Specific predictions as well as general forecasts that suggest the range of possibilities and probabilities for further alterations are set forth. Each of these sections is thus designed to offer an answer to one of the following questions: (1) What are the antecedent factors or causes of changes in the family? (2) What changes, if any, are occurring? and (3) What sort of alterations in the family are likely to take place in the near future? At this point in the study of the changing family, the answers to these important questions are only tentative, partial, and, in many instances, subject to debate. However, in raising these questions and presenting some evidence and views pertinent to them, it is hoped that an intensified interest will be taken in providing fuller and more complete replies. The fourth and final part of the volume is devoted to a consideration of some of the theoretical aspects of future analyses. Inasmuch as our predictions and prognoses of alterations are only as sound as their theoretical bases, several suggestions are made with a view toward improving current conceptualizations of familial change.

NOTES

1. Sir Henry Maine's position is set forth in his *Ancient Law* (3rd ed.; New York: Holt, 1885). For two early proponents of the theory of original matriarchate, see J. J. Bachofen, *Das Mutterrecht* (Stuttgart: Basel B. Schwabe, 1897); and J. F. McLennan, *Studies in Ancient History* (New York: The Macmillan Company, 1896).
2. Lewis Morgan, *Ancient Society* (New York: Holt, 1878); Friedrich Engels, *The Origin of the Family, Private Property, and the State* (Chicago: Kerr, 1902).

3. Edward Westermarck, *The History of Human Marriage* (5th ed.; London: Macmillan Ltd., 1921).
4. An excellent history of the family in America is contained in Arthur W. Calhoun, *A Social History of the American Family* (3 vols.; Glendale, California: Arthur H. Clark Co., 1917).
5. Pitirim Sorokin, *The Crisis of Our Age* (New York: Dutton, 1941), p. 187.
6. William F. Ogburn, "The Changing Family," *The Family*, 19 (1938), pp. 139–143.
7. Ernest Burgess, "The Family in a Changing Society," *American Journal of Sociology*, 53 (May 1948), pp. 417–422.
8. Ralph Linton, "The Natural History of the Family," in Ruth N. Anshen (ed.), *The Family: Its Function and Destiny* (New York: Harper, 1959), pp. 30–52.
9. For example, see Talcott Parsons *et al.* (eds.), *Theories of Society* (New York: Free Press, 1961), Vol. I, pp. 239–264; Kenneth E. Bock "Evolution, Function, and Change," *American Sociological Review*, 28 (April 1963), pp. 229–237; Herbert R. Barringer, George I. Blanksten, and Raymond W. Mack, *Social Change in Developing Areas: A Reinterpretation of Evolutionary Theory?* (Cambridge, Mass.: Schenkman, 1966).
10. Engels, *op. cit.*
11. Representative of the institutional approach emphasizing unidirectionality is William F. Ogburn, *Social Change* (New York: Viking Press, 1922).
12. One proponent of this structural-functional view is Marion J. Levy, Jr. See his "Aspects of the Analysis of Family Structure," in Anley J. Coale, *et al.* (eds.), *Aspects of the Analysis of Family Structure* (Princeton: Princeton University Press, 1965), pp. 1–63.

~~~~~~

PART I

Industrialization, Urbanization, & the Family

Introduction

A macroscopic approach to the study of change has been frequently employed by those interested in the family institution. In adopting such an approach to change, considerable attention has been focused on the search for highly abstract and powerful explanatory variables. Two such variables that have wide currency in discussions of familial alterations are industrialization and urbanization. Each of these variables, it should be noted, encompasses a wide range of phenomena. The term "industrialization," for instance, points to a mode of technology, a form of organization—a factory system, a type of economy —and frequently it implies a particular kind of relationship between work and worker. Similarly, the concept urbanization includes a diversity of more concrete social processes such as a direction of population movement and a reordering of institutional interchanges. In other contexts, it may refer to a shift in attitudes and values or a movement toward a specific type of solidarity and societal integration.

Regardless of the particular referents of these concepts, they have

generally been conceived as being related and co-occurring forces. Industrialization is often thought of as an antecedent to the process of
urbanization, with the two being concomitant forces once industrialization is underway. The family, as it has been studied in the context
of social change, is the dependent variable. The processes of industrialization and urbanization are viewed as stimulants to alterations in familial structures and functions. Some sociologists, reflecting this generally
accepted point of view, suggest that with increasing industrialization
family structure is altered from a consanguineous type to an essentially
conjugal form.[1] The stem family constitutes an intermediate and
transitional type between these polar extremes of family structure.

In essence, this now classical position contends that the extended
family, with its emphases on ascription, particularism, and diffuseness,
places undue restraint on the mobile labor force demanded by an
industrialized economy and interferes with efficient functioning.[2] Consequently, family structure accommodates to meet the requisites of a
changing status order. In concrete terms, this means that family size
decreases, youth are accorded considerable freedom and provided
access to facilities relevant to their advancement, and little allegiance
to any extended unit is asked. The industrialized economy, furthermore,
demands the services of only specific family members. Again, as a
matter of accommodation, the family loses or relinquishes many of its
former functions. Both in terms of structure and function the family
under the impetus of industrialization and urbanization is comparatively small, has fewer functions, and is relatively isolated. It is, in
short, a stripped-down model.

Recently, this view of the relationship between industrialization,
urbanization, and family type has been severely challenged. In the
first selection, William J. Goode presents a general discussion of the
congruity between an industrialized economy and the conjugal family.
He notes that there is a "fit" between this type of economy and family
system, but it cannot be presumed there is a natural "harmony" between the two. He illustrates, for instance, how family fertility and
familial roles are related, sometimes to the detriment of the society as
a whole. Goode also points out that a family system at times may
facilitate the change toward industrialization, that is, the family may
act as an independent variable in social change. By contrasting the
family systems in China and Japan and their attempts to industrialize,
it is shown how the patterns of inheritance, the importance of the
family in social mobility, and other family characteristics are related
to subsequent success or failure in this attempt.

Continuing this line of investigation, Sidney M. Greenfield argues in the second selection that, when examined cross culturally, an urban–industrial revolution may take place without a small nuclear unit developing as a result. Examining the work of other scholars as well as presenting evidence from his own study of Barbados, Greenfield advances the hypothesis that the small nuclear family, as the predominant type of family structure, even exists without the presence of urbanization and industrialization. With respect to the United States, he concludes that the nuclear family was brought by the earliest settlers and was present prior to the industrial revolution and the beginning of mass migration to urban areas.

Frank F. Furstenberg (selection 3) presents further evidence that the small nuclear family existed in the United States before the industrial revolution, evidence that was largely overlooked by earlier writers who posited a cause-effect relationship between industrialization and the nuclear family structure. Drawing on the accounts of European travelers, Furstenberg points up some remarkable similarities between the family of a century ago and the family of today. In particular, the system of mate selection, the marital relationship, and parent-child relationships are all shown to be quite similar. Many family strains and tensions commonly thought to result from the industrial revolution are evident in the preindustrial family and may have facilitated adaptation to the coming industrial society.

As various social scientists prior to 1950 perceived the situation, urbanization had a similar affect on the family in that it necessitated a decline in extended kin ties. Individual family members, in response to the demand for a mobile labor force brought about by industrialization, left the extended kin group for urban areas. With crowded urban conditions and the necessity for a mobility orientation, the larger family could no longer remain intact, and large numbers of children, who formerly were considered economic assets, were no longer desired. What resulted was a small unit, caught in a sea of urban anonymity and taking part in only minimal interaction with consanguinal kin.

This position too has been, in review, stringently criticized. Eugene Litwak (selection 4) presents data which show that a high proportion of geographically mobile individuals do have extended ties, although to what extent these ties are maintained is undetermined. He suggests that rather than acting as a barrier to mobility in modern industrialized society, the extended family may actually encourage geographical separation. The family structure that results is what Litwak terms a "modified extended family," a group of nuclear families bonded by affectional relations.

Focusing on intracommunity relations and the affect of varying degrees of urbanization, Scott Greer's study (selection 5) points to differentials in the general social participation of low-urban and high-urban residents. In each area within the urban community, the most important type of interaction is kin visitation. The findings indicate that, overall, the urban family is far from isolated and a high degree of urbanization may, in actuality, reinforce familial ties.

Selections 6 and 7, by Wendell Bell and by E. Gartly Jaco and Ivan Belknap, respectively, supply evidence pertaining to the relationship between suburbanization and family structure. In these studies, suburbanization is interpreted, although in different manners and on the basis of differing findings, as an attempted "quest for community." It is noted in each case that the suburban movement has modified the functions of the family. More specifically, these selections show that the families in suburban and fringe areas place greater emphasis on economic, educational, recreational, and religious functions—all historical and presumably lost functions of the American family. Although the data contained in these two selections do not directly contradict the classical view of the urban family, they do allow one to infer that the impact of urbanization has been overestimated, if not grossly exaggerated.

Directly testing the relationship of rural-urban residence to familial isolation, W. H. Key's study (selection 8) presents data on intra- and extrafamilial interaction in communities of varying sizes. Ranging from rural dwellers to residents of metropolitan areas, no consistent relationship is found in the importance accorded to interaction with either immediate or extended kin by the individuals residing in such different sized communities. It is suggested that the difficulty of the urban dweller in initiating primary contacts and the spatial isolation of some rural residents account for the high interaction rates with family members.

In selection 9, Marvin B. Sussman and Lee Burchinal present a general review of the theory and research concerning kin networks. They conclude that older theories, postulating the predominance of the nuclear structure in urban society, were selectively derived from research on immigrant groups. This led to the erroneous assumption regarding familial isolation and, subsequently, obfuscated the observation of multiple interchanges among kin. Their review indicates that frequent exchanges of aid and service, particularly among middle-class families, constitute the normal pattern of family networks rather than the exception.

In the final article in this part, Alfred M. Mirande reevaluates the positions on the isolated nuclear family in urban society and, on the basis of new findings, suggests some important qualifications to the current debate regarding the extent of kin ties. Noting the difficulty in directly testing the isolated nuclear family hypothesis without cross-cultural data, it is shown, nonetheless, that upwardly mobile families are more isolated from extended kin. Kin isolation, conversely, apparently is not related to downward social mobility, as proponents of the hypothesis maintain. Moreover, the evidence indicates sharp differences between the sexes in the extent of kinship ties, a finding consonant with the social-emotional and instrumental character, respectively, of female and male roles. Females in this study's sample are consistently more involved in extended family relations, and their interaction is less affected by the disruptive influences of social mobility. For women, household tasks and children help to engender generational continuity and continued kin relations even when their husbands are socially mobile. Finally, the data suggest that, consistent with the isolated family view, middle-class families are more detached from extended ties, but they are also ideologically less family oriented.

The articles included in Part I strongly indicate a need for revision in our theories pertaining to the relationship between industrialization, urbanization, and the family. While our views of the family as an isolated nuclear unit are largely a product of deductive reasoning, the empirical and mainly inductive works presented here point to the deficiencies of this approach. They firmly suggest as untenable the notion that industrialization and urbanization are necessary conditions for the emergence of the conjugal family. Limited evidence, on the contrary, supports the hypothesis that a nuclear family structure is a precondition to the development of the industrialization and urbanization processes. But there is not yet sufficient substantiation to settle the issue with any degree of finality. What appears certain is that industrialization and urbanization are sometimes sufficient conditions for altering family structure, but they are not necessary ones, and the precise nature of their relationship remains obscure and of greater complexity than most studies of familial change indicate.

In some measure, the debate about this crucial relationship stems from a problem of conceptualization. On one level, it is a matter of parcelling out the critical dimensions of the highly complex and multi-faceted variables of industrialization and urbanization. Particularly with respect to the term "industrialization," there seems to be little consensus as to its specific referent. Various theorists and researchers employ it in various ways, but, most frequently, its reference is left unspecified. A second problem of conceptualization concerns a confusion and misinterpretation of family structure as it has been discussed by proponents of various positions. The exponents of the isolated nuclear family interpretation have based their analyses on deductive principles and have given little attention to pertinent empirical works. In so doing, their level of analysis has focused on *ideal* rather than *actual* patterns of family relationships. Much of the debate, as a consequence, has been carried on at two quite distinct though not necessarily contradictory levels. When viewed in a cross-cultural and historical perspective, the American family is relatively small, isolated, and conjugal in form; viewed atemporally and without reference to other family systems, the American family maintains fairly extensive kin relations even in highly urbanized environments.

There is increasing evidence that to some degree most societies are undergoing the process of industrialization. For some societies the process is embryonic and slow while for others it is extremely rapid. Regardless of the particular rate experienced, it appears that a concomitant development is a movement toward some variant of the nuclear family system.[3] Even in the formerly highly traditionalist society of Japan, it has been noted, a predominant conjugal pattern is rapidly developing.[4] But as with the American case, the observation of the co-occurrence of industrialization and the emergence of the conjugal pattern does not take us far in understanding the relationship between the two, for, basically, any change relationship existing between the two patterns is likely to be sequential. Our observations, on the other hand, are largely correlational and indicate no direction of cause and effect.

It seems most reasonable to conclude at this point in the study of familial change that industrialization, urbanization, and the family are independent factors which frequently interact. The mode in which they interact is by no means simple; it suggests that the direction of causality may vary from one society to the next and from one time to the next in any given society. Clearly, it can no longer be maintained that the isolated nuclear family invariably emerges under the impetus of industrialization and urbanization.

NOTES

1. Ernest W. Burgess and Harvey J. Locke, *The Family* (New York: American Book, 1945).
2. Talcott Parsons, "The Social Structure of the Family," in Ruth N. An-

shen (ed.), *The Family: Its Function and Destiny* (New York: Harper, 1959), pp. 241–271. See also Hyman Rodman, "Talcott Parsons' View of the Changing American Family," in Hyman Rodman (ed.), *Marriage, Family and Society* (New York: Random House, 1965), pp. 262–286.
3. William J. Goode, *World Revolution and Family Patterns* (New York: Free Press, 1963).
4. Ronald P. Dore, *City Life in Japan* (Berkeley: University of California Press, 1958).

1

Changes in Family Patterns

by William J. Goode

Industrialization and the Family

Family research in the post-World War II period has documented one gross empirical regularity whose processes are not yet clearly understood—that in all parts of the world and for the first time in world history all social systems are moving fast or slowly toward some form of the conjugal family system and also toward industrialization. In agreement with the intuition of social analysts for over a century is the finding that with industrialization the traditional family systems—usually, extended or joint family systems, with or without lineages or clans—are breaking down. On the other hand, since each system begins from a somewhat different base point, the direction of change in any given family pattern may be different. The divorce rate has been dropping for half a century in Japan, and for a shorter period in certain Arab countries (e.g., Algeria), but has been rising in Western countries. The age at marriage has been dropping in most Western countries, but rising in India, the Arab countries, and (among women) in sub-Sahara Africa, yet all are moving toward some form of the conjugal system.

. . . Under the industrial system, the individual is supposed to be

Reprinted from William J. Goode, *The Family* (Englewood Cliffs, N.J.: Prentice-Hall, Inc., 1964), pp. 108–117, by permission of the author and publisher. © 1964.

hired because of his competence, and in promotion the same standards are to be applied to all who hold the same job (i.e., the standards are achievement-based and universalistic). His relationship to the job is also functionally specific—i.e., his role obligations are confined to getting the task done. Put another way, the extended family system, with its standards of ascription, particularism, and diffuseness, is ideally not permitted to interfere with the efficient functioning of a modern enterprise.[1]

Because of its emphasis on performance, such a system requires that a person be permitted to rise or fall, and to move about wherever the job market is best. A lesser emphasis on land ownership also increases the ease of mobility. The conjugal family system is neolocal (each couple sets up its own household), and its kinship network is not strong, thus putting fewer barriers than other family systems in the way of class or geographical mobility.

In these ways the conjugal family system "fits" the needs of industrialism. But the relationship may also be put another way. Since increasingly an industrializing society—consider, for example, the Arab countries, or India—creates formal agencies to handle the major tasks of any kinship groupings larger than the nuclear family, such units as lineages, clans, or even large extended families also lose their functions and thereby the *allegiance* they once commanded. Thus individual families go their own way, ignoring such extended kinship ties.

More important, elders no longer control the major new economic or political opportunities, so that family authority slips from the hands of such family leaders. The young groom can obtain his bride price on his own, and need not concern himself about the good will of his elders. The couple need not obey any one outside their family unit, since only their performance on the job is relevant for their advancement. They need not even rely on family elders for job instruction, since schools, the factory, or the plantation or mine will teach them the new skills. Nor do they even need to continue working on the land, still in the possession of the elders, since the jobs and political opportunities are in the city. Thus industrialization is likely to undermine gradually the traditional systems of family control and exchange. The terms of the role-bargaining between the generations have been altered.

. . . When Western societies underwent industrialization, the new opportunities remained in the hands of middle- or upper-class families who owned these new enterprises. Thus their bargaining power might be reduced under the new system, but not so much as that of lower-class families. By contrast, upper-strata native families in newly conquered regions, were apt to lose *more* than families toward the lower strata. Thus, after the initial period of conquest, the indigenous tribal leaders were removed in the New World. The Spanish and Portuguese rulers took all the important positions and opportunities. Native rulers lost control over their families and their political authority collapsed. Most often, however, the European empire builders have tried to rule *through* the tribal leaders, yielding few chances for economic or political advancement to the young natives, *independent* of their elders. Thus, these leaders would not lose control over their sons. On the other hand, as a larger percentage of the tribe or society is drawn into the new economic enterprises and is hired and promoted on its own merits, the leaders of large kinship groupings do lose their ability to elicit obedience to traditional family customs.

The conjugal emphasis on emotionality within the family also serves somewhat the needs of industrialism. At lower job levels, the worker experiences little intrinsic job satisfaction; at higher levels, he obtains more job satisfaction, but is also subject to rather great demands. At any level, the enterprise has no responsibility for the emotional input-output balance of the individual; this is solely the responsibility of the family, in the sense that there is nowhere else to go for it. The small family, then, deals with a problem which the industrial system cannot handle.

The "Fit" Between Industrialism and the Conjugal Family

Nevertheless, we cannot, in analyzing the interaction of the great social forces making for family change, presume some sort of natural "harmony" between the modern complex of industrialism and the conjugal family system. Both are unplanned resultants of individual desires and initiatives. Both are systems of forces, each with its own needs, and at various points either may fail to serve the needs of the other. To place everyone in his job solely on the basis of merit, for example, would require the destruction of the family system entirely. On the other hand, without a family unit to deal with the idiosyncrasies of aged parents, the emotional needs of adults, or the insecurities of children, very likely not enough adequately functioning people would be produced to man the industrial system.

This is another way of reasserting a central notion . . . that family and industrial factors or variables are *independent* but interacting. Neither fully determines the other, although both influence each other. Consequently, we cannot assume, in looking for patterns of family change, that industrial forces shape everything (unless we *define* them as including everything) to their measure. The very *resistance* of family systems to such pressures indicates their independence as a set of forces, even if the massive political and economic changes ultimately outweigh that resistance.

Since we have analyzed some of the ways in which family systems have altered to serve the needs of industrialization, we should also consider briefly how an industrial system fails to handle some of the problems created by this change toward a conjugal family system. Thereafter, we shall discuss two other types of relationships of social change (1) the resistance of family patterns to change, and (2) how a family system may facilitate industrialization.

The neolocal, independent household and its accompanying values in favor of separate lives for each couple leave the old parents in an ambiguous position. Some elements in this situation we commented on earlier—e.g., the sudden displacement of the older male from his job, the lack of land as a basis for social status, the relative unimportance of wisdom as compared with specialized technical knowledge, and the inability of the old to control the economic or social opportunities offered to young adults. In 1962 there were about 17 million people in the United States aged 65 years and over, about 9 per cent of the population, and this segment will increase in size in the future. Every study of their situation shows that they need help, although there is disagreement over where the help should come from. People no longer accept without question an obligation to care for the old, especially in a common household.

Similarly, the obligation to rear orphan children of relatives is not so definite as in the past. Modern society has, of course, invented various procedures for locating and evaluating both foster and step-parents for such children, as well as continuing until recently the older system of orphanages; but the action of the state does not fully substitute for the active kinship system of a primitive society.

In a parallel way . . . the modern conjugal system does not adequately deal with the structural disruptions caused by divorce.

Modern industrialism has offered women more economic freedom, but has not relieved them of their household tasks. Labor-saving devices merely raise the standards of cleanliness and general performance, permitting more work to be turned out, but do not reduce the hours of work. The primary status of women in all societies is that of housekeeper and mother, so that in spite of higher levels of technical training, women have not developed a commensurately high level of career-mindedness over the past half-century in Western countries. Indeed, toward the higher social strata, where more women are better educated, a lower percentage of women are in the labor force, but apparently a *higher* percentage would like to be. The modern egalitarianism within the family means that the man's energies are somewhat diverted into helping at household tasks, away from his job demands.

Industrialization and Fertility

An especially complex and important set of relations in family change may be found in worldwide efforts to reduce the birth rate in nations undergoing industrialization. In all but the highly industrialized societies, fertility is accorded high priority, but the ranks of the living are depleted by death. A high mortality rate, especially among its young people, is a heavy economic burden for a society to bear: The society invests physical maintenance for a time, but they do not live long enough to repay it. The industrial society, by contrast, develops the scientific knowledge necessary to reduce mortality, which increases further its productive efficiency.[2]

From the earliest period of socialization in most societies, the child is told that eventually he will marry and produce children. Usually, the full privileges of adulthood are not conceded until the individual has produced children. Great effort is expended to inculcate fertility values in everyone. This extensive cultural apparatus, designed to make fertility very much a part of the individual's personality needs, is in sharp contrast to the relative lack of cultural emphasis on an individual's taking care of his own life and avoiding death. Death is an intimately personal affair, and apparently human beings need very little special socialization to try to avoid it. The obligation of producing other persons, to whom we shall owe extensive and burdensome obligations, requires considerable social reinforcement.

This emphasis is necessary for the survival of the less industrialized, high mortality societies. The adjustive controls in the social structure —abortion or infanticide—come *after* conception. This relative emphasis insures quick replacement if the population is sharply reduced by war, epidemics, or famine. It would not be possible suddenly to

institute a set of high fertility values as an adjustment, since this kind
of socialization would take a generation to have any important effect.
On the other hand, to the extent that everyone in the society strongly
favors fertility, and has a set of personality needs that are satisfied
only by high fertility, it is difficult for a society quickly to take up
some contraceptive pattern when mortality is suddenly reduced and
the population begins to grow faster than the increase in productive
capacity. In several countries since World War II, the death rate has
been reduced by 25 to 50 per cent within the span of 2 or 3 years,
but with no reduction in the birth rate.

The interaction of these factors creates a special problem for the
modern era—the world's population explosion. Most societies can now
be classified as either high growth societies, or high potential growth
societies. That is, either their birth rate is already much higher than
their death rate, or their birth rate is high and their death rate is in
the process of being reduced by modern scientific techniques.

This situation arises, as noted, from the difference between the kinds
of actions needed for decreasing mortality rates, as against those required to reduce birth rates. To reduce mortality rates, the leaders of
a society require no more than a modicum of cooperation from the
bulk of the population. A clean water supply can be introduced, or a
more effective sewerage system, without a vote or without any individual decisions by those effected. Pesticides can almost wipe out
one of man's great killers, malaria, without much help on the part of
individuals. To lower mortality to the rates found in industrial societies
does of course require learning new habits. However, very great reductions in mortality can take place without much cooperation. In any
event, cooperation seems not to be difficult to obtain, since people
can be readily convinced that modern medicine and science can save
their lives, and this is a goal desired by all.

To lower the birth rate, on the other hand, requires a change in a
family pattern, an alteration in *individual* goals. Conception is an
intimately personal matter, not a mass phenomenon.

Since the socialization of all individuals has emphasized the importance of fertility, the attempt to lower birth rates requires an important shift in the attitudes, habits, and values of individuals relative
to their family roles. Indeed the situation raises the recurrent sociological question, How much can family custom be changed by conscious plan? The use of contraception is costly, and requires much
discipline. In addition, although modern religious leaders in Japan,
Islam, and India have gradually come to assert that their doctrines
do not specifically prohibit the use of contraception, in fact until

recently the main thrust of most great religious systems had been against the use of contraception, whether in Western nations, India, or China. In India a son was required to perform certain rituals upon his father's death, else the father would not be able to assume a new form in a subsequent life. The Chinese emphasis upon the unbroken link between ancestors and the living again urged a relatively high fertility. Until the 1950's the religious leaders of Islam claimed that Islamic doctrine was against the use of contraception. On the other hand, population control was relatively easily introduced in Japan, where family limitation had been common for generations.

In our own society, where the birth rate presently is well over one-third higher than that of Japan, we pity those who have not had children. Women who have had an involuntary abortion often suffer from a feeling of inadequacy if this was their first conception. Those who cannot have children often feel driven to adopt one.

Sex Roles and Fertility

Sex roles also affect fertility and the possibility of reducing it. At the present time, research projects are under way in every major nation of the world in an effort to ascertain the detailed factors which lead to conception, and these projects have been especially aimed at un-covering the variables which produce a high birth rate in less indus-trialized countries where a high rate of reproduction increases the population faster than the economic productive capacity increases. Let us look at a particular case, that of Puerto Rico.

Puerto Rico illustrates two points of some consequence here. One is that high fertility in the population at large is not any individual's particular *motivation*. Those who have many children had no special desire to keep the birth rate up or to lower it. Second, the motivations that do induce a large number of children continue to be inculcated long after the point in history when high fertility might be useful to the society.

The Puerto Rican family typically "spoils" its male children, as judged by Western standards. The appropriate relation between a husband and his wife is not one in which the man exhibits tenderness or expresses his true inner feelings to the woman, or exposes his personal weaknesses and needs. Instead he must play the role of being dominant, powerful, and *macho* (masculine). Although achievement of an intellectual or occupational character becomes increasingly im-portant, these cannot substitute at all for the male qualities of violence, courage, and virility, especially at lower-class levels where intellectual or occupational achievement is unlikely anyway. The young male's early sex experiences are likely to be with a prostitute, since young girls are guarded rather carefully. These factors mean that there is always a communication and role barrier between husband and wife, which prevent either from really understanding each other, especially with respect to sex and contraception.

Machismo is a quality which must be proved continually. The man may not rest on his laurels. In the sexual area this means that he must be sexually able, and in the reproductive area that he must continue to produce children to prove his masculinity. This is especially necessary, since so many men have little opportunity of rising in the occupational sphere. Here again is one area where the male can continue to be dominant and powerful. The woman, by contrast, can prove her maternal qualities by producing as few as one child or two. The evidence of her womanly role behavior remains as the children continue to grow. As a consequence, then, men usually oppose contraceptives, even when having children may be financially ruinous. He views their use as a discipline that he does not wish to submit to, as ego-destructive. Notice that this set of factors is not specifically Roman Catholic in origin, although of course the Church does oppose contraceptives. In fact, there is considerable anti-clericalism in Puerto Rican society. In one study of fertility in Puerto Rico,[3] a higher percentage of men than of women wanted any given number of children above the number of two. The same relationship held when the respondents were asked what was the ideal number of children their daughters should have. This attitude extends to other areas as well. For example, 28 per cent of the men, but 46 per cent of the women, approved of women working.

One interesting result in this particular case is that since men do not bother about contraceptives and indeed oppose them, women seek to learn how to prevent babies, and most utilize techniques that do not depend on the man's desire or discipline. Since most of the factors in the family structure of Puerto Rico press toward early sexual relations and conception, women have increasingly turned to sterilization as one possible solution.

The evidence from many studies in different parts of the world parallels that in Puerto Rico in at least one particular, that women are much less inclined to have a large number of children than men are, and that above a certain number of children (the number varying with the society) a majority of women actually are in favor of using some type of birth control. Typically, as in our own country, the lower classes are less inclined to utilize contraceptives. Notice that even in our own country, men have far less mistrust of the contraceptives they use than women do.

It must be emphasized, however, that we are far from understanding the psychological and social factors which change the social definition of the appropriate size of family. The complexity of this problem became evident after World War II. Prior to that time in the industrial Western countries there had been a steady long term decline in fertility. The assumption of demographers was that this pattern would continue after World War II, though it was anticipated that immediately after the war there would be the usual rise in the birth rate. When hostilities ceased, as is well known, the birth rate did rise, but remained high in many countries. In most, by now, the birth rate has dropped again. It has already begun to drop somewhat in the United States, but meanwhile the absolute rate remains high (about 22 births per 1,000 population each year) and it is much higher than in most other Western countries.

Research now going on in all class levels seeks to uncover the social and cultural factors that maintain so high a rate. A simple economic interpretation of such family changes will not suffice. In general, fertility rates rise in Western nations as we descend the social scale, but within each class division, those with more income will be somewhat more fertile. Moreover, if a simple economic interpretation were applicable, then few or no parents would have many children, since under modern circumstances they never represent a profit. Viewed in purely economic terms, children are a burden.

On the other hand, one element of the economic interpretation appears to apply, since no nation seems to have a *low* infant mortality rate for long without moving toward a low birth rate. That is to say, when nearly all infants have a long life expectancy, the family adjusts to this fact by having fewer children. Present efforts in every major industrializing country to lower infant mortality and to introduce contraceptives will presumably succeed, over the next generation, in altering this resistant family pattern.

Effect of the Family on Industrialization

Let us now consider another relationship between family factors and social change, the possibility that the family system may have an independent, facilitating effect on the modern shift toward industrialization. No full-scale research into this hypothesis has been carried out, but a few suggestive facts may be noted here. Negatively, of course, many observers have pointed out that extended and joint family systems prevented a free utilization of talent as well as the easy introduction of innovations against the power and traditionalism of family elders. Positively, it should be kept in mind that the family systems of the West have been different from those of other major civilizations for over a thousand years. Child or early adolescent marriage was not the ideal or the statistically usual. There was no ancestor worship, and *individuals,* not families, were responsible for crimes. There was no lineage or clan system, and the eldest male was not necessarily the leader of the family. Young couples were expected to live independently, for the most part.

Moreover, these differences were accentuated when the individualistic, anti-traditional ideology of ascetic Protestantism began to spread. The Puritans in the U.S., for example, defined husband and wife as loving companions rather than simply part of a family network, and their children had more freedom of marital choice than was possible in the traditional European family systems. Divorce became possible, even though disapproved. It seems likely by the time the new factory jobs opened in the late eighteenth century in England that the family system of at least part of the population was in some harmony with its new demands. Their extended kinship ties and obligations, and their links with family land, did not interfere with the new type of work obligations.

A more striking instance of the importance of family patterns in facilitating or hindering social change may be found in the contrast between the success of Japan and China in their attempt to industrialize during the late nineteenth and early twentieth centuries.[4]

Both were opened to the West at about the same time, and both faced a somewhat similar set of problems: threat of conquest, an agrarian economy, a rapid growth of population, extensive bureaucracies that had become corrupt and inefficient, an emphasis on familism not individualism, strains between town and country, and the low prestige of merchants, who would have to assume important roles in any modernizing process.

As against China's essential failure to cope with its problems, within about half a century after 1868 Japan had established heavy industries with almost no outside capital, altered its system of distribution, made both male and female literacy almost universal, and introduced a new set of social relationships, characteristic of the Western market system.

Several differences between the Japanese and Chinese family systems contributed to their varying successes in coping with the problems of industrialization. One was the pattern of inheritance. Under the Chinese family system, all sons inherited equally, so that family capital could not usually be kept intact. In Japan one son (usually the oldest) inherited all the property. Thus wealth could be accumulated, and one person could more easily make a decision to invest it.

Perhaps the most important family differences lay in the relationship between family and state. In China the personal loyalty was owed to the Emperor, but not if it conflicted with family loyalty. A man owed his first duty to his father, and through him to clan elders. Being unfilial was the greatest of Chinese sins. Of course, the Japanese man owed loyalty to his father, but the system was *feudalistic* rather than familistic: An unbroken chain of fealty linked each individual through his father and his father's leader or lord, through successively higher ranks to the great princes and the Emperor. Orders from above were backed by family pressure. The radical alterations which the Meiji leaders tried to implement called for much sacrifice—for example, former warriors might be put to work, or used as policemen—but the links of fealty between family and family, and family and state, remained strong.

The Chinese regarded nepotism as a duty. A man could not reject his family if he improved his station in life, and he was expected to carry upward with him as many members as he could. In Japan social mobility was more difficult. Ideally, in contrast to China, people should remain in their places. However, *adoption* was one important mode of social ascent in Japan. A father might even disinherit a son in order to adopt a talented young man. However, the individual so chosen rose alone. He became part of the new family, and was no longer a member of his old family. Both in fact and predisposition this pattern favored innovations under the Meiji leaders: (1) the Japanese were somewhat less handicapped by nepotism, (2) those who rose did not need to help the undeserving members of his family of birth, and (3) men could seek out talented young men for placement in positions of opportunity.

One long-term family process also lowered the capacity of the Chinese to meet the problems of the new era. Since both in fact and ideal the Chinese system permitted social mobility, but accorded the merchant a lowly social rank, a common mobility path was to acquire wealth through commerce, but then to leave that occupation. The gentry were landowners and scholars. Those who acquired wealth sought to achieve prestige and power by becoming members of the gentry or training their sons to become members. The humanistic learning of the mandarins was essentially irrelevant to the problems of the modern era. Thus there was no steady accumulation of a technical and financial tradition by the successful families. By contrast, the Japanese merchant was confined to a narrower type of mobility: financial success. He had little chance of moving out of commerce and into high social ranks. But as a consequence, Japanese merchants and banking families had developed a considerable technical knowledge and tradition and were much better prepared to cope with the complex financial problems that accompanied the rapid industrialization of Japan during the Meiji period.

It must be emphasized that these cases are extremely complex, and family variables cannot be said to be the prime creators of the dramatic contrast. Nevertheless, it seems clear that they did make an important contribution to the striking differences in the industrial achievement of the two countries.

The importance of the family as a unit in the social mobility system, and thus as a facilitating element in social change, may also be seen in another major historical event, the French Revolution. Some bourgeois families had moved into the nobility in the seventeenth and eighteenth centuries, as they had moved into the gentry in China, by acquiring wealth and beginning to live in the style of the upper stratum. This included humanistic education, or at least the support of arts and letters, fine manners, taste in clothing and furniture, and, of course, abandoning the commercial or manufacturing activities of the bourgeoisie. Those who aspired upward had to concede the superiority of the nobles, else there was no reason to move upward; but by definition, to be noble was to have been born noble. The successful bourgeois was caught in an ideological dilemma. It must be emphasized that his aim was not simply to associate with the nobility in government, or to make advantageous deals with those in power. It was rather to move his *family* and thus his family line into the nobility.

When the nobility began, over the course of the eighteenth century, to close gradually the various routes by which some bourgeois families might achieve a validation of noble status, this high stratum began to withdraw its support of the system as a whole, and instead began to view the nobility as a shackle or barrier to national progress, a violation of tenets of freedom. Moreover, the bourgeoisie furnished much of the leadership of the French Revolution in 1789.

A Concluding Comment

. . . Throughout [this selection] allusions have been made to many relations between family variables and other social variables—divorce rates, class differentials, industrialization, the distribution of authority within the family, or the breakdown of organized descent groupings. In many of these discussions, our focus was primarily on how and why these changes were taking place. However, to analyze how and why such changes occur, we must know the causal factors that cause any determinate relations. With reference to each of these patterns, only proximate and immediate forces were suggested as causes, primarily those which change the bargaining relationship between people in different social positions (e.g., how upper-class families control their youngsters more effectively than do lower-class families).

Such causal relationships, or correlations, are far from stating determinate *sequences* of change, but they are the foundation for establishing such sequences. In any event, whether we seek such determinate changes, or simpler correlations, we meet the same difficulties in theory and method. To be avoided are all theories that turn out to be only unifactorial hypotheses, suggesting that all change and all causal relations flow from some single, global factor, such as race, environment, technology, or industrialism. In the past these seemed plausible only because analysts who proposed them usually included within such global variables almost everything that needed to be explained.

Nevertheless, even such global theories have some utility, since they have as one of their aims the destruction of prior theories, and thus must muster some empirical data to support this aim. The accumulation of data helps us, then, to construct more adequate explanations. We need the facts, because our experience is narrowly confined to only a few families, and we have been taught many "facts" that were not correct. Only a few years ago, it was generally agreed, for example, that toward the upper social strata the divorce rate rose; and that divorce was more likely to lead to juvenile delinquency than was any other solution to marital difficulties.

All societies develop myths about their present family systems, as well as about the past. The "adolescent rebellion" turns out to be a most modest assault on adult values, when the data are examined. Most Americans did not once live in large, rambling houses that sheltered a numerous extended family. Most Americans lived in one-room dwellings, with perhaps a cooking lean-to attached. The finer houses were more likely to survive to the present, for reasons that are obvious. We cannot assume that modern family morals are really worse than the golden past, if we read details of individual lives in, say, the eighteenth century, in Sweden, France, Italy, or England.

The steady testing of hypotheses about how family behavior is shaped will, then, help us to develop a clear conception about both the present and the past. Perhaps we shall learn thereby much more about the reciprocal relations between family patterns and the traits of the larger society. Granted that industrialization affects the position of the wife, it seems also likely that the family system may itself affect many other social processes. For example, considerable evidence is accumulating that the socialization experiences of the boy within the family—based in turn on the structure of authority within it—may powerfully affect his later motivation to achieve, and thus the patterns of social mobility in the larger society. How family systems at different social levels utilize the economic system may shape political debate, by permitting or hindering upward mobility and thereby increasing or decreasing satisfaction with the opportunity structure.

Nevertheless, our aim in scientific work is to ascertain determinate relations, to understand the direction of causal influence, to comprehend the social process. It is not so important to prove that societal variables shape family variables, or the reverse. What is significant is to locate the prime causal relations, whatever the major variables turn out to be. The accumulation of new research data, often correcting past opinion or guess, has been progressing rapidly over the past decade. The challenge of the immediate future is both to ascertain the facts more accurately, and to develop more adequate theories to account for them.

NOTES

1. For a more extended analysis of this problem, see William J. Goode, *World Revolution and Family Patterns* (New York: The Free Press of Glencoe, 1963), Chap. I.
2. An especially good analysis of these relations may be found in Kingsley Davis and Judith Blake, "Social Structure and Fertility," *Economic Development and Social Change* (April 1956), 211–235.
3. Paul K. Hatt, *Backgrounds of Human Fertility in Puerto Rico* (Princeton: Princeton University Press, 1952).
4. Marion J. Levy, "Contrasting Factors in the Modernization of China and Japan," in Simon S. Kuznets, Wilbert E. Moore, and Joseph J. Spengler (eds.), *Economic Growth: Brazil, India, Japan* (Durham, N.C.: Duke University Press, 1955).

2

Industrialization and the Family in Sociological Theory[1]

by Sidney M. Greenfield

I

The small nuclear family found in western Europe and the United States is generally viewed in sociological theory as a consequence of the urban-industrial revolution. The present paper questions the hypothesis and suggests alternative lines of thinking.

As Western society continues to disseminate its distinctive technology to the remainder of the world, both theoretical and practical consideration must be given to the changes in social organization that accompany the introduction of the machine and the market-exchange economic system. The specific task of the sociologist and cultural anthropologist here is to seek empirically founded generalizations about cultural process, causality, and functional interdependence. For policymakers and administrators in foreign affairs and international relations have been applying ill-founded generalizations uncritically: they reason that, if certain types of social organization and urban-industrial technology and the market-exchange economic system are interrelated, they must inevitably accompany Western technology, and as a consequence, they support action programs designed to establish and foster these forms.

The dominant sociological hypothesis relating technology and social organization postulates a functional interdependence between industrialization and urbanization, the techno-economic system, with the small nuclear family as the unit of social organization. Hypotheses of functional interdependence, however, take several forms, each with different implications. As Nagel has pointed out, statements phrased in functional terms are the equivalent of those phrased in non-functional

Reprinted from the *American Journal of Sociology,* 67 (November 1961), pp. 312–322, by permission of the author and The University of Chicago Press. Copyright © 1961, by The University of Chicago Press.

terms and any statement in one terminology can be translated into the other: "The difference between a functional and a nonfunctional formulation," he states, "is one of selective emphasis; it is quite comparable to the difference between saying that B is the effect of A, and saying that A is the condition (or cause) of B."[2]

There are, however, two contrasting ways of conceptualizing sociocultural phenomena that result in significantly different meanings for statements of functional relationships. In one formulation the functional statements have approximately the same meaning as conventional causal statements while, in the other, a special type of causal implication is rendered. The most widely adopted formulation of functionalism found in social science is based upon the organic analogy. Sociocultural systems are likened to living organisms in being goal-directed, self-righting systems in which all of the parts "function" to maintain the whole in a state of equilibrium. As phrased by Radcliffe-Brown:

> The concept of function involves the notion of a *structure* consisting of a *set of relations* amongst *unit entities,* the continuity of the structure being maintained by a *life process* made up of the *activities* of the constituent units.
>
> Such a view implies that a social system (the total structure of a society together with the totality of social usages in which the structure appears and on which it depends for its continued existence) has a certain kind of unity, which we may speak of as functional unity. We may define it as a condition in which all parts of the social system work together with a sufficient degree of harmony or internal consistency, i.e., without producing persistent conflicts which can neither be resolved nor regulated.[3]

Maintenance of the state of equilibrium, then, is likened to the continuance of life in the organism; the destruction of the equilibrium is analogous to death. The system is closed, and change in the total configuration is ruled out by the basic assumptions. The state of equilibrium is based upon the efficient integration of all of the parts, each of which functions to maintain the continuing existence of the whole. As long as the system continues, then, each part is necessarily functional and its relationship vis-à-vis any other part is one of functional interdependence—all of the parts operating to achieve the goal or purpose of the whole: maintenance of the state of equilibrium. Given this self-maintaining system, we can say that both parts and whole are functionally interrelated and interdependent. By varying our perspective, however, we may view each as a functional consequence of the other, that is, any part is a functional consequence of the operation of the total system, or the whole is a functional consequence of the operation of all the parts.

In the terminology of cause and effect there may also be two perspectives: Starting from the parts, we may say that they are the cause of the whole, which is the effect of their activity, since they maintain the totality in a given state. On the other hand, however, the whole is also the cause of the parts, since the latter operate in accord with the pattern of the former, thereby becoming its effect. In this formulation, however, no causal statements can be made about relations among the parts themselves; that is, one part cannot be the cause of any other since all, taken cumulatively, are either the cause of, or are caused by, the whole. The only relationship that can exist among the parts of a self-regulating, functionally integrated, equilibrium system is that of functional interdependence.[4]

The alternative formulation of functional theory in social science modifies the assumption of equilibrium and discards the organic analogy. To those who hold this position, the empirical evidence suggests the conclusion that sociocultural systems are never in a state of complete equilibrium. They are always changing and, consequently, equilibrium is a state relative to a given period of time and, at best, only approximated. In the long run, all sociocultural systems appear to be in continuous flux and both the parts and the whole can and do change. Adherents of this opinion, then, do not generally conceptualize sociocultural systems as self-regulating and goal-directed; consequently, the specialized set of functional statements used to analyze self-regulating systems are not necessary. Functional statements in this formulation are thus the direct equivalent of causal statements, and a causal relationship is implied whether the terms "functional consequence" or "functional interdependence" are used. The term "functional consequence," however, may be read as necessary and sufficient cause while "functional interdependence" is the equivalent of sufficient cause alone.

In accord with this view the possible relationships between part and whole and part and part differ from those possible in the prior formulation. Since equilibrium is not assumed, the cause of the total system being maintained in its given state is not the functioning of the parts, nor is the cause of the operations of the units taken to be the achievement of the goal of the whole. Here the total system tends to be viewed as resulting from a process of change and adjustment among the parts. Thus, one part can and does, as the interpretation is made, exert a causal effect on the other parts and by implication on the whole. It is only after the parts have had their effect on the other units that the parts may be thought of as being functionally inter-related—the term being taken to mean operating in a state of harmony with each other for a given time. So conceptualized, the locus of the causal nexus is the part-part relationship rather than the part-whole relationship, as is the case in the alternative formulation.

II

Many students in both Europe and the United States have studied the historical conditions that have produced the distinctive modern form of the family. We select Ogburn and Nimkoff because they present the generally accepted point of view. They distinguish three basic types—the consanguineous, the stem, and the conjugal family in that temporal order. "The consanguine family and the clan," they state, "tended to break up in the course of time. . . . The family [then] took on the pattern found in historical Europe and colonial America. The consanguine family tended to disappear, especially in the western world, and the conjugal family became the predominant type." The stem family is seen as a transitional form. "With increasing industrial-ization," however, it "tends to be superseded by the conjugal family." [5]

For the United States, the base line used in the study of the family is the nineteenth century and the focal type is the rural farm family.

The American family is not a European institution transplanted to a new environment and slightly changed by this transferring. In-stead it represents an original development which so reconstructed the contributions of European culture as to bring forth a family type in its characteristics clearly distinctive from the original Eu-ropean institution.[6]

The industrial revolution, starting in the nineteenth and going into the twentieth century, is seen as the force that changed the farm family and is basically responsible for the "modern American family." Indus-trialization had several immediate consequences:

Industrial organization eventually outgrew the family. The trend was in this direction as the inventions used in handicrafts manufac-ture multiplied and the use of windmills increased. But with cheaper iron and steel, and the use of streams as a source of power applied to tools, more space was needed and more workers were required than were to be found in the household. The steam boiler was too big for the home and the power generator required more space for the machine. The factory instead of the homestead became the unit of production. The factory was too large to be manned by even a very large family.[7]

Thus, the adoption of the machine resulted in sweeping changes in social organization: factories needed laborers who could be more readily obtained in cities than on farms; urbanism and industrialization worked hand in hand to change the structure of American society; industry needed laborers and the cities grew to provide them.

In addition to ecological and demographic changes, there were significant structural-functional changes in the social system, primary among them being the expansion of the industrial factory system to assume most of the tasks formerly handled by the isolated farm family. At first, industry was only a new techno-economic system transforming methods of production. But along with the new technology there developed a set of social relations with its own specific principles of organization and stratification, and its own way of patterning interaction between individuals, into which rural people were assimilated as they moved into the cities to work.[8] One aspect of all this was the small nuclear family with its distinctive form and means of social articulation.

The argument here is concerned with social and cultural change, and a state of equilibrium is therefore not assumed. In fact, it precludes the existence of a self-regulating system since the family is being analyzed in terms of change occurring in it, in the total system, and in the other parts of the system. In formal terms the argument is that the small nuclear family found in the United States takes its present form because of the national industrialization and urbanization. Within a system in a state of change then, one part is the cause of the new form taken by another part.

Once the change is completed, however, and all of the causal factors achieve their effects, a new equilibrium in the total system is commonly assumed. For the present scholars tend to view the small nuclear family as being in a state of functional interdependence with industry and the other parts of what may be loosely called the American form of Western civilization. The family now is functional in that it operates to maintain the new equilibrium.

In Europe, the the best example of this line of thinking is presented by Max Weber who, in his *General Economic History*, for example, states the reasons for viewing the changes in the family as a function of its changing economic position that, in turn, is a function of the changes in the total society that stemmed from the industrial revolution. The concluding paragraph of Part I of the book summarizes a part of the argument:

> With the dissolution of the manors and of the remains of the earlier agrarian communism through consolidation, separation, etc., private property in land has been completely established. In the meantime, in the course of the centuries, the organization of society has changed in the direction described above, the household community shrinking, until now the father with his wife and children functions as the unit in property relations. Formerly, this was simply impossible for physical reasons. The household has at the same time undergone an extensive internal transformation, and this in two ways; its function has become restricted to the fields of consumption, and its management placed on an accounting basis. To an increasing extent, the development of inheritance law in place of the original complete communism has led to a separation between the property of the men and the women, with a separate accounting. This two-fold transformation was bound up with the development of industry and trade.[9]

A fuller reading of this and his other works completes the presentation which, though more scholarly and sophisticated, is the same in theory as is argued in the United States. Though Weber seems to imply functional interdependence of the small family and industrialization, the conceptual formulation he uses in explaining the changes in the family is the one in which parts in a dynamic system may be construed to have a causal impact on other parts. It is only after industrialization is accomplished and the new whole is created that he postulates an equilibrium in which the causal nexus is between part and whole and the parts are only interdependent.

III

In a recent paper Erwin H. Johnson questioned the hypothesis that the small nuclear family is caused by industrialization and urbanization. After examining the data from modern Japan, he concludes that the stable stem family, which is at least four hundred years old there, "is sufficiently generalized in its nature to conform to the needs of the changing technology of Japan." He then goes on to say that the traditional family, in fact, had not and "does not have to give way under . . . urban or industrial influences." [10]

Modern Japan, then, provides us with a case of both urbanization and industrialization with a family other than the small nuclear form. Garigue reports extensive kinship networks among urbanized, industrialized French-Canadians in Montreal. These extended networks of "urban French-Canadian kinship," he writes, "are no new development, but seem to have been in existence since the period of New France." He concludes:

> The collected evidence indicates no trend toward transformation of the present French-Canadian urban kinship system into the more restricted system reported for the United States. While difficulties were reported in maintaining a united domestic family or an integral kin group, there is no reason to suppose that these difficulties were caused primarily by urban living. Moreover, many cases were reported where the kin group re-formed after a period of disunity. There are many reasons for believing that the present system will continue. Far from being incompatible, kinship and urbanism among French-Canadians seem to have become functionally related. [11]

In a recent paper on Luso-Brazilian kinship patterns, Wagley, after examining data on the *parentela*—a bilateral kindred—from seven Brazilian communities, writes: "It is evident from the data provided . . . that kinship plays an important role in social, economic and even political affairs." [12] The *parentela*, he adds, operates in both rural and urban areas. In the cities, kinsmen tend to purchase apartments in the same building to facilitate the working out of kinship obligations. The studies by Firth, Young, Shaw, and Townsend in London show further evidence of the extension of kinship in urbanized, industrialized areas. [13]

Additional evidence is presented here to question the hypothesis of functional interdependence and implied causality between urban-industrial technology and the small nuclear family, challenging that part of the generally accepted hypothesis in which the diachronic formulation of sociocultural events is used. The position which assumes a static equilibrium in which functional interdependence within a closed, stable system is assumed a priori will not be argued other than to stress that even here there may be a range of family forms that can serve as functional alternatives to the small nuclear family in urbanized, industrialized systems. The additional evidence is found in an analysis of the family on the island of Barbados where the small nuclear family and fragmented kindred are present in the same form and functionally articulated with the large society in the same way as in the industrialized Western society, but without industry and machines.

We shall, then, have examples from the ethnographic record in which urbanization and industrialization are present without the small nuclear family and fragmented kindred, and the nuclear family is found in the same form and with the same functions as in industrialized Western society but without industrialization and urbanization. Taken together, these combinations seriously question a hypothesis that has received general acceptance in sociological theory before being tested by the comparative evidence.

IV

Barbados is a small, densely populated island, twenty-one miles long and fourteen miles wide, located in the Caribbean Sea at the eastern rim of the Lesser Antilles. It was first colonized by Great Britain at the beginning of the seventeenth century, and, in contrast with her other Caribbean possessions, has remained a British colony from the time of its settlement until 1956, when, with nine other English Caribbean dependencies, it became part of the Federation of the West Indies.

Today, Barbados is not a folk or peasant society. On the other hand, it is not highly mechanized and industrialized. Its economy, which is based upon agriculture, is best not considered underdeveloped since the application of additional capital has not, and, at present, cannot lead to a profitable expansion of productivity and employment opportunities for its very large population.

At present, Barbados—only 166.3 square miles in area—is one of the most densely populated areas in the world: its inhabitants numbered approximately 230,000 at the end of 1956—a density of almost 1,380 persons per square mile—and were increasing at a rate of about 2 per cent per year. Overpopulation has long been recognized as a major problem on the island.

How is this myriad of human beings supported? While its economy is based upon agriculture, in contrast with most of the world's densely populated rural areas where subsistence as well as cash crops are raised, Barbados is almost exclusively dependent upon a single cash crop—sugar. As emphasized in a recent national accounts study of the economy of Barbados,[14] agriculture, in which the growing of sugar cane predominates over all other forms of agricultural activity, is the most important contributor to the island's gross domestic product in which the processing of sugar and molasses accounts for more than half the total contribution of manufacturing. Sugar, to quote the authors of Barbados' ten-year development plan, is truly "the blood of the island." [15]

Barbadians, then, are not subsistence farmers. The island's agricultural activities are organized around the production of sugar, which is cultivated because it provides more revenue per acre than any other crop which could be grown on the island and for which a world market exists.[16] Individuals earn their livelihood in the form of wages; they produce very little for their own consumption.

Barbados, as has already been mentioned, is not an industrialized society in the general sense of the term. The concept of industrialization, however, as it is used in sociological discussions is ambiguous. The specific referent is technological—machines and factories. In general, however, it refers also to the system of social relations that organize human populations in the management of the machines. The use of one term to refer to both the technology and the social structure is regrettable since it leads to thinking of the two as inseparable: that is, the student finds it difficult to think of machine technology without the specific social patterns that have developed in Western civilization. This double referent, however, reveals more of the causal assumptions made by the early students of industrialization: the causal impact of machine technology was considered to be so great that the social relations governing the use of the machines was conceptualized as a necessary consequence of it. Both referents of industrialization must be considered independently, at least until some evidence is presented to demonstrate that there is only one way to organize a population in the use of machines.

This inadequate conceptualization is crucial, however, in the analysis of the data from Barbados since many of its social structural forms are those generally associated with machine technology in North America and Europe, although there are few factories and machines are little used except for a handful of instances in the sugar industry. This situation, itself, however, provides an additional challenge to the hypothesis which claims that industrialization—which at the beginning, at least, was purely technological—is the cause of social organization, since the consequence is present without the cause.

                                                                        V

The elementary family in Barbados, as in most of the islands of the West Indies, takes two basic forms—one conjugal or nuclear, the other subnuclear and generally matrifocal. As used here, matrifocality refers to the form of the family in which the mother-child relationship is stronger and more durable than the conjugal (husband-wife) bond. It is characterized by (1) a marginal role for the husband-father; (2) high percentages of female heads of households; (3) easy adoption and high ratios of children per household; (4) high rates of illegitimacy (by European and American standards); and (5) low rates of "legal" marriages. The conjugal or nuclear family, on the other hand, is based upon the husband-wife relationship and is characterized by the converse of the features of the matrifocal family.

The household, which generally contains at least one of the elementary kinship units, is variable. Ideally, it is composed of an isolated nuclear family which lives in a separate shelter, usually provided by the adult male. This, however, is rarely achieved by most of the population. When not composed of an isolated nuclear family, the household may consist of a number of alternative forms. The first is a nuclear family in which a mature child, invariably a daughter, has begun to have a family—often she is unmarried—before establishing a firm conjugal relationship in a separate dwelling. This extended family group, or "multi-family" household, is of three generations and is composed of one nuclear family plus one or more matrifocal units of unwed mother and children, all sharing the same house. An alternative appears when a woman and her children become established in an independent dwelling unit without an adult male. This occurs either when the members of the conjugal group separate—the male leaving— or when a woman obtains a dwelling, usually through inheritance, and occupies it with her children but without a mate. An infrequent variant of this denuded family occurs when a man is left alone with his children in a household without an adult female. These denuded family households can become extended when the children mature and begin to have offspring while they are still living at home. Here we find a three-generation unit which, generally, is composed of a woman and her children, including mature daughters and their offspring. This form, which is found throughout the Caribbean, is usually referred to as the "grandmother family." A household then, can consist of one of four alternative forms which are found distributed in the same frequencies in both the rural and urban areas: (1) a nuclear family, (2) a nuclear extended family, (3) a denuded or subnuclear extended family (male or female, but usually female-centered), and (4) a denuded or subnuclear extended family (male or female but again usually female-centered).

In form and functional integration with the total society—an at least temporary state of equilibrium is assumed for the purpose of analysis—the ideal nuclear group found in Barbados is very similar to the nuclear family found in the United States and described by Parsons.[17] The tendency toward structural and spatial isolation appears in both places; the importance of the mother in the process of the child's socialization and in the development of his personality are similar; the role of the adult male within the family as "breadwinner," responsible for supporting the entire group, is likewise analogous. More significantly, even the relationship between the individual and the larger society is the same. Individuals are all members of families linked to the larger society through the adult male who occupies a place in the local occupational system, and in both cases, the position of the latter member in the occupational system is a primary determinant of the position of the others in the social hierarchy.

Other similarities can be found in patterns of descent: Both systems are bilateral. In Barbados, where illegitimacy is common, it is usual for parents to leave wills bequeathing their property to all of their children.[18] Relations with ascending and descending generations show no tendency toward structural bias in favor of any one line of descent. Both Barbados and the United States, therefore, can be described as symmetrically multilineal.

In both cases, the tendency toward structural isolation is reinforced by the relationship between the family and the occupational system, particularly with reference to social mobility. Each nuclear family is ascribed a place in the system of stratification which is based upon the social class of the family of orientation of its adult male subject to the mobility he may achieve in his occupational pursuits. Mobility is a driving force in both societies. Kinship relationships are generally divorced from the occupational system, thus permitting conjugal units to be socially mobile, independent of kinship ties. Nuclear families striving for mobility are often best able to do so by almost total de-

nial of kinship claims, which, of course, leads to the isolation of the
conjugal family. In Parsons' terms, then, both the Barbadian and
American nuclear families can be characterized as "bilateral, structurally isolated, open, multilineal, conjugal systems." [19] The alternative
forms of the household discussed above are all variants of the isolated
nuclear unit produced by factors relating directly to the integration
of family and society.

The primary functions of Barbadian society are performed through
a highly stratified system of occupational statuses; the hierarchically
ranked positions, however, provide their occupants with wages that
vary considerably. The insular system of social stratification is tied
directly to these ranked occupational positions since they are the
primary determinant of an individual's social class. Families are
articulated with the larger society through adult males who are members of both a family and the occupational system simultaneously: the
male role is defined in terms of supporting women and children; he is
also expected to hold a position in the occupational system. In the
latter system he holds one of a series of ranked positions from which
he receives money and prestige; in the family he holds a position that
calls for the contribution of income obtained in the occupational
world. Women and children, who, in the ideal, are outside the dominant institutional complex, are linked to it through reciprocal role
obligations to a male within the family. Satisfactory performance of
the adult male role within the family requires an individual to hold a
position in the occupational system that provides him with income
sufficient to support a family.

The occupational system in Barbados, however, is so constituted
that many, if not most, of the positions at the lower end of the hierarchy provide neither the prestige nor the income necessary for the
support of a family. The occupants of these low-ranked positions are
not able to fulfil the role expectations of adult male within the family,
and if they cannot improve their occupational status after a period of
time they tend to leave the household, thereby creating a denuded,
subnuclear, matrifocal or mother-oriented group. The extended family
households, both nuclear and denuded, appear when the fathers of
the children born to girls living in parental households have not been
able to attain an occupational position with rewards sufficient to purchase a house and to establish the new family as an isolated nuclear
group.

The importance of a man to his family and his relationship to the
others, therefore, will vary directly with the income and status he
earns in the occupational world. Consequently, we may expect both

the family and the household to take different forms at varying socio-economic levels. Whether the unit is nuclear or matrifocal is, there-fore, a function of the system of social stratification and the way in which adult males link the family to society. Where adult males hold positions that provide rewards sufficient for the support of a nuclear family, the nuclear group is isolated in a separate household; where not, a subnuclear, matrifocal group appears, causing the household to take one of the forms outlined above.

On the tiny sugar-growing island of Barbados, then, we find the same small nuclear family, articulated with the larger society in precisely the same way as we find in industrialized Western society, but with-out urbanization and industrialization. The industrial revolution, in fact, has not yet come to the island.

The existence of an industrialized and urbanized society in Brazil, French Canada, England, and Japan with an extended family, and the small nuclear family—identical in form and function to the nuclear family of industrialized Western society—in Barbados without indus-trialization or urbanization provides evidence to question the hy-pothesized causal relationship between urban-industrial technology and the family. The explanation for the similarity in family form and function in Barbados and in industrialized Western society, however, may provide us with a new perspective with which to re-analyze the historical data used to support the old hypothesis.

VI

Barbados was settled by colonists who came in family groups from Great Britain. Though African slaves were later introduced to work on the sugar plantations, significant numbers of English and Irish families remained and their descendents are still there today. The institutionalized form of family now found in Barbados was brought to the island by the first settlers and later, adopted by the Negroes when integrated into the larger society through the occupational system immediately following Emancipation.[20]

The small nuclear family, the *famille particulariste* of Le Play, which is native to North Europe,[21] is known to have existed in England in the seventeenth century, prior to the colonization of the New World. Specialists in the culture of the Old World (Europe, Mediterranean, Middle East), in fact, believe it to be much older, "as old as the Vikings or older" according to Arensberg.[22] If this is the case, it antedates both urbanism and machine technology in England and the United States. Perhaps its contemporary place in modern, urban, industrialized society is related to its temporal priority to machine technology.

If, at the very beginning of the urban-industrial revolution, the inventors of machine technology already lived in small nuclear families, it is no small wonder that this form became functionally integrated with industrial technology as a new equilibrium was achieved. As North European man developed the social forms to go with the machine, it is quite probable that he reworked the social institutions with which he was already familiar. If so, the relationship between the small nuclear family and industrialization is better interpreted as one of the temporal priority of the former and not a necessary functional consequence or cause and effect in which the latter is the determinant. Further investigation of the historical material, then, may indicate that the two are related because the small nuclear family was there first. Subsequent social institutions, such as the occupational system, that went with the machine were probably adapted to, and therefore fitted with, a society organized in small families. One wonders what organizational forms urban-industrialized society might have today if these early North Europeans lived in extended families.

Some might argue that wage labor more than machine technology is the cause of the distinctive Western family. If one uses the equilibrium formulation, there is no doubt that wage labor and the small family are functionally interrelated and interdependent. The question, however, is whether a system of wage labor is a necessary and sufficient cause for the small family when an entire sociocultural system is in the process of change.

The crucial relationship between wage labor and the form of the family concerns the scale of remunerations. In the systems of North America, Europe, and Barbados, with the exception of the relative few who hold positions at the top of the hierarchy, workers earn only enough for the support of a nuclear group. While variability in wages is considerable, we rarely find a job paying enough to support more than one nuclear family. Since men are the principal wage-earners—this probably being based upon a prior cultural definition of the sexual division of labor in North Europe—they are expected to provide money for the kinship unit. The degree of possible extension of the kin group is thus related to the income earned by men. Since each nuclear unit also is expected to have its own wage-earner, it is economically independent, which brings about a weakening of reciprocal relations between members and kinsmen outside the group. Within the nuclear family, however, there is relative equality, each member having a right to a share of the income of the adult male or the goods or services it can buy.

Were the occupational system so organized as to pay one individual enough to support a larger group or to enable him to provide employment for such a unit, extended families might arise to engulf or submerge the nuclear group. Perhaps, if extended families had existed in England when the complex took its present form, the remuneration scale of modern industrial society would be very different.

In the United States, industrialization started in the Northeast, a section appropriately called New England. With reference to the family in New England, Arensberg writes, "The brittle, easily split 'nuclear' or 'democratic' ('Eskimoan') family, . . . came with [the] Yankees from England and fitted well with their egalitarian, unstratified farmer-artisan towns." [23] The small nuclear family, then, was brought to the United States from Great Britain by its earliest settlers. Therefore, it was present before the industrial revolution began in the United States. We suggest that it was reworked, as it had been several centuries earlier, in England, to provide the foundation for the new system of social organization that developed and spread with the industrial revolution. Here again, it was not the industrial revolution that produced the small nuclear family; in fact, the opposite may be true. The prior existence of the small nuclear family as the basic kinship unit of the people who industrialized both Great Britain and the United States may have been responsible for the very forms of social organization that developed along with the machines.

Furthermore, the data from Barbados demonstrates that the small nuclear family can diffuse without urbanization and industrialization just as the latter seems to be able to diffuse without the small nuclear family.

In conclusion, then, an examination of both the comparative and historical evidence indicates that, developmentally, there is no necessary and sufficient causal relationship, whether expressed in terms of necessary functional interdependence or consequence, between the small nuclear family and urbanization and industrialization. Any relationship that exists most probably results from the presence of the small family in North Europe prior to the industrial revolution.

NOTES

1. A portion of this paper was presented under another title at the annual meeting of the American Anthropological Association, Minneapolis, Minnesota, November 1960.

2. Ernest Nagel, "A Formulation of Functionalism," in *Logic without Metaphysics* (Glencoe, Ill.: Free Press, 1956), p. 251.
3. A. R. Radcliffe-Brown, *Structure and Function in Primitive Society* (Glencoe, Ill.: Free Press, 1952), pp. 180, 181.
4. Associated with the notion of functional interdependence of parts is that of functional alternatives. This refers to a limited range of parts that can perform the same function as the given part in the total system and consequently may be considered as substitutes for the given part since the equilibrium will still be maintained after the exchange.
5. William Ogburn and Meyer F. Nimkoff, *Sociology* (Boston: Houghton Mifflin Co., 1950), p. 469.
6. Ernest Groves and Gladys Groves, *The Contemporary Family* (Philadelphia: J. B. Lippincott Co., 1947), p. 140.
7. Ogburn and Nimkoff, *op. cit.,* p. 473.
8. Wirth, in his "Urbanism as a Way of Life," *American Journal of Sociology,* XL (July, 1938), 1–24, argues that the modern small nuclear family is a function of city living.
9. Trans. Frank H. Knight (Glencoe, Ill.: Free Press, 1950), p. 111.
10. "The Stem Family and Its Extensions in Modern Japan" (paper presented at the Annual Meeting of the American Anthropological Association, Minneapolis, Minnesota, 1960), p. 13.
11. Philip Garigue, "French Canadian Kinship and Urban Life," *American Anthropologist,* LVIII (December, 1956), 1098–99.
12. Charles Wagley, "Luso-Brazilian Kinship Patterns" (unpublished manuscript, 1960).
13. Raymond Firth, *Two Studies of Kinship in London* (London: Athlone Press, 1957); Michael Young, "Kinship and Family in East London," *Man,* LIV, No. 210 (September, 1954), 137–39; L. A. Shaw, "Impression of Family Life in a London Suburb," *Sociological Review,* III (December, 1955), 175–95.
14. Jeanette Bethel, "A National Accounts Study of the Economy of Barbados," *Social and Economic Studies,* IX, Special No. (June, 1960), 127–28.
15. *A Ten Year Development Plan for Barbados, 1946–56* (Bridgetown, Barbados: Advocate Press, n.d.), p. 11.
16. Lord Simon of Wythenshawe, *Population and Resourçes of Barbados* (Bloomcroft: Disbury, 1954), pp. 1–2.
17. Talcott Parsons, "The Kinship System in the Contemporary United States," *American Anthropologist,* XLV (January, 1943), 22–38. See also Talcott Parsons and Robert Bales, *Family, Socialization and Interaction Process* (Glencoe, Ill.: Free Press, 1955).
18. Sidney M. Greenfield, "Land Tenure and Transmission in Rural Barbados," *Anthropological Quarterly,* XXXIII (October, 1960), 165–76.
19. The most significant difference between the Barbadian and the American nuclear family is size. This difference, however, most critically affects the socialization and personality development of the children and not the form of the family or its articulation with the larger society (Parsons and Bales, *op. cit.,* p. 18). It is, therefore, excluded from the present comparison.

20. It is significant to note that the family form has remained the same even though it has been transferred from one ethnic group to another.
21. Frederic Le Play, Focillon, and DeLaire, *L'Organization de la famille* (Tours, 1884) (see also Edmond Demolins, *Comment la Route Crée de type social* [Paris: F. Didet, n.d., 1890?], 2 vols.; and Carle C. Zimmermann and Merle Frampton, *Family and Society* [New York: D. Van Nostrand & Co., 1937], pp. 97 ff.).
22. Conrad M. Arensberg, "Discussion of Methods of Community Analysis in the Caribbean by Robert Manners," *Caribbean Studies: A Symposium* (Mona, Jamaica: Institute of Social and Economic Studies, 1957), p. 97.

An example of what might have happened in the total society is found at the upper end of the occupational ladder where a given individual can earn enough to support more than one family.

With the acquisition of great wealth and property, we find the development of extended families, with the income-earning property accumulated by one generation providing support and prestige for several other generations. These extended families, usually patrilineages in Europe, North America, and the West Indies, develop around family property that provides income and status to all who can establish a valid genealogical connection therein.

At the lower end of the occupational scale, jobs do not provide sufficient income for a man to support even one family and the prestige rating is so low as to deny status either for himself or his family. It is here that women and children must enter the labor force to help out. The jobs available to them, however, are also at the bottom of the hierarchy. As the primary feature of the division of labor is destroyed, so is the strength of the conjugal bond. It is then that the subnuclear, matrifocal family appears.

The close functional adjustment between the isolated nuclear family and this form of stratified occupational system is related to the organization of the latter system. Since most jobs pay enough to support one family, the total system functions best when one wage-earner links one family to the social system through his wage contribution. His income and status are identified with the members of the nuclear group until the children are old enough to establish their own nuclear families, each with its own adult male wage-earner.

23. Conrad M. Arensberg, "American Communities," *American Anthropologist,* LVII (December, 1955), 1149.

3

Industrialization and the American Family: A Look Backward*

by Frank F. Furstenberg, Jr.

The proposition that industrialization destroys traditional family structures has long been accepted by sociologists and laymen alike. In industrial societies a new kind of family, the "isolated nuclear family," has been recognized; in societies presently industrializing, the older family systems are thought to be under great strain.[1] Analysts of the American family have both assumed and asserted that the transition from an agricultural to an industrial economy is accompanied by the weakening of a family system characterized by such traits as low social and geographical mobility, high parental authority over children, marital harmony and stability, dominance of husband over wife, and close ties within the extended family. It is similarly assumed that the modern family possesses few of the characteristics of the preindustrial family. Just as the older family pattern served the needs of a farming economy, it is frequently said that the modern family serves the needs of an industrial economy.[2]

Widespread acceptance of an ideal image of the pre-industrial family has limited empirical investigation of family change. Waller wrote some years ago: "According to the Victorian ideology, all husbands and wives lived together in perfect amity; all children loved the parents to whom they were indebted for the gift of life; and if these things were not true, they should be, and even if one knew that these things were not true he ought not mention it." [3] Few sociologists today would want to conceal unflattering truths about the family of three or four generations ago. However, certain widely shared beliefs about the family of today have helped to preserve what Goode has labeled "the classical family of Western nostalgia." [4]

* I would like to express appreciation to Professors William J. Goode and Sigmund Diamond for commenting on an earlier draft of this paper.

Reprinted from *American Sociological Review*, 31 (June 1966), pp. 326–337, by permission of the author and The American Sociological Association.

Goode's recent analysis of change in some of the world's major family systems suggests some general propositions that cast doubt on the traditional view of the relationship between industrialization and the family. Goode concludes: (1) there are indigenous sources of change in family systems, before industrialization takes place; (2) the relations between industrialization and family patterns are complex and still not sufficiently understood; (3) the family system itself may be an independent source of change facilitating the transition to industrialization; and (4) some apparently recent characteristics of the family may actually be very old social patterns.[5]

Each of these general propositions may be partially tested by using historical data from the United States. While this paper will touch on all four, it will concentrate on data pertaining to the fourth proposition —that certain "recent" family patterns are in fact evident in the family of a century ago. This is a particularly important theoretical point, for relatively stable family patterns would weaken the hypothesis that industrialization necessarily undermines the traditional family form. Further, it would force us to examine more carefully just which elements in the family are most responsive to changes in the economic system. A refutation of the assumption that trends in family change are well known may stimulate historians and historical sociologists to develop more precise descriptions of family systems at different periods in the past and of the family's relations with other social institutions during these periods.

It is important to recognize that the sharp contrast between the pre-industrial family and the modern family has already been diminished to some extent. Recent research has brought into question the validity of the conception of the "isolated nuclear family." [6] Increasing evidence suggests that we must modify our picture of the modern family. It seems not to be nearly so isolated and nuclear as it has been portrayed by some sociologists.[7]

Thus, we may attack from two ends the view that considerable family change has occurred in the past century. On the near end, we are beginning to get a more balanced picture of what the family of today looks like. On the far end, we have less information. This paper attempts to assemble some limited but highly useful information on the family of a hundred or more years ago. This information may be used to explore certain theoretical issues concerning family change. Although industrialization may have placed added strains on the family, the extent to which the industrial system affected the family has been greatly exaggerated. Further, I contend that not only did strains exist prior to industrialization, but some of these very tensions in the family may have facilitated the process of industrialization. The long-recognized effect of the economy on the family has too often obscured the converse—that the family may have important consequences for the economic system. To understand the complicated relationship between the economy and the family, we cannot simply view the family as the dependent variable in the relationship.

Method

The data supporting these views are drawn from the accounts of foreign travelers visiting this country during the period 1800–1850.[8] Although prior to and during this period, American technical achievements were many—a canal system, the cotton gin, the steamship, a spreading rail network, etc.—the nation was almost entirely agricultural until the decade before the Civil War. In 1850 only 16 per cent of the labor force was engaged in manufacturing and construction industries, and this percentage had not greatly changed since 1820.[9] Although the country was beginning to industrialize and urbanize, over four-fifths of the population still resided in rural areas.[10] About two out of every three workers were farmers. This ratio had decreased only slightly over the previous four decades.[11] Thus, it seems safe to assert that the impact of industrialization on the American family cannot have been great prior to 1850.[12]

Travelers' accounts are a rich source of data on the American family in the first half of the nineteenth century.[13] Many of these accounts have both literary and historical merit, and some of the writings have become famous because of their perceptive observations on American society. While the writings of Alexis de Tocqueville, Harriet Martineau, and Frances Trollope are well known, thousands of little-known accounts were written during this period.[14] Europeans, anxious to observe what was still referred to as "the New World" became the precursors of the more systematic participant observers of today.

To what extent can we place confidence in these travelers' accounts? Do they accurately portray American society as it actually was early in the nineteenth century? Naturally, the same cautions apply in using this source of historical data as apply to any other source of data. There are several methodological qualifications about the use of travelers' accounts that should be made. While these travelers may be viewed in certain respects as sociological observers of the nineteenth century, it must be remembered that they did not possess the basic qualifications of trained sociological observers. Many of the accounts of American society lack a neutral and value-free perspective. The biases of the observers are especially evident in the area of the family. For many travelers, the family was the source of great moral concern.

Without dismissing the possibility of distortion, such moral sentiment may to a degree enhance the value of these accounts as sociological data when we can ascertain and control for such biases. Generally, liberal and conservative Europeans evaluated the American family differently, reflecting their own biases. Liberals, as one might expect, viewed the American family in a more favorable light; conservatives, in an unflattering glare.[15] The possibility of bias from political persuasion is not great, however, because most of the observations reported in this paper are common to observers of all political points of view. That travelers of very different prejudices made *similar* observations enhances the reliability and validity of these observations. Where, on the other hand the observer's bias may have affected the accuracy of his accounts, I shall try to note such bias. When they do occur, these biases are more likely to be the result of the traveler's sexual status than his political status.[16]

The accounts used here do not represent a systematically selected sample of European travelers during the period. There are literally thousands of published and unpublished accounts, and a good sample of the observations of European travelers would be difficult to obtain. The sample used here is composed of forty-two accounts and selections from accounts, most of them containing extensive commentary on the family. To arrive at this sample, I examined over one hundred accounts, the majority of which made either no reference, or only an oblique reference, to family life in America.[17]

One final caution: most of the travelers base their comments on a view of the middle-class American family.[18] These travelers usually observed the family during their stay in residential hotels or during brief visits to American homes in rural areas of the country. More likely than not, these homes were middle-class. Since most of the comments and generalizations about the modern family of today also apply largely to the middle class, this limitation in the data will probably not affect the comparison adversely.

Family Observations

Courtship and Mate Selection

To begin this discussion with the first stage in the life cycle of the family, we shall discuss some of the foreign travelers' observations on the courtship patterns of American youth. The American system of courtship and mate selection is sometimes said to be one of the consequences of the urbanized and industrialized economy in the United States.[19] Free mate selection and the "romantic-love complex" are often linked to the demands of the economic system or to the weakened control by family elders in an industrialized society.[20] In fact, however, the same system of mate selection and emphasis on romantic love appear to have existed here prior to industrialization.

Although few of the travelers described the actual process of courtship in America, it is evident from their accounts that free choice of mates was the prevailing pattern as well as the social norm. Foreign visitors expressed diverse opinions on the desirability of this norm, but there was complete agreement that such a norm existed. Chevalier wrote in the 1830's that the dowry system, common in France, was almost nonexistent in the United States. He observed that American parents played only a nominal role in selecting the person their child married.[21] Parental consent was formally required, but this requirement was seldom taken very seriously. In 1842, Lowenstern wrote:

> A very remarkable custom in the United States gives girls the freedom to choose a husband according to their fancy; practice does not permit either the mother or the father to interfere in this important matter.[22]

The general expectation in America was that the choice of a mate should be based on love. Some travelers were skeptical about whether love actually dictated the marriage selection. Buckingham writes, "Love, among the American people, appears to be regarded rather as an affair of the judgment, than of the heart; its expression seems to spring from a sense of duty, rather than from a sentiment of feeling." [23] A few travelers already noted that, in spite of the previously mentioned tendency of young people to spurn financial considerations in choosing a mate, there were matches that seemed to be based on material considerations. This touch of cynicism, however, occurs in only a minority of the travelers' writings. Most of the observers praised the American marriage system because it permitted young people to select mates whom they loved and with whom they could enjoy a happy marriage. Some persons, however, noted that free mate selection resulted in certain family strains. Lowenstern states that marriage between people of different social classes, a pattern sometimes asserted to be typical of an industrial society, was not uncommon.[24] Several other travelers support this view. By no means were all the comments on interclass marriages favorable. Women, it was sometimes noted with bitterness, not infrequently married beneath themselves.[25]

Another source of strain in the marriage system in the view of some travelers, was the American habit of marrying at an extremely early age. Many observers noted that there seemed to be a great pressure for young people to marry. "In view of the unlimited freedom of the unmarried woman," Moreau writes, "it is astonishing to discover the eagerness of all to be married, for marriage brings about an absolute change in the life of the girl." [26] The tendency for an early marriage and the feelings of pressure to marry may be related to the "unlimited freedom" of which Moreau speaks.

Almost half of the travelers in the sample comment on freedom given to youth before marriage. Particularly striking to the travelers was the amount of freedom given to young women. But this freedom was tempered by considerable self-restraint. Adolescents were permitted to be alone together, but they were expected to behave according to strict moral standards. In the view of at least one observer, apparently this restraint led to a pronounced lack of responsiveness. Moreau stated that a young couple could be left alone in the house together without any fear of improper behavior. In fact, ". . . sometimes on returning, the servants find them fallen asleep and the candle gone out—so cold is love in this country!" [27]

While these extraordinary feats of self-restraint may be reminiscent of the privileges of courtly love, lauded by poets but not reported by objective observers,[28] there is general consensus among the travelers that the behavior of American women, particularly of young women, was exemplary. More often, young women in America came under criticism for being cold. No doubt, the combination of the freedom granted and the strong sanctions against misbehaving have something to do with the common observation that American women lacked warmth and spontaneity. On this matter, though, there is a dissenting view. Adby commented: "Many women, who seem cold as flint in general, give out fire enough when they find a 'blade' that suits them." [29]

The pressure to marry at an early age may have been generated by strains on the young woman. She was permitted to travel alone, to socialize with the opposite sex, and even to leave home alone for extended periods; but with this freedom went an enormous responsibility. She was expected to remain chaste, to conform to strict standards of propriety, and to respect the privileges of her freedom. The strain created by such a combination of freedom and moral restraint could well explain the tendency toward early marriage.[30]

Several observers note the problems that arise from early marriage. In her characteristically incisive way, Frances Trollope commented:

> They marry very young; in fact, in no rank of life do you meet with young women in that delightful period of existence between childhood and marriage, wherein, if only tolerably well spent, so much useful information is gained, and the character takes a sufficient degree of firmness to support with dignity the more important parts of wife and mother.[31]

The Pulszkys concurred with Trollope that American girls got too little opportunity to see life before they settled down to marriage.[32] It was also suggested that the rapid push toward marriage led young people to marry without knowing each other sufficiently; courtships were considered excessively casual. As one observer wrote, "Meet your girl in the morning, marry in the afternoon, and by six in the evening you are settled in your home, man and wife." [33]

To sum up, travelers perceived several strains in the American system of courtship and mate selection. Freedom of choice did not always lead to the selection of a mate on the basis of love; and it sometimes resulted in crossing of class lines and unwise marriages. The pressures toward early marriage seemed to result in inadequate preparation for marriage. These strains were observed by both critics and supporters of America alike. Their frequency and consistency suggest that they were very real problems. It is perhaps obvious to point out similarities in the criticisms of American marriages that were observed in the nineteenth century and the criticisms of American marriages today. At the time these criticisms were made, they were not thought to be related to incipient industrialization. The problems in the courtship process were regarded as the consequence of other political and economic factors, such as American ideological commitment to democracy, the opportunity for achievement in the society, and the emphasis on equality and individualism.[34]

The Conjugal Relation

The aspect of married life which drew the most attention was the great loss of freedom the woman suffered when she married. As already noted, single girls were granted considerable freedom before marriage. Almost a fourth of all the travelers commented on the loss of this freedom for the woman in married life. On this situation, there are no views to the contrary. Although Tocqueville[35] and Murat[36] see the loss of this freedom as voluntary on the part of the female, other observers view it as imposed upon her. A number of writers state their belief that the American wife is neglected in favor of the single woman. She is, as one traveler put it, "laid on the shelf." [37]

Why this was so, few travelers ventured to speculate. Several travelers imply that the retirement of married women from social life gives them greater moral protection.[38] Most of the writers feel that married women suffer unnecessary discrimination. Some of our contemporary sociological notions might suggest that the women, after consenting to marry, had little left to bargain with.[39] Furthermore, there were really no alternatives open to the women which would permit them to get out of the home more often and at the same time fulfill their domestic obligations. It is also possible that the intense pressures for early marriage prohibited married women from competing with single girls for men's attentions.

The primary cause for the withdrawal of married women from social life seems to have been their demanding domestic obligations. It is commonly assumed that women were more satisfied in their domestic role a century ago, before industrialization tempted them into the job market.[40] Yet the frequent complaint that married women were "laid on the shelf" belies this picture of domestic felicity. Lacking the alternative of employment, women did not face the possibility of role conflict that the modern woman may encounter. Yet boredom and dissatisfaction with this domestic withdrawal may have encouraged women into the labor market when the possibility arose some decades later.

There was general consensus that American women made dutiful and affectionate wives. Lieber wrote:

> I must mention the fact, that American women make most exemplary wives and mothers, and strange, be a girl ever so coquettish—
> yea, even a positive flirt, who, in Europe would unavoidably make

her future husband unhappy as soon as she were married, here she becomes the domestic and retired wife.[41]

The coldness that was attributed to single girls was not mentioned in the descriptions of married women. Even the most critical observers acknowledged the braveness and devotion that pioneer wives demonstrated in following their husbands into the Western wilderness.

There were a few travelers who dissented from the prevailing view that American women made good wives and mothers. A single traveler, Israel Benjamin, wrote, "The women have a characteristic, innate, and ineradicable aversion to any work and to household affairs." [42] This opinion, however, is so disparate from the vast majority of observers that it may indicate nothing more than Benjamin's generally negative attitude toward family life in America.

Although observers seemed to agree that the young women gave up an advantageous position when they married, several travelers noted that women wielded considerable power inside the home. Along with Tocqueville, these observers felt that the division of labor between husband and wife permitted the wife to have a great deal of authority over household matters.[43] One observer commented bitterly: "The reign of the women is here complete." [44] But generally, observers remarked that women deferred to their husbands' decisions in cases of disagreement. Clearly, the picture of the patriarchal household is only partially accurate. The authority of the husband was uncontested, but it seemed to be a limited authority which did not interfere with the woman's domestic power.[45] Bremer sums up the situation: "Of the American home I have seen and heard enough for me to say that women have, in general, all the rule there they wish to have. Woman is the centre and lawgiver in the home of the New World, and the American man loves that it should be so." [46]

There is a lack of consensus among the travelers on the closeness of the American family. Some observers commented that family members are united. Tocqueville interprets the close ties between husband and wife, father and sons, and between siblings as resulting from the greater equality of family members and the absence of arbitrary authority.[47]

Although Tocqueville's theory of family relations is probably sound, there was considerable opinion that family ties were not as close as in Europe. Here, the particular experiences of travelers to the United States may have created certain observational biases which cannot easily be checked. Specifically, many travelers did not observe families in their homes, but saw them in hotels and boarding houses. Families that lived in such residences were frequently engaged in business and represented the urban middle class. The observations of the urban middle class family tend to increase the appearance of similarity between the nineteenth century family and the family of today.

Most of the travelers who commented on family life in boarding houses were appalled at what they saw. Young married couples neither desired nor got privacy.[48] Young women were denied the opportunity to develop domestic skills which they would need when they moved into their own homes. Above all, boarding house life for women was exceedingly dull. Men went off to work leaving women with nothing to do. Trollope remarked that she saw the most elaborate embroidered apparel there because women had little else with which to occupy their time.[49] Several descriptions of life in the boarding house paint a dismal picture of women's pathetic attempts to occupy themselves until their husbands came home from work. A few travelers also felt the inactivity and lack of privacy endangered the wife's morals.

The claim that husbands neglected their wives for business was not restricted to accounts of boarding house life. It was one of the most frequent criticisms of American marriages. Vivid detail is supplied to give testimony to this situation. The husband left for his business early in the morning, perhaps came home for lunch, but usually did not return until late at night. This situation was frequently used to explain the dull marriages and the lack of intimacy between family members. Bishop gives a curious picture of the husband's role in the family:

> The short period which they can spend in the bosom of their families must be enjoyment and relaxation to them; therefore, in the absence of any statements to the contrary, it is but right to suppose that they are affectionate husbands and fathers.[50]

Marryat, among others, felt that the family was disintegrating in America though he was not specific about why this was so.

> Beyond the period of infancy there is no endearment between the parents and children; none of that sweet spirit of affection between brother and sisters; none of those links which unite one family; of that mutual confidence; that rejoicing in each other's success; that refuge, when they are depressed or afflicted, in the bosoms of those who love us.[51]

Thus we find there is some disagreement about the closeness of the family in America at this time, despite the widespread assumption in our generation that family life then was cohesive and intimate. Perhaps the most interesting insight on this problem is offered by Chevalier, who wrote:

> It may be objected that in the United States family sentiment is much weaker than it is in Europe. But we must not confound what is merely accidental and temporary with the permanent acquisitions of civilization. The temporary weakness of family sentiment was one of the necessary results of the general dispersion of individuals by which the colonization of America has been accomplished . . . As soon as they have their growth, the Yankees whose spirit now predominates in the Union quit their parents, never to return, as naturally and with as little emotion as young birds desert forever their native nests as soon as they are fledged.[52]

This statement suggests a reformulation of the common latter-day hypothesis that industrialization and urbanization weaken family cohesion. There are a number of general centrifugal forces which may weaken the family. These forces are not always accompanied by industrialization and urbanization. When, for example, the family cannot offer opportunities locally to its younger men and women that are equal to those opportunities elsewhere, we would expect that family ties will be weakened.

American morality drew praise from many of the European visitors. The American woman's self-imposed restraint was often attributed to the childhood freedom granted to her. Though a few of the travelers scoffed at the reputed moral purity of American women, the great majority of travelers who commented on morality found American women to be almost beyond reproach. Tocqueville[53] and Wyse[54] even indicate that there is less of a double standard for men than in Europe; moral restraints are binding on the males as well as the female. But Marryat counters, "To suppose there is no conjugal infidelity in the United States is to suppose that human nature is not the same everywhere." [55] Several travelers heard stories of infidelity but few actual encounters are reported. Martineau claims that disgrace is less permanent in the United States.[56]

Divorce

Although divorce is touched upon in the travelers' accounts, it obviously is not a matter of intense concern for most of the observers.[57] Grattan[58] and Griesinger[59] point out that a divorce is more difficult to obtain in America than in Europe. Marryat[60] and Marjoribanks[61] report just the opposite. Several observers found that divorce was increasing in this country. Wyse notes that the problem had grown to the point where divorces were said to exceed two thousand a year.[62] The fact that all the mention of divorce occurs in accounts written after 1845 suggests an increasing concern in the latter part of the century. Still, this subject was relatively neglected, and did not take on great significance until after the Civil War.

Aging

One family problem is conspicuous by its absence. This is the problem of aging. Not a single account discusses the place of old people in the society or even the position of the grandparent in the family. Indeed, the subject of the extended family is rarely, if ever, discussed. There are several possible explanations for this absence. The proportion of older persons in the population was quite small: less than 4 per cent of the population was over 60 years old.[63] Not only were there proportionally fewer old people, but they were less likely to be living in urban areas where they might be viewed as a problem to the family. In rural areas, the older person might easily live with his children. The accounts make no mention of parents living with their grown children. However, it is likely that foreign travelers, accustomed to seeing the same pattern in their own country, did not think it was worthy of notice. A careful historical study of how old people were cared for in this country would be most interesting.

Parent-Child Relations

Many travelers point out the loving care that was given to children in America. Because of early marriages and the domestic emphasis placed on the married woman's role, large families were common.[64] There was almost complete agreement that children were well taken care of in America.

The most significant observation about American children was the permissive child-rearing patterns that apparently were widespread at this time. A fifth of the sample stated that youth in America were indulged and undisciplined. Marryat put it bluntly, "Now, anyone who has been in the United States must have perceived that there is little or no parental control." [65] Many of the Europeans were shocked by the power children had over their parents, their defiance of their parents' authority, and the way the children were spoiled and pampered.

The lack of restraints on children was justified by some travelers who felt this rejection of authority was a necessary preparation for a democratic citizen. Martineau argues:

> Freedom of manners in children of which so much complaint has been made by observers . . . is a necessary fact. Till the United States ceases to be republican—the children there will continue as free and easy and as important as they are.[66]

Some observers even took delight in the spontaneity and independence shown by American children.

The above suggests that the controversy between permissive and authoritarian child-rearing has not been confined to the twentieth century.[67] Also the great respect and reverence for parental authority that is generally assumed to have existed at this time is not as pervasive as the defenders of the traditional nineteenth-century family would suggest. Furthermore, the picture of the close Victorian family is not entirely supported by these accounts. Some travelers observed disharmony as well as harmony in the family, though not enough observers commented on this subject to make any conclusive statements.

Grattan, among others, comments on the enormous push for children to grow up and become independent of their families.[68] This may be part of the "business" stereotype that is present in some of these writings, but the move toward early maturity is consistent with the prevalence of early marriages. Girls over the age of 21 were considered by some as old maids, and boys, according to Marryat,[69] left home in their middle teens. This picture may be somewhat exaggerated. Yet the impression is that children were not inclined to stay in the bosom of the family for any longer than they had to. Children are frequently characterized as self-confident, independent, poised, and mature.

This contention is supported by description of the American adolescent. Freedom is the most frequent word used to describe adolescent behavior in America. However, as already noted, the freedom which existed between the sexes was tempered by considerable restraint.

There is surprisingly little criticism of the behavior of adolescents. It is said by a few observers that there was much frivolous dancing and partying. Adolescents were not given nearly as much attention in these accounts as would be devoted to the subject today. The stress on growing up and assuming adult responsibilities seems to take precedence over what is today called "youth culture." [70]

From the little information that is reported, there appeared to be less discontinuity between the role of an adolescent and the role of an adult. This is one point where the industrialized society may have placed added strains on the family. At least there is some reason to believe that adolescence as a period of great stress had not yet been generally identified in America.

The Position of Women in Society

The final topic that emerges from the travelers' accounts is the position of women in American society. This subject has been touched upon throughout the paper. There are, however, some additional observations to be reported. Over a fourth of the travelers comment favorably on female beauty in America. Cobden describes the ladies as "petite but elegant." [71] At the same time, he notes that Boston ladies were "still deficient in preface and postscript." [72] Several writers consider the women unhealthy in appearance. It is quite interesting that so many observers find that American looks fade at an early age. Moreau expresses a common view when he writes about American women: ". . . they are charming, adorable at fifteen, dried-up at twenty-three, old at thirty-five, decrepit at forty or fifty." [73] This observation is consistent with the comments discussed earlier about the withdrawal of the older women from social life. There was probably little motivation or need for the women to keep up their appearance. In view of the strong emphasis on morality, the attractive older woman may have been viewed with a certain suspicion.

Almost all of the sample remarked that American women were treated with extraordinary deference and respect. As a matter of course, men were expected to give women any seat they desired in a public place even though someone might be sitting there and other seats be available. One traveler commented that he saw a man grab a chicken wing off another man's plate to give to a woman who had asked for it.[74] Some Europeans found this almost compulsive chivalry quite proper. To them it indicated the high esteem in which the female was held in America. Thornton wrote, "Attention and deference to women, if carried to a faulty extreme, is an error on the right side; but I deem it rather praiseworthy than faulty . . ." [75] Tocqueville suggested that the respect for women was a sign of a growing equality between the sexes.[76]

Many observers do not agree with these views. They saw the respect as superficial and deceptive. The Pulszkys had an extremely sophisticated analysis of this cult of politeness:

It appears as if the gentlemen would atone for their all-absorbing passion for business by the privilege they give to the ladies of idling time away . . . And as business is a passion with the Americans, not the means, but the very life of existence, they are most anxious to keep this department exclusively to themselves; and, well aware that there is no more infallible way to secure noninterference, than by giving the general impression that they never act for themselves, *the lady's rule* has become a current phrase, but by no means a fact in the United States.[77]

Though others do not see the degree of rationalization in the cult of politeness, there is support for the Pulszkys' view. Hall [78] and Martineau[79] state that women occupy an inferior position in American society. The elaborate courtesy and deference are only substitutes for real respect.

Although several of the observers see the American woman as satisfied with her place in society and two visitors see her fulfilling a valuable function of maintaining morality in the society, others feel strongly that the woman occupies an ambiguous position. Her lower status in the society is at odds with the democratic ideology. She cannot be considered an equal to men as long as she is confined completely to the home. The single woman must give up a good deal of her freedom when she marries. This loss of freedom is not fully compensated for by the respect she gains by mothering her husband's children and supervising his household. The discontinuity in the role of a woman is, in certain respects, similar to the conflict between career and family that exists today. It would be valuable to look at the diaries and letters of women from this period to see whether there is any indication of such a strain.

The great deference paid to women may have compensated them, in part, for this loss of standing. But many of the observers seemed to feel that the reward was not adequate compensation. It should be said, however, that some of the observers were crusaders for women's rights in Europe, and their dissatisfaction with the cult of politeness is to be expected.

Finally, it should be noted that this kind of strain, like many of the other strains in the family which we have pointed out, did not directly derive from emerging industrialization. No doubt, post-Civil War industrialization aggravated the ambiguous position of women in American society, but women by this time may have been ripe for emancipation from the home. Thus, we might find a convergence of social patterns rather than the often-assumed cause-and-effect relationship between industrialization and the emancipation of women.

Conclusion

The accounts of foreign travelers visiting the United States in the first half of the nineteenth century contain valuable observations on the American family. These observations suggest the following conclusions:

1. Changes in the American family since the period of industrialization have been exaggerated by some writers. The system of mate selection, the marital relationship, and parent-child relations in the preindustrial family all show striking similarities to those in the family of today. Family strains commonly attributed to industrialization are evident to observers of the family prior to industrialization.

2. Although the American family is for the most part viewed favorably by the foreign travelers, it is in no way viewed as a tension-free, harmonious institution. Strains resulting from the voluntary choice of mates, the abrupt loss of freedom for women at marriage, women's discontent arising from total domesticity, lack of discipline of American children, the inferior position of women in American society—these were some of the common points of stress in the American family at that time.

3. It is not unlikely that some of these tensions may have eased the adaptation to an industrial society. The lack of parental restrictions on American children and the desire for women to improve their position in society and escape the demands of domestic duties may have facilitated the growth of the industrial system.

4. It should also be pointed out that certain strains in the American family which are sources of widespread concern today were not noted by foreign travelers. Few comments were directed at adolescence, old age, or divorce, perhaps indicating that at that time these areas were not sources of strain.

NOTES

1. Talcott Parsons discusses how the family and the economy affect each other in *Family, Socialization and Interaction Process,* Glencoe, Ill.: The Free Press, 1955, especially Chapter 1. The most forceful expression of this view was made by William F. Ogburn in his *Technology and*

the Changing Family, New York: Houghton Mifflin, 1955. This view is also expressed in George C. Homans, *The Human Group,* New York: Harcourt, Brace and Company, 1950, pp. 276–280. See also David and Vera Mace, *Marriage East and West,* Garden City, N. Y.: Dolphin Books, 1959, chapter 1.

2. Two excellent books on the social consequences of industrialization summarize the supposed changes in the family produced by industrialization: Harold L. Wilensky and Charles N. Lebeaux, *Industrial Society and Social Welfare,* New York: Russell Sage Foundation, 1958, pp. 67–83; and Eugene V. Schneider, *Industrial Society,* New York: McGraw-Hill Book Company, Inc., 1957, chapter 18.

3. *The Family: A Dynamic Interpretation,* New York: Cordon Company, 1938, p. 13.

4. William J. Goode, *World Revolution and Family Patterns,* New York: The Free Press of Glencoe, 1963, p. 6.

5. *Ibid.,* chapter 1.

6. See Marvin B. Sussman's "The Isolated Nuclear Family: Fact or Fiction" in his book of readings *Sourcebook in Marriage and the Family,* Boston: Houghton Mifflin Company, 1963, pp. 48–53.

7. Marvin Sussman has done several studies on the relationship between middle-class couples and their families. See especially "The Help Pattern in the Middle-Class Family," in Sussman, *Sourcebook in Marriage and the Family, ibid.,* pp. 380–385. Note the article by Gordon F. Streib in the same reader entitled "Family Patterns in Retirement." Also see Eugene Litwak, "Occupational Mobility and Extended Family Cohesion," Bobbs-Merrill Reprint Series in the Social Sciences, Sociology-177.

8. Accounts of foreign travelers have been used in a few studies of the family. Arthur W. Calhoun made extensive use of such accounts in his three-volume study of the American family, *A Social History of the American Family,* 3 volumes, New York: Barnes & Noble, Inc., 1960 (first published 1917–1919). See also Willystine Goodsell, *A History of Marriage and the Family,* New York: The Macmillan Company, 1939, chapter 11. More recently, Lipset has used foreign travelers' accounts in making some observations about the early American family (Seymour Martin Lipset, *The First New Nation: The United States in Historical and Comparative Perspective,* New York: Basic Books Inc., 1963, especially chapter 3.)

9. U.S. Bureau of the Census, *Historical Statistics of the United States: Colonial Times to 1957,* Washington, D.C.: U.S. Government Printing Office, 1960, Series D, 57–71. It should be noted that more change appeared in the decade between 1840–1850 than in previous decades.

10. *Ibid.,* Series A, 34–50.

11. *Ibid.,* Series D, 36–45.

12. A limited amount of industrialization could be found in the Northeastern states prior to 1850. However, Wilensky and Lebeaux, and Schneider report that industrialization was quite confined until after the Civil War. Wilensky and Lebeaux, *op. cit.,* p. 49; Schneider, *op. cit.,* chapter 4. The beginnings of an industrial economy, however, were apparent in such places as Lowell, Massachusetts. A number of travelers

visited Lowell during this period and commented with great interest on the Lowell factories.

13. There are many bibliographies of accounts of foreign travelers written during this period. Two extensive bibliographies are: Max Berger, *The British Traveler in America,* New York: Columbia University Press, 1943, and Frank Monagham, *French Travelers in the United States 1765–1932,* New York: The New York Public Library, 1953.

14. Berger and Monagham each list many thousands of accounts and they are only partial listings for two countries.

15. Portions of the travelers' accounts used in this study were rated by the author and an associate and placed into three categories: positive, neutral or negative. It was found that accounts could be reliably coded. There was complete agreement in 78 per cent of the cases. Where disagreement occurred, it never involved cases where one person coded a positive evaluation and the other a negative evaluation. The traveler's general evaluation was related to his political ideology. Although this information could be obtained for only about half of the sample, it showed a distinct relationship to evaluation. All three travelers who were conservatives had a negative view of America, while only one of twelve liberals had an overall negative impression of the country.

16. The females in the sample were inclined to view the position of married American women less favorably. They were more skeptical about the desirability of the position of women in the United States.

17. The sample of accounts examined does not represent a systematic selection of travelers' accounts. A large proportion of the sample was located from the bibliography of Oscar Handlin, *et al.* (eds.), *Harvard Guide to American History,* Cambridge, Mass.: The Belknap Press, 1954, pp. 151–159, which includes a diverse selection of accounts. Handlin also edited a book of selections from travelers' accounts. This book contains some writings not listed in the *Harvard Guide.* See *This Was America,* New York: Harper & Row, 1949.

18. Middle-class, in this context, refers to persons engaged in small business, professionals, and prosperous landowners. Travelers in the sample were more likely to comment on the habits and customs of the farmers than the farmhand.

19. This is suggested in Harry Johnson's chapter on the family in *Sociology: A Systematic Introduction,* New York: Harcourt, Brace and Company, 1960, chapter 6. Parsons advocates this view in his article "Age and Sex in the Social Structure" in his *Essays in Sociological Theory,* Glencoe, Ill.: The Free Press, 1954.

20. David and Vera Mace, *op. cit.,* chapter 5; also Robert F. Winch, *The Modern Family,* rev. ed., New York: Holt, Rinehart and Winston, 1963, pp. 318–320.

21. Michael Chevalier, *Society, Manners, and Politics in the United States,* New York: Doubleday Anchor Books, 1961, p. 294. Six other travelers substantiate Chevalier's observations on the freedom of mate selection.

22. Isidore Lowenstern, "Les Etats-Unis et La Havane: souvenirs d'un Voyage, 1842," in Handlin, *This Was America, op. cit.,* p. 183.

23. James Silk Buckingham, *The Eastern and Western States of America,* 2 vols., London: Fisher, Son & Co., 1867, p. 479.

24. Lowenstern, *op. cit.* James Fenimore Cooper, the American novelist, in a book on his observations of American life, notes the same pattern of interclass marriage. See his *Notions of the Americans,* vol. I, London: Henry Colburn, 1828.
25. Among others, Sir Charles Lyell made this observation in his *A Second Visit to the United States of North America,* New York: Harper & Brothers, 1849.
26. Mederic Louis Elie Moreau de Saint-Mery, "Voyage aux États-Unis de L'Amerique, 1793–1798," in Handlin, *This Was America, op cit.,* p. 100. Similar observations on the early marriage age were made by nine other travelers.
27. *Ibid.,* p. 99.
28. Sidney Painter in his book, *French Chivalry,* Ithaca, N. Y.: Great Seal Books, 1957, presents a superb account of courtly love in mediaeval France. See especially chapter 4.
29. E. S. Adby, *Journal of a Residence and Tour in the United States of North America,* vol. 1, London: John Murray, 1935, p. 74.
30. It is possible to develop a fourfold table based on the two variables of amount of moral restraint (permissiveness toward sexual expression before marriage) and degree of freedom permitted young people to associate together. I predict that marriage age will be early when freedom to associate is high and moral restraint is also high. Where freedom to associate is high and moral restraint is low, marriage age will be somewhat later. It may be even later when freedom to associate is low and moral restraint is high. It is difficult to predict how the fourth case would turn out. A study on this problem is being undertaken.
31. Frances Trollope, *Domestic Manners of the Americans,* New York: Alfred A. Knopf, 1949, p. 118.
32. Theresa and Kossuth Pulszky, "White Red Black," in Handlin, *This Was America, op. cit.*
33. Karl T. Friesinger, "Lebende Bilder aus Amerika," Handlin, *This Was America, op. cit.,* p. 254.
34. This view is advocated by Tocqueville throughout his writings on the American family. Alexis de Tocqueville, *Democracy in America,* 2 vols., New York: Vintage Books, 1954. See especially vol. 2, chapter 8.
35. *Ibid,* chapter 10.
36. Achille Murat, *The United States of America,* London: Effingham Wilson, 1833.
37. Alex Macay uses this expression in *The Western World,* vol. 1, London: Richard Bentley, 1850.
38. Grattan suggests that married women are particularly visible and thus, to a great extent, safeguarded from moral dangers. He also notes that American women do not stop flirting after they are married. Thomas Colley Grattan, *Civilized America,* 2 vols., second edition, London: Bradbury and Evans, 1859.
39. This notion of a role bargain is implicit in Willard Waller's article "The Rating and Dating Complex," *American Sociological Review* (October, 1937), pp. 727–734 and in his book on the family, *op. cit.,* pp. 239–254. Goode uses the conception of a "role bargain" in "A Theory of Role Strain," *American Sociological Review,* 25 (August, 1960), pp. 483–496.

40. Ralph Linton, in an otherwise quite illuminating discussion of the dilemma of the modern woman, states, "Even fifty years ago the comfortably married woman looked with smug pity on the poor working girl in her drab, mannish clothes." "Women in the Family" in Marvin B. Sussman, *op. cit.*, p. 170.
41. Francis Lieber, *The Stranger in America*, London: Richard Bentley, 1835, p. 132.
42. Israel Joseph Benjamin, "Drei Jahre in Amerika 1859–1862," in Handlin, *This Was America, op. cit.*, p. 274.
43. Tocqueville, *op. cit.*
44. Benjamin, *op. cit.*, p. 273.
45. Rose Coser identifies the same pattern in the Eastern European Jewish family in her article "Authority and Structural Ambivalence in the Middle-Class Family" in the book of readings she edited, *The Family: Its Structure and Functions*, New York: St. Martin's Press, 1964, pp. 370–383.
46. Fredrika Bremer, *The Homes of the New World*, 2 vols., New York: Harper & Brothers, 1853, p. 190.
47. Tocqueville, *op. cit.*
48. Boarding house life is discussed by W. E. Baxter in *America and the Americans*, London: Geo. Routhledge & Co., 1855. Auguste Carlier associated the spread of boarding houses with the decline of domestic life in America. See his *Marriage in the United States*, Boston: De Bries, Ibarra & Co., 1867.
49. Trollope, *op. cit.*
50. Anne Bishop, *The Englishwomen in America*, London: John Murray, 1856, p. 365.
51. Frederick Marryat in Sydney Jackman (ed.), *A Diary in America*, New York: Alfred A. Knopf, 1962, p. 355.
52. Chevalier, *op. cit.*, p. 398.
53. Tocqueville, *op. cit.*
54. Francis Wyse, *America, Its Realities and Resources*, vol. I, London: T. C. Newby, 1846.
55. Marryat, *op. cit.*, p. 431.
56. Harriet Martineau in Seymour M. Lipset (ed.), *Society in America*, New York: Anchor Books, 1962.
57. The intense concern with divorce does not begin until the rise of industrialization in the post-Civil War period. Then the divorce rate slowly rises, and public discussion of divorce rapidly increases. The Census did not begin to report divorce rates until after the Civil War.
58. Gratton, *op. cit.*
59. Griesinger, *op. cit.*
60. Marryat, *op. cit.*
61. Alexander Marjoribanks, *Travels in South and North America*, New York: Simpkin, Marshall and Company, 1853.
62. Wyse, *op. cit.*
63. *Historical Statistics, op. cit.*, Series A 71–85.
64. Calhoun reports the frequency of large families in his study of the American family, *op. cit.*, vol. II, chapter 1.
65. Marryat, *op. cit.* p. 351.
66. Martineau, *op. cit.*, p. 28. Four other travelers concur with Martineau.

67. Miller and Swanson make a similar observation in their review of child-rearing practices. Daniel R. Miller and Guy E. Swanson, *The Changing American Parent,* New York: John Wiley & Sons, Inc., 1958, pp. 8–9.
68. Grattan, *op. cit.*
69. Marryat, *op. cit.*
70. Parsons, "Age and Sex in the Social Structure," *op. cit.*
71. Richard Cobden in Elizabeth Hoon Cawley (ed.), *The American Diaries of Richard Cobden,* Princeton: Princeton University Press, 1952, p. 89.
72. *Ibid.,* p. 14.
73. Moreau, *op. cit.,* p. 98. Eight other travelers make the same observation.
74. Marryat, *op. cit.*
75. Major John Thornton, *Diary of a Tour Through the Northern States of the Union and Canada,* London: F. Barker . . . and Co., 1850, p. 110.
76. Tocqueville, *op. cit*
77. Pulszky and Pulszky, *op. cit.,* p. 239.
78. Captain Basil Hall, *Travels in North America in the Years 1827 and 1828,* Edinburgh: Robert Cadell, 1830.
79. Martineau, *op. cit.*

4

Geographic Mobility and Extended Family Cohesion*

by Eugene Litwak

This is the second of two companion papers, both of which seek to demonstrate that *modified* extended family relations are consistent with democratic industrial society.[1] These papers, then, attempt to modify Parsons' hypothesis that the isolated nuclear family is the only type which is functional for such a society.[2] Because Parsons so clearly relates his hypothesis to a more general theory of class and business organization there is considerable value in keeping his point of view

* The author wishes to express his thanks to Glenn H. Beyer, Director of the Cornell Housing Research Center for permitting use of the data in this study, and to Paul F. Lazarsfeld, Arthur R. Cohen, and Bernard Barber for their helpful comments, although they are not necessarily in agreement with the author's point of view.

Reprinted from *American Sociological Review,* 25 (June 1960), pp. 385–394, by permission of the author and the American Sociological Association.

in the forefront of discussion, for its modification under such circumstances provides rich intellectual dividends.

Parsons assumes only one kind of extended family relational pattern, the "classical" type exemplified in the Polish and Irish peasant families.[3] There is some evidence, however, for the existence of a modified [4] extended family that is theoretically more relevant and empirically more predictive than either of the two alternatives posed by Parsons' hypothesis—the isolated nuclear family and the classical extended family.[5] The present inquiry supplements the earlier paper by demonstrating that modified extended family relations can be maintained despite differential geographical mobility. The first part of this paper examines the assumptions underlying Parsons' point of view as well as the modification suggested herein. In the second part empirical evidence is presented to show that extended family identification can be maintained despite geographical mobility.

Geographical Mobility and Extended Family Anomy

There are at least three arguments which support the view that extended family relations are not consistent with geographical mobility: (1) individuals who are strongly attached to their extended families will be reluctant to move even if better jobs are available elsewhere; (2) it is unlikely that identification with extended family will be retained where only one nuclear family moves while the rest of the extended family remains behind; and (3) it is financially more difficult to move a large family and locate jobs for many individuals simultaneously.

The first and third of these propositions suggest that individuals with extended family ties are unlikely to move. The second proposition suggests that if they do move individuals are unlikely to retain their extended family identification with those who remain behind. These arguments can be buttressed by the more general analysis of Homans, who points out that contact is one of the four major prerequisites for primary group cohesion.[6] Since these are familiar arguments they need not be elaborated.

Geographical Mobility and Extended
Family Cohesion

In this analysis, major attention is given to propositions which are contrary to those stated above, namely, the following: (1) individuals who are part of a modified extended family grouping are in a better position to move because the latter legitimizes such moves, and as a consequence provides economic, social, and psychological support; (2) extended family relations can be maintained over great geographical distances because modern advances in communication techniques have minimized the socially disruptive effects of geographic distance; and (3) financial difficulties of moving extended families in a bureaucratic industrialized society are minimized because family coalescence takes place when the family is at its peak earning capacity and when it is least likely to disrupt the industrial organization.

1. *Modified extended families aid geographical mobility*

Implicit in the argument that extended family relations lead to a reluctance to move is the view that extended families cannot legitimize geographical mobility. If it can be demonstrated that in current society the contrary is the case, then it can also be shown that such families have far greater facilities than the isolated nuclear family for encouraging spatial movement.

Past instances of legitimation of such movement by the extended family help to clarify the point. In situations of economic or political catastrophe (the Irish potato famine or the Russian pogroms), the extended family encouraged mobility. Given this type of situation, the extended family had at least two advantages over the isolated nuclear family. First, its greater numbers permitted easier accumulation of capital to finance the trip of any given nuclear family. This led to a push and pull kind of migration, with the migrant sending money to help those who had remained behind. Secondly, because of its close ties and size the extended family had superior lines of communication. Thus the migrant became a communication outpost for those who remained behind, providing information on jobs, housing, local social customs, and language. Those who had migrated earlier also could aid the newcomer at the most difficult point of migration.[7]

In a mature industrial society there is great institutional pressure on the extended family to legitimate differential geographical mobility among its nuclear family members. This pressure derives from the fact that the extended family can never fully control the economic destiny of its nuclear sub-parts. Although the extended family provides important aid, the major source of economic support for the nuclear family must come from its own occupational success, which is based much more on merit than nepotism. As a consequence, if the extended family wants to see its member nuclear families become successful, it must accept one of the chief prerequisites to occupational success—geographical mobility.[8]

In other words, it is postulated that a semi-independent relation links the nuclear family to the extended family. Because the extended family cannot offer a complete guarantee of occupational success it legitimates the moves of nuclear family members. On the other hand, receiving as it does significant aid in achieving many of its goals, the nuclear family retains its extended family connections despite geographical distance.

2. *Extended family identification is retained despite breaks in face-to-face contact*

There are two reasons why extended families can provide important supplements to nuclear family goal achievement despite geographical distance and therefore two reasons why extended family identification can be maintained despite breaks in face-to-face contact.[9] As noted above, the rapid development of techniques of communication has made it relatively easy for family members to keep contact despite great distances. Nor does distance, in a money economy, prevent or seriously hinder such aids to family members as help in times of illness, emergency loans or gifts, home purchase, and the like—all at long range.

3. *Geographical coalescence takes place at peaks of earning power*

Although the extended family encourages mobility when it is occupationally rewarding, it does not do so when such moves no longer bring rewards. Given the character of large-scale organizations, there are regular occasions when geographical mobility is not linked to occupational rewards, for example, when the individual is at the peak of his career. The career in the large organization is one in which the individual moves up until he reaches a position from which he can no longer advance; here he remains until he retires. Careers of bureaucrats are rarely downward. Two aspects of this situation are particularly important in the present context: (1) once a person has advanced as far as he can occupationally his working efficiency is no longer tied to geographic moves; and (2) it is at this point that the nuclear family is in the best economic position to support moves of extended family. At this period of his life, the careerist can seek a position near his extended family if he can find a job which matches his present one. Or he can encourage retired parents to settle near him. In short, it is suggested that when the extended family does coalesce it does not lead to undue financial strain (trying to locate jobs for many people simultaneously), nor is it likely to mean an irrational distribution of labor since it involves either retired people or job exchanges between people on the same occupational level.

Findings

In order to test alternative propositions about the relationship between family structure and geographical mobility, data from a survey of 920 white married women living in the Buffalo, New York, urban area were analyzed. The sample is biased in the direction of white, younger, middle-class, native-born individuals and as such is not representative of the total population.[10] However, the bias is a useful one since this is the very group which should most likely illustrate Parsons' hypothesis.[11] If it can be shown that his hypothesis does not hold for this group, then it is unlikely to hold for any division of the society.

1. *Mobility reduces extended family face-to-face contact*

The common basis for the opposing views—that geographical mobility is or is not antithetical to extended family relations—should be made explicit so that it is not mistaken for the main issue. Both positions are in agreement that geographical mobility generally reduces extended family face-to-face contact. Of the respondents in this study, 52 per cent with relatives living in the city received one or more family visits a week. In contrast, only four per cent of those with no such nearby relatives received visits this frequently.

2. *Breaks in face-to-face contact do not reduce extended family identification*

Central to the argument advanced in this paper is the view that geographical distance between relatives does not necessarily lead to a loss of extended family identification. In order to measure family orientation, all individuals were asked to respond to the following statements: (1) "Generally I like the whole family to spend evenings together." (2) "I want a house where family members can spend time together." (3) "I want a location which would make it easy for relatives to get together." (4) "I want a house with enough room for our parents to feel free to move in." These items formed a Guttman scale pattern.[12] Individuals who answered items 3 or 4 positively[13] were considered to be oriented toward the extended family. Those who answered items 1 or 2, but not 3 or 4, positively were considered to be nuclear family oriented. Those who answered none[14] of the questions positively were classified as non-family oriented.

In order to measure the effects of distance between relatives on family identification, all respondents were divided into two categories, those who had relatives living in town and those who did not. The data presented in Table 1 indicate that geographical distance does

TABLE 1

Geographical Distance Does Not Lead to a Loss of Extended Family Identification

	PERCENTAGE EXTENDED FAMILY ORIENTED	PERCENTAGE NUCLEAR FAMILY ORIENTED	PERCENTAGE NON-FAMILY ORIENTED	TOTAL
Relatives living in town	20	52	28	100 (648)*
Relatives living out of town	22	58	20	100 (272)

* In this and the following tables the figures in parentheses indicate the population base for a given percentage. For tests of significance in these tables, see note 10.

not mean a loss of identity. Those who are geographically distant from their relatives are as likely as those who live nearby to retain their extended family identification (22 and 20 per cent, respectively).

Table 1 very likely underestimates the relationship between mobility and extended family identification, since there may have been many individuals who either moved to the community because their relatives lived there or encouraged relatives to come later. In such cases family identification would have been maintained initially despite geographical distance. To deal with this question, all respondents again were divided, this time between those who spent their first 20 years in the city under study and those who were raised elsewhere. If the latter are considered to be migrants, it can be seen from Table 2 that the

TABLE 2

Migrants Are Not Less Extended Family Identified Than Non-Migrants

	PERCENTAGE EXTENDED FAMILY ORIENTED	PERCENTAGE NUCLEAR FAMILY ORIENTED	PERCENTAGE NON- FAMILY ORIENTED	TOTAL
Spent major part of first 20 years in city	18	51	31	100 (504)
Spent major part of first 20 years out of the city	23	56	21	100 (416)

migrants (23 per cent) are more likely than the non-migrants (18 per cent) to be identified with their extended families.

3. *Close identification with extended family does not prevent nuclear families from moving away*

Are people who are close to their extended families likely to leave them in order to advance themselves occupationally? To measure the likelihood of persons moving from the community for occupational reasons, the respondents were asked the following question: "Is there a good chance that your husband might take a job out of town?" Those who answered "yes" were classified as potential migrants. To test the likelihood of leaving their relatives, only respondents with relatives in town were examined. It can be seen from Table 3 that those individuals more closely identified with the extended family also were more likely to leave the city and presumably their nearby relatives (23 and 14 per cent, respectively). The same point can be made for the general population if the figures from Tables 1 and 2 are calculated to show how likely family oriented persons are to be migrants. Table 4 presents results which are consistent with Table 3. People are likely to move, then, even when they are strongly identified

TABLE 3

Strong Identification with Relatives Does Not Prevent People from Taking Jobs Elsewhere

	AMONG THOSE WITH RELATIVES IN THE CITY THE PERCENTAGE SAYING GOOD CHANCE HUSBAND WILL TAKE JOB OUT OF TOWN
Extended family orientation	23 (128)
Nuclear family orientation	18 (336)
Non-family orientation	14 (184)

with their families, and once having moved away from them, they are likely to retain their family identity.

4. Bureaucratic career and extended family mobility

The analysis is thus far consistent with the view that in modern bureaucratic society extended family relations can retain their viability

TABLE 4

People Identified with Extended Family Are as Likely or More Likely to Be Migrants Than Others

	PERCENTAGE RAISED OUT OF TOWN	PERCENTAGE HAVING NO RELATIVES IN THE CITY
Extended family oriented	51 (187)	32 (187)
Nuclear family oriented	47 (493)	31 (493)
Non-family oriented	37 (240)	23 (240)

despite differential rates of geographic mobility. To be fully consistent, however, it should be shown that extended family movement is related to career development in the way anticipated by the foregoing discussion. For it was pointed out that it is only when the individual is on the upswing of his career that mobility will be encouraged, while it will be discouraged when he reaches the peak.

In order to measure career stages individuals were asked: "Within the next ten years, do you expect the head of the household will be making: a. a great deal more than now; b. somewhat more than now; c. same as now; d. other, e.g., retired, don't know, etc." Those who said that they expected to earn "a great deal more" income were assumed to be on the upswing of their careers, those who named "somewhat more" were assumed to be fast approaching the peak, while all others were assumed to have reached the peak or plateau of their careers.[15] Table 5 confirms the view that bureaucratic de-

TABLE 5

Those on the Upswing of Their Careers
Are Likely to Be Migrants

		PERCENTAGE WITHOUT RELATIVES LIVING IN THE CITY
	WITHIN THE NEXT TEN YEARS	
Upswing of career	Expect to make a great deal more than now	39 (183)
Medium point	Expect to make somewhat more than now	29 (603)
Peak of career or plateau	Expect to make the same or somewhat less than now	16 (134)

velopment is congenial to family movement when people are upwardly mobile: 39 per cent of those on the upswing were migrants, while only 16 per cent of those who had reached their career plateaus were migrants.

Two additional bits of evidence supplement this point. First, if the hypothesis advanced in this paper is correct, the individuals who are both extended family oriented and rising in their careers should be most mobile because they have the advantage of aid from their extended families. Comparatively speaking, extended family identity should not lead to mobility when individuals have reached the career plateau. Table 6 suggests that this is the case. When individuals are moving ahead occupationally, those who are psychologically close to their families are much more mobile than those who dissociate themselves from their families (47 and 22 per cent, respectively, are mobile). In contrast, among people at the career peak, the extended family oriented are no more mobile than the non-family oriented (12 and 11 per cent, respectively).

The second bit of evidence which supports the view that extended family aid encourages mobility on the upswing of the career and discourages it otherwise involves the direction of the move. Individuals who have reached the career plateau *might possibly* still move if such moves meant bringing them closer to their extended family. To

TABLE 6

*Extended Family Identification Is Likely to Encourage
Geographical Mobility When Individuals Are on the Upswing
of Their Careers*

		Percentage Having No Relatives in the City		
	WITHIN THE NEXT TEN YEARS	EXTENDED FAMILY ORIENTED	NUCLEAR FAMILY ORIENTED	NON-FAMILY ORIENTED
Upswing of career	Expect to make a great deal more than now	47 (49)*	40 (107)	22 (27)
Medium point of career	Expect to make some-what more than now	30 (112)	31 (322)	27 (169)
Peak or plateau of career	Expect to make the same or less than now	12 (26)	22 (63)	11 (45)

* This cell reads as follows: 47 per cent of the 49 people who are extended family oriented and who expect to make a great deal more in the future have no relatives in the city.

investigate this possibility, respondents were asked: "Compared to your last house is your present house closer, the same, or farther away from your family?" Table 7 shows that where individuals are

TABLE 7

*Extended Family Identification Is Likely to Encourage Moves
Away from the Extended Family When People Are
on the Upswing of Their Careers**

	Percentage Whose Last Move Carried Them Farther from Their Families		
	EXTENDED FAMILY ORIENTED	NUCLEAR FAMILY ORIENTED	NON-FAMILY ORIENTED
Expect to make a great deal more in ten years	53 (49)†	37 (67)	48 (27)
Expect to make somewhat more	52 (112)	56 (322)	59 (169)
Expect to make the same or less	38 (26)	62 (63)	53 (45)

* Those with relatives in the city were classified together with those without relatives, since the same statistical pattern occurred in each case.

† This figure reads 53 per cent of 49 people who were extended family oriented and who expected to earn a great deal more in the next ten years moved farther away from their families.

climbing the ladder they are as likely, if not more likely, to move away from their relatives when they are identified with their extended families as when they are not (53 per cent as compared to 37 and 48 per cent). However, where individuals have reached the occupational plateau, those who are identified with their extended families are less likely to move away from them (38 per cent as compared to 62 and 53 per cent).

In short, the evidence presented here indicates that the career strongly influences the extent and the direction of geographical mobility in a manner consistent with the view that extended family relations are viable in contemporary bureaucratic society.

5. *Bureaucratic and non-bureaucratic careers*

This index of career, however, does not necessarily imply a *bureaucratic* career. Earlier discussions often assume that careers take place in a bureaucratic context. Therefore, the findings of this study should be further differentiated in terms of bureaucratic and non-bureaucratic occupations. In order to isolate the non-bureaucratic career, working-class persons whose fathers were also from a working-class occupational group were segregated from the rest of the population. Non-manual middle-class and upper-class individuals are more likely to follow bureaucratic careers, involving standard promotional steps associated with geographical mobility.[16]

In contrast, these features do not necessarily mark occupational advancement among manual workers. In this group occupational success may mean the achievement of plant seniority or the opening of a small business.[17] In such cases success is negatively related to future geographic mobility. As a consequence, a manual worker who envisions an upswing in his career may encourage family members to settle nearby because future success is closely linked to present location. Thus, it is expected that occupational advance has far different meanings for members of the working class and for the middle- and upper-class persons.

In Table 8 it can be seen that the only instances of upswings in careers leading to geographic mobility occur among members of the upper class (43 per cent of those who are on the upswing have no relatives in the community compared to 23 per cent of those who have achieved a plateau). For members of the stationary working class, occupational advancement is least likely, comparatively speaking, to result in geographical mobility (10 per cent of those on the

TABLE 8
*Only Among Upper- and Middle-Class Bureaucratic Occupations
Do Career Lines Play a Role*

	WITHIN THE NEXT TEN YEARS	Percentage Having No Relatives in the City			
		STATIONARY UPPER-CLASS*	UPWARDLY MOBILE	DOWNWARDLY MOBILE	STATIONARY MANUAL WORKERS
Upswing of career	Expect to make a great deal more than now	43 (76)†	39 (72)	40 (25)	10 (10)
Medium point of career	Expect to make somewhat more than now	42 (146)	39 (183)	26 (99)	11 (176)
Peak or plateau of career	Expect to make the same or less than now	23 (26)	13 (32)	28 (18)	12 (58)

* For a definition of occupational classification, see note 16.
† This cell should read as follows: 43 per cent of the 76 people who were stationary upper-class and who had high expectations of future economic improvement had no relatives in the city.

upswing and 12 per cent of those on the plateau have relatives in the city).

Table 8 more than any other should indicate the limitations of the present hypothesis. The latter cannot claim to explain any major features of current American society but only the behavior of members of that group which is often thought to be prototypical of future American society—those belonging to bureaucratic occupations. It is assumed here that future societies will in fact become increasingly bureaucratized. Since Parsons' analysis is largely concerned with this same group,[18] it is maintained that this study provides evidence contrary to his hypothesis.

6. *The extended family and emotional, social, and economic aid*

Extended families have a unique function in providing aid to those who are moving. This is based partly on the fact that family membership is defined in terms of blood ties and therefore is least pervious to changes in social contact, and partly on the fact that the individual receives his earliest and crucial socialization with people who eventually become extended family members. The individual might find voluntary associations of lesser help than family aid because new personal contacts must be established when one moves, and old contacts tend to have no continuing meaning when geographical contact is broken. Aid from neighbors has somewhat the same character. This point emerges clearly when newcomers to a neighborhood are compared with long-term residents in terms of the average amount of social participation in various areas of life. Table 9 shows that family contacts are as likely, if not more likely, to occur among newcomers than among long-term residents. In contrast, neighborhood and club affiliations are likely to increase the longer individuals live in the neighborhood.[19] This suggests the unique function of the extended family during the moving crisis.

Secondary Evidence

The evidence presented above consistently documents the position that extended family relations are not antithetical to geographical mobility in bureaucratic industrialized society. In fact, at times such relationships actually encourage mobility. The limits of the sample, however, place severe restrictions on the general application of these

TABLE 9

The Extended Family Meets the Needs of Recent Movers*

	Percentage Receiving Frequent Family Visits†	Percentage Belonging to More Than One Club‡	Percentage Knowing Five or More Neighbors§	Total Population
RESPONDENTS HAVING NO RELATIVES IN THE CITY				
Newcomers	22	25	38	110
Long-term residents	16	51	63	166
Difference	08	−26	−25	
RESPONDENTS HAVING NO RELATIVES IN THE CITY				
Newcomers	54	44	41	163
Long-term residents	49	43	60	485
Difference	05	01	−19	

* The respondents were divided between the newcomers or those people who had lived in their houses nine months or less and the long-term residents or all others.

† When no relatives in the city a frequent visit is defined as one or more family visits a month—either invited or non-invited. When relatives live in the city a frequent visit is defined as one or more family visits a week.

‡ This is the closest approximation to the average number of clubs to which the population belonged.

§This is the closest approximation to the average number of neighbors the respondents knew well enough to call on.

data. It is of some importance, therefore, to seek in other researches supportive evidence for extended family viability.

First, as a necessary but not sufficient condition, it should be shown that extended family relations are fairly extensive in American society today. In recent years, four studies that provide data on extended family visiting have been carried out, respectively, in Los Angeles, Detroit, San Francisco, and Buffalo. Three of these indicate that close to 50 per cent of the residents made one or more such visits a week. And three of the four investigations, on the basis of comparisons of family, neighbors, friends, and voluntary associations, conclude that the family relationships were either the most frequent or the most vital. These findings, as limited as they are, strongly suggest that extended family relations are extensive.[20]

What is of even greater interest is that these studies indicate that middle-class white persons share this viability with others and that these relations are highly important ones. Thus Sussman, in a study of middle-class white Protestant families, shows that 80 per cent of the family relationships studied involved giving aid, and in 70 per cent of the cases respondents felt that the recipients would suffer loss of status if the aid were not continued. Moreover, this aid had much more to do with standard of living than with locating jobs or helping people to advance in them through nepotism.[21] This investigation was supplemented by a study by Bell and Boat which indicates that 76 per cent of the low income and 84 per cent of the high income subjects could count on extended family aid in cases of illness lasting a month or longer; they also report that 90 per cent of the respondents indicated that at least one member of the extended family was a close friend.[22] Studies on working class families,[23] Puerto Rican families,[24] Negro families,[25] and Italian families[26] indicate that extended family relations in these cases are viable and warm.

Although these relations are of a far different character from the middle-class family contacts discussed in this paper,[27] the studies of working-class and ethnic groups do provide insight into the extension and warmth of extended family relations in all strata of contemporary society. They do not by themselves refute Parsons' formulation because he assumes that extended family relations are declining, not that they have disappeared. However, they buttress the alternative hypothesis advanced here since they do suggest a basic prerequisite of that hypothesis, namely, that extended family relations are viable in contemporary urban society.

Conclusions

It is argued, then, that these relations can retain their social significance under industrial bureaucratic pressures for geographical mobility. Evidence has been presented that is inconsistent with Parsons' hypothesis. Two theoretical points support this contrary view: first, that the extended family relationship which does not demand geographical propinquity (not examined by Parsons) is a significant form of social behavior; second, that theoretically the most efficient organization combines the ability of large-scale bureaucracy to handle uniform situations with the primary group's ability to deal with idiosyncratic situations. These two theoretical points suggest that there is both a need and a capacity for extended families to exist in modern society.

The data presented here (and in the earlier companion paper) demonstrate that persons separated from their families retained their extended family orientation; those with close family identification were as likely, if not more likely, to leave their family for occupational reasons; those on the upswing of their careers were apt to move away from their families and to receive family support; those on the career plateau were not likely to move or to move toward their family; that considerations of this kind hold only for bureaucratic occupations; and that the modified extended family seems to be uniquely suited to provide succor during periods of movement. These findings suggest interesting questions for future research. With respect to the family system, there is a need to isolate the mechanisms by which the nuclear family retains its semi-independence while receiving aid from the extended family.[28] It is also important to specify in greater detail the limits of the modified extended family organization in terms of time (does it extend over two or three generations?) and social distance (is it limited, for example, to parents and married children or siblings?). Concerning the occupational system, it is important to identify the type of bureaucratic structure which permits the family to be linked with occupations without affecting productivity.[29] For the analysis of class structure, the question arises as to how likely it is that extended family relations become significant factors blurring class identification without reducing occupational mobility.

NOTES

1. The first paper is Eugene Litwak, "Occupational Mobility and Extended Family Cohesion," *American Sociological Review,* 25 (February, 1960), pp. 9–21.
2. Talcott Parsons, "The Social Structure of the Family," in Ruth N. Ashen, editor, *The Family: Its Function and Destiny,* New York: Harper, 1949, pp. 191–192.
3. These families were marked by geographical propinquity, occupational integration, strict authority of extended family over nuclear family, and stress on extended rather than nuclear family relations.
4. The modified extended family differs from past extended families in that it does not require geographical propinquity, occupational nepotism, or integration, and there are no strict authority relations, but equalitarian ones. Family relations differ from those of the isolated nuclear family in that significant aid is provided to nuclear families, although this aid has to do with standard of living (housing, illness, leisure pursuits) rather than occupational appointments or promotions.
5. The counter hypothesis advanced in this paper is a modification of Parsons' position in that it accepts his analysis that the classical extended family is disfunctional for contemporary society, but it rejects

his view that the isolated nuclear family is the only theoretically meaningful alternative.

6. George C. Homans, *The Human Group,* New York: Harcourt, Brace, 1950, p. 36.

7. Of the large literature on this point, see e.g., Walter Firey, *Land Use in Central Boston,* Cambridge: Harvard University Press, 1947, pp. 184–186.

8. C. Wright Mills, C. Senior, and R. K. Goldsen in the *Puerto Rican Journey,* New York: Harper, 1950, p. 51, provide some indirect evidence on legitimation when they point out that the Puerto Rican migrant rarely moves out of a sense of economic necessity but because of a desire for economic betterment. They also show that these migrants rely on extended family communications before migrating (pp. 53–55). These facts illustrate that for the lowest income strata of migrants there has been a legitimation of geographical mobility for maximizing goals. This would seem to be doubly true of the middle-class migrant since he is economically better off to start with.

9. In addition to these assumptions, two more general ones should be made. First, it is assumed (in counter-distinction to W. F. Ogburn, for example, in "The Changing Functions of the Family," *Selected Studies in Marriage and the Family,* New York: Henry Holt, 1953, pp. 74–75) that extended families have not lost their functions. See Litwak, *op. cit.* Secondly, it is assumed that extensive family activity does not lead to occupational nepotism (*ibid.*); but Parsons' hypothesis states that extended family structures will collapse, or nepotism will destroy the industrial order.

10. The field study was conducted in the Buffalo area between June and October, 1952. For details of the study and the sampling, see Glenn H. Beyer, Thomas W. Mackesey, and James E. Montgomery, *Houses Are for People: A Study of Home Buyer Motivations,* Ithaca: Cornell University Housing Research Center, 1955. Some special features of the sample should be noted here. The sample cannot be considered to be a random one. Being a study designed to investigate housing, five or six different sampling procedures based on neighborhood and housing design were used. The varied nature of the sample complicates the problem of the appropriate statistical test. Therefore the argument must rest heavily on its theoretical plausibility and its consistency with other relevant studies. However, if the assumptions of a random area sample are made, and the sign and Wilcoxon signed-ranks tests are used, then all major findings are significant at the .05 level and beyond. The signs for these tests were always taken from the most complex table in which the given variables appeared.

11. Parsons, *op. cit.,* pp. 180–181.

12. Although these items were dichotomized to form a Guttman scale pattern, it is not argued that they meet all of the requirements for such a scale. See Eugene Litwak, *Primary Group Instruments of Social Control in Industrial Society: The Extended Family and the Neighborhood,* unpublished Ph.D. thesis, Columbia University, 1958, pp. 43–47.

13. The fact that only four per cent of the population answered item 4 positively means that item 3 defines extended family orientation for

most of the population. In this connection, no assumption is made that this operational definition exhausts the meaning of extended family orientation; it is only assumed that it will correlate highly with any other measures of extended family orientation.

14. Because some people may have interpreted "family" to mean only extended family it is possible that in this non-family oriented group there are some people who are nuclear family oriented. This plus the fact that the items were dichotomized to maximize their scaling properties suggests that little reliance should be placed on the absolute percentage of people exhibiting each value position but only on their differential distribution in various groups.

15. Since 95 per cent of the sample subjects were 45 or younger, and since the study was conducted during a period of great prosperity, virtually no one said he expected to earn less than now.

16. On the basis of the U.S. Census's occupational categories, the husband and the husband's father were classified into: (1) professional, technical, and kindred, and managers, officials, and proprietors; (2) clerical and kindred workers, and sales workers; or (3) all others except farmers or farm help. Husbands' and husbands' fathers' occupations were cross classified to provide four occupational categories: (1) upper-class husbands whose parents were upper-class; (2) husbands whose parents were from a higher occupational group; (3) husbands whose parents were from a lower occupational group; (4) working-class husbands whose parents were working-class. Two groups were eliminated: all individuals of farm background; and middle-class individuals of middle-class parentage (excluded because of the small number of cases). The stationary upper-class group is considered to approximate most closely the bureaucratic occupations while the stationary manual groups are assumed to be the polar opposite. Here "upper-class" does not refer to an old-line "aristocracy" but to a professional-managerial occupational grouping. By definition, all people in administrative positions in large-scale organizations and professionals are included in the upper-class or upwardly mobile occupational groups. There remains the question of whether or not they constitute a sufficiently large number within the overall classification to give a distinct direction. Gold and Slater in a study based upon a random sample of the Detroit area point out that in the one category roughly similar in age and occupation to the "upper-class" in this investigation, 74 per cent of the individuals were members of a bureaucratic organization. Martin Gold and Carol Slater, "Office, Factory, Store—and Family: A Study of Integration Setting," *American Sociological Review,* 23 (February, 1958), pp. 66, 69.

17. See, e.g., Seymour Martin Lipset and Reinhard Bendix, "Social Mobility and Occupational Career Patterns," in Bendix and Lipset, editors, *Class, Status and Power,* Glencoe, Ill.: Free Press, 1953, pp. 457–459.

18. Parsons, *op. cit.,* pp. 180–181.

19. The striking differences between respondents with relatives living in the city and those without nearby relatives, shown in Table 9, are discussed in an unpublished paper, Eugene Litwak, "Voluntary Associations and Primary Group Development in Industrial Society."

20. Morris Axelrod, "Urban Structure and Social Participation," *American*

Sociological Review, 21 (February, 1956), pp. 13–18; Wendell Bell and Marion D. Boat, "Urban Neighborhoods and Informal Social Relations," *American Journal of Sociology,* 62 (January, 1957), pp. 391–398; Scott Greer, "Urbanism Reconsidered," *American Sociological Review,* 21 (February, 1956), p. 22; Litwak, *Primary Group Instruments* . . . , *op. cit.,* p. 82.

21. Marvin B. Sussman, "The Help Pattern in Middle Class Family," *American Sociological Review,* 18 (February, 1953), pp. 22–28 *passim.*
22. Bell and Boat, *op. cit.* p. 396.
23. Michael Young and Peter Willmott, *Family and Kinship in East London,* London: Routledge and Kegan Paul, 1957, pp. 159–166.
24. Mills, Senior, and Goldsen, *op. cit.,* pp. 115, 117.
25. E. Franklin Frazier, "The Impact of Urban Civilization Upon Negro Family Life," P. K. Hatt and A. S. Reiss, Jr., editors, *Cities and Societies: The Revised Reader in Urban Sociology,* Glencoe, Ill.: Free Press, 1957, pp. 495–496.
26. Firey, *op. cit.,* pp. 184–186.
27. Cf. Litwak, "Occupational Mobility and Extended Family Cohesion," *op. cit.*
28. Cf. Eugene Litwak, "The Use of Extended Family Groups in the Achievement of Social Goals: Some Policy Implications," *Social Problems,* forthcoming.
29. Cf. Litwak, "Occupational Mobility and Extended Family Cohesion," *op. cit.;* and *Primary Group Instruments* . . . , *op. cit.,* pp. 6–30.

5

Urbanism Reconsidered: A Comparative Study of Local Areas in a Metropolis*

by Scott Greer

The investigation of the internal differentiation of urban population has been concerned chiefly with economic rank and ethnic diversity, and with the differences which accompany variations in these factors. Such

* Revised version of paper read at the annual meeting of the American Sociological Society, September, 1954. The study was carried out by the Laboratory in Urban Culture, a research facility of Occidental College, with the support of the John Randolph Haynes and Dora Haynes Foundation. I wish to express gratitude to Ella Kube, Research Associate, for assistance in the computation and analysis upon which the report is based.

Reprinted from *American Sociological Review,* 21 (February 1956), pp. 19–25, by permission of the author and The American Sociological Association.

studies throw little light upon the broad, non-ethnic, cultural differences generated in the metropolitan environment, i.e., upon "urbanism as a way of life." While there has been much concern, theoretically, with the effects of the metropolitan ambit upon all social relationships, most of the empirical basis of urban theory has been the study of small "natural areas" or the study of gross regularities in census data, arranged spatially for analysis.

Perhaps the best evidence bearing upon this larger question of "urbanism" has been the study of urban neighborhoods. The work of Donald Foley, for example, indicates that in a sample of Rochester residents (1) the neighborhood pattern still exists to some degree, but, (2) many individuals do not neighbor and do not consider their local area to be a social community.[1] Such studies approach the propositions that urban society is functionally rather than spatially organized and that urbanites are mobile, anonymous, and lacking in identification with their local area.

To gauge the generality of Foley's conclusions, however, one needs to know where the neighborhoods he studied fit in an array of neighborhoods. Because wide variation exists, the relation between the area studied and others is crucial for the hypothesis tested; most of Rochester may be much more neighborhood oriented, or much less so, than the area studied.

The Shevky-Bell typology of urban subareas is useful in this connection, for it allows any census tract to be located in three different arrays by means of three indices constructed from census data.[2] It is hypothesized that these represent three dimensions within urban social space, each statistically unidimensional and independent of the others. The dimensions are social rank, segregation, and urbanization.[3] The last largely measures differences in family structure, and, it is assumed, indicates corollary differences in behavior. Thus, when social rank and segregation are controlled, differences in the index of urbanization for specific tract populations should indicate consistent variations in social behavior. One purpose of the present research was to determine the nature of such corollary differences, and particularly differences in social participation.

This report is based upon a pilot study of differences in social participation between sample populations in two Los Angeles areas (census tracts 35 and 63).[4] The two tract populations are nearly identical with respect to two of the indices (social rank and segregation) and differ on the third, urbanization. For simplicity in presentation the tract with the higher urbanization index score (tract 63) will hereafter be called the high-urban tract, the other (tract 35) the low-urban tract.

The two sample tracts compare as follows. *History:* the low-urban tract is in an area that thirty years ago was separately incorporated for a brief time; the high-urban tract has always been a part of Los Angeles proper. *Location:* the low-urban tract is approximately fifteen minutes from the city center by auto; the high-urban tract is about half as far. (The low-urban tract is adjacent to the competing centers of Glendale and Pasadena.) *Social rank:* both tracts fall within the large middle range, being slightly above the median for the County. The social rank index for the low-urban tract is 68, for the high-urban tract, 66, as of the 1950 census of population, based upon the standard scores developed by Shevky with 1940 census data. *Ethnicity:* in neither tract does the foreign-born and non-white population amount to more than 5 per cent. *Urbanization:* the two tracts represent the extremes of the middle range of the urbanization index, within which a majority of the Los Angeles County census tracts lie. The low-urban tract had an urbanization index of 41, the high-urban tract, 57. There are much more highly urban tracts at middle rank, and much lower ones, in the County. The sample is weighted against the instrument, so that if striking and consistent variations appear in this middle range, they probably indicate more extreme variations at the poles.

The Field Procedure and the Sample

The field study included scheduled interviews on the participation of adult members of households in formal organizations, neighboring, cultural events, visiting, domestic activities, the mass media, the kin group, and other social structures.

Visiting was measured by questions concerning friends or relatives who were visited regularly at least once a month. The respondent was asked to give the address of the residence visited, both as a control over the accuracy of the information, and as a clue to social space position in the Shevky-Bell typology. Neighboring was measured by Wallin's "Neighborliness Scale," which was developed for a similar population in Palo Alto, California.[5] The scale assumes that neighborliness is unidimensional and can be measured by a small battery of questions referring to the degree of interaction with neighbors. The reproducibility for the present sample has not yet been determined.

Cultural events were recorded and categorized in the manner devised by Queen, in his studies of social participation in St. Louis.[6] Individuals were asked about their attendance in the past month at movies, classes, and study groups, athletic contests, lectures, and speeches, museums and exhibits, musical events, and stage shows. They were also asked the location of the event and who accompanied them. Special schedules of questions were developed for the purpose of describing participation in formal organizations of various sorts, definitions of the local area, domestic participation, neighborhood play of children, and other aspects of participation which will not be reported here.

An area random sample was interviewed in each tract, with 161 respondents in the low-urban tract, 150 in the high-urban tract. These households represented approximately 7 per cent of the population of the two census tracts chosen. The housewife was the respondent, and the response rate was over 85 per cent, being higher in the low-urban area. Interviewers were advanced and graduate students at Occidental College, and the average interview time was approximately one hour.

The two samples of households compare as follows:

Income: 20 per cent of the households in each area had less than $3,000 annually; 37 per cent in the low-urban area and 31 per cent in the high-urban area had annual incomes between $3,000 and $5,000, 35 per cent in the low-urban area and 38 per cent in the high-urban area had over $5,000 annually. Those who did not know or declined to state were 8 per cent in the low-urban area, 11 per cent in the high-urban area. The chief difference was a preponderance of middle income households in the low-urban area, with somewhat more heterogeneity in the high-urban area. *Occupation:* using the blue collar-white collar break, the samples were identical. In both areas, 72 per cent of the employed respondents were white-collar. Seventy-two per cent of the husbands in each area were in clerical jobs or higher.

Education: if education is divided into three classes, elementary or less, some high school or completed high school, and some college or more, the low-urban sample is slightly more homogeneous. Both respondents and husbands are 60 per cent high-school educated, with approximately 15 per cent below and 25 per cent above this class. In the high-urban sample the middle category accounted for only 50 per cent, with approximately 25 per cent below and 25 per cent above this class.

Such differences are not great but seem to indicate a consistent tendency towards somewhat more heterogeneity in the high-urban sample. It includes a slightly higher proportion of low-income, low-education persons, and also a slightly higher proportion of high-income, high-education persons. The high-urban sample is also more heterogeneous with respect to ethnicity. Although the percentage of non-white and foreign-born is similar in the two samples (9 for the low-urban sample, 11 for the high-urban) differences in religious affiliation indicate more ethnic diversity in the high-urban sample.

The low-urban area sample is much more homogeneous and Protestant in affiliation and preference. The high-urban sample, however, includes sizeable representations of the minority American religious beliefs: Jews and Roman Catholics are, together, only 20 per cent of the low-urban sample; they are 37 per cent of the high-urban sample. This heterogeneous and non-Protestant population in the high-urban sample is probably, to a large degree, made up of second and later generation ethnic individuals. Since the census tracts with high indexes of segregation in middle economic ranks are usually found in the more highly urbanized areas of the Skevky-Bell grid, it is likely that "later generation ethnics" (not identified in census data) are also concentrated in the more highly urbanized tracts of the middle social rank.

Such a correlation between second and later generation ethnic populations and urbanization, however, does not allow the reduction of the urbanization dimension to the ethnic component. In truth, many of these individuals are in process of leaving their ethnic status behind. Instead, it may be said that one of the attributes indicated by the urbanization index is apt to be the presence of second and later generation ethnics in the midst of acculturation. Such heterogeneity between faiths and within faiths is one of the conditions that give highly urbanized populations their particular characteristics.

Empirical Findings

Table 1 gives differences in participation between two areas with respect to the localization of community. The low-urban sample differed sharply and consistently in the direction of more participation in the local community. Their neighboring score was higher, they were more apt to have friends in the local area, and these constituted a larger proportion of all close friends, i.e., those visited at least once a

TABLE 1
Local Community Participation in Two Urban Areas

TYPE OF SOCIAL PARTICIPATION	LOW URBAN*	HIGH URBAN*
Per cent of respondents with high neighboring scores (Scale types 2 through 5)	67†	56†
N of respondents	(162)	(150)
Per cent of respondents with friends in the local area	50	29
N of respondents	(162)	(150)
Per cent of all respondents' friends who live in local area	41	25
N of all friends	(441)	(316)
Per cent of respondents attending cultural events in local area, of those attending any cultural events	45	18
N attending any events	(101)	(92)
Per cent of respondents' formal organizations which meet in:		
Local area	62	26
Other areas	35	71
No response	3	3
N of organizations	(126)	(67)
Per cent of respondents' formal organizations with the majority of members residing in:		
Local area	57	33
Other area	18	18
Scattered over the city	23	45
No response	2	4
N of organizations	(126)	(67)
Per cent of husbands' formal organizations (as reported by respondent) which meet in:		
Local area	21‡	5‡
Other areas	73	86
No response	6	9
N of husbands' organizations	(104)	(57)
Per cent of husbands' formal organizations (as reported by respondent) with the majority of members residing in:		
Local area	25	10
Other area	23	12
Scattered over the city	45	77
No response	7	1
N of husbands' organizations	(104)	(57)

* P (χ^2) <.01, with exceptions noted below.
† P (χ^2) slightly above .05 level: $\chi^2 = 3.77$.
‡ P (χ^2) between .01 and .02 levels.

month. They were more apt to go to cultural events such as movies, athletic contests, stage shows, and study groups, in the local area, and they were more apt to use local commercial facilities of certain types.

The low-urban sample had a higher rate of membership and participation in formal organizations other than church, and, more important, a larger proportion of their organizations were local in nature. A large majority of the respondents' organizations held meetings in the local area, and although the husbands' organizations usually met outside the area, still a much larger proportion met locally than did in the high-urban sample. Furthermore, the members of formal organizations to which the low-urban sample belonged were more apt to live in the immediate local community. In the high-urban sample other members were most apt to be scattered over the metropolis as a whole.

Further indication of the differential importance the local based organization had for these two samples is the greater familiarity of the low-urban sample with local community leaders. (See Table 2.)

TABLE 2

Respondents' Ability to Name Leaders of the Local Area and of Los Angeles

	LOW URBAN	HIGH URBAN
Per cent of respondents who could name at least one local leader	32*	21*
N of respondents	(162)	(150)
Per cent of respondents who could name at least one Los Angeles leader	38†	37†
N of respondents	(162)	(150)

* P (χ^2) between .02 and .05 levels.
† Difference not significant.

While the samples were equally able (and unable) to name Los Angeles leaders, there was a significantly higher proportion who could name local leaders in the low-urban area sample. This probably indicates a uniform engagement of the middle-rank populations in the affairs of the metropolis as a whole, but definite variations in their interest and involvement with respect to local affairs.

It is sometimes stated, almost as an axiom, that the urban milieu results in the extreme attrition of kin relations. The present study indicates this to be questionable. The most important single kind of social relationship for both samples is kinship visiting. A large majority of both samples visit their kin at least once a month, and *half of each sample visit their kin at least once a week.* These data, reported in Table 3, are consistent with the findings of Bell in his comparable study of social areas in the San Francisco Bay Region.[7]

TABLE 3
Kin Visiting in Two Urban Areas

PER CENT VISITING KIN	LOW URBAN*	HIGH URBAN*
Once a week or more often	49	55
At least once a month, but less than once a week	24	21
A few times a year, but less than once a month	11	8
Never	5	9
No kin in Los Angeles	11	7
N of respondents	(162)	(150)

* No significant difference between low and high urban area samples.

Both samples indicated complacency with their neighborhood and said they were satisfied with it as a home, but in giving their reasons for liking it, they tended to differ. The low-urban sample described their area as a "little community," like a "small town," where "people are friendly and neighborly." The high-urban sample, on the other hand, most frequently mentioned the "convenience to downtown and everything," and spoke often of the "nice people" who "leave you alone and mind their own business." The high-urban sample seemed less committed to remaining in their present area—a higher proportion stating that there were other neighborhoods in the city in which they would rather live.

A tendency toward differential association with populations at a similar level of urbanization is indicated in the visiting patterns of the two samples outside their local areas. The residences of close friends and the meeting places of social circles are almost mutually exclusive for the two samples. Furthermore, when the census tracts in which are located the homes of the friends they visit are categorized by urbanization scores, clear differences appear. The low-urban sample is more apt to have friends in other low-urban areas, while the high-urban sample is apt to visit in other high-urban areas. (See Table 4.) When it is recalled that these two samples are almost identical with respect to social rank and segregation, the importance of the urbanization dimension is underlined. These visiting patterns refer to well structured friendship relations of probable importance. Such differ-

TABLE 4

*Residence of Friends Visited, Outside of the Local Area
by Urbanization Index Score**

	LOW URBAN†	HIGH URBAN†
Per cent of friends living in tracts with urbanization index score of		
1–20	13	12
21–40	35	25
41–60	41	33
61–80	8	19
81–100	3	11
N of friends visited	(180)	(162)

* Friends' addresses which could not be coded (80 in the Low Urban area, 65 in the High Urban) are excluded.
† P (χ^2) <.001.

ential association may result from proximity, as well as selective visiting by levels of urbanization. The relative importance of proximity will be measured through the use of the intervening opportunities model. However, even if such differential association is to a large degree a function of spatial proximity, its significance in certain respects would remain. For, if populations at given levels of urbanization interact more intensely within those levels than with other populations, such interactions should result in fairly stable networks of informal communication and influence. The content of such communication should vary with urbanization.

Summary and Interpretation

In order to investigate empirically the complex of notions surrounding the nature of urban social behavior, the Shevky-Bell typology, applied to sub-areas in Los Angeles County, was used to select two neighborhoods which differed clearly on the index of urbanization. Social rank was not used as the chief factor accounting for differential social participation, as was the case in the studies of Komarovsky, Goldhamer, and others.[8] Instead, rank was controlled, and the urbanization dimension was tested for broad differences in social participation.

It should be noted that this study investigates the effects of urbanization at a *particular* level of rank and segregation; at other levels, the effects of urbanization remain problematical. It is hoped that future studies will clarify, for example, the effects of differential urbanization at higher and lower social ranks, as well as in segregated populations. The Shevky-Bell typology, based upon a three dimensional attribute-space model of urban society, calls attention not only to three separate factors, but also to the possibility that the particular effects of one may be transformed as either or both of the others vary.

However, the urbanization dimension was the focus of the present study. It was not identified with the older notion of urbanism which implies that all city populations are changing in the direction of atomistic, mass society.[9] Instead, it was assumed that there is a continuum of alternative life-styles at the same economic level and that these are concentrated in different urban sub-areas. In this framework, the low-urban areas are just as characteristic of modern urban society as are the high-urban areas. Both types continue to be alternatives in the urban complex. In this view, the Shevky-Bell index of urbanization is a putative means of identifying such variations in "ways of life." Instead of concentrating on urbanism as *a* way of life, the present study was focused upon the variations possible.

Two social aggregates, inhabiting tracts with similar economic rank and ethnicity but varying with respect to the urbanization index, were sampled. The sample populations were then studied by means of reported social participation.

The findings are consistent with the hypothesis that, where rank and ethnicity are equal, differences in the urbanization index will indicate differences in social behavior. Had the index identified populations not significantly different, doubt would have been cast upon its utility at the level of individual social behavior, for the urbanization dimension of modern society, as conceived by Shevky in his theoretical structure, implies such differences in social behavior.[10] However, the present study indicates that the index, constructed primarily with items related to family structure, does identify differences in social participation which are associated with variations in family structure but not derived solely from them. The general validity of the hypothesis must rest upon further studies in Los Angeles and other urban complexes. Although this study and that of Bell indicate the urbanization dimension does affect social participation to an impressive degree, the regularity with which these differences form a continuum at this intersection of social rank and segregation, and the nature of the hypothesized continuum, remain to be spelled out. Still, in the interpretation of the findings here reported, the following implications come to mind:

1. The local area in the contemporary American metropolis may be viewed as attracting population, not only by the economic rank and ethnic composition of the population already in the area, but also by the degree of urbanization characteristic of the area—the way of life common to the older inhabitants.

2. Such areas may attract populations on at least two different functional bases: (1) the demographic and the cultural character-istics of the older settlers who give the area its "tone," may attract people as seems true in the low-urban sample, or (2) the area as a socially neutral, but convenient base of operations for various seg-mental interests, may attract people as in the high-urban sample. Such different principles of attraction would tend to produce greater homogeneity of background and interest in low-urban areas, and from this similarity a higher degree of community-type behavior and of conformity would be expected.

3. A continuum is hypothesized for non-segregated, middle-rank areas. At one pole lie the local areas which select a predominantly "old American" population with similar jobs, aspirations, incomes, who wish to raise children, neighbor, participate in local community groups, and, in brief, carry on a life in many ways similar to that of the small towns described by Warner and his associates.[11] At the other pole lie those areas of the city which are more heterogene-ous, with fewer children and little interest in the local area as a social arena. Such areas may approach, in many ways, the ideal type of urban environment hypothesized by Wirth.[12]

4. In this perspective, the local area is important as a framework for interaction, as a "social fact," just where it is least representative of the total urban society. The small community, as studied by Warner and others, is a very poor example of the urban complex, since it will include the fewest elements of urban society as a whole. At the same time, the high-urban tract as a sample of urban society is only slightly less biased, for in it the local area as a social fact dis-appears altogether. Thus it is not possible to use either the model of a small, spatially enclosed community or the stereotype of the continually more atomistic mass society in describing social partici-pation in the contemporary metropolis.

There are, however, certain common structural threads running through the fabric of modern society. As Paul Hatt noted, the indices developed by Warner and others to measure social status may be gen-eralized to the total society, since the various methods correlate highly with one universal attribute—occupation.[13] The present approach is, then, to ask: How does this attribute become defined and organized, how does it influence participation, in different sub-areas of the metropolis?

A tentative answer is that the individual's social position is defined differently and his social participation is patterned differently as the focus shifts from the low-urban populations to the high-urban populations. One may envisage the low-urban areas as somewhere between the small town and the conventional picture of metropolitan living. Where the local area is a social fact, where common interests and associations obtain, generalizations derived from small community studies may have validity. For here the individual's status will result, in part, from participation in a known and used local organizational structure and from family ties that are publicly understood.

When, however, high-urban populations are considered, social participation is organized around position in other organizational contexts, as for example, the corporation, politics, the labor union, or perhaps, as Riesman has suggested, categories derived from the popular culture of the mass media.[14] Here also are many individuals whose life, aside from work, is ordered by participation in small informal groups, and informal groups only, floating within the vast culture world of the market and the mass media. In such populations the locally defined community is largely irrelevant to status and participation. Associations are spread geographically, but ordered and concentrated in terms of selected interests. Family, in this context, is still important. It is slightly more important in the high-urban sample described. But it is probably much more private in its reference. In fact, kin relations may be seen as growing in importance just because of the diminished reliance placed upon neighborhood and local community.

What has been sketched above is a tentative model which will allow the use of contributions from earlier research (studies of small cities, natural areas, the apartment house family, the suburban fringe) within a framework which integrates and orders them in relation to one another. Such a frame of reference also relates, eventually, to the increasing importance of large-scale organizations in a society which allows many alternative life patterns for individuals at the same functional and economic level.

NOTES

1. Donald L. Foley, "Neighbors or Urbanites? The Study of a Rochester District," *The University of Rochester's Studies of Metropolitan Rochester,* Rochester, New York, 1952.
2. Eshref Shevky and Wendell Bell, *Social Area Analysis,* Stanford, California: Stanford University Press, 1955. See also, Eshref Shevky and Marilyn Williams, *The Social Areas of Los Angeles,* Berkeley and Los Angeles: The University of California Press, 1948.
3. For a description of the statistical analysis and testing of the typology, see Wendell Bell, "Economic, Family, and Ethnic Status," *American Sociological Review,* 20 (February, 1955), pp. 45–52.
4. The extension of the study to include two additional sample tracts will be reported later; results are generally consistent with the findings reported here. Rank and segregation are the same in the added tract samples, but the new tracts extend to the extremes of the urbanization index within middle economic rank.
5. Paul Wallin, "A Guttman Scale for Measuring Women's Neighborliness," *American Journal of Sociology,* 49 (November, 1953), pp. 243–246.
6. Stuart A. Queen, "Social Participation in Relation to Social Disorganization," *American Sociological Review,* 14 (April, 1949), pp. 251–256.
7. Wendell Bell (with the assistance of Maryanne Force and Marion Boat), "People of the City," (processed) Stanford University Survey Research Facility, Stanford, California, 1954.
8. Mirra Komarovsky, "The Voluntary Associations of Urban Dwellers," *American Sociological Review,* 11 (December, 1946), pp. 868–896; Herbert Goldhamer, "Voluntary Associations in the United States," unpublished Ph.D. thesis, University of Chicago, 1942.
9. See Louis Wirth, "Urbanism as a Way of Life," *The American Journal of Sociology,* 44 (July, 1938), pp. 1–24.
10. Shevky and Bell, *op. cit.,* especially Chapter II.
11. See, for example, W. Lloyd Warner and associates, *Democracy in Jonesville,* New York: Harper & Brothers, 1949.
12. Wirth, *op. cit.*
13. Paul K. Hatt, "Stratification in the Mass Society," *American Sociological Review,* 15 (April, 1950), pp. 216–222.
14. David Riesman, in collaboration with Reuel Denny and Nathan Glazer, *The Lonely Crowd, A Study of the Changing American Character,* New Haven: Yale University Press, 1950, especially Chs. X, XI, XII.

6

Familism and Suburbanization: One Test of the Social Choice Hypothesis*

by Wendell Bell

Introduction

Social Choice and Population Types

Within certain population types, the relationship between the food economy and population growth fairly well resembles the conditions described by Malthus.[1] These societies, described by Notestein as having high growth potential[2] and described by Schultz as having endogenous relationships between the agricultural economy and population changes,[3] contain populations which tend to expand to the limits of the food supply. In these societies, the "positive checks" of Malthus operate to control population size; birth rates remain high and relatively stable, variations in population growth being tied to variations in the death rate. Although a large proportion of the world's people still live under such conditions, it has been demonstrated that in other societies, especially large-scale industrial societies, population changes cannot be explained by changes in the agricultural sector of the economy.[4] These societies are freed from the Malthusian limits, and population variations within them will be an expression of a wide range of alternatives for individuals, death rates being characteristically low and stable and variations in population growth being tied to variations in the birth rate rather than to variations in the death rate. Thus the pressure of the population on the food supply no longer explains population growth in such societies as the United States, and other

* A paper read at a joint session of the American and Rural Sociological Societies, Washington, D.C., Aug. 31, 1955. This research was accomplished with the cooperation of the Center for Metropolitan Studies, Northwestern University. Walter C. Kaufman made important contributions to this paper.

Reprinted from *Rural Sociology,* 21 (September–December 1956), pp. 276–283, by permission of the author and *Rural Sociology.*

explanatory concepts are needed. A range of available choices which may affect the birth rate have been postulated. These include *familism, upward vertical mobility,* and *consumership,* among others.

The Three Alternative Choice Patterns Defined

By familism is meant investment in the familial system of the society; marriage at young ages, a short childless time-span after marriage, large families, and other such characteristics are indicators of familism. By upward mobility is meant movement into social positions of greater prestige, property, and power.

These are fairly common notions and many writers have discussed the relationship between the family and economic systems, usually positing an inverse relationship between familism and upward vertical mobility.[5] Recent writers have pointed out, for example, that the investment of time and money in family life may have deleterious consequences for upward mobility; and, conversely, that the investment of time and money in one's career may limit one's family life by delaying marriage or postponing children.

Those persons who eschew investment in either career or family and prefer having as high a standard of living as possible in the present represent the consumership choice pattern.[6] These persons expend their efforts on "having a good time," "living it up," or "enjoying life as much as possible," and they do this in ways which are unconnected with family or career goals.[7]

The Hypothesis

There is some evidence that these alternative choice patterns and the recent shift of population to the suburbs may be linked together, although there does not seem to be complete agreement concerning which choice patterns are most reflected in the suburban shift. Demographic comparisons between central cities and their suburbs have shown that there is generally a higher socio-economic status group in the suburbs, suggesting that vertical mobility was involved in the suburban move.[8] On the other hand, these comparisons also have shown for the suburbs a larger family size, more married males, more intact families, and more women not in the labor force, suggesting that a preference for familism was reflected in the outward move. Statistically analyzed surveys as well as impressionistic articles by popular writers have reflected one or another aspect of these two themes, and in some cases both themes are present.[9]

The hypothesis of this study is *that the move to the suburbs expresses an attempt to find a location in which to conduct family life which is more suitable than that offered by central cities,* i.e., *that persons moving to the suburbs are principally those who have chosen familism as an important element of their life styles.* This is not offered as a complete explanation of the move to the suburbs. The sheer growth of our cities has brought about an expansion into the areas around them. This hypothesis concerns the selective or differentiating factors involved in the movement.

The Sample

One hundred interviews were obtained in two adjacent suburbs in the Chicago metropolitan area. These were Park Ridge and Des Plaines, both of which have had relatively large increases since the end of World War II. Park Ridge increased 37.6 per cent between 1940 and 1950 and about 44.6 per cent between 1950 and 1955. Des Plaines has had a somewhat larger relative growth, increasing its population 57.5 per cent between 1940 and 1950 and about 80 per cent between 1950 and 1955. Both have increased every decade since 1880; the largest relative increase over the years in each case occurred during the 1920's. Both suburbs are primarily residential in character, and are located along a Chicago and Northwestern Railway commuter line. Park Ridge has a somewhat higher average income, occupation, and education than does Des Plaines; and the sample, having been drawn from both places, contains a relatively wide range with respect to economic status characteristics. Thirty-two per cent of the sample are classified as blue-collar; 24 per cent, lower white-collar; and 44 per cent, upper white-collar.[10]

A sample of dwelling units was randomly drawn from those areas where about 30 per cent or more of the housing consisted of post-World War II building. Substitution of next-door neighbors was allowed in case the selected respondent refused or was not at home. Half of the field work was done on the weekends in order to obtain about an equal split between men and women respondents. The interviewing was done during the early summer of 1955. Most of the interview schedule was memorized by the interviewers, and the average interview was about 30 minutes long.

The Findings

Sixty-eight per cent of the respondents had been living in Chicago just prior to their present move to the suburbs; 24 per cent came from nearby areas, mostly other suburbs, outside of Chicago; and only 8 per cent came from other places. Persons of lower socio-economic status were more likely to have moved from Chicago than were those of higher socio-economic status—88 per cent of the blue-collar, 62 per cent of the lower white-collar, and 57 per cent of the upper white-collar persons reported their last residence within the city limits of Chicago.

Characteristically, the suburbanites interviewed had been apartment dwellers before moving to their present residence, 65 per cent so reporting. Thus the shift to these two suburbs typically involves not only a move from the central city, but also entails a move from an apartment to a house.

The bulk of each interview was devoted to probing the reasons the respondent gave for moving to the suburbs. The reasons given for the move were classified into five broad categories (Table 1). Four-fifths

TABLE 1

Broad Classes of Reasons Given for Moving to the Suburbs, and Percentage of Respondents Mentioning Each Type

TYPE OF REASON	PER CENT*
Better for children	81
Enjoy life more	77
Husband's job	21
Near relatives	14
Other	3

* Since many respondents gave more than one reason, the sum of the percentages does not equal 100.

of the respondents gave reasons which had to do with bettering conditions for their children. Three-fourths of these responses concerned physical features of the suburbs in contrast to those of the city (Table 2). More space outside the house with less traffic and cleaner areas were cited as allowing the children to play out of doors "like children should," with much less worry and supervision on the part of the parents. Also, the fresh air, sunshine, and other features of "the outdoors" were mentioned as providing a "more healthy" life for the

TABLE 2

Percentage Distribution of Specific Reasons in the
"Better for Children" Category

SPECIFIC REASONS FOR MOVING TO THE SUBURBS	PER CENT
Physical reasons ($N = 172$)	*72.3*
More space outside house	19.7
More space inside house	14.3
"The outdoors" (fresh air, sunshine, etc.)	12.6
Less traffic	11.8
Cleaner	6.3
No neighbors in same building	3.8
Quiet	2.1
No stairs	1.7
Social reasons ($N = 66$)	*27.7*
Better schools	10.2
"Nice" children to play with	9.2
Other children to play with	2.5
More organized activities	2.5
Home of own (security)	1.7
Adults "nice" to children	0.8
Better churches	0.8
Total reasons in this category ($N = 238$)	100.0

children. Living in a single-family detached house—instead of next to, above, or below other persons as in an apartment—was cited as giving the children more freedom to run and play in the house without the constant repressive demands of the parents. Also, the additional space inside the house, according to the respondents, allows the children to have a place of their own within the house, and permits them to "be children" without constantly "being on top" of their parents. Naps are less interfered with in the quiet of the suburbs.

Only a quarter of the responses having to do with moving for the children's sake referred to social factors. The most frequent reason was the belief that the schools would be better in that classes would be smaller, more individual attention would be given by the teachers, and the teachers in the suburbs would be more interested in the children as well as generally more competent than those in Chicago. Other features concerning the social aspect of suburban living thought to be better for children were the following: other children of about the same age to serve as playmates for the respondent's children;

more organized activities available for children; owning one's own home, which gives the children a sense of security they could never get in an apartment; other adults in the suburbs have children and, therefore, the adults treat all children with understanding; and better churches in the suburbs to which the children can go.

In 9 per cent of these responses (a third of those classed as "social") there were words to the effect that there were "nicer" children in the suburbs to serve as playmates for one's children. When this reason was given, extensive probing was employed to determine whether or not an upward mobility motif was involved. In one case this seemed to be so. The mother said, "We moved here mainly because of my daughter. The environment and schools are better, and her companions are of high caliber." (Interviewer probed "high caliber.") "I mean more highly educated families." (Interviewer asked what difference that made.) "If it's a girl I suppose you're thinking of who she's going to marry and grow up with." (Pause.) "When it comes down to it, it's a matter of income isn't it? We want to give our child the best possible chance." (Interviewer asked what she meant by "chance.") "So she can enjoy life to the fullest and live graciously, I suppose."

This case was an exception, however, for probing indicated that other respondents giving this response seemed to be referring to their belief that there are fewer "juvenile delinquents" and "bad" influences among their children's playmates in the suburbs. Thus, the response generally seems to indicate a maintenance of present social status rather than upward mobility aspirations for children.

Three-fourths of the respondents (Table 1) gave reasons for their move to the suburbs which have been classified as "enjoying life more." These are shown in detail in Table 3. In these reasons, social features were mentioned more often than the physical features of the suburbs as being important influences in the decision to move. The respondents expected more friendly neighbors, greater participation in the community, and easier living at a slower pace than they had had in the city.

Another theme was the "people-like-ourselves" idea. Some respondents said they wanted to live in a neighborhood where people had the same age, marital, family, financial, educational, occupational, or ethnic status as themselves. Ten per cent of the repsonses fell into this category, and extensive probing seemed to indicate that the mobility motif was not involved. Instead, it appeared that it was more a matter of feeling more comfortable and having more in common with persons of similar interests. For example, a white-collar man living in a predominantly blue-collar block indicated that he would

TABLE 3

Percentage Distribution of Specific Reasons in the
"Enjoy Life More" Category

SPECIFIC REASONS FOR MOVING TO THE SUBURBS	PER CENT
Physical reasons (*N* = 141)	*44.1*
"The outdoors" (fresh air, sunshine, etc.)	13.1
Gardening and "puttering around the house"	10.9
Quiet	7.2
Less crowded	6.6
Cleaner	4.1
More modern conveniences in house	2.2
Social reasons (*N* = 179)	*55.9*
Friendly neighbors	14.1
Feeling of belonging	8.8
Easier living, slower pace	8.1
Home of own (investment)	7.2
Privacy	4.1
Age, marital, and family status the same	4.1
Financial status the same	3.1
"Higher class" of people	2.8
Education the same	1.2
Racial stock the same	1.2
Friends moved here	0.9
Occupational level the same	0.3
Total reasons in this category (*N* = 320)	100.0

move elsewhere in the suburbs because he didn't have much of a common interest with his neighbors. He went on to say that his chief concern, although by no means his only one, was the fact that none of his neighbors played bridge.

Only 9 per cent of the respondents indicated that one of their reasons for moving to the suburbs was that they expected a "higher class" of person to be living there as compared with the central city. When probed on this point, the respondents referred to higher education and income, better occupations—especially engineering and sales occupations—good manners, quiet rather than loud and boisterous habits, a gracious manner of living, and intelligence. Certainly, a mobility motif must be admitted in most of these cases, but even here some persons seemed to be trying to find a group of persons "like themselves" with which to live, rather than trying to "better themselves" socially.

The physical features which attracted these suburbanites were the fresh air, sunshine, growing trees and other characteristics of the "open country" in contrast to the central city; also, the opportunity to garden and to "putter" around their "own home" was important. The quiet, lack of congestion, and cleanliness of the suburbs were also mentioned, as was the fact that a new house with modern conveniences was to be had in the suburbs for a lower price than its equivalent in the city.

As is also shown in Table 1, a fifth of the respondents said that the husband's job was a factor in their move to the suburbs. Of these, more than half were transferred without a promotion or increase in salary or were just moving closer to a job which they had held for some time. The others, 9 per cent of the respondents, indicated that their move was a consequence of upward mobility, although none felt that their move was consequential for future increases on the job.

Social Choice Types

The following interpretation should be accepted with caution since these findings may not hold for the movement into suburbs of different types from those studied here. Even though a fairly wide range with respect to value of homes and occupations of the respondents was included in the sample, different reasons for moving may be found in other types of suburbs, such as industrial suburbs or suburbs in which only families of the very top socioeconomic stratum reside. For the two suburbs studied, however, the findings are quite convincing.

The respondents were classified with respect to the dominant theme underlying their reasons for moving to the surburbs. Upward vertical mobility does not seem to be greatly associated with choosing to live in the suburbs, despite the contention of some recent writers. In fact, only 10 per cent of the respondents could be classified as having upward mobility aspirations involved in their move to the suburbs, and even here most of these persons also had other reasons for moving.

On the other hand, 31 per cent of the respondents can be classified as exemplifying pure familism, and a familistic orientation entered into the decision to move to the suburbs in a total of 83 per cent of the cases. That familism as it enters into the suburban move is largely "conjugal familism" is indicated by the fact that only a relatively small percentage of the respondents moved in order to be closer to relatives not living with them while a much larger percentage indicated that they moved "because of the children." In fact, several who moved because of the children also noted that it was a little farther away from their relatives—a condition which they considered desirable.[11]

In many of the responses which were categorized as familistic, it was evident that the respondents tended to think of the move to the suburbs in terms of the move from an apartment to a house. Thus, some respondents pointed out that if they could have found the same house in the city they would have preferred to live in the city. Although they realized such sections did exist within the city, they also noted that homes in them cost more than in the suburbs. Also in these responses there was the definite notion that the move from apartment to house was mutually beneficial for parent and child. In fact, several of the wives, according to their own testimony, had been on the verge of nervous collapse living with small children in an apartment. Since moving to a house in the suburbs, they reported they were no longer "nervous."

In general, the respondents reported moving because of the children, but they also reported that since they had lived in the suburbs they had learned to enjoy "suburban living" so much that they would never move back to the city. Seven per cent of the respondents, however, said that they would move back to an apartment in the city as soon as their children were married.

Ten per cent of the respondents were classified as pure examples of the consumership pattern, and an additional 43 per cent gave consumership reasons along with other reasons.

The three original life styles did not seem adequate to account for all of the responses given. A fourth theme, labeled the "quest-for-community," was apparent. This was the idea of moving to the suburbs to get more friendly neighbors, greater community participation, and a sense of belonging to the community. About 73 per cent of the respondents included such reasons as important factors in their decision to move to the suburbs, and usually this was in conjunction with the familistic orientation.

Thus the data support the hypothesis that the new suburbanites are largely persons who have chosen familism as an important element in their life styles, and in addition suggest a relationship between the desire for community participation or sense of belonging and the move to the suburbs.[12]

Dewey concluded from his study of suburbanization in Milwaukee County that the ". . . movement into the rural-urban fringe is not a desire to escape anything that is inherent in urbanism as a way of life. . . ." [13] The data of the present study, only partially reported here,[14] confirm that suburbanites, in general, desire the advantages of modern technology and many of the facilities of urban "culture." However, if anonymity, impersonality, defilement of air and land by industry, apartment living, crowding, and constant nervous stimulation are inherent in "urbanism as a way of life," as some writers have said, then the findings of this study necessitate the conclusions that the suburbanite *is* seeking an escape from many traditional aspects of city living. The suburbanite seems to be seeking a way of life in which family, community, and immediate enjoyment through living the "good life" are dominant and interdependent ends.

NOTES

1. Thomas Robert Malthus, *An Essay on the Principle of Population as It Affects Future Improvement of Society,* 1798.
2. Frank W. Notestein, "Population—The Long View," in Theodore W. Schultz, *Food for the World* (Chicago, Ill.: University of Chicago Press, 1945).
3. Theodore W. Schultz, *The Economic Organization of Agriculture* (New York: McGraw-Hill Book Co., 1953).
4. *Ibid.*
5. E. Digby Baltzell, "Social Mobility and Fertility within an Elite Group," *Milbank Memorial Fund Quarterly,* 31 (Oct., 1953), pp. 411–420; Jerzy Berent, "Fertility and Social Mobility," *Population Studies,* 5 (Mar., 1952), pp. 244–260; Ernest W. Burgess and Paul Wallin, *Engagement and Marriage* (Chicago, Ill.: Lippincott, 1953); Theodore Caplow, *Sociology of Work* (Minneapolis: University of Minnesota Press, 1954); Rudolph Heberle, "Social Factors in Birth Control," *American Sociological Review,* 6 (Dec., 1941), pp. 794–805; John F. Kantner and Clyde V. Kiser, "The Interrelation of Fertility, Fertility Planning, and Intergenerational Social Mobility," *Milbank Memorial Fund Quarterly,* 32 (Jan., 1954), pp. 69–103; E. E. Lemasters, "Social Class Mobility and Family Integration," *Marriage and Family Living,* XVI (Aug., 1954), pp. 226–232; Sverre Lysgaard, "Social Stratification and the Deferred Gratification Pattern" (unpublished Ph.D. dissertation, Purdue University, 1952); Alva Myrdal, *Nation and Family* (New York; Harper & Bros., 1941); Ruth Reimer and Clyde V. Kiser, "Economic Tension and Social Mobility in Relation to Fertility Planning and Size of Planned Family," *Milbank Memorial Fund Quarterly,* 32 (Apr., 1954), pp. 167–231; Warren S. Thompson, *Population Problems* (3rd ed.; New York: McGraw-Hill Book Co., Inc., 1942); Charles F. Westoff, "The Changing Focus of Differential Fertility Research: The Social Mobility Hypothesis," *Milbank Memorial Fund Quarterly,* 31 (Jan., 1953), pp. 24–38; and Robert F. Winch, *The Modern Family* (New York: Henry Holt & Co., 1952).

6. There is a characteristic economic consumption pattern associated with each of the choice patterns. Certain types of purchases should be more typical of those who have chosen familism, other types more typical of those who are upward-mobile, and still other types more typical of those classified in the "consumership" pattern as the term is used here.

7. A more complete statement of these three choice patterns and their implications has been made by Scott A. Greer, in "Working Papers Toward a Theory of Social Choice" (mimeo., Occidental College, 1955).

8. For example, see J. Allan Beegle, "Characteristics of Michigan's Fringe Population," *Rural Sociology,* XII:3 (Sept., 1947), pp. 254–263; Donald J. Bogue, "A Few Facts about Chicago's Suburbs," Chicago Community Inventory (1954); Beverly Duncan, "Demographic and Socio-economic Characteristics of the Population of the City of Chicago and the Suburbs and Urban Fringe: 1950," Chicago Community Inventory (1954); U. S. Bureau of the Census, *Census of Population: 1950,* Vol. IV, *Special Reports,* Pt. V, chap. A, "Characteristics by Size of Place."

9. E.g., see Richard Dewey, "Peripheral Expansion in Milwaukee County," *American Journal of Sociology,* 54 (Sept., 1948), pp. 118–125; E. Gartly Jaco and Ivan Belknap, "Is a New Family Form Emerging in the Urban Fringe?" *American Sociological Review,* 18 (Oct., 1953), pp. 551–557; Harry Henderson, "The Mass Produced Suburbs" (in 2 parts), *Harpers,* Vol. 207 (Nov. and Dec., 1953), *passim;* Myles W. Rodehaver, "Fringe Settlement as a Two-Directional Movement," *Rural Sociology,* XII:1 (Mar., 1947), pp. 49–57; Nathan L. Whetten, "Suburbanization as a Field for Sociological Research," *Rural Sociology,* XVI:4 (Dec., 1951), pp. 319–330; and William H. Whyte, Jr., "The Transients" (in 4 parts), *Fortune,* 49 (May, June, July, and Aug., 1953), *passim.*

10. Professionals, managers, officials, and proprietors were classified upper white-collar; clerical and sales workers were classified lower white-collar; and craftsmen, foremen, operatives, private household workers, service workers, and laborers were classified blue-collar. None of the sample dwelling units contained persons reporting the occupations of farm laborer, farm manager, or farm proprietor.

11. Cf. Jaco and Belknap, *op. cit.*

12. An excellent discussion related to this point can be found in Sylvia Fleis Fava, "Suburbanism as a Way of Life," *American Sociological Review,* 21 (Feb., 1956), pp. 34–37.

13. Dewey, *op. cit.,* p. 125.

14. Data were also collected concerning the features of suburban life which the respondents liked or disliked "after having lived there for a while."

7

Is a New Family Form Emerging in the Urban Fringe?

by E. Gartly Jaco & Ivan Belknap

One modern school of family sociologists, represented chiefly by Zimmerman, considers the present urban American family an alarming instance of disintegration in the familial process. This disintegration is believed to have reached such extremes that the family can no longer adequately discharge vital functions such as reproduction and socialization. Writers of this school imply that American, and Western civilization generally, faces the dilemma of social collapse through failure of the family functions, or a return to some form of the large rural or semi-rural family system.[1]

Another school considers the modern urban family to be making a reasonably satisfactory adjustment to population density, secondary relations, and diversity of urban institutions.[2] Most demographers apparently agree that basic population trends have been in harmony with the assumptions of this latter school.[3] Urban sociologists also have generally accepted the present urban "companionship," or small family as necessarily typical of urban communities.[4] Burgess and Locke consider this type of family as one "which seeks to combine the values of both the old rural and the modern urban situations." [5]

It is the purpose of this paper to point out certain trends that may be leading toward the emergence of a variant type of urban family which may be able to maintain sufficient fertility and integration to satisfy the Zimmerman requisites and yet function adequately in the urban community. This variant type of urban family seems to be locating in the urban "fringe," [6] as a product of changing ecological and demographic forces in metropolitan regions, and as a new functional adjustment of the family to the urban way of life. Because this family apparently represents primarily an adjustment to or a product of the peripheral metropolitan ecological area, it might be tentatively termed the "fringe family." [7]

Reprinted from *American Sociological Review*, 18 (October 1953), pp. 551–557, by permission of the authors and The American Sociological Association.

This new family form may be only temporarily connected, however, with the urban fringe. The new family type should not be construed as being permanently or intrinsically bound up with the "fringe." The "fringe family" label is offered only as a provisional, heuristic term which implies that this family form is initially a product of contemporary urban fringe development. This form may eventually spread to other ecological areas. Further research is needed, therefore, before a precise term pertaining to the social structure of this new family type can be given.

Satisfactory proof of the existence of such family form in significant numbers will require restudy of parts of current urban family sociology. In view of the present status of sociological data on the fringe, however, such proof will require considerable field research. Little attention has been paid by sociologists to any family form associated with the outskirts of the city.[8] Also little systematic research has been done on the fringe as a social unit. At present, census and vital statistics data are inadequate for a thorough statistical analysis of the fringe; the former offering only data for 1950 on Standard Metropolitan Areas (these will not be useful for comparisons until 1960); and the vital statistics have no fringe definition at all. The census category of "rural nonfarm" is for the present about the only index of the fringe, but it includes many non-fringe components.

Trends Toward the Fringe Family

The following trends in American society do not prove conclusively the existence and operation of a fringe family. They do, however, indicate a very strong probability of the development of this form. Demographic, ecological, labor force, and stratification data justify the inference that such concerted forces *must* be affecting and sustained by the family system existing in such an area.

Demographic

Birth order is obviously an index of increasing or decreasing family size. The boom in first order of births during the war years has evidently not been sustained recently.[9] However, an analysis of higher birth orders between 1942 and 1949 (comparative percentages computed by dividing the number of each birth order by total live births) reveals some noteworthy changes. (Regional Summaries appear in

114   E. GARTLY JACO & IVAN BELKNAP

Table 1.[10]) Every state reporting has an increase in third order of births in 1949 over 1942. For fourth order of birth, 43 out of the 47 states reporting had equal or greater percentages for 1949 over 1942; the four states having less in 1949 were Arkansas, New Mexico, Tennessee, and West Virginia, the latter having the greatest disparity

TABLE 1

*Percentages of Third, Fourth, Fifth, and Sixth Birth Orders in U.S. by Regions, 1942 and 1949 ***

	Birth Order							
	Third		Fourth		Fifth		Sixth	
REGION	1942	1949	1942	1949	1942	1949	1942	1949
New England	12.3	16.1	6.2	7.4	3.4	3.5	2.0	1.9
Middle Atlantic	12.0	15.1	5.9	6.6	3.2	3.1	1.9	1.6
East North Central	12.9	16.5	6.7	7.8	3.6	3.8	2.2	2.1
West North Central	13.7	16.8	7.6	8.4	4.5	4.3	2.8	2.4
South Atlantic	13.2	15.4	8.3	8.6	5.6	5.3	4.0	3.7
East South Central	13.3	14.8	9.0	8.9	6.3	5.9	4.7	4.2
West South Central	12.5	16.1	7.2	8.9	4.6	5.4	3.1	3.5
Mountain	14.4	17.2	8.3	9.1	5.2	4.9	3.3	2.9
Pacific	11.9	17.1	5.5	7.3	2.8	3.1	1.6	1.6

* Compiled from *Vital Statistics of the United States,* U.S. Government Printing Office, Washington, D.C., Part II, 1942 and 1949.

of only one per cent. Apparently the fourth order of birth was the peak increase in 1949 over 1942, since only 17 states had equal or higher percentages of fifth orders in 1949. For the sixth order of birth, only nine states showed an increase in 1949. In sum, between 1942 and 1949, all states had higher third order of births in 1949, and 43 out of 47 for fourth order. Seventeen states showed a consistent gain in third through fifth orders in 1949 over 1942: Louisiana, Maryland, New Hampshire, Oregon, South Carolina, Texas, California, Connecticut, Idaho, Illinois, Michigan, Minnesota, New Jersey, New York, Ohio, Washington, and Wisconsin. The first six states were consistently higher in percentages from the third through the fifth birth orders. For the U. S. generally, Whelpton's cohort study substantiates our results in his 1925 cohort's experience.[11]

Kiser has pointed out the increase in fertility ratios since 1940 which are

proportionately heaviest among groups previously characterized by lowest fertility. Thus the percentage increases have been larger in the Northeast than in the South, larger among whites than non-whites, larger among urban than rural-farm populations, and probably larger in the "upper" than in the "lower" socio-economic classes.[12]

Further data of a demographic order are suggested by Firey's finding of an excess of children under 10 years of age in the fringe of Flint, Michigan, in 1945.[13] Scaff's study of a California suburb showed that the "commuting population adds young families and comparatively larger families to this community." Furthermore, "without question, the presence of the commuter group in the community introduces younger adults and children and helps to balance an age distribution that is otherwise heavily weighted by elderly people." [14]

While the census area of rural non-farm is not strictly identical to that of the urban fringe area, it does include the latter and offers a crude index of trends in the fringe. In 1949, for the first time, the number of children under 5 years of age per 1,000 women was higher in the rural non-farm area than in both urban and rural farm areas, showing a steadier and higher rise than for urban areas, while in 1949, the rural farm amount dropped.[15] Further, the per cent distribution for 4 persons per household in 1950 was highest for rural non-farm areas as compared to both urban and rural farm areas.[16]

A recent study indicates an increase both in intra-urban and inter-urban migration to fringe areas.[17] A sustained drop in rural-urban migration and in immigration points in the direction of even further growth for the fringe.

Thus, with a spurt in higher birth orders and excess numbers of young children associated with a jump in fringe in-migration, a trend toward increased family size in the fringe can be deduced.

Ecological

Perhaps the most significant single index of the increase in the fringe population is the comparative rates of growth between 1940 and 1950: central cities grew 13 per cent; the hinterland increased 5.7 per cent; but the outlying parts of central cities showed a jump of 34.7 per cent.[18]

Home ownership is directly related to large families, both in urban and rural areas.[19] Census figures show that home ownership has increased 53.9 per cent between 1940 and 1950,[20] a change which may stimulate or be stimulated by larger families. The rate of home ownership in rural non-farm areas from 1930 through 1950 has been closer to that of the rural farm than to that of the urban area.[21]

An increase in the processes of concentration of population and decentralization of services is mentioned by Hauser[22] and Blumenfield.[23] Therefore, the growth of the urban fringe need not represent a deconcentration of urban population from central cities, but may indicate rather an expansion of urban population into broader territory. Many fringe areas exist apart from central city political boundaries only for a brief time until they become incorporated into the central city. However, the data accumulating on the ecology of the urban community do indicate a continuing increase in the distribution of the United States population into the fringe areas.

Labor Force

Whetten and Mitchell's study of a Connecticut suburb showed that "white-collar" workers predominated among occupational groups.[24] However, movement to the fringe is not confined to the middle and upper economic levels. The spread of the concept of the guaranteed annual wage in American industry, taken with the increase in fringe population, indicates a drift to the fringe and to single-family dwellings by the so-called "blue-collar" workers.[25] The bearing of the guaranteed wage on the possibility of home ownership in this latter group is clear enough. Moreover, by "living out" and "working in," as Liepmann puts it, the blue-collar worker may paradoxically increase his family stability as he increases his job mobility. By living in the fringe, that is, the worker ceases to be tied to a particular factory or combination residential-occupational area in the city. He is free to change his jobs without the disruption of family stability caused by residential relocation.[26]

With the increasing employment of women, single as well as married, many women who eventually marry and become mothers return to their early forms of work after their children reach a more independent age (Table 2). Increased employment of married women is conducive to fringe living. Being employed in an area distant from residence minimizes the conflict between the mother's familial and nonfamilial roles. It seems highly probable that the increase of employment of women in the higher age groups is partly an index of employment of fringe family mothers.[27]

Liepmann has pointed out that fringe families encourage and even require "secondary earners," particularly in lower economic groups.[28]

TABLE 2

Percentage of Women in U.S. Labor Force, by Marital and Familial Status, 1949 *

STATUS	PER CENT IN LABOR FORCE
All women in labor force	22.5
Women without children	28.7
With children under 6	10.0
With children some 6–11 only	24.7
With children some 12–17 only	31.3

* Adapted from A. J. Jaffe and C. D. Stewart, *Manpower Resources and Utilization,* New York: Wiley, 1951, Table 4, p. 133.

There are equally cogent reasons for the employment of higher status fringe mothers in view of the increasing costs of educating children, intensified by the inflation which has persisted since World War II. Lower age at marriage makes such employment of mothers consistent with a higher birth rate, while their superior education permits them to seek employment affording an economic surplus after they have paid for maids, kindergartens, and other maternal surrogates for the youngest children.

Social Stratification

Scaff holds that "education and membership in a profession become a badge of acceptance" in suburbs.[29] Coupled with its matricentric orientation, social stratification in the fringe is probably more distinct and overt than is apparent in the central city, where the "elite" is composed of professionals and their wives or widows, while industrial workers occupy lower social strata. If so, then social cleavages in the fringe may be disparate, and fixed along occupational lines.

Furthermore, if industrial workers make up the lower social strata and participate less in the suburban community, as Scaff's study indicates, then commuting by such a population may be viewed as "escape from status." That is, by "working in and living out," a worker may absent himself from his inferior social position during the working day. This would be especially true if the wife and older children are also employed. Indeed, such flexibility may make more tolerable the occupancy of a lower social position in the fringe.

The Structure of the Fringe Family

If one follows the clues suggested by current urban population and economic trends in the light of what is already known about the modern suburban family a number of inferences on the structure of the fringe family becomes possible. Some of the more important of these inferences involve the probable fringe family roles and the integration of this family at various stages of the institutional life cycle.

When the family selects the fringe for the sake of rearing children, this selection can be regarded as involving emphasis on the reproductive-socializing roles of father and mother. There is evidence that some movements to suburbs are carried out to improve the educational and recreational life of children.[30] This improvement is a reciprocal affair, since in its very nature it involves not only a greater control over the children's environment but a strengthening of the significance of the parental roles and the associated roles of the siblings. This strengthening of parental roles has already been examined for the mother by Mowrer, and by Burgess and Locke in their studies of the matricentric suburban family.[31] With the increasing employment of mothers, the shorter work day and week, and the spread of relatively higher incomes among many employed classifications, the father will come to play a more prominent role in the family and the community than was possible either in the companionship or suburban matricentric family. In general it seems likely that all the family roles in the fringe family may be enhanced by proximity of members, and by mutual functional significance.

The Burgess viewpoint of family sociology, with certain qualifications, holds that the companionship family is more in line with other urban social institutions. In view of the powerful stress required by this form on the intrinsic husband-wife relationship rather than on the father-mother bond, the companionship family may represent less of an adaptation than a negation of the family's important functions. There is an implication in this position that as the family "gives in" and loses its historical functions, it becomes better adjusted to the urban environment.[32] Hence the fringe type of family offers at least a compromise between familistic and companionship forms while maintaining at least an apparent emerging adaptation to the urban environment.

Implicit in the strengthening of the parental bonds in the fringe family is an increased control over the courtship process, and perhaps solidarity in the old age family roles.[33] In the central city, anonymity and diversity of interaction minimizes parental control over children in the realm of courtship and dating. In the fringe, the courtship process can be confined in some degree to peer groups selected by parents in tacit agreement with other parents of like status. This represents a compromise between parental mate choice for the children, and the theoretical free choice implied in the dating pattern of the urban youth culture. This actuarial kind of control over the courtship process by fringe parents obviously gives greater continuity to the family process as experienced by both parents and children. This continuity, together with the heightened significance of the member relationship, may be one explanation of the greater number of children in the fringe.

Summary and Discussion

Burgess and Locke list six long-time family-related trends which have been disrupted by the recent war and speculate about their continuation after the war. These are: (1) The declining birth rate; (2) The consequent smaller size of the family; (3) The increase in proportion of the married to those of marriageable age; (4) The decrease in the age at marriage; (5) The increase in the proportion of all women, and of married women gainfully employed; (6) The decline in the historic functions of the family—economic, educational, recreational, religious, and protective.[34] The apparent assumption is that, should these trends be only temporarily disrupted by the recent war, and should they continue as in the past, the companionship family will become institutionalized in the United States.

Trends pointed out in the preceding discussion, however, indicate that particularly for the rapidly increasing U. S. fringe area, a somewhat different picture is appearing: (1) Sustained fertility through higher orders of birth; (2) A consequent increase in the size of the fringe family; (3) Marriage rates for males higher in the rural non-farm areas than in both urban and rural farm areas; (4) Decrease in the age at marriage continuing; (5) Employment of both single and married women increasing, particularly for the higher age groups and with mothers of children from 12 to 17 years of age; (6) The historic functions of the family seemingly better retained in the fringe—the economic, with employment of mothers as secondary workers; the educational, in the selection of "better" schools for children; the rec-

reational, in the encouragement of participation of children in selected peer groups and social sets; the religious, in belonging to and
supporting the "right" churches, and the protective, in addition to the
preceding, in providing the best care and rearing practices of medical
and mental science.

There is some indication, therefore, that the interruption of the
long-term trends listed above by Burgess and Locke may have become
sustained in the fringe family. We can say definitely, at least, that this
interruption has been associated with an enormous increase in the
fringe population between 1940 and 1950, and that the concept of the
fringe family may serve sociology as one useful research hypothesis
for the analysis, in a relatively unexplored area, of the demographic,
ecological, community structure and working force trends we have
mentioned.

If a family form of the type suggested here is beginning to appear
in the urban fringe, several current postulates in the social-psychology
of personality development will also have to be reconsidered.[35] To
urban sociological study, the presence and operation of this family will
mean new possibilities and problems if the present trends continue
toward fringe expansion of population, decentralization and subsequent relocation of industry and services in the fringe.

For the determination of the structure and function of the fringe
family and the community processes associated with it, nine hypotheses
are here suggested for further research:[36]

1. More Protestant than Catholic or Jewish families appear to
live in the fringe. If so, Protestant fertility may be rising, Catholic
fertility declining, and Jewish fertility destined to continue at a low
rate.

2. More whites than non-whites live in the fringe. If this is true,
white fertility may rise, Negro fertility decline even further.

3. Social stratification may be more fixed and disparate in the
fringe than in the central city. Analysis of stratification in the fringe
should show new class criteria, and should suggest answers to such
questions as whether social classes are becoming more or less numerous and rigid in the United States.

4. The inhabitants of fringe areas are experimenting with new
forms of age and sex social organization. New perspectives on the
urban cultural life cycle for childhood, youth, maturity and old
age for both sexes should appear in systematic studies of the fringe.

5. In the fringe the kinship system is assuming a more prominent
function as the basis of status. Is the strengthening of kinship in

this sense making the family as important as occupation in determining status in the urban community? If occupation is still maintaining major importance as a status-basis in the fringe, is the kinship system becoming more important in maintaining occupational lines?

6. A strengthening of sibling as well as parental family roles occurs in the fringe family compared to the central city family. This changed significance of the sibling roles should extend the range of kinship association among age peers and modify current urban voluntary association practices.

7. When contrasted to the central city, the fringe presents the following differential demography: higher fertility, larger families, more marriage, more children, greater number in the labor force, more home ownership, greater fluidity, less mobility, lower mortality, more aged persons, lower age at marriage.

8. There is a higher rate of family participation in social institutions in the fringe than in the central city. Re-alignment of the family with urban institutions has tremendous significance for the study of contemporary social organization.

9. More parental control of marriage occurs in the fringe than in the central city. The influence of parents on courtship in the fringe may be such as to bring about new types of mate selection and courtship patterns differing from those associated with the urban companionship family.

The foregoing propositions are not meant to be exhaustive. It seems certain, however, in view of the evidence now at hand, that the verification of a few of these hypotheses should begin a new chapter in urban family sociology. Moreover, this verification will have decided implications for demography, ecology, and social psychology.

NOTES

1. See C. C. Zimmerman, *Family and Civilization,* New York: Harper, 1947, who concludes that "unless some unforeseen renaissance occurs, the family system will continue headlong its present trend toward nihilism" (p. 808). Also E. Schmiedeler, *An Introductory Study of the Family,* New York: Appleton-Century-Crofts, 1947 (revised). The dilemma consists in the fact that in neither case can the present structure of social organization be maintained.

2. E. W. Burgess and H. J. Locke, *The Family,* New York: American Book Company, 1945; and J. K. Folsom, *The Family and Democratic Society,* New York: John Wiley, 1943. For a discussion of both schools,

see R. F. Winch, *The Modern Family,* New York: Henry Holt, 1952, pp. 472–474, and W. Waller and R. Hill, *The Family,* New York: Dryden Press, 1952, pp. 17–20.

3. The recent jump in fertility and marriages is generally regarded as a temporary phenomenon, holding that as knowledge and practice of contraception and other effects of urban life continue to reach the high-fertility segments of U. S. population, the downward trend will be resumed. See F. W. Notestein, "The Facts of Life," *The Atlantic Monthly,* 177 (June, 1946), pp. 75–83, and his "The Population of the World in the Year 2000," *Journal of American Statistical Association,* 45 (September, 1950), pp. 335–349. C. V. Kiser's review of P. K. Whelpton's *Cohort Fertility* supports this contention in general, though less emphatically. See "Fertility Trends and Differentials in the United States," *Journal of American Statistical Association,* 47 (March, 1952), pp. 25–48.

4. See L. Wirth, "Urbanism as a Way of Life," *American Journal of Sociology,* 44 (July, 1938), pp. 1–24; N. Anderson and E. C. Lindeman, *Urban Sociology,* New York: Knopf, 1928; B. A. McClenahan, *The Changing Urban Neighborhood,* Los Angeles: University of Southern California Press, 1929; E. R. Mowrer, *Family Disorganization,* Chicago: University of Chicago Press, 1927; W. F. Ogburn, *Social Characteristics of Cities,* Chicago: 1937; S. A. Queen and L. P. Thomas, *The City,* New York: McGraw-Hill, 1939; C. F. Ware, *Greenwich Village,* Boston: Houghton-Mifflin, 1935; H. W. Zorbaugh, *The Gold Coast and The Slum,* Chicago: University of Chicago Press, 1929. This typical family is described as (1) small in size; (2) equalitarian in member relations; (3) individualistic in terms of family formation and functioning; (4) tending to be located in multiple family dwellings; and (5) lacking many of the functions of the rural family.

5. Burgess and Locke, *op. cit.,* p. 143.

6. The fringe herein considered includes suburbs, satellite cities, and any other territory located immediately outside central cities whose labor force is engaged in non-farm activities.

7. This is not to take issue with either school. The type of family Zimmerman holds to be basic we regard as functional in rural areas. The companionship type of family is associated with *central cities.* However, with the current growth of fringe areas around central cities, we feel that a new urban family form is developing within this fringe. If this is the case, it would be a serious oversimplification to continue to regard the "companionship" family as typical of the entire urban community. Some urban sociologists are suggesting that the urban family forms need restudy. See, for example, Svend Riemer, *The Modern City,* New York: Prentice-Hall, 1952, pp. 255–259.

8. It has come to the authors' attention just before going to press that Cavan has also discussed the development of new family processes in the urban fringe. (See R. S. Cavan, *The American Family,* New York: Thomas Crowell Co., 1953, Ch. 4.) See also the discussion of the suburban matricentric family by E. R. Mowrer, *The Family,* Chicago: University of Chicago Press, 1932; and by Burgess and Locke, *op. cit.,* pp. 131–134. Also R. E. L. Faris, *Social Disorganization,* New York:

Ronald Press, 1948, pp. 462–465; and G. A. Lundberg, M. Komarovsky, and M. McInery, *Leisure: A Suburban Study,* New York: Columbia University Press, 1934.

9. Kiser, *op. cit.,* p. 25, among others. Demographers have tended to concentrate fertility analysis to either first or second or "very high" birth orders, ignoring the middle range which is significant to our thesis. See, for example, F. W. Notestein, "The Population of the World in the Year 2000," pp. 337 ff.

10. Massachusetts is omitted from the New England region because of an absence of birth order data.

11. Kiser, *op. cit.,* Fig. 1, p. 30.

12. *Ibid.,* p. 38.

13. W. I. Firey, *Social Aspects to Land Use Planning in the Country-City Fringe,* Michigan State College Agricultural Experiment Station Special Bulletin No. 339, East Lansing, June, 1946, pp. 17–18.

14. A. Scaff, "The Effect of Commuting on Participation in Community Organizations," *American Sociological Review,* 17 (April, 1952), p. 217.

15. Bureau of the Census, *Statistical Abstract of the United States,* Washington, D. C., 1951, Table 24, p. 20.

16. *Ibid.,* Table 33, p. 25.

17. R. Freedman, *Recent Migration to Chicago,* Chicago: University of Chicago Press, 1950.

18. From P. K. Hatt and A. J. Reiss, Jr. (editors), *Reader in Urban Sociology,* Glencoe, Illinois, Free Press, 1951, p. 68.

19. M. Parten and R. J. Reeves, "Size and Composition of American Families," *American Sociological Review,* 2 (October, 1937), p. 664.

20. Bureau of the Census, *op. cit.,* Table 866, p. 723.

21. *Ibid.,* same table; also Table 871, p. 725.

22. P. M. Hauser, "The Changing Population Pattern of the Modern City," in Hatt and Reiss, *op. cit.,* pp. 165–182.

23. H. Blumenfield, "On the Growth of Metropolitan Areas," *Social Forces,* 28 (October, 1949), pp. 59–64.

24. N. L. Whetten and D. Mitchell, "Migration from a Connecticut Suburban Town, 1930–1937," *American Sociological Review,* 4 (April, 1939), pp. 173–179.

25. For a discussion of this possibility, see A. J. Jaffe, "Population Trends and City Growth," in Hatt and Reiss, *op. cit.,* pp. 188–189.

26. K. K. Liepmann, *The Journey to Work,* New York: Oxford University Press, 1944, pp. 10–12. Logically, this should apply to the white-collar worker as well.

27. A. J. Jaffe and C. D. Stewart, *Manpower Resources and Utilization,* New York: Wiley, 1951, p. 133, show that the rate of married women in the labor force increases as the age of their children increases.

28. In this process the family assures itself some safety through economic diversification, while at the same time it develops in what is probably an equalitarian direction. (Liepmann, *op. cit.,* pp. 19–25). Liepmann states further, ". . . The family as a whole benefits from the varied employment of its members. It is economically safer for the family not to have all its eggs in one basket, i.e., not to depend on one industry

which may decline while others prosper. Domestic life, moreover, is enriched by a variety of occupational interests among the family," p. 24.

29. Scaff, *op. cit.*, p. 220.

30. Arthur Jones found in a study of a Philadelphia suburb that 80 per cent of its families had moved there to give their children better educational and recreational opportunities. (*Cheltenham Township*, Philadelphia: University of Pennsylvania Press, 1940, pp. 51–52.)

    Strictly speaking, the parental roles of mother and father represent the center of the family functions, rather than the husband-wife roles. The central-city companionship family stresses the latter; the fringe family the former.

31. E. R. Mowrer, *The Family*, Chicago: University of Chicago Press, 1932; Burgess and Locke, *op. cit.*, pp. 131–134.

32. See Zimmermann, *op. cit.*, Ch. 2.

33. It seems very likely that the extension of one's family of procreation into some supervision and control of his children's courtship process may give greater integration to his family of old age (gerontation). This would be an important development in view of the present trend toward an aging population, and the present isolation of grandparents in the terminal segment of the urban family life cycle.

34. Burgess and Locke, *op. cit.*, p. 750.

35. Particularly those theories centering on the consequences to the developing child of membership in a family unit which is relatively small in numbers, feeble in social extent and power, and self-centered. See for a sociological treatment of these theories, Bossard, J. H. S., *The Sociology of Child Development*, New York: Harper, 1948, Chapter III.

36. Each of these hypotheses may have corollaries which can be deduced in the process of setting up the research. Each of them must also be comparatively primitive in view of the current status of data on the fringe.

8

Rural-Urban Differences
and the Family

by William H. Key

A considerable body of theory has arisen dealing with rural-urban differences in the family. The assertion in many cases, and the inference in others, is that the extended family is most important in

Reprinted from *The Sociological Quarterly*, 2 (January 1961), pp. 49–56, by permission of the author and *The Sociological Quarterly*.

rural areas and that the nuclear or conjugal family stands as a relatively independent unit in urban localities. Davis, Loomis, and Beegle, and Burgess and Locke are but a few of those who have held that the disintegration of the extended family has proceeded farther in the city than in the country.[1] These and other students of the family[2] in their comparisons of rural and urban life also suggest that people are so individualized in the city that they have little or no time to spend with members of their immediate families, and that in urban settings as contrasted with the rural settings there are few if any intrafamilial co-operative activities.

This particular hypothesis of the disintegration of the family in urban areas is but one of a number of related hypotheses which collectively and in their simplest form hold that urban areas are strongholds of secondary groups and inimical to primary groups.

Wirth and Redfield have advanced similar arguments that an increase in population size, heterogeneity, and density produces a decline in the importance of primary groups.[3] Yet in recent years there has been an increasing body of theory suggesting the opposite of the above hypothesis, e.g., that the family in urban areas has gained in importance in providing companionship, affection, and other primary group relationships for its members.[4] Few direct comparisons have been made between samples of rural and urban dwellers to test the validity of such hypotheses. Most of the evidence adduced has been from secondary sources relying on historical works, census data, or on the evidence derived from studying individual communities at one period in time.[5] The lack of direct comparison in a range of communities is a gap in our evidence. One of the major difficulties preventing direct testing of this hypothesis has been a methodological one. We lack valid scales to directly compare the interaction patterns of rural and urban dwellers. It is the purpose of this paper to report work on a scale of social participation by which such comparisons can be made. We chose the concept social participation since all or most of the aforementioned hypotheses suggest that individual members of the family (or any primary group) participate in family (or any primary group) activities less in the urban areas than in rural areas, and that there is a comparatively consistent decline in such participation as one goes from rural to urban. The pioneer work in this area has been performed by Queen and by Bernard and we began with the scales they had developed.[6] *A priori*, we divided participation into functional areas and developed a scale for each area.[7] We further developed the scale through preliminary interviews conducted in St. Louis and St. Louis

County and later pre-tested the revised schedule in Fayetteville, Arkansas. After making minor modifications, the research was conducted as described below.

We delineated six areas for which scales were developed—neighboring, informal groups, formal groups, work, immediate family and the extended family. Questions were chosen initially from the works of Queen and Bernard, and other questions were added from suggestions by colleagues and from a review of the literature. Each of the sample of questions was tested for unidimensionality by the Guttman technique and each met the criteria of the Guttman schema and are hereinafter designated as scales.[8]

In this paper we are presenting the results of the research as applied to one area of interaction, the family. We divided the family into two areas for which we adopted the terms immediate family and extended family.[9] The questions used in the final scale and the final weights given to the answers used from these scales are given below. Using these questions resulted in ten empirical scale types for the sample reported below.

Scale for Measurement of Participation in the Extended Family[10]

1. How often do you visit in the homes of relatives whether here or elsewhere?
   - At least once a month   2
   - At least once a year but less than once a month   1
   - Less often than once a year   0
2. How often do you engage in activities with relatives outside your homes?
   - At least once a month   1
   - Less often than once a month   0
3. How often do you borrow things from or lend things to relatives?
   - At least once a week   3
   - At least once a month but less than once a week   2
   - At least once a year but less than once a month   1
   - Less often than once a year   0
4. How often do you do favors other than lending for relatives?
   - At least once a week   3
   - At least once a month but less than once a week   2

At least once a year but less than once a month   1
Less often than once a year   0

5. Do you visit more with friends or relatives?
       As much or more with relatives   1
       More with friends   0

Scale for Measurement of Participation in the Immediate Family[11]

1. How often do you spend evenings at home with your immediate family when no outsiders are present?
       Six or seven evenings a week   3
       Three to five evenings a week   2
       One or two evenings a week   1
       Less than one evening a week   0

2. How often do you eat meals with at least one member of your immediate family?
       Two or more meals a day   2
       One meal a day   1
       Less than one meal a day   0

3. How much of the average day during the work week do you spend with your immediate family?
       One-half or more of the average day   2
       One-fourth to one-half of the average day   1
       Less than one-fourth   0

4. How much of the average day do you spend with your family on weekends?
       One-half or more   2
       One-fourth to one-half   1
       Less than one-fourth   0

5. How often do you engage in activities besides work away from home when no member of your immediate family is present?
       Less than once a month   2
       Once a month but not once a week   1
       At least once a week   0

6. Does your family celebrate birthdays?
       Sometimes or often   1
       Never   0

The sample[12] consisting of 357 individuals, on which this study is based, was chosen from the Midwestern states. The population was subdivided into rural dwellers (those living in unincorporated places), village dwellers (incorporated places of less than 2500), residents of small towns (2500–25,000), of medium-sized cities (25,000–100,000) and of metropolitan areas (more than 100,000). One locality was chosen from each of these five categories. Localities were chosen on the basis of accessibility. Dwelling units within the localities were listed and numbered. A probability sample of dwelling units was chosen using a table of random numbers. Since the numbers of interviews in each of the subsamples was small we used rigorous controls and made return visits in the event a contact could not be made on the initial visit. Substitutions were allowed only in the event of a refusal on the part of the occupants or a vacancy. Refusals were few, comprising in total 3 per cent of those approached. Substitutions were made from a list of alternate households chosen by random numbers. We decided beforehand to divide our sample into 50 per cent male and 50 per cent female and predesignated the sex of the respondent to be interviewed in a given household. All adults (i.e., those over twenty years of age or married individuals fulfilling adult roles) of the pre-designated sex were interviewed in a household. If the household contained no adults of the sex given, the adult head of the household was interviewed. For this reason we failed to achieve our balanced sex ratio.

The sample was compared to census data on sex, age, race, and schooling, and no significant difference was detected. Since age seemed so important to the subject under study the age-distributions in the several components of the sample were compared. The result showed that the subsamples did not vary significantly among themselves in age distribution.

We also tested the relationship between social class and social participation. Since there is no one measure of social class available which permits ranking of individuals from such diverse areas, we chose two status measures, the Warner, "Index of Status Characteristics" for the urban areas and the Sewell, "Short Form of the Farm Family Social Status Scale," for the rural areas. Correlations between these measures of socioeconomic status and our measures of social participation in either the immediate or extended family were consistently negative but not statistically significant.

A casual inspection of Table 1 is enough to indicate that there are no straight line trends from rural to urban. Of particular interest is the similarity of distribution of the mean scores for participation with relatives compared with the mean scores for immediate family participation.

TABLE 1

*Means of Scores for Participation with the Immediate Family
and Participation with Relatives Outside the Immediate
Family Presented by Population Groups and Sex*

POPULATION GROUPS	IMMEDIATE FAMILY			EXTENDED FAMILY		
	Total	Male	Female	Total	Male	Female
Rural	9.56	9.60	9.10	6.22	6.10	6.40
Village	7.86	8.73	7.42	5.19	5.20	5.19
Small urban	8.10	8.73	8.08	5.50	6.40	5.04
Medium-sized city	8.37	8.78	8.08	5.92	6.00	5.91
Metropolitan areas	8.51	9.20	8.20	5.87	7.00	5.25

I would like to emphasize two points in connection with these data: (1) the differences among the subsamples are significant only within the category female for participation in the immediate family, and (2) while the differences are not significant, except as previously noted, the distribution in both cases is that of a "V" curve, with the low point coming in the village and small urban category, rather than the hypothesized straight line rural-urban relationship. Since these findings do not support the hypotheses advanced at the beginning of this article, I would like to advance an alternative hypothesis which may account for such findings.[13]

Let us recall that it has been commonly assumed that life in an urban area tended to pull families apart because of the diverse contacts, particularly those in secondary groups, which individuals have. As Wirth puts it, "The family as a unit of social life is emancipated from the larger kinship group characteristic of the country, and the individual members pursue their own diverging interests in their vocational, educational, religious, recreational, and political life." [14] This view has not been substantiated for this sample, and there seems to us to be a more satisfactory explanation for our data. It is probable, in line with the theory of the effects of primary groups on personality, that any reduction in the number of satisfactory primary contacts makes those that remain seem more rather than less important.[15] It is the difficulty of making satisfactory primary contacts outside the family that makes the immediate and extended family more important. In the urban areas are large numbers of people with whom persons have contact and the fleeting and specialized nature of these contacts mean that they cannot be of a primary nature and therefore completely satisfactory. In the rural area, spatial isolation tends to force

association with one's family. It is the absence of either spatial or social isolation which could account for the relatively low rate of family
interaction in the village and small urban localities. In such a setting,
intrafamilial contacts may be replaced by satisfactory contacts with
friends of long standing, while the whole village or neighborhood takes
on the characteristics of a primary group and isolation is at a minimum. From the standpoint of interaction, the family is less important
in the village than in any other population grouping.[16]

In the case of the extended family, it is possible that there is a
more special explanation for the emphasis on its disintegration in urban
sociology. It seems likely (without doing extensive historical research)
that the hypotheses of the disintegration of the extended family developed early in the history of urban sociology when attention was focused on recent immigrants to the city, and before these individuals
had had an opportunity to establish families. In other words, while
there might have been a noticeable lack of contact with relatives during and immediately following the period of greatest immigration
to the city, this seems to have been a temporary phenomenon produced
by migration rather than by the city as such, and when possible (i.e.,
after time had elapsed and immigrants had attracted more of their kin
or had produced and reared children on their own), isolation in the
city increased pressure for association with such kin.

It is recognized that the hypothesis advanced to account for the
variations discovered needs further testing and that it will undoubtedly
be modified as consideration is given to the related variable of ecological position and social status. However, *the problem of intracity difference was not the focal point in this study* but will probably be the
focus of further research as will the relationship of frequency of participation to such variables as types of city, recency of immigration,
period in the life cycle of the family and composition of the household. Our research was intended to test the simple hypothesis advanced
at the beginning of this article and has indicated that, in the form
in which it is usually presented, it is not supported by our findings.

NOTES

1. Kingsley Davis, *Human Society* (New York: Macmillan, 1949), pp.
   422–27; Charles P. Loomis and J. Allan Beegle, *Rural Social Systems*
   (New York: Prentice-Hall, 1951), pp. 87–88; Ernest W. Burgess and
   Harvey J. Locke, *The Family* (New York: American Book Co., 1945),
   Chs. 3 and 4.
2. Don Martindale and Elio D. Monachesi, *Elements of Sociology* (New

York: Harpers, 1951), pp. 415–16; James H. S. Bossard, *The Sociology of Child Development* (New York: Harpers, 1948), pp. 56–57; Robert E. L. Faris, *Social Disorganization* (New York: Ronald Press, 1948); Meyer Nimkoff, *Marriage and the Family* (New York: Houghton Mifflin, 1947), pp. 143–45, for a few representative selections.

3. Louis Wirth, "Urbanism as a Way of Life," *American Journal of Sociology,* 44:1–24 (July, 1938); Robert Redfield, "The Folk Society," *American Journal of Sociology,* 52:293–308 (Jan., 1947).

4. For two examples of this viewpoint see Svend Riemer, *The Modern City* (New York: Prentice-Hall, 1952), p. 258; and Stuart Queen and David Carpenter, *The American City* (New York: McGraw-Hill, 1953), p. 265.

5. Morris Axelrod, "Urban Structure and Social Participation," *American Sociological Review,* 21:13–19 (Feb., 1956).

6. Stuart A. Queen, "Social Participation in Relation to Social Disorganization," *American Sociological Review,* 13:251–57 (1948); Jessie Bernard, "An Instrument for the Measurement of Neighboring with Experimental Application" (unpublished doctoral dissertation, Washington University, 1935).

7. Work on the scales was carried out co-operatively with Dr. Robert Schmidt, now with the University of Minnesota, Duluth Branch. Dr. Schmidt subsequently used the scales in some research conducted entirely within the St. Louis Metropolitan Area.

8. Louis Guttman, "The Cornell Technique of Scale and Intensity Analysis," *Educational and Psychological Measurement,* 7:247–79 (1947). These scales met all the requirements of the Guttman system. Reproducibility: Extended family .95, Immediate family .96; Predictability: Extended family .90, Immediate family .81. Predictability has not been given the emphasis of reproducibility, but it is implicit in Guttman's formulation. Predictability is the ratio of actual to possible errors. Acceptable levels of predictability are assumed to be .50. We are indebted to Dr. David B. Carpenter, of Washington University, for the analysis of predictability.

9. A note of caution should be introduced, however, with respect to that of the immediate family. While this scale met the requirements of the Guttman technique, there was an unusual concentration of cases in the upper scores, i.e., nine and ten. Almost two-thirds of all cases (240 of 357) were concentrated in these two scores. In dealing with a group such as the family this was not an unexpected distribution, but it would be desirable to continue work on this scale until questions could be selected which would increase the effective range.

While we are not here giving consideration to the important problem of item selection, we have considered the question at length in William H. Key, "Rural-Urban Social Participation" (unpublished doctoral dissertation, Washington University, 1953), Ch. 2 and App. 2. We recognize that this selection of the particular items (questions) to be used is arbitrary and there may and probably will be disagreement with our particular selection of items. *Ex post facto* we recognize that some alternative selection of items might have been a more efficient one, e.g., the heavy concentration of cases in the two upper scores of the scale measuring participation in the immediate family restricts the effective range of the scale. However, if the theory behind the Guttman hypothesis is correct, the selection of a different sample of items would not affect the main relationships.

10. A relative was defined as any individual with whom a "blood" relationship was recognized or an individual who bore a recognized "blood" relationship to the informant's spouse if he or she were married.

11. The immediate family was defined as all individuals occupying a separate household and related by marriage or by "blood." Unattached individuals living in rooming houses were considered as constituting separate households.

12. Details concerning the sample are available in Key, op. cit., Ch. 2. Urbanism was defined demographically. For a similar definition and an exposition of reasons why the definition is in demographic rather than behavioral terms, see Stuart Queen and David Carpenter, The American City (McGraw-Hill, 1953), Chs. 2 and 3.

13. It is, of course, possible that significant differences would be found if a scale of sufficient discrimination could be developed, and it is certainly possible that there are unrecognized defects in study design and sampling. We are concerned about the size of the sample, especially in the village. In defense of the sample, however, it should be pointed out that (1) the universe from which the sample was chosen represented only adults, and therefore the size of the universe from which the sample was chosen was not as large in relation to sample size as first appears; (2) no substitutions in the sample were allowed. Each person was chosen before interviewing began, and recalls were made (sometimes as many as seven) until the interview was completed. We could have increased the size of the sample by a less rigorous procedure, but we preferred to be content with fewer cases rigorously chosen and personally interviewed.

14. Wirth, op. cit., 44:1–24 (1938).

15. For an excellent criticism of the theory of the demise of primary groups in an urban environment, see Richard T. LaPiere, A Theory of Social Control (McGraw-Hill, 1954), especially pp. 9–24.

16. Readers interested in this point should consult the work done by Mel Spiro. Dr. Spiro reports research in a community in which the de-emphasis of the family has been carried to the extreme and in which most familial functions are carried on by the community rather than the family. See Melford Spiro, "Is the Family Universal?" American Anthropologist, 56:839–46 (Oct., 1954); and his Children of the Kibbutz (Cambridge, Mass.: Harvard University Press, 1958).

9

Kin Family Network: Unheralded Structure in Current Conceptualizations of Family Functioning*

by Marvin B. Sussman
& Lee Burchinal

Introduction

Most Americans reject the notion that receiving aid from their kin is a good thing. The proper ideological stance is that the individual and his family should fend for themselves. The family in this instance is nuclear in structure and consists of husband and wife and children. Further investigation would probably reveal that most of these rejectors are receiving or have received financial and other types of aid from their kin long after the time they were supposed to be on their own. After marriage many are involved within a network of mutual assistance with kin, especially with parents. Moreover, one would find that independence of the nuclear family of procreation is being maintained. Where independence is threatened, it is probably due to other causes. The rejection of the idea of receiving aid from kin and actually being helped by them is another case of discrepancy between belief and practice.

Discrepancies between belief and practice of "ideal" and "real" behavior are common in our society. In family sociology the reason is "academic cultural lag"; the lag between apparently antiquated family theory and empirical reality. The theory stresses the social isolation and social mobility of the nuclear family while findings from empirical studies reveal an existing and functioning extended kin family system closely integrated within a network of relationships and mutual

* Graduate School, Western Reserve University, and published as Journal Paper No. J-4197 of the Iowa Agricultural and Home Economics Experiment Station, Ames, Iowa, Project No. 1370.

assistance along bilateral kinship lines and encompassing several generations.[1]

The major purpose of this paper is to reduce the lag between family theory and research in so far as it concerns the functioning of the American kin family network and its matrix of help and service among kin members. The procedure is to review relevant theory and conclusions derived from research on kin family networks completed by sociologists and anthropologists. Appropriate modifications of existing theory which posits the notion of the isolated nuclear family are then suggested.[2]

Nuclear Family Theory

Durkheim, Simmel, Toennies and Mannheim have stressed that the family in urban society is a relatively isolated unit. Social differentiation in complex societies requires of its members a readiness to move, to move to where there are needs for workers and where there are opportunities for better jobs.

American social theorists such as Linton,[3] Wirth,[4] and Parsons[5] support this position. Parsons suggests that the isolated nuclear family system consisting of husband and wife and offspring living independent from their families of orientation is ideally suited to the demands of occupational and geographical mobility which are inherent in modern industrial society. Major obligations, interactions and nurturance behavior occur within the nuclear family. While bonds exist between the nuclear family and other consanguineous relatives and affinals of the kin group, these lack significance for the maintenance of the individual conjugal family.

Family sociologists generally accept the isolated nuclear theory as promulgated above. They report the changes in the structure and functions of the American family system which have occurred as the system has adapted to the demands of a developing industrial society. There is general agreement that the basic functions reserved for the family are procreation, status placement, biological and emotional maintenance and socialization.[6] However, these functions are generally analyzed in the context of the "isolated" nuclear family. The functions of intergenerational and bilateral kin family networks regarding the process of biological and emotional maintenance or socialization are given little attention by theorists or analysts. The conclusion reached is that demands associated with occupational and geographical mobility have brought about a family pattern in urban areas consisting of relatively isolated nuclear family units which operate without much support from the kinship system.

The textbooks are written by family sociologists. Few among them, either texts on the sociology of the family or those written for marriage and family preparation courses, give theoretical or empirical treatment to the maintenance of the family system by the mutual assistance activities of the kin group. Among the texts examined, only one considers in any detail financial arrangements among kin members.[7] One result of the review of basic family and preparation for marriage texts regarding current knowledge of the functioning of the kin network and its matrix of help and service is that the theory of the isolated nuclear family prevails.

Discussion of the Theoretical Argument

The lack of research until the 1950's and the almost complete omission of the topic, kin family network and its matrix of help and services, in family texts are closely related. If the generalized description of the American family system as atomistic and nuclear were valid, there would be very little exchange of financial help or services within the kin family network. Parental support of married children or exchange of services and other forms of help among kin members would be comparatively rare and hence, unimportant.[8] Research would be unnecessary and discussion of the subject, except in crisis situations, could be safely omitted from textbook discussions. However, accepting this theory as essentially valid without considerable empirical substantiation has contributed to errors in descriptions of kin family networks and aid patterns among families. A new empiricism emerging in the late 1940's questioned the persistence of the isolated nuclear family notion and presented evidence to support the viability of kin family network in industrial society.

The ideal description of the isolated nuclear character of the American family system cannot be applied equally to all segments of American society. Regional, racial, ethnic, and rural and urban, as well as socio-economic status differences in modified extended relations and family continuity patterns are known to exist. Family continuity and inheritance patterns of families in several social strata have been described.[9] Among upper-class families direct, substantial and continuous financial support flows from the parents, uncles, aunts, and grandparents to the children both before and after marriage. Only by receiving substantial kin support can the young high-status groom and his bride begin and sustain their family life at the financial and social level which is shared by their parents, other relatives and their friends. This support frequently includes obtaining a position for the husband in his or his in-law family's economic enterprise.

Members of lower-class kin groups generally have few financial resources with which to assist married children. Among certain European ethnic groups some effort is made to assist the young couple at marriage; the notion of a dowry still persists. Generally, however, there is little knowledge, tradition or tangible forms of assistance transmitted to children which directly aids children in establishing or enhancing their socio-economic status.[10] Kin support in this class most frequently takes the form of providing services and sharing what financial resources are available at the time of crises or of exchanging nonmonetary forms of aid. Marginal financial resources and the impact of unemployment hits all kin members alike.[11]

The description of the isolated, nuclear American family system, if valid, is most suited to the white, urban, middle-class segment of American society.[12] Presumably, the leisure time of the members of these families is absorbed in the activities of secondary, special interest social groups. Since urban, lower-class family members participate less than middle-class family members in voluntary organizations, it is believed that social activities of adult lower-class family members are restricted to informal visiting patterns. Visiting with relatives would be a significant proportion of all of their social relations. However, prevailing sociological theory suggests that the disparities between an extended kin family system and the requirements of a mobile labor force and intergenerational family discontinuities generated by social mobility should be reflected in the lack of continuity among lower-class families as well as among middle-class families.

The degree to which urban lower- or middle-class families function as relatively isolated from their extended kin family systems is critical for all subsequent discussions of the question of kinship network, and its matrix of help and service. Unless there is a reasonable frequent occurrence of primary group interaction among kin members, very likely there will be an insignificant help pattern.

The emphasis on the atomistic character of urban families has contributed to incorrect assumptions concerning interaction within the kinship matrix. It has led family sociologists to incorrectly assume that assistance among kin members was comparatively rarely sought or offered. A reconsideration of these assumptions is necessary. The bases of reconsideration are logical constructs and empirical realities set forth in the following data.

Family Network and Mutual Aid: Conceptualization and Research

A theory is here considered to be composed of logically interrelated propositions which explain phenomena. Concepts are elements of a theory, defining what is to be observed. Concepts by themselves cannot be construed as a theory. They require integration into a logical scheme to become a theory.

The existence of a modified extended family with its intricate network of mutual aid in lieu of the isolated nuclear family notion is probably more of a conceptualization than a theory. However, it approaches the state of being a theory since it is not an isolated concept but is integrated with other propositions concerned with the maintenance over time of the family and other social systems of the society.

Family networks and their patterns of mutual aid are organized into a structure identified as a "modified extended family" adopted to contemporary urban and industrial society.[13] This structure is composed of nuclear families bound together by affectional ties and by choice. Geographical propinquity, involvement of the family in the occupational placement and advancement of its members, direct intervention into the process of achieving social status by members of nuclear family units, and a rigid hierarchical authority structure are unrequired and largely absent. The modified extended family functions indirectly rather than directly to facilitate the achievement and mobility drives of component families and individual members. Its tasks complement those of other social systems. By achieving integration with other social systems, concerned with the general goals of maintenance and accomplishment of these systems, the extended family network cannot be considered as an isolated or idiosyncratic concept. Its elements require organization as logically interrelated propositions and whereupon it should emerge as a theory replacing the prevalent one of the isolated nuclear family.

Our concepts die hard and one way to speed their demise is to examine the evidence supporting the new ones. Evidence and measurement are difficult terms to define. When do you have evidence and

Functional Analysis of Parental Aid to Married Children

Familial Variables Affecting Economic Support

1. Family values
   a. Neo-familism
   b. Individualism vs. organizationism
   c. Developmental values (permissiveness)

2. Position of family in the social structure
   a. Social class
   b. Residential location
   c. Occupation (bureaucratic-entrepreneurial)
   d. Status aspiration
   e. Ethnic group membership

3. Family economic position
   a. Wealth relative to class
   b. Security against retirement and catastrophy
   c. Perception of own economic position as relatively risk-free

4. Family structure
   a. Number of children
   b. Degree of family integration
   c. Patterns of role differentiation
   d. Ordinal position of children

5. Relation to married child
   a. Son or daughter
   b. Parent-child harmony
   c. Parental approval of marriage
   d. Age at marriage

Types of Parent-Child Economic Support

1. Goods
   a. Furnishings at wedding and at later periods during marriage
   b. Hospitality gifts
   c. Use of parent's equipment: automobiles, rent free house, summer cottage, appliances, food gifts, transfer of property

2. Money
   a. Given at wedding, childbirth, holidays, and anniversaries
   b. Education
   c. Low interest or interest free loans
   d. Endowments
   e. Subsidized visits and vacations

3. Services
   a. Emergency and crises: care of family members
   b. Babysitting
   c. Boarding of grandchildren
   d. Shopping
   e. Recreation
   f. Home decorating
   g. Garden and yard work
   h. Home construction

Intervening Variables

1. Amount of aid
2. Expectation for aid and regularity
3. Stage in family cycle
4. Disguise of aid
5. Parental expectations
6. Husband's or wife's parents
7. Parental approval of marriage
8. Emotional attachment to parents
9. Geographical distance
10. Family status
11. Married child's image of in-law
12. Generalized attitudes

Consequence for Family Patterns

1. Husband-wife relations: friction, power, harmony
2. Intergenerational integration: parental power
   a. Occupational choice
   b. Mobility
   c. Mate-choice
3. Higher fertility
4. Support for aged parents
5. Lower divorce (teen marriages)

Consequence for Individual Personality

1. Dependency
2. Striving and achievement motivation
3. Anxiety and security
4. Freedom to concentrate on arts, politics, family life

General Societal Consequences

1. Reduction or implementation of geographical and occupational mobility
2. Population growth
3. Economic and occupational striving
4. Cultural development
5. Individualistic vs. other directed values

Societal Supports and Constraints on Parental Aid

1. Economic and technological
   a. Productivity and affluence
   b. Inflation
   c. Tax system
2. Group structure
   a. Burocratization
   b. Professionalization
   c. Suburbanization

3. Demographic structure
   a. Lengthened education
   b. Early age at marriage
   c. Early child bearing
   d. Lengthened life span
4. Values . . .

when have you achieved a measurement? The reader will have to judge. The approach here is to examine the writings and research emerging from several disciplines. In some cases the work is focused on testing hypotheses or describing relationships relevant to the new conceptualization. In others, the discussions and findings emerge incidentally to the major purpose of the study. These are cases of serendipity. They occur more frequently than one would expect and add to the uncertainty of the notion of the isolated nuclear family.

One assumption of the isolated nuclear family conceptualization is that the small nuclear family came into existence in Western Europe and the United States as a consequence of the urban-industrial revolution. Furthermore its small size is ideally suited for meeting requirements of an industrial society for a mobile workforce. The effect of the urban-industrial revolution is to produce a small sized family unit to replace the large rural one. This assumption can be challenged. A study of different societies reveals that industrialization and urbanization can occur with or without the small nuclear family.[14]

If household size reflects in any way the structure and characteristics of the joint extended family in India, then little changes have occurred in this system during the period of industrialization in India from 1911 to 1951.[15]

The uprooting of the rural family, the weakening of family ties, and the reshaping of the rural family form into a nuclear type as a consequence of the industrial revolution are disclaimed for one Swiss town in a recent investigation. On the contrary many fringe rural families were stabilized and further strengthened in their kin ties from earning supplementary income in nearby factories. Able-bodied members obtained work nearby and no longer had to leave the family unit in search of work. Families which moved closer to their place of employment were accommodated in row houses; these units facilitated the living together of large family groups.[16] These findings question the impact of industrialization upon the structure and functioning of the pre-industrial family.

It is difficult to determine if the conditions of living during the transition from a rural to an industrial society ended the dominance of the classical extended family and replaced it with a modified kin form, or if it was replaced by the nuclear one. The question is whether the modified extended family has existed since industrialization occurred; is it a recent phenomenon or an emergent urban familism, a departure from the traditional nuclear form; or is it non-existent? The evidence to support either of these positions is inconclusive.

It remains however that the family network described variously as "an emergent urban familism" or "modified extended family" exists and functions in the modern community.

The family network and its functions of mutual aid has implications for the functioning of other social systems. With the growth of large metropolitan areas and concomitant occupational specialization, there is less need for the individual to leave the village, town, city or suburb of the urban complex in order to find work according to his training. Large urban areas supply all kinds of specialized educational and occupational training. The individual can remain in the midst of his kin group, work at his specialty and be the recipient of the advantages or disadvantages preferred by the kin family network. If individuals are intricately involved within a kin family network, will they be influenced by kin leaders and be less amenable to influence by outsiders; will they seek basic gratifications in kin relationships in lieu of the work place or the neighborhood; will they modify drastically current patterns of spending leisure time thus affecting current leisure forms and social systems?[17]

Empirical evidence from studies by investigations in a variety of disciplines substantiate the notion that the extended kin family carries on multitudinous activities that have implications for the functioning of other social systems of the society. The major activities linking the network are mutual aid and social activities among kin related families. Significant data have been accumulated on the mutual aid network between parents and their married child's family in a number of separate and independent investigations.[18-20] The conclusions are:

1. Help patterns take many forms, including the exchange of services, gifts, advice and financial assistance. Financial aid patterns may be direct as in the case of the young married couples Burchinal interviewed; or indirect and subtle, such as the wide range of help patterns observed by Sussman, Sharp and Axelrod.

2. Such help patterns are probably more widespread in the middle and working-class families and are more integral a feature of family relationships than has been appreciated by students of family behavior. Very few families included in available studies reported neither giving nor receiving aid from relatives. However, these relationships until recently have not been the subject of extensive research.

3. The exchange of aid among families flows in several directions, from parents to children and vice versa, among siblings, and less frequently, from more distant relatives. However, financial assistance generally appears to flow from parents to children.

TABLE 1

Direction of Service Network of Respondent's Family and Related Kin by Major Forms of Help

MAJOR FORMS OF HELP AND SERVICE	Direction of Service Network				
	BETWEEN RESPONDENT'S FAMILY AND RELATED KIN PER CENT*	FROM RESPONDENTS TO PARENTS PER CENT*	FROM RESPONDENTS TO SIBLINGS PER CENT*	FROM PARENTS TO RESPONDENTS PER CENT*	FROM SIBLINGS TO RESPONDENTS PER CENT*
Any form of help	93.3	56.3	47.6	79.6	44.8
Help during illness	76.0	47.0	42.0	46.4	39.0
Financial aid	53.0	14.6	10.3	46.8	6.4
Care of children	46.8	4.0	29.5	20.5	10.8
Advice (personal and business)	31.0	2.0	3.0	26.5	4.5
Valuable gifts	22.0	3.4	2.3	17.6	3.4

* Totals do not add up to 100 per cent because many families received more than one form of help of service. Marvin B. Sussman, "The Isolated Nuclear Family: Fact or Fiction," *Social Problems* 6 (Spring, 1959), 338.

4. While there may be a difference in the absolute amount of financial aid received by families of middle- and working-class status, there are insignificant differences in the proportion of families in these two strata who report receiving, giving or exchanging economic assistance in some form.

5. Financial aid is received most commonly during the early years of married life. Parents are probably more likely to support financially "approved" than "disapproved" ones, such as elopements, interfaith and interracial marriages. Support can be disguised in the form of substantial sums of money or valuable gifts given at the time of marriage, at the time of the birth of children, and continuing gifts at Christmas, anniversaries or birthdays. High rates of parental support are probably associated with marriages of children while they are still in a dependency status; those among high school or college students are examples.

6. Research data are inadequate for assessing the effects of parental aid on family continuity and the marital relations of the couple receiving aid. Few studies report associations between the form and amount of aid given with the parents' motivations for providing aid. Additional studies on these points are necessary before the implications of aid to married children can be better known.[21]

Social activities are principal functions of the kin family network. The major forms are interfamily visitation, participation together in recreational activities, and ceremonial behavior significant to family unity. Major research findings are:

1. Disintegration of the extended family in urban areas because of lack of contact is unsupported and often the contrary situation is found. The difficulty in developing satisfactory primary relationships outside of the family in urban areas makes the extended family *more important* to the individual.[22]

2. Extended family get-togethers and joint recreational activities with kin dominate the leisure time pursuits of urban working class members.[23]

3. Kinship visiting is a primary activity of urban dwelling and outranks visitation patterns found for friends, neighbors, or co-workers.[24–28]

4. Among urban middle classes there is an almost universal desire to have interaction with extended kin, but distance among independent nuclear related units is a limiting factor.[29]

5. The family network extends between generational ties of conjugal

units. Some structures are identified as sibling bonds,[30] "occasional kin groups"[31] family circles and cousin clubs.[32] These structures perform important recreational, ceremonial, mutual aid, and often economic functions.

Services performed regularly throughout the year or on occasions are additional functions of the family network. The findings from empirical studies are:

1. Shopping, escorting, care of children, advice giving and counselling, cooperating with social agencies on counselling and welfare problems of family members, are types of day-to-day activities performed by members of the kin network.[33, 34]

2. Services to old persons such as physical care, providing shelter, escorting, shopping, performing household tasks, sharing of leisure time, etc. are expected and practiced roles of children and other kin members. These acts of filial and kin responsibility are performed voluntarily without law or compulsion.[35-42]

3. Families or individual members on the move are serviced by units of the family network. Services range from supplying motel-type accommodations for vacationing kin passing through town, to scouting for homes and jobs for kin, and in providing supportive functions during the period of in-migration and transition from rural to the urban pattern of living.[43-47]

4. Services on occasions would include those performed at weddings or during periods of crisis, death, accident, disaster, and personal trouble of family members. A sense of moral obligation to give service or acknowledgement of one's kin appropriate to the occasion is found among kin members. The turning to kin when in trouble before using other agencies established for such purposes is the mode rather than the exception.[48-51]

5. General supportive behavior from members of the kin family network facilitate achievement and maintenance of family and community status.[52] Supportive behavior of kin appears to be instrumental in affecting fertility rates among component family members.[53]

A convergence of many of these findings occurs in the work of Eugene Litwak. In an extensive study of a middle class population Litwak tests several hypotheses on the functional properties of the isolated nuclear family for an industrial society: (a) occupational mobility is antithetical to extended family relations; (b) extended family relations are impossible because of geographical mobility. His findings summarized briefly are: (1) The extended kin family as a structure exists in modern urban society at least among middle class families; (2) Extended family relations are possible in urban industrial society; (3) Geographical propinquity is an unnecessary condition for these relationships; (4) Occupational mobility is unhindered by the activities of the extended family, such activities as advice, financial assistance, temporary housing, and the like provide aid during such movement; and (5) The classical extended family of rural society or its ethnic counterpart are unsuited for modern society, the isolated nuclear family is not the most functional type, the most functional being a modified extended kin family.[54]

Conclusions

There exists an American kin family system with complicated matrices of aid and service activities which link together the component units into a functioning network. The network identified by Litwak as extended family relations is composed of nuclear units related by blood and affinal ties. Relations extend along generational lines and bilaterally where structures take the form of sibling bonds and ambilineages, i.e., the family circle or cousin club.

As a consequence of limited historical work and particularistic developments in theory and research in sociology there is uncertainty concerning the impact of industrialization upon the structure and function of the pre-industrial family. Was the extended classical type found in rural society replaced by a nuclear one, or did it evolve into the modified kin form described in this paper? It is suggested that the notion of the isolated nuclear family stems from theories and research on immigrant groups coming into the city to work during the period of urbanization in Western society.[55] Anomie in family behavior resulted from individual and institutional failure to make appropriate adjustments required by this migration. The coldness and indifference of the workplace and the city as a steel and concrete bastion contributed to a feeling of aloneness and isolation. The basic concern of the in-migrant was survival in an unknown man-made jungle. Survival was related to dependence upon small family units. These could make quicker and more complete adjustments to the new ways of urban life. The ethos of a competitive and expanding industrial society supported the flexibility of movement now possible by an atomistic unit. Every man is for himself, every man should be unencumbered by ties that will hinder his economic or social progress, and every man should seize opportunities to better himself. One assumption of this position is that early urban man had little time for concern or activity with kinsmen. A more logical assumption is that isolation, a depressive workplace, and uncertainty produced greater reliance upon kin. Once new immigrants became established in the city they served as informants, innkeepers, and providers for later kin arrivals.[56] Once these followers arrived the kin family network then functioned most effectively to protect and acculturate their members into urban ways.

Major activities of this network are that members give to each other financial aid and goods of value, and a wide range of services at specific times and under certain conditions. The aid and service provided within the network supplement rather than displace the basic activities of nuclear family units. Kinship behavior assists more than negates the achievement of status and occupational advance of component families and their members.

The main flow of financial aid is along generational lines, from parents to young married children and from middle-aged parents to aged parents. Such aid is not restricted to emergencies, but may be given at various occasions such as support for education, to start a family, at time of marriage, to begin a career, and the like.

The network is used among middle-class families as a principal source of aid and service when member families or individuals are in personal difficulty, in times of disaster and crisis, and on ceremonial occasions. There are some indications that established working-class families are following the same pattern. Some situations cannot be handled by the nuclear unit alone, e.g., destruction of the family home by a tornado; while other situations involve more than one nuclear family or individual member, e.g., the death of an aging parent. In such situations there are mutual expectations of going to the aid of kin. Aid is sought from the most immediate kin chiefly along sibling or generational lines. Then it is followed by help from more distant kin.

In many instances everyday or weekly activities link together the members of the kin family network. Joint participation in leisure time activities are possible because of reduction of the work week. Visiting among kin is facilitated by high speed highways and other conveyances of a modern transportation system. Constant communication among kin members is possible by the widespread adoption on all class levels of the telephone as a household necessity.[57, 58]

The feasibility of the kin network in modern society is due to the existence of modern communication and transportation systems which facilitate interaction among members; a bureaucratic industrial structure suited to modern society which removes the responsibility for job placement from the network will still permit the network to concentrate on activities intended to aid the social and economic achievement of network members;[59, 60] and expansion of metropolitan areas in which individuals can obtain educational, occupational and status objectives without leaving their kin area. Kin members can live some distance from each other within the metropolitan area and still have relationships within the network. Nuclear units function autonomously. Decisions on what and when to act are responsibilities of the nuclear family. Influence may be exerted by the kin group upon the nuclear units so that the latter may make the "right" decision. However the kin group seldom directs the decision or action of the nuclear family in a given situation. Immunity from such control is guaranteed by legal and cultural norms which reaffirm the right and accountability of the nuclear family in such situations. The role of the family kin network is supportive rather than coercive in its relationship with the nuclear family.

Understanding of the family as a functioning social system interrelated with other social systems in society is possible *only by rejection of the isolated nuclear family concept.* Accepting the isolated nuclear family as the most functional type today has led to erroneous conclusions concerning the goals and functions of these other social systems. In social service fields, for instance, institutions establish goals and programs concerned with caring for individuals and families who are unable to fend for themselves. Institutions assume that the family unit is a small and isolated unit easily injured and upset by the many problems it faces in contemporary society. The therapeutic approach is to treat the individual or at best the members of the nuclear family. The kin network is overlooked. Often nuclear families respond hesitantly to the overtures of these institutions; the nuclear unit prefers to find solutions to its problems within the family kin network. When such solutions are impossible then the specialized service institution may be used. How the operations of the kin family network effect the functioning of other social systems is yet to be established. Their positive or negative effects are unknown. Some beginning research on this problem is now underway.[61]

NOTES

1. The authors adopt Eugene Litwak's interpretation of the modified extended family. It is one that "does not require geographical propinquity, occupational nepotism, or integration, and there are no strict authority relations, but equalitarian ones." See "Geographical Mobility and Ex-

tended Family Cohesion," *American Sociological Review,* 25 (June, 1960), p. 385. The components of the system are neolocal nuclear families in a bilateral or generational relationship. This system is referred to as the "Kin Family Network."

2. The implications of parental support to the married child's family for the functioning of the American Family System is discussed in another paper. The major question is whether parental aid affects the independence of the married child's family. "Parental Aid to Married Children: Implications for Family Functioning" forthcoming in *Marriage and Family Living,* November, 1962.

3. Ralph Linton, "The Natural History of the Family," in Ruth N. Anshen, *The Family: Its Function and Destiny* (New York: Harpers, 1959), pp. 45–46.

4. Louis Wirth, "Urbanism As a Way of Life," *American Journal of Sociology,* 44 (July, 1938), pp. 1–24.

5. All by the same author, see Talcott Parsons, "The Kinship System of the Contemporary United States," *American Anthropologist,* 45 (January–March, 1943), pp. 22–38; "Revised Analytical Approach to the Theory of Social Stratification," in R. Bendix and S. M. Lipset, eds., *Class, Status, and Power* (Glencoe, Illinois: Free Press, 1953), p. 166 ff.; "The Social Structures of the Family" in Ruth Anshen, *op. cit.,* p. 263 ff.; Parsons and Robert F. Bales, *Family, Socialization and Process* (Glencoe, Illinois: Free Press, 1955), pp. 3–33.

6. Compare Robert F. Winch, *The Modern Family* (New York: Hole, 1952), and William J. Goode, "The Sociology of the Family," in Robert K. Merton, Leonard Broom and Leonard S. Cottrell, Jr., eds., *Sociology Today* (New York: Basic Books, 1959), pp. 178–96.

7. Evelyn M. Duvall, *Family Development* (Chicago: Lippincott, 1957), pp. 129–33, 206–10.

8. See Reuben Hill, *Families Under Stress* (New York: Harpers, 1949).

9. W. Lloyd Warner and Paul S. Lunt, *The Social Life in a Modern Community* (New Haven, Connecticut: Yale University Press, 1941). See also Cavan, *The American Family, op. cit.,* pp. 119–87, for a review of other studies of social status differentials in family behavior.

10. R. E. L. Faris, "Interactions of Generations and Family Stability," *American Sociological Review,* 12 (April, 1947), pp. 159–64.

11. Ruth S. Cavan, "Unemployment-Crisis of the Common Man," *Marriage and Family Living,* 21 (May, 1959), 139–46.

12. Someone has facetiously suggested the samples of white, urban, middle-class Protestant respondents be labeled as WUMP samples. If family sociologists continue to draw samples principally from this segment of our social structure or wish to limit generalizations to this segment, there would be more than a facetious basis for arguing for the merit of the convenient shorthand expression represented by WUMP.

13. Eugene Litwak, *op. cit.,* p. 355. See also by the same author, "Occupational Mobility and Extended Family Cohesion," *American Sociological Review,* 25 (February, 1960), p. 10.

14. Sidney M. Greenfield, "Industrialization and the Family in Sociological Theory," *American Journal of Sociology,* 67 (November, 1961), pp. 312–22.

15. Henry Orenstein, "The Recent History of the Extended Family in India," *Social Problems,* 8 (Spring, 1961), pp. 341–50.
16. Rudolph Braun, *Industrialisierung Volksleben* (Erbenback-Zierrich: Reutsch, 1960).
17. A. O. Haller raises interesting questions on the significance of an emerging urban familism. See "The Urban Family," *American Journal of Sociology,* 66 (May, 1961), pp. 621–22.
18. Marvin B. Sussman, "The Help Pattern in the Middle Class Family," *American Sociological Review,* 18 (February, 1953), pp. 22–28. For related analyses by the same author see, "Parental Participation in Mate Selection and Its Effect Upon Family Continuity," *Social Forces,* 32 (October, 1953), pp. 76–81; "Family Continuity: Selective Factors Which Affect Relationships Between Families at Generational Levels," *Marriage and Family Living,* 16 (May, 1954), pp. 112–20; "Activity Patterns of Post Parental Couples and Their Relationship to Family Continuity," *Marriage and Family Living,* 27 (November, 1955), pp. 338–41; "The Isolated Nuclear Family: Fact or Fiction," *Social Problems,* 6 (Spring, 1959), pp. 333–40; "Intergenerational Family Relationships and Social Role Changes in Middle Age," *Journal of Gerontology,* 15 (January, 1960), pp. 71–75.
19. Harry Sharp and Morris Axelrod, "Mutual Aid Among Relatives in an Urban Population," in Ronald Freedman and associates, eds., *Principals of Sociology* (New York: Holt, 1956), pp. 433–39.
20. Lee G. Burchinal, "Comparisons of Factors Related to Adjustment in Pregnancy-Provoked and Non-Pregnancy-Provoked Youthful Marriages," *Midwest Sociologist,* 21 (July, 1959), pp. 92–96; also by the same author, "How Successful Are School-Age Marriages?" *Iowa Farm Science,* 13 (March, 1959), pp. 7–10.
21. Further analyses on the implications of parental aid to married children are found in a paper, "Parental Aid to Married Children: Implications for Family Functioning," forthcoming in *Marriage and Family Living,* November, 1962.
22. William H. Key, "Rural-Urban Differences and the Family," *Sociological Quarterly,* 2 (January, 1961), pp. 49–56.
23. F. Dotson, "Patterns of Voluntary Association Among Urban Working Class Families," *American Sociological Review,* 16 (October, 1951), pp. 689–93.
24. Morris Axelrod, "Urban Structure and Social Participation," *American Sociological Review,* 21 (February, 1956), pp. 13–18.
25. Scott Greer, "Urbanism Reconsidered," *American Sociological Review,* 21 (February, 1956), pp. 22–25.
26. Wendell Bell and M. D. Boat, "Urban Neighborhoods and Informal Social Relations," *American Journal of Sociology,* 43 (January, 1957), pp. 381–98.
27. Marvin B. Sussman and R. Clyde White, *Hough: A Study of Social Life and Change* (Cleveland: Western Reserve University Press, 1959).
28. Paul J. Reiss, "The Extended Kinship System of the Urban Middle Class" (Unpublished Ph.D. Dissertation, Harvard University, 1959).
29. E. Franklin Frazier, "The Impact of Urban Civilization Upon Negro Family Life," in P. K. Hatt and H. S. Reiss, Jr., editors. *Cities and Society* (Glencoe: Illinois, Free Press, 1957, rev. ed.), pp. 495–96.

30. Elaine Cumming and David M. Schneider, "Sibling Solidarity: A Property of American Kinship," *American Anthropologist,* 63 (June, 1961), pp. 498–507.
31. Millicent Ayoub, "American Child and His Relatives: Kindred in Southwest Ohio," project supported by the Public Health Service, 1961. Dr. Ayoub is continuing her studies under the subtitle, "The Nature of Sibling Bond." She examines the solidarity or lack of it between siblings in four focal subsystems and at different stages of the life cycle.
32. William E. Mitchell, "Descent Groups Among New York City Jews," *The Jewish Journal of Sociology,* 3 (1961), pp. 121–28; "Lineality and Laterability in Urban Jewish Ambilineages," read at the 60th Annual Meeting of the American Anthropological Association in Philadelphia, Pa., November 16, 1961; and William E. Mitchell and Hope J. Leichter, "Urban Ambilineages and Social Mobility," unpublished paper based on research from the project, "Studies in Family Interaction" sponsored jointly by the Jewish Family Service of New York City and the Russell Sage Foundation.
33. Sussman, *op. cit.,* "The Help Pattern in the Middle Class Family."
34. Hope J. Leichter, "Kinship and Casework," paper read at the meetings of the Groves Conference, Chapel Hill, North Carolina, 1959; "Life Cycle Changes and Temporal Sequence in a Bilateral Kinship System," read at the annual meetings of the American Anthropological Association, 1958; Washington, D.C. "Normative Intervention in an Urban Bilateral Kinship System," paper read at the meetings of the American Anthropological Association, 1959.
35. John Kosa, Leo D. Rachiele and Cyril O. Schommer, S. J. "Sharing the Home with Relatives," *Marriage and Family Living,* 22 (May, 1960), pp.129–31.
36. Alvin L. Schorr, *Filial Responsibility in a Modern American Family,* Washington, D.C.; Social Security Administration, U.S. Department of Health, Education and Welfare, 1960, pp. 11–18.
37. Peter Townsend, *The Family Life of Older People: An Inquiry in East London* (London: Routledge and Kegan Paul, 1957).
38. Michael Young and Peter Willmott, *Kinship and Family in East London* (Glencoe, Illinois: Free Press, 1957).
39. Elizabeth Bott, *Family and Social Network* (London: Tavistock Publications, Ltd., 1957).
40. See *Adjustment in Retirement,* by Gordon F. Streib and Wayne E. Thompson, *Journal of Social Issues,* 14 (1958). Streib and Thompson have done the most creative thinking and analysis of data on these points. Streib's paper "Family Patterns in Retirement," pp. 46–60 in this issue is most pertinent.
41. Ethel Shanas, "Older People and Their Families," paper given at the meetings of the American Sociological Association, September, 1961. A more complete report is in *Family Relationships of Older People,* Health Information Foundation, 1961.
42. The best treatment of uses of leisure during the later years of life is found in Robert W. Kleemeier, ed., *Aging and Leisure* (New York: Oxford University Press, 1961). See particularly the chapters by Wilensky, Streib and Thompson.

43. M. B. Sussman and R. C. White, *op. cit., Hough: A Study of Social Life and Change.*
44. C. Wright Mills, Clarence Senior and Rose K. Goldsen, *Puerto Rican Journey* (New York: Harper Bros., 1950), pp. 51–55.
45. James S. Brown, Harry K. Schwarzweller, and Joseph J. Mangalam, "Kentucky Mountain Migration and the Stem Family: An American Variation on a Theme by LePlay," paper given at the meetings of the American Sociological Association, September 1, 1961.
46. Peter H. Rossi, *Why Families Move* (Glencoe, Illinois: Free Press, 1955), pp. 37–38.
47. Earl L. Koos, *Families in Trouble* (New York: Columbia University Press, 1946).
48. Sussman, *op. cit.,* "Family Continuity: Selective Factors Which Affect Relationships Between Families at Generational Levels."
49. Seymour S. Bellin, *Family and Kinship in Later Years,* N.Y. State Dept. of Mental Hygiene, Mental Health Research Unit Publication, 1960.
50. Sharp and Axelrod, *op. cit., Mutual Aid Among Relatives.*
51. Enrico L. Wuarantelli, "A Note on the Protective Function of the Family in Disasters," *Marriage and Family Living,* 22 (August, 1960), pp. 263–64.
52. Bernard Barber, "Family Status, Local-Community Status, and Social Stratification: Three Types of Social Ranking," *Pacific Sociological Review,* Vol. 4, No. 1 (Spring, 1961), pp. 3–10. In this paper Barber challenges the current conceptualization of social class for designating an individual's position, and power within a community. He differentiates social class position, family status and local-community statuses into three types of social ranking. Each one has its own structure and functions; each allocates position, power and prestige; and each has its own range of variation. The family kin network and support received from it determines family status. President Kennedy's family and its extended family relations illustrates the point of this thesis.
53. David Goldberg, "Some Recent Developments in Fertility Research," Reprint No. 7, *Demographic and Economic Change in Developed Countries,* Princeton University Press, 1960. Recent fertility research has focused upon the relationship of family organization to differential fertility since variations in family planning and family size cannot be explained by differences in socio-economic status. One variable of family organization is the family kin network. Goldberg observes, "—and incidentally one which may ultimately prove fruitful in cross-cultural studies, is a consideration of the relative benevolence of the environment in defraying the economic and social costs of having children. Here it is hypothesized that the greater the amount of help available from one's community or kinship system the weaker the desire to prevent or postpone pregnancy." *Ibid.,* p. 9.
54. Eugene Litwak, "The Use of Extended Family Groups in the Achievement of Social Goals: Some Policy Implications," *Social Problems,* 7 (Winter, 1959–60), pp. 177–87; *op. cit.,* "Occupational Mobility and Extended Family Cohesion"; *op. cit.,* "Geographical Mobility and Family Cohesion."
55. Key, *op. cit.,* "Rural-Urban Differences and the Family," p. 56; Sussman, *op. cit.,* "The Isolated Nuclear Family: Fact or Fiction," p. 340.

56. Key discusses this point in his paper "Rural-Urban Differences and the Family," *op. cit.* From studies on immigration to the United States and geographical movement of families within the country one concludes that family members perform invasion or scout roles and then attract other kin into their communities and neighborhoods.
57. Several empirical studies are currently in progress on the extensity of kin family network functions in metropolitan areas. Robert W. Habenstein and Allan D. Coult are conducting one in Kansas City on "The Functions of Extended Kinship in an Urban Milieu." "The purpose of this research is to discover, describe, and analyse the social correlates and functions of extended kinship in representative samples of blue collar and white collar socio-economic classes in Kansas City," p. 1, Research Proposal, July 1, 1961.
58. A second study is being undertaken by Marvin B. Sussman and Sherwood B. Slater in Cleveland, Ohio. "The objectives of the Cleveland Study are to investigate the working and middle-class families; to compare the kinship networks of 'illness' and 'non-illness' families; to estimate the normative form of kinship networks for social class and family life cycle stages to variations in normative patterns," p. 1, Research Plan, September 27, 1961.
59. One investigation being conducted by John Bennett is concerned with the variations in business operations due to kinship behavior. Business organization practice according to current theory operates with bureaucratic, universalistic, and impartial norms. Bennett is investigating the compatibility and conflict between these bureaucratic norms and those which characterize the kinship network, particularistic behavior for idiosyncratic situations. "Kinship in American Business Organization," meetings of the Central States Anthropological Society, May, 1961.
60. William Mitchell, "Lineality and Laterality in Urban Jewish Ambilineages," *op. cit.,* finds some integration of kinship and business activity. There is a tendency to "Throw business to kin members."
61. Hope J. Leichter, *op. cit.,* see note 34.

10

The Isolated Nuclear Family Hypothesis: A Reanalysis*

by Alfred M. Mirande

The nuclear family in the United States has been described by Parsons, Williams, and other sociologists as relatively isolated and independent of extended kinship ties.[1] In recent years, however, the isolated family hypothesis has been challenged by several investigators who maintain that help and visiting patterns between the nuclear family and extended relatives are very prevalent, and the isolation and independence of the American family from kinship ties has been grossly exaggerated. Sussman, for example, has posed the question, "The Isolated Family: Fact or Fiction?" and concluded that it is mostly fiction. His research revealed extensive networks of mutual assistance and activity among interlocking nuclear families in an urban setting.[2] In two urban samples, Greer found that visiting with kin was the most important single type of social relationship. A large majority of these respondents saw relatives at least once a month.[3] Similarly, Axelrod reported that residents of Detroit were more likely to participate socially with relatives outside of the immediate family than with friends, neighbors, or co-workers.[4] In addition, Litwak has questioned one of the basic assumptions underlying the isolated family view, namely that social and geographical mobility tend to weaken extended family bonds. According to Litwak, mobility strengthens rather than weakens extended family cohesion.[5]

In spite of the increasing concern with extended family relationships, the status of the isolated family hypothesis is still unclear. The hypothesis as proposed suggests that the family in American society is *relatively* isolated, relative, that is, to families in less urbanized and industrialized societies. Therefore it can be tested directly only with

* The data employed in this paper were obtained through research supported by the National Science Foundation under grants G 24969 and GS 779. I am indebted to Harry J. Crockett, Jr. and Lewis Levine for giving me access to these data.
Written especially for this volume.

cross-cultural data. Yet an indirect test of the hypothesis can be made within American society by an analysis of subhypotheses which follow directly from the isolated family position. This paper will examine some of these hypotheses and present data which bear on the controversy over the isolated nuclear family. The variables considered in relation to extended family participation are social mobility, social class, and sex.

Method

The data employed in this study were obtained from residents of Hillsboro, North Carolina, a community of approximately 5,000 inhabitants. A random sample of 275 was selected from the 1,121 dwelling units normally occupied by white residents.[6] An interview was conducted with a member of each household.[7]

Extensive occupational information was contained in the interview schedule. Occupations were classified as manual or nonmanual.[8] Married women were classified according to the occupation of their husbands. Intergenerational social mobility was measured by comparing the respondent's occupation with the occupation of his father. Respondents who moved from a manual to a nonmanual occupation were termed upwardly mobile, those who moved from a nonmanual to a manual occupation were downwardly mobile. Female mobility was determined by comparing the occupation of her husband with the occupation of her father.

Several questions in the interview pertained to participation with extended relatives. The two questions considered here ascertained the number of relatives seen regularly and the amount of time usually spent with relatives during a given week. Because persons without relatives in the community have less opportunity to interact with relatives, the analysis was limited to respondents with at least one relative living in Hillsboro.

Findings

Social Mobility and Extended Family Participation

As stated earlier, the isolated family hypothesis can only be tested directly with comparative cross-cultural materials, but several subhypotheses can be tested within American society. Proponents of the isolated family position maintain that strong extended family bonds are inconsistent with the needs of a complex society.[9] Presumably the high rates of social and geographical mobility characteristic of urban-industrial societies are not conducive to the development of a complex network of kinship ties. If social mobility disrupts extended family relations cross culturally, it should have a similar effect within a particular society.

The foregoing leads to the hypothesis that social mobility and extended family participation will be inversely related. The findings support this hypothesis with upward but not with downward mobility. It is shown in Table 1 that upwardly mobile respondents spend less time with relatives and see fewer relatives regularly than stable respondents. Specifically, among nonmanual respondents only 27 percent of the upwardly mobile usually spent three hours or more per week with relatives, compared to 67 percent of the stable. A *gamma* correlation of $-.68$, significant at less than the .01 level, was obtained between these two variables. A similar pattern was found with respect to the number of relatives seen regularly. Sixty-four percent of the upwardly mobile and 76 percent of the stable respondents saw four or more relatives regularly. These differences were also statistically significant ($p < .01$).

While upward mobility has a detrimental effect on extended family participation, downward mobility seems to enhance family participation. From Table 1 it is clear that downwardly mobile persons are

TABLE 1

Social Mobility and Extended Family Participation

*Percentage Spending Three Hours or More with Relatives Per Week**			
Manual		Nonmanual	
Stable	66(N = 82)	Stable	67(N = 24)
Downwardly mobile	75(N = 12)	Upwardly mobile	27(N = 11)
G = .22	p < .01	G = −.68	p < .01

Percentage Seeing Four or More Relatives Regularly			
Manual		Nonmanual	
Stable	66(N = 87)	Stable	76(N = 25)
Downwardly mobile	85(N = 13)	Upwardly mobile	64(N = 11)
G = .49	p < .01	G = −.29	p < .01

* The information on hours spent with relatives was not obtained for seven respondents.

more active than stable persons on both measures of family participation. For example in the manual occupational category, 85 percent of the downwardly mobile saw four or more relatives regularly; only 66 percent of the stable saw this many relatives. The differences between the stable and downwardly mobile categories in participation with relatives were statistically significant with both measures of family participation (p < .01).

These findings indicate that the effects of downward mobility on extended family ties are very different from the effects of upward mobility. Upward social mobility disrupts intergenerational family continuity; downward mobility does not. The upwardly mobile individual is exposed to groups with values, beliefs, and life styles which are different from those of the groups he encountered during childhood and adolescence. He is moving into a more desirable position and is therefore predisposed to establish effective interpersonal relations with others of similar status and disassociate himself from his previous contacts. The downwardly mobile person, on the other hand, is entering a less desirable position. He probably continues to use the previous status as a reference point and retains some rewards by continued association with persons of higher status.[10] Perhaps, in addition, downward mobility leads to a strengthening rather than a weakening of extended family ties because the position of the downwardly mobile person is defined as temporary by extended relatives and an effort is made to help him regain a higher status.

Sex Differences in Extended Family Participation

In view of the recent interest in the way the nuclear family relates to extended relatives, it is surprising that possible sex role differences in extended family participation have been virtually unexplored.[11] In the United States much has been done to bring about the emancipation of women, but the female role still revolves primarily around domestic tasks. Although the proportion of gainfully employed women has risen sharply, their employment is typically temporary or sporadic. Even those employed on a full-time basis seldom view such employment as their primary role. By and large, American women still appear to derive their major gratifications from activities and functions carried out in the home.[12] This domestic orientation would lead one to expect that the wife would generally be more active than the husband in maintaining extended family ties.

The data presented in Table 2 indicate that women are more family oriented than men. Women are more active than men on both measures of family participation. Sixty-nine percent of the females spent three hours or more with relatives, while only 55 percent of the males spent this much time with relatives. The differences between men and women in time spent with relatives approach statistical significance. Similarly, 73 percent of the females and 64 percent of the males saw four or more relatives regularly.

TABLE 2

Sex Differences in the Effect of Social Mobility
on Extended Family Participation

Percentage Spending Three Hours or More with Relatives Per Week*	
Male 55(N = 54)†	Female 69(N = 75)†
Stable 60(N = 45)	Stable 70(N = 61)
Mobile 33(N = 9)	Mobile 64(N = 14)
G = −.50 p < .01	G = −.14

Percentage Seeing Four or More Relatives Regularly	
Male 64(N = 56)‡	Female 73(N = 80)‡
Stable 66(N = 47)	Stable 69(N = 65)
Mobile 56(N = 9)	Mobile 87(N = 15)
G = −.22 p < .01	G = .49 p < .01

* The information on hours spent with relatives was not obtained for seven respondents.
† Chi square between male and female was 2.540 p < .10.
‡ Chi square between male and female was 1.037 p < .25.

Two conclusions can be drawn from the findings presented thus far: (1) upward social mobility adversely affects extended family participation, and (2) women participate more with extended relatives than men. The task at hand is to demonstrate the consequences of the second finding for the first. Women usually derive social status from their husbands and it is only indirectly, through marriage, that they experience social mobility.[13] Social mobility should therefore be less disruptive of extended family relations among women than men. Table 2 shows the relationship between social mobility and family participation for both men and women. From this table it is clear that social mobility does impede extended family participation to a greater extent among men than women. The same pattern was found with both measures of family participation, but it was more pronounced in terms of time spent with relatives. In the male subsample, 60 percent of the stable respondents spent three hours or more with extended relatives, compared to 33 percent of the mobile respondents. Mobile and stable females are much more similar in time spent with relatives. Seventy percent of the stable and 64 percent of the mobile females spent three hours or more with relatives.

An interesting finding was uncovered with the second measure of family participation. As expected, stable men saw more relatives than mobile men but, surprisingly, mobile women saw more relatives than stable women. Eighty-seven percent of the mobile females and 69 percent of the stable females saw four or more relatives regularly. Thus, women maintain active contacts with relatives even when they are socially mobile. In fact, mobile females are more active than stable males according to both measures of family participation.

Class Differences in Extended Family Participation

Proponents of the isolated nuclear family hypothesis suggest that the prototype of the isolated and independent nuclear unit is found in the middle class.[14] In the middle class there is a strong emphasis on individual achievement and a parallel de-emphasis of extended family obligations. The value that the nuclear family should be self-sustaining and independent is believed to be most widely internalized in the middle class. Kinship ties are supposedly more important at the extremes of social class hierarchy. In the upper-upper class, endogamy and overall kinship solidarity are effective instruments for maintaining positions of status and power.[15] Family lineage is used to gain access into status groups, and there is enough wealth to maintain a semblance of an extended kinship network with some control over members. Extended family ties are stressed in the lower class for different reasons. Geographical mobility is minimal in the lower class. Lower-class persons are isolated, both physically and socially, from the larger society, and they participate in few social activities outside of those which involve relatives.[16]

A number of researchers have questioned the assumption that the nuclear family in the middle class is isolated from extended relatives by presenting empirical evidence which ostensibly demonstrates the importance of extended family ties in the middle class.[17] Unfortunately, such research has tended to focus exclusively on middle-class respondents rather than on interclass differences. It is difficult to draw conclusions concerning the importance of kinship among middle-class persons without comparable data for lower-class persons.

One of the two measures of family participation used in this study supports the assumption of the isolated family position that kinship is emphasized less in the middle class. Table 3 shows that persons with nonmanual occupations spent less time with relatives than those with manual occupations. Fifty-four percent of the nonmanual respondents spent at least three hours per week with relatives. Sixty-seven percent of the manual respondents devoted this much time to family activities. The *gamma* correlation between time spent with relatives and social class was −.26 (p < .01). There was no significant difference between manual and nonmanual respondents on the number of relatives seen. Nonmanual respondents were only slightly more likely to see relatives. Seventy-two percent of the nonmanual and 68 percent of the manual persons saw four or more relatives regularly (*gamma* = .10).

TABLE 3

Social Class and Extended Family Participation

*Percentage Spending Three Hours or More with Relatives Per Week**
Manual   67(N = 94)
Nonmanual   54(N = 35)
G = −.26 p < .01

Percentage Seeing Four or More Relatives Regularly
Manual   68(N = 100)
Nonmanual   72(N = 36)
G = .10

* The information on hours spent with relatives was not obtained for seven respondents.

It will be recalled that all of the hypotheses in this study were tested only with persons who had at least one relative living in the community. This control had an important effect on the relationship between social class and extended family participation. Restricting the analysis to persons with relatives living in Hillsboro had the effect of reducing the differences between manual and nonmanual respondents on family participation. Because nonmanual persons are more likely not to have relatives in the community they appear to be even less family oriented when the hypothesis is tested without taking into account whether or not one has relatives in the community. For example, 33 percent of those with nonmanual occupations spent three hours or more with relatives; 56 percent of those with manual occupations spent this much time with relatives (*gamma* = $-.45$, p < .01).[18]

Thus, some of the relationship between social class and extended family participation can be attributed to extended relatives being less accessible to middle-class persons. Nonetheless, given the opportunity, they are still less likely to participate with relatives than lower-class persons. While it is frequently assumed that middle-class individuals are less family oriented because they are more apt to be isolated from relatives, the opposite explanation is seldom offered. Perhaps they are isolated from relatives because they are less family oriented. The direction of causality cannot be determined from these data, but the two factors do appear to be reinforcing rather than mutually exclusive. The lack of familism in the middle class facilitates geographical mobility; once isolation from relatives occurs, it tends to decrease familism further.

Conclusion

Although the controversy concerning nuclear family isolation can be settled conclusively only by comparison of family participation in societies with varying degrees of urbanization and industrialization, several propositions concerning kin participation in the United States are implicit in the isolated family view. Some of these propositions were tested in this study. The findings were, with certain qualifications, consistent with the isolated family hypothesis.

According to the isolated family view, kinship is less important in societies where social mobility is very prevalent. In this study, upward social mobility was associated with isolation from extended kin, but downward mobility did not lead to kin isolation. In fact, downward mobility seemed to increase familism. The differential effects of upward and downward mobility on family participation may be due to the meaning that is attached to each of these types of mobility in American society. In an achievement-oriented society, there is a great deal of upward mobility and downward mobility constitutes aberrant behavior. Perhaps traditional success goals are so widely internalized in the society that the low status occupied by the downwardly mobile person is defined as temporary by ego and extended relatives as well. Thus, downward mobility may have the effect of increasing rather than decreasing family cohesion.

The nuclear family has usually been considered as a unit in kinship participation, and possible differences in the way husbands and wives relate to extended relatives have not been studied systematically. The sex differences in family participation in this study are consistent with the social-emotional female role and the instrumental male role. Women were strikingly more ˎfamily oriented than men. Moreover, social mobility was less disruptive of extended family ties among women than men. For women, children and household tasks serve as bases for intergenerational family continuity, and they are able to maintain kin relations even when their husbands are socially mobile.

Middle-class persons were less involved with the extended family, as proponents of the isolated family hypothesis suggest. This lack of involvement is due, in part, to physical isolation from relatives, but kinship is less important in the middle class even when relatives are accessible.

These findings reveal a need to focus on differential kinship emphasis in American society, not only for its own sake but also as an indirect test of the isolated family hypothesis. Social class, social mobility, and sex differences in extended family participation were uncovered in this study.[19] Further research will undoubtedly suggest other variables that relate to kinship involvement.

NOTES

1. Talcott Parsons, "The Kinship System of the Contemporary United States," *American Anthropologist,* 45 (January, 1943), pp. 22–38; Robin Williams, "Kinship and the Family in the United States," *American Society,* 2nd ed. (New York: Alfred A. Knopf, 1960), Chap. 4.
2. Marvin B. Sussman, "The Isolated Nuclear Family: Fact or Fiction," in Robert F. Winch, Robert McGinnis, and Herbert R. Barringer (eds.), *Selected Studies in Marriage and the Family,* rev. ed. (New York: Holt, Rinehart and Winston, 1962), pp. 49–57.
3. Scott Greer, "Urbanism Reconsidered: A Comparative Study of Local Areas in a Metropolis," *American Sociological Review,* 21 (February, 1956), 19–25.
4. Morris Axelrod, "Urban Structure and Social Participation, *American Sociological Review,* 21 (February, 1956), 13–18.
5. Eugene Litwak, "Geographical Mobility and Extended Family Cohesion," *American Sociological Review,* 25 (June, 1960), 385–394. Also see his "Occupational Mobility and Extended Family Cohesion," *American Sociological Review,* 25 (February, 1960), 9–21.
6. For a full description of the sample, see Lewis Levine and Harry J. Crockett, Jr., "Speech Variation in a Piedmont Community: Postvocalic r," *Sociological Inquiry,* 36 (Spring, 1966), 204–226. Also see Alfred M. Mirande, "Kinship, Friendships, and Voluntary Associations

in a Small Piedmont Community" (Doctoral dissertation, University of
Nebraska, 1967), Chap. 2.

7. The Kish method was used in selecting the member of the household
to be interviewed. Leslie Kish, "A Procedure for Objective Respondent
Selection Within the Household," *Journal of the American Statistical
Association,* 44 (September, 1949), pp. 380–387.

8. Persons from farm backgrounds and single females were not ranked.
Farm occupations are so varied that they almost defy accurate classification, and the occupations of single females seldom reflect their true
class position.

9. Parson, *op. cit.;* Williams, *op. cit.*

10. For research findings which indicate that downwardly mobile persons
continue to identify with the middle class, see Harold Wilensky and
Hugh Edwards, "The Skidder: Ideological Adjustment of Downward
Mobile Workers," *American Sociological Review,* 24 (April, 1959), pp.
215–231; Cecil L. French, "Correlates of Success in Retail Selling,"
American Journal of Sociology, 66 (July, 1960), pp. 128–134.

11. Habenstein and Coult have studied sex differences in extended-family
relations, but their measures of familism are very different from those
employed in this study; see Robert W. Habenstein and Allan D. Coult,
The Function of the Extended Kinship in Urban Society (Kansas City,
Mo.: Community Studies, Inc., 1965), pp. 16–19.

12. For a discussion of social-emotional and instrumental functions as they
relate to sex roles, see Talcott Parsons, "The American Family: Its Relations to Personality and to Social Structure," in Talcott Parsons, *et al.,
Family, Socialization and Interaction Process* (New York: Free Press,
1955), pp. 3–22.

13. Talcott Parsons, "Age and Sex in the Social Structure of the United
States," *Essays in Sociological Theory,* rev. ed. (New York: Free Press,
1954), p. 94.

14. Parsons, "The Kinship System," *op. cit.;* Williams, *op. cit.*

15. Several community studies have noted the importance of kinship in
the upper class. See, for example, W. Lloyd Warner and Paul S. Lunt,
The Social Life of a Modern Community (New Haven: Yale University
Press, 1941), Vol. I, p. 104; Allison Davis, Burleigh B. Gardner, and
Mary E. Gardner, *Deep South* (Chicago: University of Chicago Press,
1941), Chap. 4.

16. Floyd Dotson, "Patterns of Voluntary Association Among Urban
Working Class Families," *American Sociological Review,* 16 (October,
1951), pp. 687–693; Mirra Komarovsky, *Blue-Collar Marriage* (New
York: Random House, 1964), p. 238.

17. See, for instance, Marvin B. Sussman, "The Help Patterns in the Middle
Class Family," *American Sociological Review,* 18 (February, 1953), pp.
22–28; and the two articles by Litwak, *op. cit.*

18. Manual respondents also saw more relatives regularly, but the relationship was not as strong with this measure of family participation (*gamma*
$= -.26$, $p < .01$).

19. This study was conducted in Hillsboro, North Carolina, and generalizations are limited to this small community. But there is reason to believe

that the same relationships would be found in other settings. The hypotheses were supported in a community where kinship ties appear to be very important. They would probably receive even stronger support in communities where kinship is less important and there is greater variation in extended family participation.

PART II

Changes in Family Structure & Functions

Introduction

Social-scientific interest in familial change is not confined to a consideration of the global factors associated with such alterations. A substantial concern centers on relatively specific changes and their relationship to various and less complex social factors. From a theoretical point of view, analyses of this sort contribute to the delimitation of the pertinent variables involved in directly measurable relationships. When change is examined at this level of analysis, in other words, a greater number of the influencing conditions may be identified and taken into account. Such studies also indicate with greater precision which aspects of the family are changing. Thus various investigations focus on relatively narrow and circumscribed areas of the family, for example, sex-role patterns, family norms, and socialization practices. While still seeking the antecedent and contributing factors of these alterations, they generally do so on a less abstract level. Employing this level of analysis, the selections included in Part II give concrete assessments of several discrete units of change.

Concentrating on changes in motivational factors leading to large families, for instance, Lois W. Hoffman and Frederick Wyatt (selection 11) examine three contributing social trends.[1] New definitions in women's roles and in parental roles as well as the increasing theme of alienation in modern society are suggested as being instrumental in motivating families to have three or more children. Particularly for the middle class, these trends appear to be significant. A large number of children may be one means of solving the dilemma faced by the woman in choosing between the alternative roles now available to her. Modern views of child rearing have made the mother role more rewarding, even though the housewife role has become less desirable. Finally, additional children may overcome the adult's sense of aloneness, providing companionship and a fusion of self with others not otherwise attainable in mass society.

Turning to quite a different matter, selection 12 analyzes the implications of sexual freedom. Sexual freedom, primarily premarital permissiveness, is often viewed as a threat to family formation and stability, ultimately challenging the need for the family group.[2] Assessing the results of the current "sexual revolution," Hallowell Pope and Dean D. Knudsen point to a number of social pressures buttressing traditional sexual standards. Limiting the analysis to a white-collar and college-educated population, the social conditions of stability and change are set forth. Despite the availability of effective contraceptives, abortion, out-of-wedlock births, and the possibility of marriage following premarital intercourse, the desire to maintain family continuity and prestige are seen as opposing these countervailing forces toward permissiveness. Among the advantaged social strata, the changes in sexual standards are not so much a revolution as a continuing evolution.

Focusing on the normative pattern pertaining to spouse roles, evidence is presented in selection 13 supporting the hypothesis that the equalitarian family has become institutionalized in our society. William G. Dyer and Dick Urban maintain that the family is no longer in a state of flux between a patriarchal and equalitarian type, but that in most areas, full institutionalization of equalitarian norms has already taken place. Especially in the areas of child rearing, decision making, and recreation, equalitarian norms are clearly defined and prevalent. Only in the two areas of household tasks and finance is institutionalization incomplete. In these areas marital tension and conflict are expected to result, but needed adjustments in the handling of finances appear more problematic. With a few notable exceptions, adjustment appears to be toward equality.

One of the more significant changes impinging on the family has been the increase in women's roles and the alternative relationships open to them, participation in the labor force being prominent among these. Although there has been a striking rise in the number of working married women and mothers, Ruth E. Hartley (selection 14) contends that this has not been accompanied by an abandonment of traditional family responsibilities. The expansion of feminine roles and participation in them, in fact, may have enhanced woman's ego and sense of self-satisfaction. The effect of these alterations on men's roles seems to be small and only of tangential importance. More significant in the attempt to assay future changes is the fact that children apparently do not perceive any precipitous alterations in sex roles which may lead to future confusion. Much of the concern about radical shifts in sex roles that might foster instability in the family appears, therefore, to be without foundation. The trends in role patterns are toward greater equalitarianism but without the drastic consequences hypothesized by many writers.

In selection 15, Daniel Miller and Guy Swanson outline some of the general changes in family structure and parent–child relations. Not only have the members of the modern family become increasingly equal, but they have developed unique specializations and differences. Husband and wife complement one another or form what the authors term a "colleague" family. Miller and Swanson view this change largely as an outgrowth of the reordering in the world of work. Large bureaucratic organizations, by their very nature, demand the specialization of functions and complementary roles. This in turn requires that considerable emphasis be put on "getting along." In the "bureaucratic" home, therefore, child training in human relations and adaptation are emphasized, parental functions give way to formal rules and are subject to the checks of technical knowledge, and children increasingly serve as outlets for the "creative management of social relations."

Complementing Miller's and Swanson's analysis of the changing parent, Urie Bronfenbrenner (selection 16) examines changes in socialization practices and child behavior. With time, it appears that the most effective socialization techniques (formerly employed exclusively by middle-class parents) have been adopted by parents of other social strata. However, a number of qualifying factors enter into this trend. Clearly, there are sex differences irrespective of class factors, and some social-class differentials still emerge in the effectiveness of the techniques used. Despite this, the predominant movement in

American society appears to be toward an equalitarian, bureaucratic family, emphasizing achievement drives as supported by the now prevailing socialization techniques.[3]

J. M. Mogey, selectively evaluating some historical and empirical evidence, proposes that over the past one hundred years the legal and customary authority of the father has declined. At the same time, the number of broken families has increased. Although the author carefully points out that the connection between the two phenomena is not necessarily causal, it is hypothesized that the role of the father is extremely critical in determining family stability. Some evidence suggests that the father role has been redefined, and, as a consequence, the husband-father has experienced increased involvement in family activities. Despite the decline in paternal authority, reintegration of the family is the result.

Taking the body of family law as a point of departure, Herma H. Kay (selection 18) analyzes the major changes in the mores reflected in legal materials. She notes that, under common law, the rights of husband and wife were considered as one, and the one legal person was the husband. With marriage, the woman lost certain property rights, relinquished her ability to enter into contracts, and was denied the right to recover damages. Similarly, the husband's parental authority had legal primacy. From 1850 to the present, however, there has been a continuing trend toward greater legal equality for married women. Children's rights also have been gaining legal recognition to the point that the individuality of nuclear-family members is a major emphasis of family law. Kay concludes that the transfer of family functions and curbing of paternal authority, reinforced and promulgated by the law, need not cause undue concern. Current law provides for further growth in equalitarian, familial relationships.[4]

Concluding this section, J. Milton Yinger (selection 19) presents a synoptic view of several aspects of the changing American family. Taking note of institutional strains, the ambiguity in role expectations, child-training methods, parent–child relationships, and sibling interaction, Yinger explores the implications of these phenomena and the attendant changes in them for family-service agencies and the community at large. He concludes that many problems and tensions of family members can be understood only in the context of the total changing society and not separately or in isolation.

When familial units of change are less abstractly conceptualized as in these studies, the balance between persistence and alteration can be more readily evaluated. Overall, it would appear that many of the structural and functional features of the American family are changing in only a gradual manner. For example, with respect to sex roles and the authoritative relations between parents and children, the alterations that have taken place are ones of degree rather than radical mutations.

Most outstanding, perhaps, is the trend toward greater equality in the relationships among nuclear-family members. As noted in several of these selections, greater equalitarianism is evinced in a number of spheres. The tendency is most notable in spousal relationships, but here, as in other areas, change has been uneven. Greater equalitarianism also has emerged in parent–child relationships; again, however, the shift has been gradual and has occurred in only certain areas of these relationships. But the evidence suggests further changes in the direction of equality.

While many of the social scientists represented here indicate, implicitly at least, the continuance of these trends, a few stipulate structural constraints on familial change. With respect to alterations in our sexual norms, for instance, it is suggested that the system of stratification plays a prominent role in retarding the furtherance of permissive norms. Furthermore, social class is viewed as a restraining factor in the adoption of certain socialization techniques.

Significantly, these studies, variously and sometimes tacitly, point out some of the integrative aspects of ongoing change. In this context, the evolutionary changes in family size are seen as fostering a greater opportunity for the fusion of self with others and, for women, the attainment of a more meaningful and less ambiguous role. The shift to the "colleague" type of family is also interpreted as an integrative alteration, inasmuch as it is accompanied by increased complementarity in familial roles. And even though change in parental and paternal authority is obvious, the fact that decline has been gradual suggests that it has not been altogether dysfunctional or disintegrative.

Despite the greater specificity these studies afford us, it is clear that our knowledge of change, even on this level, is wanting. Our hypotheses and propositions, lacking in precision, are confined to statements of "more than" or "less than." Our analytical tools, unfortunately, presently are not capable of indicating the precise degree of change. Although not an inherent part of this methodological problem, considerable improvement in the measurement of alterations could be achieved (even with respect to our "more or less than" statements) if adequate baseline studies were undertaken. Elementary as such a procedure is, the assessment of change has been severely restricted by its absence. Related to this, of course, is the element of time under consideration. Given the historical evolution of research in the social sciences, empirical evidence for previous epochs is unavailable. Even what is available to the past three or four decades often does not lend itself to the precise formulations that have been attained in other substantative and less temporally oriented areas of social analysis. Until this is accomplished, the effort to control events, in the scientific sense of the term, necessarily must remain imperfect.

NOTES

1. With regard to family size, marriage and divorce rates, role relationships, and the implications of these patterns, a striking parallel exists between changes in American and British families. For example, see Norman Dennis, "Secondary Group Relationships and the Pre-eminence of the Family," *International Journal of Comparative Sociology,* 3 (1962), pp. 80–90.
2. Actually, George P. Murdock, on the basis of 158 societies, found that premarital sexual relations are permitted in about 70 percent of the cases; see his *Social Structure* (New York: Macmillan, 1949). To date, no general sociological explanation of either the occurrence or nonoccurrence of premarital restrictions has been formulated. The threat of permissiveness to family formation is only one explanation, and it does not appear to hold in most cases. Given a great deal of contradictory evidence, it would seem that the prevalence of permissiveness or restrictiveness can be largely attributed to historical happenstance.
3. A quite different and interesting mode of child rearing, when compared with the American pattern, is that found in the Israeli kibbutz. See, for example, Melford E. Spiro, *Children of the Kibbutz* (New York: Schocken, 1965).
4. For various legal changes pertaining to the Russian family, see Rudolf Schlesinger (ed.), *Changing Attitudes in Soviet Russia: The Family in the U.S.S.R.* (London: Routledge and Kegan Paul, 1949).

11

Social Change and Motivations for Having Larger Families: Some Theoretical Considerations [1]

by Lois W. Hoffman & Frederick Wyatt

In recent years there has been an increase in the size of the American family. This is especially marked in the middle class where more families have three or four children than formerly. Furthermore, it has been established that this increase is due not only to medical advances or to ineffective family planning; it is largely the result of choice. Freedman, Whelpton, and Campbell (8),* interviewing a national sample of married women between 18 and 39, found that almost three-quarters of their sample *expected* to have families of two, three, or four children; a similar number felt that three or four children would be *ideal*. The authors also reported that the number of children considered ideal has increased even since 1941 when 27 per cent considered four or more children ideal; in 1955, as many as 49 per cent considered four or more ideal.

The increase in family size is usually assumed by writers on the subject to be the result of technological advances and economic prosperity which have removed some of the hardships of parenthood. This view assumes that there is a relatively unchanging desire for large families and that fertility rates are determined by whether the current social setting facilitates or impedes the expression of this desire. However, it is possible that the very *motives* for reproduction are not fixed but respond to social change, and that the current increase in family size is in part a reflection of increased motivations for larger families.

Studies of motivations for reproduction can be broadly classified as psychoanalytic and demographic. The psychoanalytic studies (1, 2, 3, 5) have been concerned with motivations for pregnancy *per se* rather than for having large families, and all of them have tended to view the

---

* [Numbers in parentheses refer to references at the conclusion of this selection.]

Reprinted from *Merrill-Palmer Quarterly*, 6 (1960), pp. 235–244, by permission of the authors and *Merrill-Palmer Quarterly*.

motivation for reproduction as fixed—more or less unresponsive to the social milieu. The demographic studies dealing with psychological motivations (12, 14, 16, 17, 19, 20, 21, 22) have been interested in family size and in fertility *trends*, but they have not investigated the psychological motivations related to social change.

The approach presented in this paper deals specifically with motivations for having larger families and with the social changes that may underlie these motivations. (Thus, only those facets of the motive for reproduction which might be seen as responsive to recent social change and which seem most relevant to having three or more children will be taken up.[2]) We will consider three groups of social trends that may have influenced women's attitudes toward maternity: changes that have occurred in the woman's role; changes in the parent role and the concept of parenthood; and the loneliness and alienation that seem to characterize individuals in our society.

Changes in the Woman's Role

Technological advances have brought about the following changes:

1. Housework has become less time-consuming.
2. The remaining household tasks are the dullest and most un-creative (e.g., dusting). Areas where formerly a woman could make a special contribution as homemaker have been lost through the greater availability of commercial products (e.g., package mixes) and through standardization of techniques (e.g., the modern cookbook).
3. There are more women employed outside the home and greater opportunities for women to find such employment.
4. A housewife's time has potential monetary value, and, because of mass production efficiencies, performance of tasks in the industrial setting is more efficient than their performance in the home. In most cases, it is more economical for the woman to work for wages and buy commercial products than to spend her time making products at home for her own family.

These conditions mean that being a housewife without children or a mother whose children are all in school is not a full-time job, not a creative job, and not a functionally efficient job.[3] This was not the case thirty years ago, nor is it true today for the woman who has a preschool child.

At the same time a change has taken place in the notions of what a woman should expect from life. There seem to be more opportunities and desires for personal happiness and self-fulfillment. Perhaps "choice" and "freedom" are the key words. A woman's life has become much less circumscribed. There are more choice points in her life, more paths available, more opportunities for activity and impulse expression; and the possibility that she will make the accompanying decisions for herself is greater. These are not, however, unmixed blessings; presumably they can produce doubt and anxiety, as Fromm, among others, has suggested (9).

In addition, the Protestant Ethic seems to be still very much alive in the United States.[4] In some ways it may be stronger than ever. The present-day "idle rich" are more likely to be involved in public works than in the the pursuit of sheer pleasure. The conspicuous use of leisure seems to have become the creative or efficient use of leisure. The do-it-yourself projects are not just an answer to inflation but have become a sign of the productive use of leisure time and a great source of prestige and esteem. There seems to be an orientation toward a full and useful life which combines creativity and contribution.

To these we add another consideration: the woman of today who has borne two children is younger, more attractive, healthier, and more energetic than her mother or grandmother was after her second child, and she has a longer life ahead of her.

What can this young and vigorous woman look forward to when her second and last child enters school? If she does not choose employment, she can anticipate a life of housework which she very likely considers dull, or at least an insufficient contribution to her family or the world. For some women, particularly in the upper middle or upper class, unpaid work in voluntary organizations may fill out their lives. Many women, however, who do not choose employment, may feel they have chosen a path of "boondoggling," and their neighbors will disapprovingly concur. Work is virtue. The mother of five children and the employed mother are both hard workers, but the mother of two school-age children who is not employed is a woman of leisure.

In contrast, having a child is highly creative—both in the physical sense of producing it and in the social sense of molding it. The decision to have another baby is a decision to break the established daily routines. With a new baby the woman introduces a major change in her life and in the lives of her family. Furthermore, the care of the infant provides an area where the woman is not replaceable. In America, few other persons would be entrusted with the total care of an infant.

In addition, the care of a very young child is a full-time job, and while it often may not seem efficient, there are no acceptable alternatives.

Thus, the third (or later) child may be the expression of a need for creativity or for change. This child may be an escape from outside employment, boredom, unwelcome leisure, guilt about inactivity or non-contribution, and censure. It may also be an escape from independence, impulsivity, and, very much as Fromm discusses it, an "escape from freedom."

In addition there is today a considerable diffusion of sex roles and the definition of the woman's role is ambiguous. Bearing and mothering children are important as proofs of femininity. Not only is this the traditional feminine role, but it is now especially important because it enables the woman to avoid entering the occupational role. Employment may involve competition with one's husband and the woman may want to avoid this, not for fear of losing, but for fear of winning. The need to perceive the man as more competent is deeply rooted, and, if the woman's employment is a potential threat to this perception, it will be avoided in order to preserve the woman's sense of femininity, the man's masculinity, and the integrity of the marriage.[5] Thus, since employment is such a viable alternative, some women will be motivated to have a large family in order to avoid employment.

Mishler and Westoff (14) offer the hypothesis that excessive dependency needs are incompatible with the desire for pregnancy. The formulation presented here would lead to a different expectation. The third child can be seen as a prolongation of the period of the mother's dependency in relation to the husband. Not only is pregnancy itself an opportunity for the legitimate expression of dependency needs, but to the extent that remaining at home is a more dependent relationship to the husband than employment, prolonging this period prolongs dependency. This is assuming that we are not dealing with pathological dependency where legitimacy of roles is not a consideration. While extreme dependency needs might allow the woman to languish in the traditional role of full-time homemaker with no young children, occupation, or community activities, she must be prepared to defend this point to to herself and her friends or acknowledge her self-indulgence. Furthermore, personality needs are usually not unidimensional, and seemingly opposite tendencies often coexist. Thus, for some women the dependency dimension is a salient one but it involves both needs for being dependent on others and having others dependent on oneself. For such women, the ideal situation might be having an infant dependent on them while, at the same time, both the infant and the mother are dependent on the father.

Changes in the Parent Role

In the past decade the United States has become increasingly a child-centered culture, and a closely related development is the popularization of psychology. The role of the parent in socializing the child has been emphasized in the popular culture to the point where theories about heredity are now rarely heard. The stress on child rearing and the widespread conviction that a child is what his parents have made him have had two important effects on the parental role. First, they have added challenge and importance to the child-rearing function, making it a creative and ego-involving area, for mothers at least. Being a "good mother" no longer means simply keeping the children fed and clothed but implies that one is skilled in a mysterious and difficult art. The creative aspect of the mother role is particularly important when highlighted against the background of the increased standardization and mechanization of the housewife role and the increased desire for self-fulfillment, mentioned earlier. Thus some women will be motivated for motherhood because of the challenge it imposes, this challenge being all the greater in contrast to other aspects of the woman's role.

At the same time, and largely because the skills for being a good mother are not being communicated at the same rate as is the emphasis on being a good mother, the child-rearing function is fraught with anxiety. Paradoxically, this very anxiety may operate as a motivation for reproduction, particularly for later pregnancies. The rare mother who is satisfied with her performance in rearing the first and second child may either have more children because of the gratifications it offers, or cease to, in the knowledge that she has done well. Many mothers, however, will, consciously or unconsciously, be disappointed with their handiwork, guilty and anxious about their failures. People respond differently to anxiety, but the situation often limits the possibilities. For example, the mother cannot run away from the child who is the focal point of her anxiety. A more appropriate solution is either to try to do better with the next one or bury her anxiety in activity. Both of these are well served by having many children. With many children, she has less involvement in one, more chances to alleviate her own sense of responsibility through the individual variations offered by her products, and less time to experience anxiety. Furthermore, it is likely that her job performance does improve with practice and so this particular defense may be reinforced by reality. In addition, the attention of others, and perhaps even her own involvement, may become focused on the quantity rather than the quality.

A trend that is closely related to the emphasis on the parent's responsibility for the child's personality and to the filtering of psychology to the grass roots is an increased acknowledgment of hostile feelings toward one's own parents. Analytic writers have sometimes discussed the first pregnancy as a hostile wish to replace one's mother. There is a modern way that child bearing can express hostility toward the mother. Today's young woman who has more children than her own mother and who often does so with a show of greater ease (e.g., being physically active throughout her pregnancy) says in effect to her mother: "What was all the fuss about? I can do a better job, on a bigger scale, and with very little effort on my part." Thus, the larger family may be an expression of hostility toward the mother. Such inter-generational conflict may not be new except in form. It is possible that the generation which mothered two-child families had exactly the same motivation, but since their mothers had large families instead of small, the form of their protest was different. These women may have been saying in effect to their mothers: "I am intelligent enough, genteel enough, and sufficiently in control of my own life, that I can have only one or two children instead of seven."

There is one other way in which the particular emphasis on child rearing might operate as a stimulus to the motivation for larger families. The modern young mother is neither drudge nor disciplinarian but warm, active, and a companion to her children. This is a more attractive model for a woman and, hence, the mother role is a becoming one. The slim, vigorous, well-groomed woman with four children has an advantage over another woman who is not a mother. This latter point may be true only because of the transitional nature of the present situation where the stereotype of the haggard mother still exists as a contrast. Attractiveness in a mother seems doubly attractive, and the more children, the greater the emphasis to her attractiveness.

The Loneliness and Alienation Theme

Several contemporary writers have discussed a "loneliness" and "alienation" quality as characterizing modern life. Briefly, this is described as feeling insignificant, lost and alone. This is not a new trend on the social scene, nor is it new to social scientists. Durkheim discussed it over fifty years ago (7). Like Fromm after him (9) he attributed it, in part, to Protestantism and to the lack of group affiliation. More recently, Riesman has similarly discussed it in connection with the

breakdown of moral traditionalism (18). The loneliness and alienation of modern man have also been attributed to changes in productive modes, the complexity of modern politics, urbanism, the loss of
religious conviction, the absence of extended family ties, and increased
geographical mobility. Thus, while it is not a new trend, it may be an
evergrowing one, and we will consider it as a possible basis for fertility
motives.

Pregnancy itself is in some ways the fulfilled fantasy of the lonely
child. The pregnant woman has a secret companion who is hers alone.
The companion is always with her and communicates only to her. Like
the imaginary friend of the lonely child, it is a creature of her own
making.

Even after the child is born, elements of this fantasy continue. The
infant's total dependency on the mother may suggest almost a fusion
of the mother with the child. This is related to our earlier suggestion:
for some women, having a child totally dependent on them is highly
gratifying; at the same time they find it gratifying to be dependent
themselves. Both circumstances involve close relationships, the antithesis
of loneliness. Although these motives may not be readily articulated,
they may help to make pregnancy and mothering pleasurable experiences both in the past and in anticipation.

Furthermore, a child may represent a tie between the mother's life
and "immortality." Modern man may feel himself to be insignificant
—sometimes acutely and depressingly aware of the evanescent quality
of life. The creation of a child may involve the feeling that something
of the self will continue after death. This theme has been explicitly
put forth in certain religions, and it may operate independently among
many persons. This motivation for fertility is not a new one, but it
may be one that has become increasingly important as the belief in the
"hereafter" loses ground. Another motive for pregnancy may be the
desire to re-create the self. The child represents to the mother herself as
a child. This brings the mother still closer to "immortality" and at the
same time involves a connection to the past: the child that the mother
once was is re-created and will live on after she is dead.

Since the child develops out of the mother and is at first entirely a
part of her, the mother is sometimes able to envisage herself in two
roles at the same time. She can feel as *mother* with all attendant rewards of status and self-regard and she can feel as the *child*. She can
in this way relive her own childhood and give herself as child all the
love and affection which she wanted in her own life, but did not always receive. In short, by having a baby, a mother has an opportunity

for remaking her own life in fantasy. She can treat her infant as she wanted her mother to treat her. Women also imagine sometimes that in the child they are reproducing the husband in order to be his mother. In all these instances women repeat characteristic fantasies of their own early girlhood.

There is one other motivation for children which seems to have significance for avoiding feelings of aloneness. Participation in a secret ritual and entering into a special status group have often been thought of as means by which aloneness is avoided through merging the self with the group. Both Durkheim (6) and Fromm (9) talk of this in explaining the existence of certain social institutions. Motherhood itself is such a group; the ritual is the bearing of a child. Through childbirth and child rearing the woman joins a special society. The society has many members and with each of them she automatically has common bonds. Kluckhohn (13) has discussed the advantages a woman has in an unfamiliar culture in establishing rapport with other women. These advantages come from sharing a common status with similar role prescriptions. Thus, simply by becoming a mother, a woman becomes part of a group and has a bond with many other persons. Furthermore, with successive children one joins more exclusive groups with whom there are even closer bonds and one does not lose membership in the larger group. In fact, with each successive child one gains a certain amount of status as an expert ("Yes, it was that way with my first, but you'll find with the second . . .").

Most of the motivations that have been organized around the loneliness theme do not deal specifically with motivations for successive children. However, the gratification of these needs with the first birth may make pregnancy and mothering events of great pleasure. Thus the motivation for later pregnancies may be the recapturing of this gratifying experience.[6]

Summary and Implications

It is our view that the recent increase in family size in America may reflect in part a change in women's motivations for reproduction and that this change may be a response to certain social trends. The first group of trends we discussed dealt with some of the changes in the role of women which have resulted from technological developments. Thus, for many women the role of housewife has ceased to be a satisfying or even legitimate full-time pursuit. In addition, maternal employment has increased to the point where it is a conscious possibility to most women when their youngest child enters school. In combination, these trends mean that the woman may have to choose between the housewife role and the employment role. For those women who view both alternatives negatively, having another baby can postpone the choice. The new baby represents an opportunity for the woman to avoid employment and leisure, to have a socially acceptable role which is creative and demands her very special attention, and also enables her to remain dependent and to continue in a traditionally feminine and circumscribed pattern.

We have also taken the cultural emphasis on child rearing and the prevalent belief in environmentalism and the importance of the mother's role as a social trend that may influence fertility rates. Thus creativity and significance have been added to the role of mother just at the time they are disappearing from the housewife role. Even the anxiety which many mothers feel as a result of this emphasis may provide a motivation for larger families through the desire to have a less intense investment in one child and to bury the anxiety in activity. Furthermore, modern child-rearing notions with their greater emphasis on warmth and companionship have made the mother role a more becoming one. Thus, technological advances have removed much of the drudgery from both the mother role and the housewife role, but modern views of child rearing have added new meaning to the mother role while the housewife role has been left empty of potential gratifications.

Several social trends have been seen by social scientists as leading to feelings of loneliness and alienation. We have pointed out how pregnancy and motherhood might provide satisfactions for the needs induced by these feelings. Thus a new baby or a large family may mean to the mother companionship, a fusion of the self and the child, a tie with immortality, and a meaningful status in society.

We would not expect that these social factors will affect all women equally. First of all, fertility is not always a matter of free choice. Subfecundity, religious attitudes against birth control, and ignorance about contraceptive methods may all influence fertility rates. Secondly, social trends may affect certain segments of society more than others. There may be some subgroup variations in the amount of time required by the housewife role and in its potential for creative satisfactions; for some groups the employment alternative will be more viable than for others; child-rearing beliefs are not uniform; and the social conditions that lead to alienation vary. Thirdly, there are personality differences that are relatively independent of the social trends although they interact with them in determining the attitude of the mother toward having another child or toward planning a large family. Thus, for example, a need for dependency may provide a motive for pregnancy only because of the existence of pressure toward employment.

Because of these subgroup differences and individual personality differences, much of this theory could be tested within the current social setting. Specified groups could be compared as to attitudes toward pregnancy and toward having another child as well as to actual fertility rates. These groups would be defined in terms of their social situation (e.g., the child-rearing beliefs prevalent in the individual's social milieu, maternal employment rates, geographical mobility, ties to the extended family) and in terms of personality factors (e.g., the woman's feelings about leisure, impulsivity, femininity). We would expect these social and personality variables, which reflect and interact with the social trends, to influence the meaning of a new baby and a large family.

In addition, the theory presented here has certain implications for social prediction. It suggests that the recent increase in family size, particularly in the middle class, reflects not only economic affluence but also an increased desire for children. It is not merely that having children is less burdensome; they are actually wanted more. If this is so, it has considerable significance for predicting population shifts. For example, if certain social trends have brought about an increased desire for reproduction, an economic recession without a corresponding change in these trends might fail to bring about a decrease in family size. If the motivation for large families is strong enough, many other "luxuries" might be given up before giving up the "luxury" of a third or fourth child. On the other hand, if economic hardship succeeded in bringing about a decrease in family size, this response might prove costly in terms of mental health.

NOTES

1. The authors wish to thank Joseph Adelson, Ronald Freedman, Gerald Gurin, Martin L. Hoffman, E. Lowell Kelly, and Elliot Mishler for reading an earlier draft of this paper and making many helpful suggestions.
2. Mishler and Westoff (14) point out that decisions concerning the first and third births are especially significant for population trends. The decision regarding the first child is usually one of timing. This would probably affect eventual family size only in that it influences the age and circumstances of the couple when the decision for the third child is made. Thus, it seems more parsimonious in the present context to consider these factors as they influence the decision about a third child at the time

the decision is made, rather than to study the original reasons for the timing of the first birth.

3. These points are discussed in more detail by Cyrus (4), and data supporting them have been reported by Hoffman (11).
4. Empirical evidence for this is presented by Morse and Weiss (15).
5. This point is discussed in more detail by Hoffman (10, 11).
6. Also of relevance to the theme discussed in this section is a point made by Ronald Freedman that the family itself is important as a primary group anchor in avoiding loneliness and alienation. The family of procreation has become the only primary group with any permanence. Therefore, the desire for the larger family may be a response not only of women, for whom reproduction has a special significance, but also of men.

REFERENCES

1. Benedek, Therese. *Psychosexual functions in women.* New York: Ronald Press, 1952.
2. Benedek, Therese. Parenthood as a developmental phase. *J. Amer. Psychoanal. Ass.,* 1959, 7, 389–417.
3. Bibring, Greta. Some consideration of the psychological process in pregnancy. In *The psychoanalytic study of the child.* Vol. 14. New York: International Universities Press, 1951. Pp. 113–121.
4. Cyrus, Della. Problems of the modern homemaker-mother. In J. T. Landis and M. C. Landis (Eds.), *Readings in marriage and the family.* New York: Prentice-Hall, 1952. Pp. 392–402.
5. Deutsch, Helene, *The psychology of women.* New York: Grune and Stratton, 1944. 2 vols.
6. Durkheim, E. *The elementary forms of the religious life.* (Trans. J. W. Swain.) London: Allen and Unwin, 1915.
7. Durkheim, E. *Suicide.* (Trans. J. A. Spaulding and G. Simpson.) Glencoe, Ill.: Free Press, 1951.
8. Freedman, R., Whelpton, P. K., and Campbell, A. A. *Family planning, sterility, and population growth.* New York: McGraw-Hill, 1959.
9. Fromm, E. *Escape from freedom.* New York: Rinehart, 1941.
10. Hoffman, Lois W. Effects of the employment of mothers on parental power relations and the division of household tasks. *Marriage and Family Living,* 1960, 22, 27–35.
11. Hoffman, Lois W. The motivation of mothers for outside employment. In I. Nye and Lois W. Hoffman (Eds.), *The working mother.* Chicago: Rand McNally, 1963.
12. Kiser, C. V., Mishler, E. G., Westoff, C. F., and Potter, R. G., Jr. Development of plans for a social psychological study of the future fertility of two-child families. *Population Studies,* 1956, 10, 43–52.
13. Kluckhohn, Florence. The participant observer technique in small communities. *Amer. J. Sociol.,* 1940, 46, 331–343.
14. Mishler, E. G., and Westoff, C. F. A proposal for research on social psychological factors affecting fertility: concepts and hypotheses. *Current Research in Human Fertility* (Proceedings of a Round Table at the 1954 Annual Conference). New York: Milbank Memorial Fund, 1955. Pp. 121–150.

15. Morse, Nancy C., and Weiss, R. S. The function and meaning of work and the job. *Amer. Sociol. Rev.,* 1955, 20, 191–198.
16. Notestein, F. W., Mishler, E. G., Potter, R. G., Jr., and Westoff, C. F. Pretest results of a new study of fertility in the United States. *ISI Bull.,* 1958, 36 (Pt. 2), 154–163.
17. Pratt, Lois V. The relationship of non-familial activity of wives to some aspects of family life. Unpublished doctoral dissertation, University of Michigan, 1955.
18. Riesman, D., Glazer, N., and Denny, R. *The lonely crowd.* New York: Doubleday Anchor Books, 1953.
19. Westoff, C. F., Mishler, E. G., and Kelly, E. L. Preferences in size of family and eventual fertility twenty years after. *Amer. J. Sociol.,* 1957, 62, 491–497.
20. Westoff, C. F. The social-psychological structure of fertility. *Proceedings of the International Population Conference, Vienna, 1959.* Pp. 355–366.
21. Whelpton, P. K. and Kiser, C. V. Social and psychological factors affecting fertility: VI. The planning of fertility. *Milbank Mem. Fund Quart.,* 1947, 25, 63–111.
22. Whelpton, P. K. and Kiser, C. V. (Eds.). *Social and psychological factors affecting fertility.* Vol. 4. *Further reports on hypotheses and other data in the Indianapolis study.* New York: Milbank Memorial Fund, 1954. Pp. 801–1086.

1 2

Premarital Sexual Norms, the Family, and Social Change*

*by Hallowell Pope &
Dean D. Knudsen*

Family sociologists have often considered current American family institutions in the context of social change. But, curiously, the causes for

* This is a revised version of a paper read at the annual meeting of the Southern Sociological Society, April 1964. It is one of a series of papers written in connection with the Unwed Motherhood Study conducted by the Institute for Research in Social Science of the University of North Carolina under grant #006 from the Social Security Administration. Charles E. Bowerman is project director, Donald P. Irish and the senior author are research associates, and the junior author was a research assistant. The authors would like to acknowledge the suggestions and help of the project staff members as well as members of the Institute for Research in Social Science and the Department of Sociology at the University of North Carolina. Bernard Berk also supplied helpful criticism.

Reprinted from *Journal of Marriage and the Family,* 27 (August 1965), pp. 314–323, by permission of the authors and the National Council on Family Relations.

the changing American family have not been systematically formulated, largely because the search for causes has not been guided by explicit theory. The family specialist's approach to change has too often been descriptive, with a grab bag of variables being introduced to "account" for change. This vague, eclectic approach has resulted in the inability to identify core arguments, to formulate them precisely, and then to subject them to empirical test. Not only is our understanding of the process of change limited, but we are also faced with the inability to predict future changes. Systematic understanding of the process of social change would provide the tools whereby predictions rather than forecasts could be made; these predictions could be stated so that the passage of time would provide an empirical test of them and, more importantly, of the theory on which they were based.[1]

This paper is an attempt to further the systematic investigation of changes in American family institutions by consideration of the so-called "sexual revolution" against traditional standards—premarital chastity for the woman, the double standard for the man. This revolution has been written about, analyzed, researched, and, above all, worried about by several generations. Except in rare instances, the "revolution" in sexual standards is now accepted as an accomplished fact.[2] Such analysis as there is focuses on the forces that are producing "sweeping" changes and overlooks the forces promoting maintenance of traditional standards. This paper presents an alternative interpretation of the facts regarding changing sexual standards in the United States during this century; it also points out that there are strong social pressures that are inhibiting changes in our traditional sexual standards. It discusses reasons why norms governing premarital intercourse have *not* become rapidly more permissive, and why they are not likely to do so in the near future, in spite of pressures in that direction. It then characterizes those social conditions under which conservative standards are maintained and those under which permissive standards are allowed. The analysis is intended to apply only to the advantaged— the white-collar worker, the college educated, those with middle- and upper-level incomes. This limitation is necessary because present sexual standards, those that are likely to emerge, as well as the reasons for their emergence are different for the various social strata.[3]

By this paper, the authors hope to accomplish an appreciation of the fact that any valid theory used to explain changes in American sexual standards must account for the social supports of traditional standards as well as the pressures that undermine them. Any simplistic notion that traditional standards maintain themselves only by inertia in the face of pressures toward change will be found wanting.

Changes in Sexual Standards
and the Evidence

After the Second World War, the Kinsey Reports stimulated wide-spread discussion of American sexual standards, particularly those governing premarital intercourse. Many explanations were offered for what often was interpreted as a trend toward permissiveness as the dominant American premarital sexual standard. Among the many contributing factors mentioned were: technological changes, rationality, anonymity, altered familial functions, equal status for women, freedom of the young, the dating system, the romantic love complex, automobiles, an acceptance of play morality, coeducational colleges, and so forth. But several studies show that shifts in American sexual standards, though real, are not nearly as dramatic as trumpeted in the popular press or by pessimistic moralists.

Evidence about shifts in sexual standards is scarce; some "evidence" is no more than inference from studies describing behavior.[4] Kinsey's data, for example, show that no change took place among the middle strata in incidence of premarital intercourse among those women born after 1900. Further, much of the shift occurring for women in the 1920's was due to increased incidence of intercourse with their future husbands.[5] In the late 1940's, Ehrmann interviewed white college students who were unmarried and predominantly middle class. His results indicate how slowly change has occurred in comparison to what some feared would happen following the "gay 'twenties." [6] Many of his college males still adhered to the double standard. Only 24 percent of these men experienced intercourse with their love mates, but 60 percent experienced sex relations with girl friends. Their personal codes for behavior allowed less than half (47%) of these college men to have sex relations with their love mates, but allowed about three-quarters (72%) of them to have sex relations with their girl friends. For the females, behavioral adherence to the abstinence standard was common: 17 percent had experienced intercourse with love mates, less than ten percent with friends or acquaintances. The personal codes of only 14 percent of the female students allowed them intercourse with their love mates, and less than ten percent felt that intercourse with boy friends or acquaintances was permissible.[7] In 1959, Ira Reiss found that among white college students in Virginia, 46 percent of the men and only four percent of the women held standards that allowed premarital intercourse.[8] In 1963, from a national probability sample of adults, Reiss found that among whites, less than one-third of the men and less than one-tenth of the women held standards accepting premarital coitus.[9]

The available data indicate that since World War II, there has not been a mass retreat from chastity standards among the advantaged groups. The change since World War I in premarital sexual standards among the middle and upper strata seems to have been one of increased permissiveness for women only under certain conditions. Standards intolerant of promiscuous premarital intercourse remain, so that "concurrent" promiscuity is still condemned. However, "serial" promiscuity with different love mates has become more permissible. There appears to have been a decline in adherence to the double standard among men as well as a decreased acceptance of it by women. Convergence toward a single standard for men and women has occurred— a standard of "permissiveness with affection." [10] That is, strong affection or love is becoming an accepted condition for premarital intercourse. This standard has not replaced the formal standard of chastity for women or the double standard for men, but it is making inroads into both of them.[11]

What accounts for this moderate change in sexual standards, the convergence on a norm of permissiveness with affection, and the associated decline of the double standard? This gradual trend has occurred even though the family is faced with declining functions, the dating system, romantic love, and other forces for change. Following is an analysis of the forces for stability and also a brief conjecture about the future—the next generation or two.

The Advantages of Legitimacy for the Advantaged

Any analysis of premarital sexual norms, as Kingsley Davis has pointed out, must start from an analysis of marriage and parenthood. The first question should be, "Will unmarried motherhood be allowed?" rather than, "Will premarital coitus be permitted?" If the conclusion is that unmarried motherhood will be proscribed normatively, the next question is, "Will parenthood be disassociated normatively from coitus?" [12] The control of premarital intercourse is closely connected with the maintenance of the family; any analysis that deals with change in premarital sexual standards and does so independently of change in norms governing family formation is mistaken—in reasoning, if not in fact.

Those social strata with advantages to protect will strive to maintain their advantaged position. For groups with prestige or power, legitimate birth maintains secure and unambiguous status placement and supports the transmission of social power and honor from generation to generation. Members of these strata have good reason to support norms ensuring legitimacy and have the means to do so. In addition, because small numbers of persons violate these norms, negative sanctions can be concentrated upon transgressors. Among advantaged strata, premarital intercourse is proscribed because children born to unwed parents have illegitimate status. In a recent article, Goode has supported this argument with cross-cultural data. He found that a stratum's lack of prestige and power is associated with its lack of commitment to the norm of legitimacy.[13]

However, there are social arrangements, some based on technological innovations, that circumvent unwed parenthood in spite of premarital intercourse. These social arrangements include the following:

1. Premarital intercourse may be permitted, but only between those partners who will later marry.
2. Institutionalized means may be available for the legitimation of children born out of wedlock, for example, through adoption.
3. Abortion (or infanticide) may be tolerated or encouraged, allowing the separation of conception from parenthood.
4. Contraception may be permitted, allowing separation of premarital coitus from parenthood.[14]

Commitment to norms of chastity will lessen to the extent that one or more of the above social arrangements permits the disassociation of premarital intercourse and illegitimate birth. So long as premarital intercourse *might* produce an illegitimate child, norms prohibiting it will be supported among the advantaged.[15]

Premarital Coitus, Legitimacy, and Normative Change

These four social arrangements and the degree to which they have been and are likely to become cultural alternatives can now be considered. This allows interpretation of past changes in premarital sexual norms in the United States as well as prediction of future changes.

1. One of the various contraceptive techniques would seem to offer the best possibility of breaking the link between intercourse and conception. In the past, contraception could have allowed norms to develop that condone premarital coitus provided some contraceptive technique was used. Contraceptives permitted the violation of chastity standards in the past, but the availability of contraception did not do much to help create more permissive *standards.* Contraceptive techniques *in practice* have been, and still are, too risky—especially for the advantaged girl with everything to lose and only an unwanted child to gain. Even among middle-class married couples practicing birth control, there are large numbers of "accidental" children.[16] Attempted use of contraception among guilt-ridden, poorly informed, and inexperienced couples would often misfire; the number of accidental pregnancies among the unmarried is enough to keep parents fearful and daughters apprehensive. Unless our middle classes develop a much more open attitude toward sex and allow more practically oriented school instruction about it, contraception will not become sufficiently effective to foster a general normative change within the next generation or two.

However, within advantaged groups, some parents will train their children in more liberal sexual attitudes, and these children will be able to take advantage of traditional contraceptive methods or the newer oral contraceptives which have the advantage of keeping one's preparation for "safe" coitus continuous. Students in some colleges will continue to be exposed to liberalizing influences, and this in conjunction with access to information about up-to-date contraceptive techniques will encourage some students to develop permissive sexual attitudes. But the extent of permissiveness on college campuses is often overdrawn or based on information from colleges with liberal atmospheres.[17] To understand the changes that are taking place, it must be determined whether these liberal attitudes are spreading from campus to campus, especially whether they are spreading to and within the bigger universities. And should the conservative pressures exerted in many colleges, especially those with religious affiliations, be ignored?

Even granting that a significant and increasing proportion of college students will develop more liberal standards as a result of their college experiences, will they keep their permissive attitudes and pass them on to their children? Although children are known to perceive their parents as more restrictive than themselves, the reasons for this perception are not known.[18] Is it because of historical change, with each generation becoming progressively more permissive, or is it because each generation becomes more restrictive as it grows older and has children? The authors suspect that both effects are present. Knowing what standards the present generation holds while in college does not indicate what standards they will attempt to pass on to their children. Again, it is wise to remember that accidental and unwanted pregnancies both before and after marriage are not an uncommon experience for recent generations. Will such parents be open and frank regarding sex with their children and have the confidence to instruct and encourage their children in the use of contraceptive techniques when the official morality says safety through restraint is the proper way?

Certain conditions will generate strong pressures against traditional chastity standards; among these pressures is the growing number of women in the labor force. This leads to the association of unmarried men and women on the job. Such couples are often free of family or community controls and in a position to engage discreetly in illicit sex relations. In the case of a premarital pregnancy, the girl has the financial resources, mobility, and independence necessary to dispose of the baby with a minimum of fuss—through adoption or abortion. Opportunity for heterosexual contact within the context of the search for intimacy and the American emphasis on fun morality, freedom, and the commercialization of sex generates strong pressures against restrictive standards among working couples.[19] Under such conditions, norms emphasizing mutual satisfaction and responsibility toward one another rather than toward family and community may develop. But will such standards be carried away from the situations that generate them? After marriage and parenthood, the authors would expect many to retreat from the liberal standards of their "irresponsible youth."

2. Abortion is technically available for prevention of a birth after an unwanted pregnancy. A number of women have used this currently illegal avenue to avoid the stigma of an illicit birth.[20] Abortion avoids the social problems that are caused by the birth of a fatherless child. Seemingly, this would provide a practical means of avoiding illegitimacy, and if it were to be encouraged or even just tolerated, a more permissive attitude could be expected to develop toward premarital intercourse. What is the likelihood that within the next few generations, abortion will become a legal and subsequently a generally accepted means of avoiding illegitimate births?

Abortion has never been normatively prescribed in the United States and is generally considered by religious and social agencies alike to be a negative and antisocial control of birth.[21] The abhorrence with which abortion is publicly greeted precludes its consideration as a way to avoid illicit birth, either by the person contemplating illicit sex relations or by parents suspicious about what happens to their daughter while out on a date. Our cultural tradition even blocks use of abortion as a means of resolving pregnancies within wedlock except when the health of the mother and/or the fetus is endangered. In the future, as in the past, religious and most legal and medical professional groups will resist attempts to legalize abortion except under restricted conditions. More likely than any sudden change is a process of relaxation of the restrictions placed on legal abortion—such as making abortion permissible for not only physical but also for mental health reasons. It is highly unlikely that abortion will in the near future become tolerated as the means whereby illegitimacy will be circumvented after a premarital pregnancy.[22]

3. In the past, the ease with which the advantaged girl left home temporarily, had her child adopted, and then returned home to re-enter the marriage market unencumbered may have contributed to a change in sexual standards. Adoption could, if properly handled, avoid the stigma of an acknowledged illegitimacy, dispose of the baby in an acceptable manner, and avoid unpleasantness with the father's family. If there is a continued high demand for illegitimate babies of middle-class couples, this will contribute to a slackening public and private concern over illegitimacy. Norms could develop which would make it permissible for a middle-class girl to have a baby if she put it up for adoption. However, the adoption market may become overloaded, due either to an oversupply of babies or to increased stringency of selection procedures for adopting parents.[23] Heightened concern over illegitimate children could then be expected among middle-class parents. The end result would be attempts to promulgate and enforce chastity standards. Because it is unlikely that adoption will ever conveniently absorb enough illegitimate children, this social arrangement will not support more permissive sexual standards.

4. A final social arrangement, namely, marriage between sex partners who conceive a child out of wedlock, avoids illegitimate birth. By establishing and strengthening norms that ensure marriage between couples who premaritally conceive, the middle-class parent would protect the position of his family. Within the context of American culture, the following norms, which are mutually reinforcing, are likely to be supported: (1) couples should be committed to marriage before engaging in premarital sex relations; (2) couples considering marriage or sex relations should be in love with one another; and (3) marriage between the natural parents should take

place following a premarital pregnancy. The linking of commitment to marry with the emotional attachment of love would make the desired outcome—marriage—highly likely in case of a premarital pregnancy. It is the normative solution most likely to be adopted by advantaged strata if they are forced to retreat from chastity standards. The trend in changing sexual norms, if any is yet clearly discernible, is in this direction.

This "solution" to the problem of premarital sexual relations is compatible with other changes that are taking place in American family institutions: (1) As women gain social equality, the double standard becomes increasingly more difficult to maintain. The middle-class woman seeking premarital sexual privileges will seek them with the man she loves. (2) The "irrationality" of romantic love has been under attack from family life professionals, such as family sociologists, who have some influence over the education of youth. With parental support, these professionals would be able to encourage young people even more than now to pick their courtship partners on the basis of marriageability. This would allow an easy resolution of the dilemma created by a premarital pregnancy. Such changes will cause more advantaged persons in the future to condone intercourse, but only between potential marital partners.[24]

This paper has drawn its conclusions primarily from the premise that the threat illegitimacy poses to the social position of the advantaged will cause them to institute the norm of permissiveness-with-affection-plus-commitment-to-marry. However, there are obviously other forces that will generate norms different from and more permissive than this one. Such a factor is the relative freedom with which our youth interact during the courtship period and the relative absence of adult surveillance of them. Our courtship system is to a great degree participant-run; youths themselves are in control of the role bargains made in the courtship market.[25] Parents attempt to teach restraint to their children, especially their daughters, but when a child enters high school, and even more so when he or she departs for college, peer group influences compete with direct parental control and with attitudes internalized within the family of orientation. The pressures on youths in their peer groups are different from those acting on their parents and tend to generate different sets of norms than those supported by their parents.

Under conditions of relative status equality between the sexes, one would expect that the bargaining power of each partner in a dating relationship would be relatively equal and that norms stressing equal commitment and mutual responsibility would develop. Male exploitation of affection to obtain sexual favors or female exploitation of sex to obtain affection will be rejected, and norms of mutual responsibility will be stressed. Affection and sex will have to come from both sides of the partnership in equal measure. However, illegitimacy is less salient a threat to youth than to parents of established families, and youth will not stress the commitment to marry as much as their parents. And to the extent that contraceptive techniques are available and believed effective, there will be further pressure to disassociate sex and affection from a commitment to marry. The pressures toward acquiring the safety of a "steady" in a competitive dating market, the relatively equal bargaining power of the sexes, and the fear of exploitation of one's feelings will lead youth to prescribe sex relations only within the protective cocoon of mutual affection. The youth norm of permissiveness with affection can be expected to compete with the adult norm of permissiveness-with-affection-plus-commitment-to-marry.[26]

Other forces will also lead to support of the norm of permissiveness-with-affection-plus-commitment-to-marry, or even of the more conservative norm of premarital chastity. These forces will act more on youth than on the parental generation. If there is an increased emphasis on rational-scientific criteria for mate selection (e.g., through the influence of marriage and the family courses[27]), there will be increased fear of the "affection trap." Dating couples will avoid overcommitting themselves, either through sex or affection, so as to avoid a premature marriage. Either partner will be wary of committing himself or herself to premarital intercourse, fearing it might lead to marriage (due to pregnancy or to premature emotional involvement). Partners will delay committing themselves to one another as long as possible—until they are sure. This kind of courtship will be a progressive commitment, weighed at every step. Intercourse would result only when each partner was definitely willing to marry. Such courting procedures foster the same norms that advantaged parents would support, but for different reasons—not for fear of illegitimacy but for fear of acquiring an undesirable marital partner.

Advantage, Legitimacy and Social Change: A Summary

Premarital sexual norms are intimately connected with maintenance of family lines and position. Through group pressures and control over sanctions, advantaged strata will resist the development of norms that threaten their high position and support those that maintain family prestige and continuity. Among the advantaged, changes in sexual standards have successfully been resisted for the past 30 years. In the future, some concession to changed social conditions will cause more of the advantaged to adopt the premarital sexual standard of permissiveness with affection. But this step will be resisted strongly unless those social arrangements that allow separation of premarital coitus from unwed parenthood are also adopted.

The desire of those in advantaged social positions to maintain a high position for themselves and their children comprises an important element in the dynamic situation that determines change or stability in standards governing sexual intercourse before marriage. The traditional chastity standard cannot be treated merely as a brake that slows down but cannot stop changes toward permissiveness. The struggle between those forces fostering permissiveness, such as equal rights for women and the dating system, and those forces fostering restrictiveness outlined above will be continued in the families of the future. Because these two opposing forces are nearly equal in strength, change in the foreseeable future will be gradual, and the American sexual revolution will remain but a continuing evolution.[28]

NOTES

1. Science, of course, phrases future possibilities as predictions rather than as forecasts. Predictions may be incorrect forecasts for three reasons: (1) the necessary and sufficient conditions specified by the prediction do not occur; (2) the prediction is wrong—that is, even though the necessary and sufficient conditions do occur, the predicted events do not take place; and (3) the conditions specified in the prediction are irrelevant for the prediction being attempted. In each case, the implications for the relationship between theory and fact are very different. In the first case, the prediction is wrong, not because adequate understanding is lacking, but because the required antecedent conditions do not occur. In the second and third cases, the prediction is wrong because understanding is faulty. Only in the latter two cases is theoretical revision definitely needed. In this paper, the reader may disagree with the authors' predictions either because of theoretical differences or because he judges the empirical conditions to be different than do the authors. The first type of disagreement calls the theoretical analysis into question; the second, only the assessment of the facts.

   The analysis of social change and the American family has a number of classics. Cf., Carle C. Zimmerman, *Family and Civilization*, New York: Harper & Row, 1947; William F. Ogburn, "The Family and Its

Functions," *Recent Social Trends,* New York: McGraw-Hill, 1933, Ch. 13; Ernest W. Burgess and Harvey J. Locke, *The Family: From Institution to Companionship,* New York: American Book Co., 1945; and W. F. Ogburn and Meyer F. Nimkoff, *Technology and the Changing Family,* Boston: Houghton Mifflin, 1955.

In addition, there have been more recent signs of interest in the analysis of change in the family field: Reuben Hill, "The American Family of the Future," *Marriage and Family Living,* 26 (February 1964), pp. 20–28; and Bernard Farber, *Family: Organization and Interaction,* San Francisco: Chandler, 1964. Finally, for a world perspective, see William J. Goode, *World Revolution and Family Patterns,* Glencoe, Ill.: Free Press, 1963.

As the above indicates, there are a variety of strategies one might employ to understand social change in the family. The authors have chosen to consider the middle-class family as governed by a normative system and to interpret the impact of extrafamilial social factors (e.g., occupational institutions) or nonsocial factors (e.g., technological) on the norms defining the family structure. The authors further argue that certain features of our family institutions, namely those governing family formation, serve as structural anchors; that is, variations in norms within the family institution are limited in their variation by those norms defining these systemic anchor points. A basic change in a familial norm must in most cases be associated with a change in these anchor points. For example, if married women are to be allowed employment, traditional patriarchal ideas governing interaction between the spouses will have to be modified.

2. In a paper written in 1937, Theodore Newcomb pointed out that the 1930's were less different from the 1920's in sexual standards than many "scarehead writers" had feared. See "Recent Changes in Attitudes toward Sex and Marriage," *American Sociological Review,* 2 (December 1937), pp. 659–667.

3. In a projected paper, the authors intend to examine the social conditions associated with permissive premarital sexual standards. In the United States, permissive standards appear in those same strata in which the matrifocal family is most frequent—among deprived Negroes and whites. In these groups, the woman forms a series of liaisons rather than formally contracting marriage. She does this when marriage offers limited, if any, advantages, and when no wealth or tradition is present to be conserved by and transmitted through a family line.

4. For a discussion of the past trends in behavior and changes in standards, see Ira L. Reiss, *Premarital Sexual Standards in America,* Glencoe, Ill.: Free Press, 1960. Also see: William M. Kephart. *The Family, Society, and the Individual,* Boston: Houghton Mifflin, 1961, pp. 350–352; and Winston Ehrmann, *Premarital Dating Behavior,* New York: Henry Holt, Bantam edition, 1960, who reports on the incidence of premarital sexual intercourse by sex as reported by various investigators, pp. 39–44. See Nelson N. Foote, "Sex as Play," in *Sexual Behavior in American Society,* ed. by J. Himelhoch and S. F. Fava, New York: W. W. Norton, 1955, pp. 237–243, for a summary of the evidence from Kinsey's data indicating a decline in the double standard. Finally, see Winston Ehr-

mann, "Social Determinants of Human Sexual Behavior," in *Determinants of Human Sexual Behavior,* ed. by George Winokur, Springfield, Ill.: Charles C Thomas, 1963, pp. 142–143, for a general review of knowledge about sexual behavior from a sociological perspective.

5. The data: among ever-married women born before 1900, 27 percent were sexually experienced; this increased to 51 percent for those born in in the 1900–1910 decade and did not increase from this figure even for those women born in the 1920–1929 decade. The proportion of ever-married women who experienced coitus with other than their husbands-to-be only increased one percent (5.5 percent to 6.5 percent) from those born before 1900 to those born between 1920–1929. Reiss, *op. cit.,* p. 230, Table 4.

6. One example of a statement forecasting fast change: "In contrast with the slow tempo of many cultural changes, the trend toward premarital sex experience is proceeding with extraordinary rapidity. . . . If the drop should continue at the average rate shown for those born since 1890 virginity at marriage will be close to the vanishing point for males born after 1930 and for females born after 1940. . . . It will be of no small interest to see how long the cultural ideal of virgin marriage will survive as a moral code after its observance has passed into history." Lewis M. Terman, *Psychological Factors in Marital Happiness,* New York: McGraw-Hill, 1938, pp. 321–323.

7. Ehrmann, *op. cit.,* p. 224, Table 5.2.

8. Ira L. Reiss, "Sociological Studies of Sexual Standards," *Determinants of Human Sexual Behavior, op. cit.,* p. 134, Table XIV.

9. Ira L. Reiss, "Premarital Sexual Permissiveness among Negroes and Whites," *American Sociological Review,* 29 (October 1964), p. 691, Table 2. See also, Ira L. Reiss, "The Scaling of Premarital Sexual Permissiveness," *Journal of Marriage and the Family,* 26 (May 1964), pp. 188–198.

10. Here, the authors follow Reiss's terminology. See Reiss, *Premarital Sexual Standards in America, op. cit.*

11. The above is not meant to imply that no significant changes have taken place since 1900. It only argues that *standards* governing premarital intercourse have changed less than is often believed. It is true that some forms of heterosexual behavior defined previously as immoral are now acceptable—for example, petting. Some argue most girls remain "technical" virgins only and that the increase in heavy petting is indicative of the change that has occurred. But this "technical" virginity is crucial sociologically, as the remainder of this paper tries to demonstrate. For a discussion of changes in Western countries in sexual norms and behavior before marriage, see Goode, *op. cit.,* pp. 35–39.

12. See Kingsley Davis, *Human Society,* New York: Macmillan, 1949, pp. 399–401. An analysis consistent with the present one in most respects is found in Robert F. Winch, *The Modern Family,* New York: Holt, Rinehart, and Winston, Rev. Ed., 1963, pp. 608–635.

13. William J. Goode, "Illegitimacy in the Caribbean Social Structure," *American Sociological Review,* 25 (February 1960), pp. 21–30. For a brief but excellent summary of Goode's views on legitimacy and illegitimacy, see: W. J. Goode, *The Family,* Englewood Cliffs, N.J.: Prentice-Hall, 1964, pp. 19–30.

Contrary to Kingsley Davis's treatment and, in some respects, contrary to Goode's treatment in the above article, there is no need to make assumptions about societies or strata having system properties or maintaining steady states. The only necessity is the assumption that upper-status parents, or those responsive to their influence, will strive to prevent illegitimate births by creating, promulgating, and implementing norms proscribing premarital intercourse. They can effectively do this through political pressure, pressure on educational agencies, influence in religious organizations and over mass media productions, as well as by direct influence over and control of their own children. Before expecting the advantaged strata to tolerate the disruptive consequences of illegitimacy, it would be necessary to expect them to ignore the importance of family in the maintenance of their privileged position.

14. If the authors were to extend their analysis to include cross-cultural variations as well as those through time, they would have to consider the impact of factors other than those applicable to the American situation. For example, infanticide is a possible method of eliminating an illegitimate child; it need not be considered further here because in the United States, adoption and abortion are available as more acceptable cultural alternatives. Sterilization, if it could be made temporary, might be another way of avoiding conception after coitus, but contraception achieves the same effect and is the most likely cultural alternative to be chosen in a country with a high educational level. In the United States, people could learn to use contraceptive techniques effectively.

There are relatively high illegitimacy rates and, at the same time, liberal sexual attitudes, including the widespread acceptance of intercourse between engaged couples, in some modern Western societies—for example, Denmark. There, even the unwed mother and her child are not the objects of opprobrium—the general population in Denmark holds an understanding and sympathetic attitude toward them. This points to the possibility that illegitimacy and permissive sexual norms may be accepted by advantaged strata under conditions other than when cultural alternatives allow the circumvention of illegitimacy after premarital intercourse.

However, an analysis of sexual standards and illegitimacy in Denmark supports the above analysis in large part. The following conditions in Denmark allow the more complete disassociation of premarital intercourse and illegitimate birth than is true in the United States: (1) A long tradition in Scandinavia permits premarital intercourse between potential spouses, but if a child should result, the couple is expected to marry eventually and is held responsible for the "illegitimate" child. Thus, officially recorded illegitimacies may not be illegitimacies socially. (2) Adoptions of illegitimate children are possible, and the unwed mother is aided in the placement of her child. (3) Criminal abortions are widely utilized to avoid the birth of an illegitimate child and are relatively easily obtained. Apparently, the population is more tolerant of abortion than in the United States. (4) Contraception is, of course, practiced. (As in the United States, there is widespread ignorance about it.) These cultural traits and social practices mean that illegitimate status for a child is a less likely outcome after premarital intercourse in Denmark than in the United States; as a result, advantaged groups in Denmark can tolerate more permissive norms.

But in spite of the above, it is likely that advantaged groups in Denmark both experience and tolerate more actual social illegitimacy and at the same time, hold more permissive norms regarding premarital sexual intercourse than do comparable groups in the United States. Another reason for the greater tolerance of illegitimacy in Denmark is that the unwed mother is given more government protection. She is provided less grudging assistance by public agencies than in the United States. Also, the father is legally required to contribute to the support of the child. Because she is helped by the state and little stigma is attached to this help, the unwed mother is better able to get along until she can marry or have her child adopted; she need cause only a minimum of trouble to her family. If legal protection and public assistance were more readily available to the premaritally pregnant daughters of advantaged parents in the United States (and if assistance by social welfare agencies carried no stigma), advantaged parents might be less resistant to the development of permissive sexual attitudes here.

One additional point needs to be made: there has not been an upward trend in the illegitimacy rate in Denmark during this century. It may be that structurally Denmark generates and can tolerate somewhat more illegitimacy than is true for the United States but that the structural factors resulting in illegitimacies have not varied appreciably in recent times in Denmark. Thus, in Denmark, since more permissive sexual attitudes are not related to more and more actual illegitimacy, these liberal standards can be accepted. In the United States, since actual social illegitimacy has increased, liberal sexual standards are likely to be resisted by the advantaged.

See Sydney H. Croog, "Aspects of the Cultural Background of Premarital Pregnancies in Denmark," *Social Forces,* 20 (December 1951), pp. 215–219; Goode, *World Revolution and Family Patterns, op. cit.,* pp. 35–39; Harold T. Christensen, "Cultural Relativism and Premarital Sex Norms," *American Sociological Review,* 25 (February 1960), pp. 31–39; and the articles on Scandinavian countries in *The Encyclopedia of Sexual Behavior,* ed. by Albert Ellis and Albert Abarbanel, New York: Hawthorn Books, 1961.

15. An additional reason can be found for why the advantaged will attempt to uphold retrictive sexual standards. The moral stance taken by advantaged strata is not independent of the behavior and standards held by those in more disadvantaged strata. Persons in positions of advantage will attempt to uphold their standards as the legitimate yardstick for all. Thus they differentiate themselves from those who do not hold these standards or who do not conform to them. In addition to avoiding the internal disruption illegitimacy produces in their family system, the advantaged will attempt to maintain restrictive sexual standards as a part of "middle-class morality" in the attempt to capitalize on their moral worthiness as a part of their constant struggle to maintain their high position in the prestige hierarchy.

In the United States, discrimination against ethnic and minority groups has been justified by pointing out the moral unworthiness of such groups.

For example, the loose sexual behavior and standards of Negroes is one of the favorite "proofs" by whites that Negroes are inferior. Constant attempts have also been made to question the morality of those being supported by welfare, attempts to define them as the undeserving poor—attempts that will justify decreased welfare allotments. Though this degradation of the disadvantaged is done in a haphazard manner and not by the organized action of class-conscious strata, our educational system, our mass media, and our political system act so that the disadvantaged are defined as unworthy because they do not meet middle-class moral standards. Thus bills are introduced in state legislatures proposing to declare women who have had illegitimate children morally unfit and incompetent mothers so that their children may be placed in foster homes or so that they may be sterilized; in the public mind, these bills give official backing to the definition of lower-class (or ethnic group) behavior as immoral.

16. Married white Protestant women, using appliance methods of contraception only, reported that 21 percent of their pregnancies were accidental (conception occurred when some method was being used to avoid it). See Ronald Freedman, Pascal K. Whelpton, and Arthur A. Campbell, *Family Planning, Sterility, and Population Growth,* New York: McGraw-Hill, 1959, p. 208, Table 6-17. This study was based on a national sample chosen to represent white married women between the ages of 18 and 39 who were living with their husbands.

On the basis of numerous talks with girls from colleges throughout the country, journalist Gael Greene reports: "By her own description, the average college girl is 'pitifully naive' about conception and 'even less informed about contraception,'" *Sex and the College Girl,* New York: Dell Publishing Co., 1964, p. 160.

17. The difference between colleges and, presumably, between groups on the same campus can be striking. Reiss, "The Scaling . . . ," *op. cit.,* p. 195, Table 8, reports 62 percent of students in a white Virginia college accepting abstinence whereas the same was true of only 18 percent of students in a white New York college. Such variations need to be explained; in addition, the relation of standards to behavior must be more thoroughly investigated.

18. For evidence that the younger generation sees their parents as more restrictive than themselves plus evidence that the older generations are, in fact, more restrictive, see Harry A. Grater, "Behavior Standards Held by University Females and Their Mothers," *Personnel and Guidance Journal,* 38 (January 1960), pp. 369–372, and Reiss, "Premarital Sexual Permissiveness . . ." *op. cit.,* p. 692. See also Robert R. Bell and Jack V. Buerkle, "Mother and Daughter Attitudes toward Premarital Sexual Behavior," *Marriage and Family Living,* 23 (November 1961), pp. 390–392.

19. The above is based on Vincent's discussion in his study of unwed mothers in California. It is notable that the greatest increase in the illegitimacy rate has been among women aged between 25 and 34 between 1938 and 1957—over three times that of the 15–19 age group. These are the women most likely to be working and independent of their families. In spite of the large increase in the illegitimacy rate among

older women, the greatest concern is with the adolescent unwed mother. The older women and their children are not a social problem because they do not burden the taxpayer and because they provide childless couples with adoptable infants. See Clark E. Vincent, *Unmarried Mothers*, Glencoe, Ill.: Free Press, 1961, p. 54 and pp. 86–96.

20. For a summary of the Kinsey figures on abortion, see Clifford Kirkpatrick, *The Family*, New York: Ronald Press, 2nd Ed., 1963, pp. 359–360.

21. "The woman who has an abortion has, from the Planned-Parenthood point of view, wasted life. . . . Abortion destroys life; . . . [and] is negative and anti-social." Edward F. Griffith, *A Sex Guide to Happy Marriage*, New York: Emerson, 1952. See also the discussion of penalties for abortion as they are associated with the Judeo-Christian tradition in Richard M. Fagley, *The Population Explosion and Christian Responsibility*, New York: Oxford U. Press, 1960, p. 108.

22. It is possible that conditions such as extreme population pressure would lead to the acceptance of abortion as a corrective measure (cf. Japan), but in a Western-educated society, with its Judeo-Christian background, contraception would probably be tried first. In contrast to abortion, contraception may be practiced in private by illicit lovers. Thus, there may be a split between public morality and private behavior and morality—witness the data on sexual practices reported by Kinsey and the public reaction to them. Use of contraception and private acceptance of it may increase without public acknowledgment or acceptance. Such a condition may pave the way for a sudden shift toward public acceptance of contraception used by unmarried couples when it is suddenly realized that many such couples have been using contraception for some time.

Unlike contraception, abortion cannot usually be kept a private matter between the illicit lovers. Also, the abortionist involved is subject to legal and professional controls. Changes in the number of abortions or individual shifts in attitudes toward abortion will generate discussion within professional groups and by the public. (The inaccessibility of information about this illegal practice may lead to an exaggerated fear of its extent and the threat it poses to society.) Shifts toward a more liberal view of abortion are less likely to have their way paved by prior widespread private use of abortion and by an acceptance of it by the private morality. This would be changed if an easy, reliable, and safe technique for induced abortion were developed which would be carried out by the pregnant girl herself—if such a technique were allowed to become widely known.

23. "One of the most important factors influencing adoption for a number of years has been the discrepancy between the number of families wanting to adopt a child and the number of children legally available for adoption. With ten or more families applying to adopt for every child legally available for adoption, it was impossible for adoption agencies to meet the demand for children. . . . Recently there seems to be a tendency in the opposite direction. A number of agencies are concerned about the decrease in applications for adoption of normal white infants." *Readings in Adoption*, ed. by Evelyn I. Smith, New York: Philosophical Library, 1963, pp. 530–531.

24. The pattern of marriage following premarital conception is common now. Christensen's work using record linkage shows that nearly one-fifth of first marital births in an Ohio sample were premaritally conceived. However, it is likely that these couples marry more from fear of detection than from following a norm of marriage to the person with whom one premaritally conceives. This is indicated by the large number of couples who marry almost immediately after the pregnancy is determined or even suspected. As the pattern of marriage after premarital conception became accepted and institutionalized, there would be much less anxiety generated and fewer quick marriages. This is the pattern shown by a more sexually permissive culture investigated by Christensen. It should be clear from the present argument, however, that post-conception marriages will become required normatively among the advantaged and will not remain a matter of personal choice. Otherwise, the threat to social position and honor would remain.

For a recent summary of Christensen's work, see Harold T. Christensen, "Child Spacing Via Record Linkage: New Data Plus a Summing Up from Earlier Reports," *Marriage and Family Living*, 25 (August 1963), pp. 272–280.

Clark E. Vincent reports from his study of unwed mothers in California (*Unmarried Mothers, op. cit.*, pp. 82–91) that those from advantaged groups had predominantly felt themselves to have been in a "love relationship of some duration" with their sex partners. Can this data be interpreted as indicating that the norm of permissiveness with affection but *without* commitment to marry is already spreading among the advantaged? The present authors think not. Many of these women probably expected or assumed that they would marry the father of their child—especially if they became pregnant. They were most likely following the norm of permissiveness-with-affection-plus-commitment-to-marry, but the commitment may not have been mutual.

Below is described a likely result for those women engaging in premarital intercourse in a culture with restrictive sexual attitudes. Once the woman finds that she is pregnant premaritally, she develops guilt feelings and blames her erstwhile lover for her plight. Her family and friends are likely to interpret the male as the "sexual exploiter" (see Vincent, *op. cit.*, pp. 73–82) and to consider him unworthy as a marriage partner. The premaritally pregnant girl is charged with finding someone more suitable. A girl who is genuinely in love with an illicit sex partner can decide that she does not want to marry him, especially if he is hesitant about "making an honest woman of her." Evidence from the study of unwed motherhood in North Carolina comparing whites (more restrictive standards) and Negroes (more permissive standards) supports this interpretation: whites who are premaritally pregnant more often marry (usually the child's father) before giving birth; but among those who have given birth and who marry, whites less frequently marry the natural father than do Negroes.

25. See Goode, "Illegitimacy in the Caribbean Social Structure," *op. cit.*, for a discussion of courtship systems as market systems in which role bargains are struck. That is, ". . . in any role relationship both ego and alter are restricted in what services they may agree to perform for one

another, by the expectations of others and thus by the sanctions which others will apply. . . . All courtship systems are market systems in which role bargains are struck. They differ from one another with respect to the commodities which are more or less valuable on that market (beauty, personality, kinship position, family prestige, wealth) and who has the authority to do the marketing. Modern Western societies seem to constitute the only major historical civilization in which youngsters have been given a substantial voice in this bargaining (Imperial Rome might be added by some historians)." (p.28.)

26. In a recent book written for teen-agers, one widely read family life specialist stresses mutual responsibility in her discussion of sex controls. She also tells the teen-ager to recognize the investment parents have in their children and that parents want children to be a credit to the family ("one impulsive moment may break the social standing of years"). Teen-agers are urged to view their sexual behavior within the context of the larger goals they have in life and are told that the ability to achieve depends on deferring immediate gratifications. For the most part, this book represents the normative position which advantaged parents are expected to take, but, in addition, it recognizes the position that advantaged youths are formulating. The author attempts to interpret the parental position to teen-agers, stressing the ruined reputations and damaged life chances which premarital intercourse can cause. See Evelyn Millis Duvall, *Love and the Facts of Life,* New York: Association Press, 1963, especially pp. 228–230, 260–263, and 334–342.

27. Reuben Hill compared the emphasis given to different concerns by the first marriage textbook in 1934 and by three 1963 marriage texts. This comparison can be an index to how the family professionals, through their writing, teaching, and counseling, will attempt to shape the future of our family system. Hill's content analysis shows that in 1963, the most frequently mentioned area of concern is the general topic of "better mate selection." This topic is getting about twice as much attention in 1963 as it did in the 1934 text. And, interestingly enough, Hill lists the following as subtopics under this general heading: "More mutuality in sex relations, less exploitation," and "Single high or single permissive standard for premarital sex." Neither topic is mentioned as a concern of the 1934 text. See Hill, *op. cit.,* pp. 24–28.

28. As contraceptives become more efficient and gain wider acceptance, confidence in them will increase. Among groups that gain complete confidence in available contraceptive techniques, a norm of permissiveness with contraception will likely develop. Though this norm is probably developing now, its wide acceptance is several generations in the future.

13

The Institutionalization of Equalitarian Family Norms

by William G. Dyer & Dick Urban

A basic postulate held by many sociologists in the area of the family is that the American family is in a stage of transition from the older patriarchal family to a system of a democratic, equalitarian arrangement.[1] It is the contention of Burgess and Locke that the roles of the father and mother were highly institutionalized in the rural, patriarchal family, but that social change has brought a change in the marital roles. In the present family arrangement, the roles of the father and mother are no longer highly institutionalized and happiness in the family comes as the husband and wife work out their role definitions between them.[2]

However, a process of logical inference from other propositions in the field of the behavioral sciences gives rise to a hypothesis that the equalitarian family has become institutionalized in American society.

Theoretical Formulation

Following the model outlined by Merton for building theory,[3] a paradigm of theoretic analysis may be stated as follows:

1. In a normless situation, members of a group will form new norms to direct behavior.[4]
2. Social change has broken down the old family norms in American society.[5]
3. New norms will be formulated around predominate values.
4. A predominate value in America is equality between men and women.[6]

Reprinted from *Marriage and Family Living,* 20 (February 1958), pp. 53–58, by permission of the authors and the National Council on Family Relations.

5. Therefore, new family norms can be expected to be formed in America around equality between husband and wife.

The above formulation constitutes a theory for it provides a system of explanation of relationships but stated in a manner that allows the derivation of hypotheses. Propositions one and two appear to have been validated by research. Propositions three and four have been less validated and should be considered assumptions. The test of the derived hypothesis gives weight to the validity of the propositions and assumptions from which it has been derived.

Basic to this research is the concept of institutionalization. Parsons has defined this to mean those standards which have been internalized by members of a society which orient their behavior. Conformity to these standards both satisfy the needs of the individual and maximize the favorable reactions of others with whom he is interacting.[7] It is assumed that institutionalization follows the establishment of norms in a social system.

Methodology

In testing the above general hypothesis, the sample of necessity limits the generalization of the main hypothesis which is stated in terms of American society as a whole.

Sample

The sample consisted of two strata: (1) single students both male and female of the Brigham Young University and (2) married male students and their wives, most of whom were not students. This breakdown was felt advisable to see if the same role expectations were found among single and married people. If a norm is institutionalized, we would expect it to be relatively constant for both married and single people.

Three hundred single students divided equally between males and females were interviewed in classes which were randomly selected from all upper and lower division courses offered in one school quarter. One hundred married couples were selected at random from the married students' campus housing area. All were interviewed in the fall of 1955.

Background Factors

Since Brigham Young University is a church-related school, approximately 97 per cent of all persons interviewed, both married and unmarried, were members of the Church of Jesus Christ of Latter-Day Saints (Mormon). This may represent a bias factor in the findings, but a pre-test taken at Iowa State College indicated substantially the same results. Christopherson's study[8] substantiates what appears also to be the case in the study, that despite the patriarchal tradition in the Mormon Church the actual behavior of young Mormon people conforms rather closely to general societal behavior regarding family roles.

The married couples were slightly older than the single group; the mean number of years married was 3.6, and the mean number of children among the married group was 1.27 with only sixteen couples being childless. Both married and unmarried subjects were similar regarding home community (most coming from small towns or cities between 10,000 and 100,000); marital happiness of parents; and year in school, with nearly equal numbers from each of the four college years. Generally, age, year in school, religion, community of origin, and marital happiness of parents remained constant in all analyses between married and single students.

The Questionnaire

To test the central hypothesis of institutionalization of equalitarian family norms, the field of family activities was divided into five areas, following the procedure set up by E. E. Dyer.[9] The areas were childrearing, decision making, finances, household tasks, and recreation. Sub-hypotheses derived from the major hypothesis would hold that in each of these areas a system of equality of action would be found.

Following pre-tests at Iowa State College and Brigham Young University, the schedule was administered to the sample of students. Questionnaires were of two types: one for the single students indicating their expectations of future marital roles, and the other for married students indicating both their actual marital roles and the roles they desired. The latter was included because of a recognition of disparities that often exist between ideally held norms and actual behavior. Comparisons between married and single students were made between the single students' ideally held expectations and the married students' actual behavior and ideal behavior.

Treatment of Data

If equalitarian family norms are institutionalized, we would expect the majority of the members of both single and married groups to respond in the same way. If the norms are not institutionalized, we would expect a fluctuation in response. There is a question whether institutionalization can be considered dichotomously—is a norm either institutionalized or not, or is institutionalization a matter of degree? The researchers considered institutionalization to be a matter of degree and assumed that the higher the level of agreement the greater the degree of institutionalization.

Responses to the various questions were scaled along a continuum of equality. For each question regarding activity the person could respond that the activity should be handled by: (1) huband alone, (2) husband mostly, (3) about equally, (4) wife mostly, (5) wife alone. If the pattern of family activity is centered around equality, we would expect most of the responses to be checked around response three "about equally," and if it is institutionalized we would expect the majority of the people to respond the same way.

Chi-square analysis was used to compare responses between males and females both single and married, between single and married males and females for both the actual and desired behavior of the married persons, and between the actual and desired responses for married males and females.

Findings

Child-rearing

Child-rearing covers ten areas:

Item No.	Item
20	Disciplining children
21	Deciding when to have children
22	Deciding how many children to have
23	Taking care of children's physical needs
24	Being children's playmate
25	Determining and supervising games children may play
26	Deciding who will be children's playmates
27	Deciding children's jobs in home

28 Deciding children's voice in family decisions
29 Deciding children's spending money

The level of majority agreement for all areas covered under child-rearing is with but one exception above 60 per cent agreement in terms of equality of activity. The exception is in response to the question 23 where the majority response was "wife mostly." It would appear that equalitarian action in child-rearing is the norm for all groups in the sample although some areas (items 24, 25, 26, 27) show less agreement than others.

Decision Making

Areas covered here were:

Item No.   *Item*

16 Who should be boss of the family?
17 Who should be head of the family?
18 Who should have the final word in family decisions?
50 Who should have charge of home-planning, management and housework?
51 Who should determine how leisure time is to be spent?
52 Who should determine the family budget and money matters?
53 Who should decide the type and number of recreational activities?
54 Who should deal with the children?

In this area the majority agreement is above the 60 per cent level in terms of equality of action for all areas considered but one. The one exception was in terms of "who should be the head of the family." Majority agreement for all groups was that the husband should be head although the disparity between married and single women is significant. A significantly greater number of married women felt that the husband alone should be head, while more single girls responded that this function should be handled equally. All groups distinguished between "head of the family" and "boss of the family." The majority in each group felt that no one person should be "boss."

Again there is some disparity in the levels of agreement for the various groups but the pattern appears to be in terms of the norm centering around equality between men and women in decision making. For certain items (51, 52, 53, 54) the married men and women desire more equality of action than is now the case with them.

Finances

Finances include:

Item No.	Item
57	Decides how much for necessities (food, fuel, rent)
58	Decides how much for luxuries (periodicals, TV, etc.)
59	Decides how much for entertainment and recreation
60	Decides what personal items for wife will be bought
61	Decides how much for wife's personal items
62	Decides what personal items for husband will be bought
63	Decides how much for husband's personal items
64	Handles money for groceries
65	Decides on large purchases
66	Handles money for household
67	Handles charge accounts

There appears to be generally too much disparity in response to conclude that a norm of equality has been established. There is above 70 per cent majority agreement around equality regarding deciding how much is spent for family necessities (item 57), how much is spent for family extras (item 58), what is spent for entertainment and recreation (item 59), and who decides on large purchases (item 65). For all other areas the level of majority agreement is 69 per cent or below. Even for such areas as "who should handle the money for groceries and household expenses," and "who should decide what and how much the husband and wife should spend on personal items" there is no one response where there is a high level of agreement. Traditional family functions appear not to be clearly defined and new norms in these areas are not clearly established.

Household Tasks

This includes:

Item No.	Item
14	Wife should be mother, etc., or have career
15	Husband should help with household tasks
32	Doing dishes
33	Grocery marketing
34	Yard and garden work
35	General housecleaning

36 Making beds
37 Washing clothes
38 Ironing clothes
39 Sewing and mending
40 Planning and cooking meals
41 Planning and organizing housework
42 Planning what groceries to be bought
43 Making household repairs
44 Painting
45 Moving furniture
46 Doing "heavy" odd jobs
47 Planning what furniture is to be bought
48 Planning what insurance is to be held
49 Planning and managing upkeep of car
55 Separate jobs and responsibilities

In this area as in no other does the hypothesis of equalitarianism of activity break down. Regarding household tasks, there appears to be more a traditional division of labor that apparently is still a part of the orientation of college students. It is interesting to note that in many of those activities most generally considered to be male or female work there is not a high level of agreement indicating that these tasks may not be as strictly defined as before. Such is the case with such areas as who should plan what groceries are to be bought (item 42), painting around the house (item 44), yard and garden work (item 34), grocery marketing (item 33), making household repairs (item 43), and moving furniture (item 45).

However, if two categories are combined, namely (1) you alone (doing the job) and (2) you mostly, mate helping some, a clearer definition of behavior emerges in some areas. Such activities as general house cleaning, making beds, washing clothes, planning and cooking meals, and planning and organizing housework are seen as generally being women's work. For the men, doing heavy odd jobs generally falls in their division of labor. It appears that there is more agreement as to the jobs that are predominately female than those that are mostly for men.

Only two areas were seen to be clearly the responsibility of both—planning what furniture is to be bought and planning what insurance is to be held. It may be that these two items really belong in the area of decision making where the equalitarian pattern is more clearly the norm.

In this area there is little evidence that the norm is towards equal sharing in activity. It is much more the case that the norm is still towards a division of labor of men's and women's work with the men's work being less clearly defined.

Recreation

In the area of recreation, the norm appears to be decidedly around equality or shared activity. Only "hobbies" is seen to be an individual activity and even here the highest response of agreement is that it should be shared.

Items of Significant Difference

In terms of the general hypothesis of the study, we would expect to find few differences between groups if the norms are institutionalized where items are analyzed by use of chi-square.

The trend shown in the analysis of levels of majority agreement is substantiated, for in the areas of child-rearing, decision making, and recreation there is a high level of agreement while finances and household tasks show many more significant differences when tested by chi-square.

It is interesting to note that there is generally high agreement between married men and married women in terms of both their actual practice and their desires around the areas investigated. There is much less agreement between single men and single women and between single men and women and the married group. However, even here the major differences are found in the areas of finances and household tasks.

Child-rearing

In the area of child-rearing the major differences appear between the single women and the married women for three questions (items 24, 25, 27). In every case the differences are in terms of a greater response for equality of action on the part of single women. More married women than single women see these child-rearing activities as more their individual responsibility as determined by their actual practice. However, when the single women's responses are compared with what the married women desire their role to be, the differences cancel out, for the married women desire more equality of activity between themselves and their husbands. Item 23 is concerned with taking care of the children's physical needs and there is no difference between what the single women expect and what the married women do. However, there is a difference between the single women and what the married women desire, for they desire more equality.

Finances

The greatest differences in financial matters are between single men and single women, single men and married men, and single women and the desires of married women.

For those items of differences between single men and single women (items 57, 58, 59, 63, 65) the difference in every case is due to a greater expectation of equality on the part of the single women. More single men expect the wife to decide most of the time how much is spent for family necessities and they expect that they will decide more of the time how money will be spent for luxuries, entertainment, husband's personal items, and large family purchases.

Comparing single men and married men, the married men both practice and desire more equality of function. The single men more often see the handling of money as either a function of the wife's or the husband's role and less a joint activity. This trend is constant for every item of difference (items 60, 62, 64, 65, 66).

The difference between single women and married women is that the single women see those items (items 64, 66, 67) in terms of a division of labor either handled more by women or their husbands. The married women both in practice and desire feel these activities should be more equally shared between husband and wife.

Household Tasks

Differences in agreement in the area of household tasks appear most often between single men and single women, single men and married men, and single women and married women.

Comparing the single men and the single women, the men more often see themselves helping with household tasks, making beds, helping in general housekeeping, washing clothes, ironing clothes, and doing sewing and mending than is expected by the single girls. The single girls see all of the above activities more as their individual responsibility. In the area of the more traditional male activities, the single men feel these are more their responsibilities (yard and garden work, and heavy work around the house) while the single women expect to help more in these tasks.

The differences are not clear between single and married men. Generally the single men see household tasks in terms of more a division of labor than do the married men, but there are reversals of this in some areas. Married men behave more equally in grocery marketing, planning what groceries are to be bought, painting, and moving furniture than the single men expect to do. But the single men expect to help more in ironing clothes and sewing and mending than do the married men. Regarding doing dishes and doing yard and garden work there is a wide diversity of response among the married men while the single men see this more in terms of the traditional division of labor.

A comparison of single women and married women shows that generally the married women behave more in terms of equality of activity. Married women expect the grocery marketing, painting, and moving furniture to be done more equally than do the single girls who see these more in terms of division of labor. However, the married women do the dishes alone more and expect the husband to keep the car up alone while the single girls expect to have more equality in both.

Discussion of Findings

It appears that in three of the five areas investigated the main hypothesis of the institutionalization of equalitarian family norms is substantiated. These areas are child-rearing, decision making, and recreation. In two other areas, finances and household tasks, the responses are disparate enough to conclude that they are not institutionalized to a high degree around any one given response. However, within the areas of finances and household tasks there are certain tasks that appear to be institutionalized around the equalitarian norm. But certain of the household tasks appear to follow a traditional division of labor, and there is a high degree of agreement between the men and women of the study which is the criterion used to determine institutionalization.

One would expect to predict that the greatest amount of tension and conflict would appear and the greatest adjustments be made in those areas of least institutionalization. However, the item analysis would tend to disprove this at least for certain areas under household tasks. Even though there are differences in the expectations between single men and single women, the differences often occur in that both expect to help the other in the other's traditional tasks while expecting to do their own tasks alone. This should tend to minimize difficulty of adjustment and lead to greater harmony.

But in the area of finances, a different picture emerges, and it appears that there are real differences between single men and single women. Single women expect much more to handle finances equally while single men expect more division of labor. We would tend to predict more conflict in this area than any other between newly married couples.

It also appears that there is generally high agreement between married men and women. As compared to the single men and women, the married people operate more in terms of equality of action, although this is not always the case. In the individual item analysis, there are few areas of disagreement between married men and their wives. The differences between single men and married men and single women and married women and the lack of difference between married men and women tends to support the idea that changes are made in behavior after persons are married as they begin to adjust the marital role expectations they held while single. Generally it appears the adjustment is towards equality although there are notable exceptions.

We would tend to conclude that the major hypothesis that family norms are institutionalized around equality of action between husband and wife cannot be accepted without qualification. Institutionalization appears to be the case in certain areas of family activity but not in others as determined by the areas examined in this study and for the sample of the population investigated.

NOTES

1. Ernest W. Burgess and Harvey J. Locke, *The Family: From Institution to Companionship,* New York: American Book Co., 1953, p. vii.
2. *Ibid.,* Chapter 16.
3. Robert Merton, *Social Theory and Social Structure,* Glencoe: Free Press, 1949, pp. 92–96.
4. Muzafer Sherif, *The Psychology of Social Norms,* New York: Harper Bros., 1936.
5. Burgess and Locke, *op. cit.*
6. Robin M. Williams, Jr., *American Society,* New York: Alfred A. Knopf, 1955, pp. 409–417.
7. Talcott Parsons, *The Social System,* Glencoe: Free Press, 1951, p. 38.

8. Victor A. Christopherson, "An Investigation of Patriarchal Authority in the Mormon Family," *Marriage and Family Living,* 17 (November, 1955), pp. 328–333.

9. Everett E. Dyer, "A Study of Role and Authority Patterns and Expectations in a Group of Urban Middle-class Two-income Families." Unpublished Ph.D. Thesis, University of Wisconsin Library, 1955.

1 4

Some Implications of Current Changes in Sex-Role Patterns [1]

by Ruth E. Hartley

In recent times it has been the fashion to cry havoc and sound the alarm when discussing alleged changes in sex role patterns. The topic itself has had a certain bandwagon effect so that one could scarcely open a Sunday supplement without being faced with scare headlines about women in pants and the dire consequences of contact with dishwater to the male psyche.[2] All sorts of "experts" have had a heyday with "mannish" women and "emasculated" men, on the basis of very little evidence for the existence of either in unusual proportions. In view of undisputed interest in this topic, it seems desirable to take a sober look at the facts and make a considered assessment of the changes that actually have taken place, or are taking place, on the basis of systematically collected empirical evidence.

When we make such evidence the criterion for our evaluations, we find there is surprisingly little to go on. For one thing, to talk of *change* in sex role patterns implies comparison with some state before the change took place. In this case, it demands that we establish some temporal baseline, i.e., we must answer the question: change since when? An examination of the popular press seems to indicate that much of the recent and current hysteria had its beginnings in conditions at the close of World War II, when some of the women who had been lured out of private life for service in wartime industries and as substitutes for men withdrawn from essential public services refused

Reprinted from *Merrill-Palmer Quarterly,* 6 (1959–1960), pp. 153–164, by permission of the author and *Merrill-Palmer Quarterly.*

to be pushed back again. The cries of anguish of the would-be per-
suaders are preserved in most of the post-1945 issues of the "slick"
magazines addressed to homemakers. Our assumption, therefore, is
that the change we are assessing must have taken place roughly within
the last twenty years, between the beginning of World War II and
now. If this is the case, we must look for reliable empirical material,
preferably in quantitative form, depicting sex role patterns around
1940 and a set of siimlar measurements of current patterns, and
compare them, before we can really know what, if anything, has
happened to sex role patterns within the last two decades.

Anyone who has tried to find sets of validly comparable sex role
data gathered over a twenty-year interval will acknowledge that the
pickings are rather sparse. We have some statistics for who-does-what
in limited samples of current families,[3] but with what shall we compare them? This just does not seem to have been a burning question
in 1940—certainly not important enough for any systematic records
to have been made.

The best evidence we have deals with only a small segment of sex
role activities in adulthood and derives from census data. I refer, of
course, to the figures depicting the striking rise in the number of
women in the labor force during the last twenty years. Before we
consider this evidence as a definitive criterion of change, however, I
would like to quote a few words of caution by Smuts, who has been
intimately involved in the intensive study of human resources conducted by the Conservation of Human Resources Project.[4] He writes:

> The only source of comprehensive data on the number of working
> women and their occupations is the U.S. Census. Before 1940 the
> Census counted these persons, aged ten years and over, who were
> "gainfully occupied." A gainfully occupied person was defined, es-
> sentially, as one who pursued with some regularity an activity which
> produced money income. Since 1940 the Census has counted persons
> in the "labor force," which is a much more precise approach. The la-
> bor force includes all persons aged fourteen and over who work for
> pay or profit for any length of time during a given week or who
> seek such work; and those who work for fifteen hours a week or
> more in a profit-making family enterprise, even if not paid. . . .
>
> Comparison of Census data on women's employment in different
> years must be undertaken with extreme caution. The definition of a
> gainfully occupied person was much narrower in 1890 than in later
> years. The 1890 Census counted a person as gainfully occupied only

if he reported an occupation "upon which he chiefly depends for support, and in which he would ordinarily be engaged during the larger part of the year." This definition excluded most of the large number of women who earned money through homework and many of those who worked irregularly away from home. In addition, a great many who qualified under the definition were not counted. Because most women did not work regularly for pay, and because the Census instructions emphasized the circumstances under which women should not be counted as gainfully occupied, Census takers were likely to be careless in recording women's work. This tendency was reinforced by the *ad hoc* character of the Census organization and by the tendency of the respondents to reflect the prevailing views of women's proper role by concealing the employment of female members of the family. As a result of all these circumstances, any woman who was both a housekeeper and a paid worker, or a student and a paid worker, was likely to be recorded only as a housekeeper or student.

It is particularly important to keep this in mind when evaluating analyses of long-term trends in women's work. The increasing employment of women shown by the Census data reflects not only the growing employment of women for pay, but also the growing willingness of respondents to report women's work, the broadening of Census definitions, improvement of the Census organization and procedures, and the decline of homework, which could be more easily overlooked than work away from home (20,* pp. 157–159).

It seems clear from the above that even Census data are not a reliable indicator of the extent of social changes. Granting the validity of these qualifications, however, it still seems evident that there are more women in the labor force than ever before, and of these a larger proportion are wives and mothers than ever before. This is one definite change in sex role activity for which we have evidence and we might start our search for implications by asking what impact this change has had. First, however, it would be well to again attend to some admonitions from Smuts:

> Emphasis on the new work of women, however, should not be allowed to obscure an equally important fact. Today, as always, most of the time and effort of American wives is devoted to their responsibilities within the home and family circle. This is true even

* [Numbers in parentheses refer to references at the conclusion of this selection.]

of those who are in the labor force. Since 1890 the demands of paid work have become much lighter. The normal work week has decreased from sixty to forty hours; paid holidays and vacations have become universal; and most of the hard, physical labor that work once required has been eliminated. Because of these developments, many women can work outside the home and still have time and energy left for home and family. Moreover, most working mothers do not assume the burdens of a full schedule of paid work. Among employed mothers of preschool children, four out of five worked only part time or less than half the year in 1956. Among those whose children were in school, three out of five followed the same curtailed work schedule. And even among working wives who had no children at home, only a little more than half were year-round, full-time members of the labor force (20, pp. 36–37).

As the last quotation suggests, this change in feminine roles apparently does not mean that women are abandoning their traditional family responsibilities to seek personal glory in the market place. It does not even seem to mean that women are particularly intent on competing with men, contrary to the accusations that have been frequently hurled at them. On this point, Smuts remarks:

Today, as in 1890, the great majority of working women have little interest in achieving success in a career. . . .

In recent years employers have been able to attract millions of additional women into the labor force without changing the relative levels of men's and women's pay, or greatly expanding women's opportunities for advancement. The decade between 1945 and 1955 was one of booming prosperity, labor shortages, unprecedented peacetime demand for women workers, and unprecedented increase in the number of women working. Yet, in 1955, the median wage and salary income of women who worked full time was still less than two-thirds that of men—almost exactly the same as it was in 1945. This suggests that it is not particularly important to a great many working women whether or not they earn as much as men, or have equal opportunities for training and promotion. What they seek first in work is an agreeable job that makes limited demands. Since they have little desire for a successful career in paid work, they are likely to drift into the traditional women's occupations. They are willing to become teachers, though they could earn more as engineers; willing to take factory and service and clerical jobs that hold little hope of substantial advancement (20, p. 108).

These observations by Smuts have been supported by many studies of adolescent girls and young women in high schools and colleges distributed widely over the country (3, 4, 18, 19). We might legitimately ask if there are implications we can validly derive from this particular change in the role patterns of one sex. Below, we will consider the data we have as they apply to the women themselves, to their husbands, and to their children, as far as it is possible and valid to separate the three.

From lengthy interviews with about forty working mothers,[5] divided almost equally between professional and nonprofessional levels, the implication emerges that this change in sex role pattern is more a matter of form than function. Most of the working mothers we interviewed consider their work as an aspect of their nurturant function. It is another way in which they can serve families. They do not substitute work for family obligations—they *add* it to the traditional roster of womanly duties and see it as another way of helping their husbands and providing for the needs of their children. Their husbands are still seen as the major and responsible breadwinners—the mothers consider themselves merely as "helping" persons in this area.

The opportunity to help in this way has happy consequences for many. They feel a greater sense of freedom of choice, less coercion by blind fate, more integrity as persons, less frustration and less harrassment by economic problems. The stimulation they receive from contact with others on the job and the change in physical surroundings between home and work even seem to make housework more satisfying and less like drudgery. The really bitter complaints about the hatefulness of household tasks tend to come from the nonworking women we interviewed rather than from those who worked at an outside job. That these salutary effects of the freedom to work may not be confined to our small sample is suggested by the findings of Hoffman, who in a study of 89 working mothers and 89 nonworking mothers, matched in pertinent variables, found that working mothers, in comparison to nonworking mothers, are warm, helpful, supportive and mild in their discipline, suggesting more relaxed and satisfied persons (9).

The freedom to work has, however, not been achieved without psychic penalty. The guilt some working mothers feel about their "self-indulgence" in going to work is marked and may have negative consequences to their daughters and to society at large. Typically, these "guilty" mothers do not work out of dire necessity; they enjoy their work and provide well for their absence from the household. Yet they seem to feel that there is something not quite legitimate about their preference for working and almost invariably give their children the impression that they work only because they need the money. "What other excuse would I have for working?" one such mother asked the interviewer. It seems to us that this situation reveals a questionable state of social values which induces women to feel that they have not a natural right to work at something congenial to them, which makes a positive contribution to the community, and which need not deprive their school-age children to any significant degree. That this anxiety is a socially induced one is suggested by Williams,[6] who found that working mothers whose social contacts were mainly with others in a similar situation did not suffer these difficulties, while working mothers whose contacts were mainly with more traditionally oriented families experienced great discomfort. Perhaps as more and more mothers work, the social climate inducing these feelings will dissipate. Meanwhile, however, these attitudes are resulting in a strongly negative perception of the work situation in general on the part of many children (it is something one does only out of necessity) and a damaging lack of candor between parent and child. It is also, we feel, producing an ego-crippling effect on the female children involved, since it exerts a necessarily restrictive influence on the development of the child's self-concept (6, 7, 24).

Perhaps the most widely discussed area of concern related to this change in women's roles deals with its effect on men. The more sensational statements have implied the immediate emasculation of any male whose wife spends some time at money-earning. What does sober fact reveal? One traditional element of masculinity in our society is the dominance of the male in his family. Dominance implies control over other persons as well as control over possessions. Hoffman (9) suggests that control in the family situation might function in two ways: as *activity-control*, referring to control a person has over a given area of activities, regardless of whether or not this control has an important effect on others, and as *power*, defined as the degree to which one person makes decisions which control another person's behavior or makes decisions about objects which affect another person in an important way. In relation to activity-control, Hoffman found that working wives had less control and their husbands more than in families where wives did not work. In relation to the power component, no difference was found between working women and matched nonworking women. Although the husbands of the working wives may have participated more in household tasks after the women went to work than they had before, this apparently did not perceptibly affect the quality of their status in the family group.[7]

Actually, we still have very little reliable information concerning the effect of the woman's work role on the man's domestic role. Blood and Hamblin report that the husbands of working women participate in domestic activities to a greater extent than the husbands of nonworking women (1). Our own data, coming from children's perceptions rather than adult reports, suggest that the class variable is more significant in relation to male participation in traditionally female household tasks than the work status of the wife.[8] Boys with working mothers assign domestic tasks to men more frequently than do boys with nonworking mothers (p = .05), it is true, but boys from working-class and lower-middle homes exceed boys from upper-middle-class homes by an even greater margin in making such assignment of roles (p < .01). This finding might suggest that assumption of the work role by women of lower economic strata might have more impact on traditional male roles than the same phenomenon at higher economic levels, where outside persons substitute for the wife in domestic tasks more frequently. Careful examination of our data, however, reveals that in the class comparison boys from homes with nonworking mothers contributed the bulk of the male domestic role assignments!

It is interesting to note, in passing, that the boys in our sample were more prone to assign traditionally feminine domestic tasks to men than were the girls (.2 > p > .1). This may mean that these tasks are gradually being incorporated into the male self-concept, so that we may expect acceptance of an increasingly egalitarian division of all life tasks and a parallel diminution of rigid judgmental evaluations about the "manly" or "unmanly" nature of specific activities. A bit of clarification is necessary here, however. Male domestic involvement is regarded by our subjects as a "helping" role, with the major responsibility for household management and child care still unquestionably the woman's job. This feeling about male domestic participation echoes the feeling we have noted about the woman's participation in the work world: the activity is subordinate in importance both to the major responsibility of the sex involved and to the weight of the responsibility borne in the given area by the opposite sex. We are not witnessing an elimination of differences—only an amelioration.[9]

A few more items from the data collected in our study of the development of concepts of women's social roles might be of interest here. These deal with the apparent connections between a mother's work status and her children's concepts of the future roles of themselves and others. We found, for example, that the presence of a working mother made no difference in the assignment of nondomestic work roles to women by girls but was a significant variable (at the .05 level) with the boys. When we asked our female subjects about their own future plans, however, the work status of the mother was an important differentiating variable. Significantly more daughters of nonworking mothers mentioned housewife as their first choice of future occupation than did daughters of working mothers (p < .05). Significantly more daughters of working mothers said they thought they would work after they had children than did the others (p < .05). Similarly more daughters of working mothers tended to choose nontraditional vocations (among choices other than housewife) than did the daughters of nonworking mothers.

Despite the effect of working mothers on boys' assignment of work roles to women, significantly more girls indicated plans to work after marriage than there were boys who said they expected their wives to work (p < .01). This disparity echoes a common finding (15) and indicates a force which we believe serves to slow the movement of women into the work world.[10]

Differences in plans for the future expressed by daughters of working mothers as compared with daughters of nonworking mothers may be explained in part by differences in their perception of the work role as such. This is suggested by the comparative proportions of children of working and nonworking mothers who made relatively positive and relatively negative interpretations of a pictured situation in which a woman was leaving her child to go to work.[11] Although about 64 percent of our subjects (N = 108) sensed some discomfort in this situation for the woman in the picture, only 37 percent of the children of working mothers interpreted her attitude as negative toward the work itself. In contrast, approximately 54 percent of the children of nonworking mothers thought that the woman must feel negative toward her work. These findings, combined with the others already described, suggest that the changes that have already taken place in sex role patterning will inevitably lead to extension of themselves, provided their orderly development is not interrupted by widespread social or economic crises.

The desirability of such extension may be a moot point. Some preliminary findings reported by Bronfenbrenner[12] from a study of family structure and personality development seem to be relevant here.

Studying the effects on children of parental absence, he gathered data from 450 students in the tenth grade of a small city and from their teachers. Parental absence was defined by a variable called "saliency" or the general extent to which a particular parent appears to be actively present in the child's world.

Bronfenbrenner found that the effect of parental absence on the child seems to depend on whether the missing parent is of the same or opposite sex and how much time the remaining parent spends in the home. The crucial person seems to be the parent of the same sex.

In relation to responsibility, for example, so long as the same-sex parent was present a good deal of the time, the child of either sex was rated as above average. If the same parent was in the high-absence group, and the opposite-sex parent was also absent a great deal, the responsibility rating dropped drastically. Similarly, if the remaining parent was in the high-presence category, the subject received a low rating. But if the same-sex parent was absent a great deal, and the opposite-sex parent present only an intermediate amount, the child received the highest mean rating on responsibility in the sample. Thus, if a boy's father was away from home a good deal, and his mother was either away excessively or present excessively, he tended to be rated low in responsibility. If the mother avoided either extreme, the son tended to be rated exceptionally high. Similarly for girls: if the mother was excessively absent, the relative presence or absence of the father seemed to determine the responsibility rating.

The implications of this study for our topic are intriguing. For one thing, it suggests that, in the traditional family set-up where the father is usually absent a great deal of the time, the continuous availability of the mother may be detrimental to her sons; they may be better served were the mother to be legitimately involved away from the home on a part-time basis. For girls, on the other hand, an optimal pattern would seem to be one in which the father is home somewhat more than ordinarily obtains, if the mother carries full-time responsibilities outside the home. The sex role pattern which seems to be currently increasing, with fathers fully employed and mothers employed part time, would seem to promise more for the development of boys than of girls. However, since the same-sex parent is still present a good deal of the time for girls, the latter seem not likely to be penalized.

Effects of parental presence and absence seem to differ markedly with differences in the socioeconomic status of the family, the father's level of education and his work orientation (whether quality oriented or not). The differential impacts of such variables as these may account for apparent inconsistencies in findings presented by studies focusing on different respective segments of the population. Thus we find many apparent contradictions between findings reported by the Gluecks (5) who studied mainly families of low socioeconomic status and those reported by Hoffman, Blood and Hamblin, and Bronfenbrenner, who either concentrated on middle- and upper-middle-class subjects or included a significant number of such subjects in their samples. Recognizing this state of affairs, we must limit any implications drawn from the data we have discussed to the type of population from which the data were collected. With this qualification in mind, a few general observations seem to be warranted.

The direction of current sex role change seems to be toward consistently greater egalitarianism, with leadership centered in families of higher educational levels. As the tendency toward the spread of higher education continues, we can expect more and more families to share this pattern. If psychologists are correct in assuming that one can give to others only what one has as part of the self, increased feelings of self-fulfillment and freedom of action which seem to accompany current developments in women's roles should lead to a lessening of crippling maternal possessiveness and a diminution of "momism."

The implications for men are less clear. It is unfortunately evident that socialization techniques used with boys continue to saddle many of them with irrational and damaging anxieties about their ability to implement the male role (8, 11, 12). These anxieties are frequently accompanied, as one might expect, by extreme conceptual rigidities and limitations in self-definition and by a tendency toward defensive hostility. It is obvious that any change in the *status quo* would cause discomfort to such anxious individuals, and an increase in the apparent capability of females, whom they are taught at all cost to avoid emulating and whom they are pressured to best in order to validate their masculinity, would be particularly threatening. Perhaps we are approaching an era of more confident women and more anxious men. Frankly, this is pure speculation. It might be instructive to keep an eye on the sex ratio of male and female psychiatric referrals. At present they show a complete reversal between childhood and adulthood, with males far in the lead before adolescence and females coming out way ahead after adolescence (2, 14, 17, 21, 23). If significant changes in the relative proportions of satisfaction and threat impinging on each sex accompany changes in sex role patterns, the gap between female and male referrals should lessen.

There is one possibility of more generalized male difficulty which relates to ego-development in childhood rather than functioning in adulthood. Current socialization practices in relation to male children can create even greater difficulties than they do at present as the permissible role activities of girls widen. It is conceivable that the widespread use of negative sanctions, generally phrased in the unspecific and semantically confusing adjuration not to be a "sissy," may be responsible for more and more limitation in permissible activity for boys as girls enter into more and more formerly exclusively masculine activities (10, 16). There is some indication that in certain localities this is happening (22). However, this suggestion may be borrowing trouble. There is no indication at present that activities cease to be regarded as suitably masculine just because girls also engage in them, if they have been considered acceptable before girls joined the fun.

In conclusion, I should like to emphasize the following five points:

1. Concern about a possible increase in children's confusion about sex roles because of alleged changes seems to be without foundation. For one thing, children are not aware of the changes since they do not have the time perspective for this. They react to the picture as they perceive it at any given moment, and changes in social roles are not so precipitous as to create contradictions from moment to moment. Let us beware of projecting our adult confusions on the children, and try to profit from them to create child-handling techniques that will ensure the necessary psychic flexibility that future developments will require.

2. Whatever changes have taken place seem to be mainly new means of fulfilling established and accepted functions and to imply no radical reversals of these.

3. There seems to be no realistic basis for the guilt many working mothers of school-age children feel about their work. Some of the evidence available at present suggests that it might, in fact, be desirable for some mothers to take part-time jobs.

4. There is no necessary implication of threat or damage in any perceptible current change in sex role activity. The real problem of adjustment to sex roles seems to be rooted in the differential pressures associated with respective developmental stages in each sex. Among males the pressures seem to be more exigent before adulthood; among females, during and after adolescence. In each case, special pressure toward limitation and restriction is identifiable during the periods for which comparative rates of breakdown are greatest for each sex.

5. In view of the above, current trends toward greater freedom of action for women would seem to be positive in implication, if the implied evaluative egalitarianism is also extended to the male sex. This seems to be taking place only in a very limited fashion, with the leadership centered in families of upper educational levels. Ego-strengthening

socialization processes applied to male children seem to be of central importance for the smooth synchronization of change in sex role activity patterns.

NOTES

1. This paper is based on an address delivered at the annual meeting of the New York Society of Clinical Psychologists, May 23, 1959. The data reported here were collected as part of a project supported by Research Grant M-959 (C, C-1, C-2, C-3) from the National Institute of Mental Health, Public Health Service. The author wishes to thank Dr. Frank Hardesty, Research Associate on the project, for his skill in collecting a large portion of the data reported here and for his cooperation in handling the analysis.
2. See, for example, these articles: Ward Cannel, "Is the American Male Man or Mouse?" *Washington Daily News,* Dec. 11, 1958; Bruno Bettelheim, "Fathers Shouldn't Be Mothers!" *This Week Magazine,* Apr. 20, 1958; Jean Libman Black, "Husbands Shouldn't Do Housework!" *This Week Magazine,* Sept. 8, 1957; Dorothy Barclay, "Trousered Mothers and Dishwashing Dads," *New York Times Magazine,* Apr. 28, 1957; Mike Wallace and John A. Schindler, "Are the Two Sexes Merging?" *New York Post,* Oct. 17, 1957.
3. One source is an unpublished study by Lois W. Hoffman, Ronald Lippitt, and others, at the Research Center for Group Dynamics, University of Michigan, in which 450 middle-class families in Detroit were surveyed. The study was reported by John Sembower in *The New York Journal,* November 12, 1957, under the headline "Hear Ye, O Husbands, Dusting's Not Thy Destiny. . . . " References to results of this survey can also be found elsewhere (1, 9, 13).
4. Established at Columbia University in 1950 as a cooperative research undertaking, the Project has led to major publications concerning the uneducated, the Negro potential, the ineffective soldier, and women as workers.
5. These interviews took place as part of a study of children's concepts of women's social roles and were used to gather data concerning the background of the children who were subjects as well as to assess the attitudes of the interviewees concerning the satisfactions and frustrations of woman's role from the adult's point of view. Each interview took from 1½ to 2½ hours to administer.
6. From a preliminary statement of findings by Dr. Robin Williams in correspondence with the author.
7. This opinion is also supported in the paper by Blood and Hamblin (1).
8. The raw data yielding these comparisons came from the responses of approximately 150 boys and girls, 5, 8, and 11 years of age, to the following statement: "Suppose you met a person from Mars and he knew nothing about the way we live here, and he asked you to tell him about girls (your age) in this world; what would you tell him girls need to know or be able to do?" These same questions were asked in relation to boys, women, and men.

224   RUTH E. HARTLEY

9. This amelioration is not characteristic of sex role patterns only—it is
   only one aspect of a pervasive social trend. Turning again to *Women
   and Work in America,* we find Smuts pointing out: "The increasing employment of middle-class, middle-aged wives is but one aspect of a
   series of developments that have tended to eliminate sharp differences
   in American society. . . .
       "Rural and urban ways of life have come closer together. Many local
   and regional peculiarities have been all but erased as a result of increased industrialization. The vast gulf between the very rich and the
   very poor has been narrowed. Status distinctions among occupations
   have been blurred as the wages of manual labor have risen, and the
   brutalizing aspects of manual work in the last century have been abol-
   lished. The spread of free public education has reduced the cultural and
   economic advantages of the well-born. For present purposes, at least,
   the most important of the fading contrasts in American life is the contrast between the activities of men and women" (20, pp. 66–67).
10. This opinion was supported by materials collected from parents of our
   subjects. From interviews with 90 mothers, divided approximately
   equally among working and nonworking, we got the impression that the
   husband's attitude toward his wife's working often served as the deciding factor when neither economic necessity nor preschool children were
   involved—and some of the unhappiest women we talked with were
   among those who prevented from working because there was no
   economic necessity for them to do so and their husbands could not conceive of any other valid reason. The unhappiest husbands we interviewed
   were those who aspired to upper-middle-class status, whose wives were
   compelled to work for economic reasons; their wives were not particularly unhappy about working.
11. The materials from which these data were derived were elicited in the
   following way. A picture showing a woman with a briefcase leaving the
   half-open door of a house through which a small child watched was
   presented to each subject. The interviewer said, "This little girl is at
   home and her mother is going to work. How does the mother feel about
   going to work? What makes you think so?" Other questions elicited reasons for the mother's working, alternatives to her working, and feelings
   of the child.
12. Personal communication from Dr. Urie Bronfenbrenner giving a preliminary report of findings.

REFERENCES

1. Blood, R. O. and Hamblin, R. L. "The effect of the wife's employment
   on the family power structure," *Soc. Forces,* 1958, 36, 347–352.
2. *Department of Mental Hygiene, Annual Report for 1956.* Albany:
   Dept. Ment. Hyg., 1957.
3. Douvan, Elizabeth M. and Kaye, Carol. *Adolescent Girls.* Mimeo-
   graphed paper, University of Michigan.
4. Empey, L. T. "Role Expectations of Young Women Regarding Marriage
   and a Career," *Marriage and Family Living,* 1958, 20, 152–155.

5. Glueck, S. and Eleanor. "Working Mothers and Delinquency," *Ment. Hyg., N.Y.,* 1957, 41, 327–352.
6. Harte, Joan B. *Modern Attitudes Toward Women.* Issued as a separate by the Auxiliary Council to the Association for the Advancement of Psychoanalysis, 220 W. 98th St., New York 25, N.Y., 1950.
7. Harte, Joan B. *Women in Our Culture.* Issued as a separate by the Auxiliary Council to the Association for the Advancement of Psychoanalysis, 1953.
8. Hartley, Ruth E., "Sex Role Pressures and the Socialization of the Male Child," *Psychol. Rep.,* in press.
9. Hoffman, Lois W., "Effects of the Employment of Mothers on Parental Power Relations and the Division of Household Tasks," *Marriage and Family Living,* 1960, 22, 27–35.
10. Jones, Mary C. "A Comparison of the Attitudes and Interests of Ninth Graders." Paper read at Society for Research in Child Development, Bethesda, Md., March, 1959.
11. Lynn, D. B. "A Note on Sex Differences in the Development of Masculine and Feminine Identification," *Psychol. Rev.,* 1959, 66, 126–135.
12. Lynn, D. B. "Sex Differences in Identification-Development," *Sociometry,* 24 (December, 1961), 372–383.
13. Miller, D. R. and Swanson, G. E. *The Changing American Parent: A Study in the Detroit Area.* New York: John Wiley & Sons, 1958.
14. *Patients in Mental Institutions 1955: Part II. Public Hospitals for the Mentally Ill.* Publ. Hlth. Serv. Publication no. 574. Washington, D.C.: Govt. Printing Office.
15. Payne, R. "Adolescents' Attitudes Toward the Working Wife," *Marriage and Family Living,* 1956, 18, 345–348.
16. Rosenberg, B. G. and Sutton-Smith, B. "A Revised Conception of Masculine-Feminine Differences in Play Activities," *J. Genet. Psychol.,* 104 (June, 1964), 259–264.
17. Schwartz, E. F. "Statistics of Juvenile Delinquency in the United States," *Ann. Amer. Acad. Polit. Soc. Sci.,* 1949, 261, 9–20.
18. Slocum, W. L. *Occupational Planning by Undergraduates at the State College of Washington.* Pullman, Wash.: State College of Washington, 1954.
19. Slocum, W. L. and Empey, L. T. *Occupational Planning by Young Women.* Pullman, Wash.: State College of Washington, 1956.
20. Smuts, R. W. *Women and Work in America.* New York: Columbia University Press, 1959.
21. *Statistical Report for the Year Ending June 30, 1955.* Sacramento: Department of Mental Hygiene, 1955.
22. Sutton-Smith, B. *The Games of New Zealand Children.* Berkeley: University of California Press, in press.
23. Ullman, C. A. Identification of Maladjusted School Children. *Publ. Hlth. Monogr., no. 7.* Washington, D.C.: Govt. Printing Office, 1957.
24. Wenkart, Antonia. *The Career Mother.* Issued as a separate by the Auxiliary Council to the Association for the Advancement of Psychoanalysis, 1947.

15

The Changing American Parent

by Daniel Miller & Guy Swanson

The Family and Bureaucracy

. . . the family has been in historical times in transition from an institution with family behavior controlled by the mores, public opinion, and law to a companionship with family behavior arising from the mutual affection and consensus of its members. The companionship form of the family is not to be conceived as having already been realized but as emerging. . . .

The most extreme theoretical formulation of the institutional family would be one in which its unity would be determined entirely by the social pressures impinging on family members. The ideal construction of the family as a companionship would focus upon the unity which develops out of mutual affection and intimate association of husband and wife and parents and children. . . .

Of the historical and existing types of families the large patriarchal type most closely approximates the ideal construction of the institutional family. . . . The modern American family residing in the apartment-house areas of the city approximates most nearly the ideal type of companionship family, in which the members enjoy a high degree of self-expression and at the same time are united by the bonds of affection, congeniality, and common interests.[1]

When Burgess and Locke wrote this now widely influential description of the family, World War II was in process. The thinking of sociologists in the United States was still powerfully dominated by the spectacle of the growth of cities and the spread of city ways of life in the wake of industrial capitalism. First through Western Europe and the United States and then in the Orient and every other part of the world reached by a burgeoning commerce and industry, the cities

Reprinted from Daniel Miller and Guy Swanson, *The Changing American Parent* (New York: John Wiley & Sons, Inc., 1958), pp. 197–206, by permission of the authors and publisher. Copyright 1958.

had grown and changed. The industrial and, often, entrepreneurial society had begun to appear, and the traditional pattern of the family had shifted to accommodate to these new forces. Generally, in all these places, the preindustrial family was patriarchal, patrilineal, and patrilocal. That is, the father held the principal authority, children were considered more closely "related" to his family than to the parents and brothers and sisters of their mother, and the family lived in close association with the husband's relatives. Among non-literate societies this pattern was broken most typically when the methods of production were such that wife and, perhaps, children could participate on an almost equal basis with the husband. Such is the case in those simple economies where almost every able-bodied member aids in the gathering of food through collecting nuts and fruit, wild vegetables and cereals, and insects and small animals. Hunting big game, caring for large herds of animals, or conducting agriculture on a large scale require more specialized skills and greater strength. The wife could not participate in full equality in such activities and simultaneously manage the home. The surplus of wealth was not sufficient to hire baby sitters, although, in certain peak periods of activity, the younger children might care for any infants in the family while the mother and older children worked to bring in the harvest or plant the seeds for the next crop.[2]

The city life that developed with industrialism was one of those conditions that change the family. In the Western world it typically meant that husband and wife had to leave the large group of relatives in the rural area and take up independent residence in the city. The family was no longer as completely patrilocal or patrilineal as before. It continued to be patriarchal.[3] With certain notable exceptions, as in textiles and pottery making, the strength of males and their lesser responsibilities for the care of children made them the principal breadwinners in an age in which much heavy common labor was in demand. Women worked in industry when poverty forced them to and their strength and level of skill would permit.[4]

The continuous extension of machine techniques and the growth in size of enterprises whittled away at patriarchal patterns, especially in the middle classes. Women could handle an increasing number of jobs as physical strength was replaced by machine power. Fewer children and the easing of many burdens of housekeeping freed women for employment that substantially increased family incomes. The surplus of wealth produced by industry enabled an increasing number of wives to hire someone to take over at least a part of their household duties while they were away at work. Wages and salaries were lower for women, and their services in greater demand in offices as well as in many blue-collar occupations. The equality of wife with husband grew. It increased in the economy and, ultimately, before the law at the polls, and in the making of family decisions.[5]

We find some striking examples of the outcome of these trends in the relations between men and women in the most urbanized parts of the middle classes at the period of the Civil War in the United States and, especially, after the First World War. Suffragette leaders in the nineteenth century were, of course, not typical of their sex, nor were the professional women or the women who found their way into the bohemias of the great cities in the early 1900's. They do give us extreme versions of trends that were spreading rapidly among the female population. There were the women who thought of the attachment to the household and children as servitude imposed by the lusts and self-ishness of men and by the outmoded society which they saw males forcing on women. Some of them refused to take even their husband's names which they thought of as badges of servility. They were violently determined equals. They were in that state of revolt given whimsical and pointed form in James Thurber's classic sketches of "The War Between Men and Women." [6] The flapper style was their sign. The dress was emancipatedly short, its hips and bosom were manly flat. Its waist was at an unmotherly low. The wearer was one of the boys.

It was into this urban, industrialized family that there came romantic love in the modern sense. If husband and wife, parent and child were not bound together as tightly as before with the old ties of kin supports and the heavy dependence of woman on man, a new basis for their relation had to develop. It was, as Burgess and Locke suggest, shared affection. In this remaining bond, the relation had to be more intense and sure than before. Romantic love became the test. It was a passion for another person so great that that one was singled out from all others as the only fully satisfying object in the world; so intense that, at the slightest chance of its failure, appetite fled, words were inadequate, and the world barren until it was resumed. And with romance went the criteria of common interests and compatibility. In the relations of equals, interests had to be common and compatible or the marriage failed.

It is our impression that the companionship family described by Burgess and Locke represents, not the growing wave of the family's future, but one of those sudden surges of history that are swallowed in even mightier currents. We, like Burgess and Locke, see the new trends documented best among the middle classes, those parts of the population which we believe were the first to experience these new social conditions. The companionship family is an end product of the entrepreneurial society. The bureaucratic order makes different demands on husbands and wives, and on parents and children.

We should like to draw a new and speculative model of the emerging type of family and to speak of it as the *colleague* family. By this term we want to imply that the tendencies which Burgess and Locke describe have in part been consolidated for large parts of the population. Women and men are increasingly equal; they are also separate and different. Specialization, that distinctive characteristic of the bureaucratic way of life, has, we believe, created new conditions for relations in families. In our view, the companionship model began as a demand that women should be able to do all the things open to men. It was still a man's world and women tried to enter it by becoming masculine. But the conditions that brought equality and companionship did not stand alone. The same machine technology that enabled women to enter the economy, made the distinctive character of the male role less necessary. The woman, however, was not transformed overnight. The male partner now had to expect to get to know her interests and to share her work in domestic life and in the arts. Further, the older demands that the male be aggressive and independent and dominating decreased with the growth of the greater security and of routinized channels of occupational advance through the more passive means of education and faithful service. In large areas of life it became acceptable and even required that men, like women, have some of the skills and preoccupations traditionally associated with the other sex.

Even in the late stages of the companionship family it was a parliamentary order. Husband and wife were fairly equal partners whose vote on many subjects was of the same weight. We feel that the distinctive characteristics of the bureaucratic order have led to what might be called a neotraditional family. The specialization on the job has entered the home, and the equal partners have been able to see that differences in talent, interest, and function, as long as they are complementary, do not threaten equality. Instead, they may enrich and promote the common life. For this reason we call this type of family the "colleague" family. As specialists at work may find in each other skills they lack, but skills they equally need, and as they may defer to one another's judgment on the grounds of differing competence without feeling that they have personally lost in prestige, so husband and wife may now relate in this way.

One direction in which this trend toward specialization has led is that of the professionalization of the wife's functions. She can no longer learn them satisfactorily from her mother's tutelage and example. They must be rationalized. Their intuitive processes must give way to formal rules and special technical knowledge. They are subject to improvement as the instruments they use are subjected to critical appraisal and functional selection. The women's magazines provide a kind of in-service training, supplemented with the post-graduate work of the mother's study clubs, the meetings with the specialists at the nursery school, the cooking classes, and the growing number of handbooks for preparing unfamiliar or exotic foods.

The aesthetic style conspicuous in latter-day entrepreneurial homes was starkly functional. Its lines were straight, the angles sharp. The model was the machine, designed as a tool and having its beauty in the perfect expression it gave to the purposes for which it was designed. It was a design of economy. The styles since the Second World War have made room for the unexpected corner, the design included for its own sake, the curved and even undulating line. Clothing, painting, and all the arts, domestic and fine, show signs of a general humanizing trend that expresses convenience while leaving room for changing interests and for experiences that may provoke new tastes.

We believe there has been a general strengthening of some of the traditional family patterns along revised lines. We should guess that the requirements for personal stability made by large specialized organizations, together with the economic security they provide, will begin to slow and then lower the rate of divorce and separation in the population and will raise again the criteria of competence and the gifts of homemaking to renewed importance in the choice of a marriage partner. We also find evidences in the novel, the newspaper, the motion picture, television, and the popular magazine that the formal social controls of the large scale organizations are being extended to shape the family and to provide a new sense of obligation.

It is not likely that the children are as subordinated in the household as they were in times past, or that they are the equal decision makers of some companionship families. They are more in the nature of junior partners, who are wanted and needed and whose opinions are sought and given careful consideration, but who must have proper seniority before being admitted to full participation in deciding the family's course.

There is also a renewed interest in limiting the child's freedom. As Wolfenstein says, even the U.S. Children's Bureau pamphlet, *Infant Care,* has changed, after a decade of emphasizing the desirability of freedom for the expression of childish impulses, now saying that children need to have some limits set. Many advisers of parents have gone even further in recent years to say that children *want* such limits, that, without them, the world is too unstructured and uncertain for the child's comfort. Some advisers add that, since the child's untutored desires are without limit, he can find happiness only if he is given limited, hence feasible, goals.

The child who is to be trained for the intricate human relations of the bureaucracy is not ready for adulthood, even after receiving an intensive basic course in responsibility training. He must learn the nuances of human relations and must be able to clarify them in his own thinking so that he can study his own relations to others and gain better control over himself and his associates. This training, together with the child's growing independence in our society, requires that parents spend more time with children. The family is again the school for the job, only now it is the school for the job's human relations, not its technical skills.

In the companionship family of the individuated-entrepreneurial society the child was expected to meet other children as friends. That word has long been in the language, but the word's traditional meaning does not capture the singular content it came to have under entrepreneurial conditions. In those circumstances, a man was often cut off from kin and community. He needed warmth and support and some secure human relations. These needs were likely to be met in his contacts with one or two close friends.[7] With them, in part by contrast with the rest of his social life, there was a complete interchange of thought and feeling. The friend did what kin and neighbors might have done at an earlier time. The loyalty of friend to friend was sometimes as great as that between brothers. The intense pattern we have found in romantic love is here, the same mutual choice based on unique complementarity of need, but it does not, of course, contain quite the same weight of responsibility and permanence as the marriage relation. One of the special joys of such a role as that of friendship was that it could, at least in law, be broken without complications other than the emotional shock.

To a great extent the relations of parents and children in the family were modeled along the lines of the role of friends. A father was supposed to be a "pal" or a "buddy" or a "friend" to his children. But, like parental patterns, the nature of friendship is changing. The child increasingly meets his peers as colleagues whose favor he must court and whose respect he must win. He cannot acceptably choose one or two with whom to strike up companionship. He must learn to fit in smoothly with all of them. Since, with many, he does not feel a truly close comradeship, he must learn to produce a relationship that uses the symbols of genuine friendship as its currency without the actual commitment of the real thing. He must learn to be a "nice guy"—affable, unthreatening, responsible, competent, adaptive. It is this kind of skill in which the parents must train him. Without the help of kin and community and without the assistance of a set of rigorous controls built into the child in his early days—controls that would soon be outmoded in a changing world—the parents must spend more time at this task if the children are to be "a credit" to them.

Much of the recent discussion by demographers of the size of families has proceeded on the assumption that parents would limit their children to the smallest possible number if only the means were available. The spread of knowledge about cheap, effective, and available contraceptives to much of the population has made this reputed desire a possible choice for most families, yet the birth rate has increased. Not only are more couples having children but more of them are having second and third children. These are not the large families of eight or ten that were relatively common in the 1800's. Nor are they the childless or one child marriages that were common in the early twentieth century. A new kind of expectation about desirable family size has appeared.

The beliefs of some students of population that most parents desire to keep the number of children to the minimum seems rooted in observations of the middle classes in the entrepreneurial society. Among entrepreneurial middles, each additional child was a strain on the slender resources on which the family's possible social ascent was based. For the parents interested in the children's future, larger family size meant that fathers and mothers could offer less help toward an education and a "start in life" to each boy and girl.

We may expect that the greater security of the bureaucratic middle classes, especially lower middle families, together with the lesser opportunities for social advance through individual enterprise, takes away some of the forces against having more children and permits a rise in the birth rate. But this situation would be true only if there were some powerful positive forces to promote such a rise. It is our impression that parents in the bureaucratized family, like those in the older agricultural family, find children a fulfillment, without many of the difficulties that went with the raising of a family under entrepreneurial conditions. For the wife they are a necessary canvas on which professionalized skills of homemaking can be expressed. For both husband and wife they are an outlet for creative management of social relations, for the parents' learning new things about themselves, and for demonstrating their conventionality and adaptability and "maturity" in the bureaucratic world. If the family is secure in the new sense that the children can find employment near the home of the parents and, with swift transportation and communication, can be part of the parental families for a long time to come, then there is also a renewed sense of self-continuity and self-realization through children that comes to the couple with a family.

Further, the parents in this new order, unlike those of the entrepreneurial society, have a kind of wisdom that their children will continue to need and that cannot be obtained except by long experience in the stable and complex relations of large organizations. The parents may not have their children's new technical skills. This was a gap that made for isolation if not alienation between generations in the entrepreneurial society. The bureaucratic parents do have relevant, hard-bought skills in making the critical judgments of social situations that their children will need. We may expect, then, a reappearance of the parent as the counselor and aid of the children after they become adults and parents in their own right. In this way it is likely that bureaucratic conditions enhance the function of children as a means of self-continuity and companionship for their parents. This, in turn, makes having children more desirable.

Our own data did not enable us to examine the possibility that the birth patterns of bureaucratic families would show a greater tendency to have children or to have more children than would those of entrepreneurial families. This was the case because we did not have information for families having no children. We sampled only those households in which one or more children eighteen years or younger were living. What we have done is to examine the birth patterns obtained by the Detroit Area Study in a different year, 1954. In that year, unlike the one in which we collected our information, the sample consisted of a random sample of adults in dwelling units in the area.[8] Table 1 gives the results. An inspection of this table does not show any differences in the likelihood of having children among older (forty years of age and beyond) entrepreneurial and bureaucratic wives. Among younger wives, however, a slight but consistent trend appears. We find that bureaucratic wives are more likely than entrepreneurial wives to have some children instead of being childless. This finding appears in all of our comparisons except that between wealthier

TABLE 1

Number of Children Ever Had by White Wives Living in the Detroit Area in 1954: By Social Position

| | Wives Aged 39 Years or Less | | | | | | | | Wives Aged 40 Years or More | | | | | | | |
| | Family Income: Less Than $6000 | | | | Family Income: $6000 or More | | | | Family Income: Less Than $6000 | | | | Family Income: $6000 or More | | | |
NUMBER OF CHILDREN EVER HAD	UM*	LM†	UL‡	LL§	UM*	LM†	UL‡	LL§	UM*	LM†	UL‡	LL§	UM*	LM†	UL‡	LL§
Entrepreneurial Wives																
3 or more	1	3	1	4	6	0	5	0	0	5	8	8	4	4	10	6
2	0	2	4	2	6	3	4	1	0	2	7	7	6	4	6	5
1	0	2	0	3	1	3	0	3	0	0	3	5	2	2	1	1
0	1	0	2	2	1	3	2	4	2	1	6	5	2	1	2	4
Total	2	7	7	11	14	9	11	8	2	8	24	25	14	11	19	16
Bureaucratic Wives																
3 or more	2	7	9	13	9	12	7	4	0	5	2	6	1	8	13	1
2	1	7	11	12	5	5	13	2	0	3	6	2	8	4	6	4
1	2	3	11	3	6	7	9	10	0	0	1	0	3	3	5	1
0	1	1	1	4	4	7	6	4	0	3	1	4	2	5	2	1
Total	6	18	32	32	24	31	35	20	0	11	10	12	14	20	26	7

* UM = upper middle class.   † LM = lower middle class.
‡ UL = upper lower class.   § LL = lower lower class.

upper middle-class families in the two integration settings. In one other case, that between entrepreneurial and bureaucratic wives in the less wealthy families that have a lower middle-class status, no comparison is possible since entrepreneurial lower middles include no child ess families and since the total number of such families is smaller than that for bureaucratic lower middles. The probability of obtaining six out of seven comparisons in the predicted direction by chance alone is slightly greater than five in a hundred. Table 1 shows no convincing entrepreneurial-bureaucratic differences in childlessness for older wives nor in the number of children had by wives in any income or social class group. We can also report that the birth patterns in this table are not affected by the distribution of Protestants and Roman Catholics in the population or by the number of years for which these couples were married. Thus, even though we do not have strong support for our expectations, these results do suggest that our ideas may have enough merit to be pursued further.

NOTES

1. Ernest W. Burgess and Harvey J. Locke, *The Family from Institution to Companionship* (New York: American Book Company, 1945), 26–27.
2. Leonard T. Hobhouse, G. C. Wheeler, and Morris Ginsberg, *The Material Culture and Social Institutions of the Simpler Peoples, An Essay in Correlation* (London: Chapman and Hall, Ltd., 1915), contains descriptions of various family patterns and their relation to economic and other conditions. For somewhat different interpretations consult Julian H. Steward, "The Economic and Social Basis of Primitive Bands," in Robert H. Lowie (ed.), *Essays in Anthropology* (Berkeley, California: University of California Press, 1936), 331–350.
3. A classic example of this pattern is described in Conrad M. Arensberg, *The Irish Countryman* (London: The Macmillan Co., Ltd., 1937).
4. It is doubtful that the use of women for physically lighter work is a simple function of their lesser muscular strength. Certainly women in the Soviet Union seem to be employed for the heaviest kinds of manual labor.
5. As Albert Reiss points out, the worlds of parents and children were further separated by the compulsory attendance laws that put children in the schools instead of the parental world of work, and by the child labor laws that gave youngsters a special status through enforcing idleness.
6. *The New Yorker Twenty-fifth Anniversary Album: 1925–1950* (New York: Harper and Bros., 1951), unpaginated.
7. An important discussion of the forms and conditions of friendship appears in Jyotirmoyee Sarma, "The Social Categories of Friendship,"

unpublished doctoral dissertation, Department of Sociology, The University of Chicago, 1946.

8. The very methods used in the present study to place respondents in a particular social class were also employed in the DAS for 1954. However, the 1954 study did not gather all the data for placing respondents in the entrepreneurial or bureaucratic settings that we had obtained in the previous year. Specifically, the 1954 study did not have information on the number of supervisory levels in the work situation or on the portion of its income that the family earned in the form of profits, fees, and commissions. With these restrictions, the definitions of entrepreneurial and bureaucratic found in 1954 were identical with the ones we used in the present study.

16

The Changing American Child—
A Speculative Analysis[1]

by Urie Bronfenbrenner

A Question of Moment

It is now a matter of scientific record that patterns of child rearing in the United States have changed appreciably over the past twenty-five years (Bronfenbrenner, 1958).* Middle class parents especially have moved away from the more rigid and strict styles of care and discipline advocated in the early Twenties and Thirties toward modes of response involving greater tolerance of the child's impulses and desires, freer expression of affection, and increased reliance on "psychological" methods of discipline, such as reasoning and appeals to guilt, as distinguished from more direct techniques like physical punishment. At the same time, the gap between the social classes in their goals and methods of child rearing appears to be narrowing, with working class parents beginning to adopt both the values and techniques of the middle class. Finally, there is dramatic correspondence between these observed shifts in parental values and behavior and

* [References in parentheses are listed alphabetically at the conclusion of this selection.]

Reprinted from *Journal of Social Issues,* 17 (1961), pp. 6–18, by permission of the author and The Society for the Psychological Study of Social Issues.

the changing character of the attitudes and practices advocated in successive editions of such widely read manuals as the Children's Bureau bulletin on *Infant Care* and Spock's *Baby and Child Care.* Such correspondence should not be taken to mean that the expert has now become the principal instigator and instrument of social change, since the ideas of scientists and professional workers themselves reflect in part the operation of deep-rooted cultural processes. Nevertheless, the fact remains that changes in values and practices advocated by prestigeful professional figures can be substantially accelerated by rapid and widespread dissemination through the press, mass media of communication, and public discussion.

Given these facts, it becomes especially important to gauge the effect of the changes that are advocated and adopted. Nowhere is this issue more significant, both scientifically and socially, than in the sphere of familial values and behavior. It is certainly no trivial matter to ask whether the changes that have occurred in the attitudes and actions of parents over the past twenty-five years have been such as to affect the personality development of their children, so that the boys and girls of today are somewhat different in character structure from those of a decade or more ago. Or, to put the question more succinctly: has the changing American parent produced a changing American child?

A Strategy of Inference

Do we have any basis for answering this intriguing question? To begin with, do we have any evidence of changes in the behavior of children in successive decades analogous to those we have already been able to find for parents? If so, we could take an important first step toward a solution of the problem. Unfortunately, in contrast to his gratifying experience in seeking and finding appropriate data on parents, the present writer has, to date, been unable to locate enough instances in which comparable methods of behavioral assessment have been employed with different groups of children of similar ages over an extended period of time. Although the absence of such material precludes any direct and unequivocal approach to the question at hand, it is nevertheless possible, through a series of inferences from facts already known, to arrive at some estimate of what the answer might be. Specifically, although as yet we have no comparable data on the relation between parental and child behavior for different families at successive points in time, we do have facts on the influence of parental treatment on child behavior at a given point in time; that is, we know that certain variations in parental behavior tend to be accompanied by systematic differences in the personality characteristics of children. If we are willing to assume that these same relationships obtained not only at a given moment but across different points in time, we are in a position to infer the possible effects on children of changing patterns of child rearing over the years. It is this strategy that we propose to follow.

The Changing American Parent

We have already noted the major changes in parental behavior discerned in a recent analysis of data reported over a twenty-five year period. These secular trends may be summarized as follows:

1. Greater permissiveness toward the child's spontaneous desires
2. Freer expression of affection
3. Increased reliance on indirect "psychological" techniques of discipline (such as reasoning or appeals to guilt) vs. direct methods (like physical punishment, scolding, or threats)
4. In consequence of the above shifts in the direction of what are predominantly middle class values and techniques, a narrowing of the gap between social classes in their patterns of child rearing.

Since the above analysis was published, a new study has documented an additional trend. Bronson, Katten, and Livson (1959) have compared patterns of paternal and maternal authority and affection in two generations of families from the California Guidance Study. Unfortunately, the time span surveyed overlaps only partially with the twenty-five year period covered in our own analysis, the first California generation having been raised in the early 1900's and the second in the late '20's and early '30's. Accordingly, if we are to consider the California results along with the others cited above, we must make the somewhat risky assumption that a trend discerned in the first three decades of the century has continued in the same direction through the early 1950's. With this important qualification, an examination of the data cited by Bronson et al. (1959) points to still another, secular trend—a shift over the years in the pattern of parental role differentiation within the family. Specifically:

5. In succeeding generations the relative position of the father vis-à-vis the mother is shifting with the former becoming increasingly more affectionate and less authoritarian, and the latter becoming relatively more important as the agent of discipline, especially for boys.

"Psychological" Techniques of Discipline and Their Effects

In pursuing our analytic strategy, we next seek evidence of the effects on the behavior of children of variations in parental treatment of the type noted in our inventory. We may begin by noting that the variables involved in the first three secular trends constitute a complex that has received considerable attention in recent research in parent-child relationships. Within the last three years, two sets of investigators, working independently, have called attention to the greater efficacy of "love-oriented" or "psychological" techniques in bringing about desired behavior in the child (Sears, Maccoby, and Levin, 1957; Miller and Swanson, 1958; 1960). The present writer, noting that such methods are especially favored by middle class parents, offered the following analysis of the nature of these techniques and the reasons for their effectiveness.

Such parents are, in the first place, more likely to overlook offenses, and when they do punish, they are less likely to ridicule or inflict physical pain. Instead, they reason with the youngster, isolate him, appeal to guilt, show disappointment—in short, convey in a variety of ways, on the one hand, the kind of behavior that is expected of the child; on the other, the realization that transgression means the interruption of a mutually valued relationship. . . .

These findings [of greater efficacy] mean that middle class parents, though in one sense more lenient in their discipline techniques, are using methods that are actually more compelling. Moreover, the compelling power of these practices is probably enhanced by the more permissive treatment accorded to middle class children in the early years of life. The successful use of withdrawal of love as a discipline technique implies the prior existence of a gratifying relationship; the more love present in the first instance, the greater the threat implied in its withdrawal (Bronfenbrenner, 1958).

It is now a well established fact that children from middle class families tend to excel those from lower class in many characteristics ordinarily regarded as desirable, such as self-control, achievement, responsibility, leadership, popularity, and adjustment in general.[2] If, as seems plausible, such differences in behavior are attributable at least in part to class-linked variations in parental treatment, the strategy of inference we have adopted would appear on first blush to lead to a rather optimistic conclusion. Since, over the years, increasing numbers of parents have been adopting the more effective socialization techniques typically employed by the middle class, does it not follow that successive generations of children should show gains in the development of effective behavior and desirable personality characteristics?

Unfortunately, this welcome conclusion, however logical, is premature, for it fails to take into account all of the available facts.

Sex, Socialization, and Social Class

To begin with, the parental behaviors we have been discussing are differently distributed not only by socio-economic status but also by sex. As we have pointed out elsewhere (Bronfenbrenner, 1961), girls are exposed to more affection and less punishment than boys, but at the same time are more likely to be subjected to "love-oriented" discipline of the type which encourages the development of internalized controls. And, consistent with our lines of reasoning, girls are found repeatedly to be "more obedient, cooperative, and in general better socialized than boys at comparable age levels." But this is not the whole story.

. . . At the same time, the research results indicate that girls tend to be more anxious, timid, dependent, and sensitive to rejection. If these differences are a function of differential treatment by parents, then it would seem that the more "efficient" methods of child rearing employed with girls involve some risk of what might be called "oversocialization" (Bronfenbrenner, 1961).

One could argue, of course, that the contrasting behaviors of boys and girls have less to do with differential parental treatment than with genetically-based maturational influences. Nevertheless, two independent lines of evidence suggest that socialization techniques do contribute to individual differences, *within the same sex*, precisely in the types of personality characteristics noted above. In the first place, variations in child behavior and parental treatment strikingly similar to those we have cited for the two sexes are reported in a recent comprehensive study of differences between first and later born children

(Schachter, 1959). Like girls, first children receive more attention, are more likely to be exposed to "psychological" discipline, and end up more anxious and dependent, whereas later children, like boys, are more aggressive and self-confident.

A second line of evidence comes from our own current research. We have been concerned with the role of parents in the development of such "constructive" personality characteristics as responsibility and leadership among adolescent boys and girls. Our findings reveal not only the usual differences in adolescents' and parents' behaviors associated with the sex of the child, but also a striking contrast in the relationship between parental and child behaviors for the two sexes. To start on firm and familiar ground, girls are rated by their teachers as more responsible than boys, whereas the latter obtain higher scores on leadership. Expected differences similarly appear in the realm of parental behavior: girls receive more affection, praise, and companionship; boys are subjected to more physical punishment and achievement demands. Quite unanticipated, however, at least by us, was the finding that both parental affection and discipline appeared to facilitate effective psychological functioning in boys, but to impede the development of such constructive behavior in girls. Closer examination of our data indicated that both extremes of either affection or discipline were deleterious for all children, but that the process of socialization entailed somewhat different risks for the two sexes. Girls were especially susceptible to the detrimental influence of over-protection; boys to the ill effects of insufficient parental discipline and support. Or, to put it in more colloquial terms: boys suffered more often from too little taming, girls from too much.

In an attempt to account for this contrasting pattern of relationships, we proposed the notion of differential optimal levels of affection and authority for the two sexes.

The qualities of independence, initiative, and self-sufficiency, which are especially valued for boys in our culture, apparently require for their development a somewhat different balance of authority and affection than is found in the "love-oriented" strategy characteristically applied with girls. While an affectional context is important for the socialization of boys, it must evidently be accompanied by and be compatible with a strong component of parental discipline. Otherwise, the boy finds himself in the same situation as the girl, who, having received greater affection, is more sensitive to its withdrawal, with the result that a little discipline goes a long way and strong authority is constricting rather than constructive (Bronfenbrenner, 1960).

What is more, available data suggest that this very process may already be operating for boys from upper middle class homes. To begin with, differential treatment of the sexes is at a minimum for these families. Contrasting parental attitudes and behaviors toward boys and girls are pronounced only at lower class levels, and decrease as one moves up the socio-economic scale (Kohn, 1959; Bronfenbrenner, 1960). Thus our own results show that it is primarily at lower middle class levels that boys get more punishment than girls, and the latter receive greater warmth and attention. With an increase in the family's social position, direct discipline drops off, especially for boys, and indulgence and protectiveness decrease for girls. As a result, patterns of parental treatment for the two sexes begin to converge. In like manner, we find that the differential effects of parental behavior on the two sexes are marked only in the lower middle class. It is here that girls especially risk being over-protected and boys not receiving sufficient discipline and support. In the upper middle class the picture changes. Girls are not as readily debilitated by parental affection and power; nor is parental discipline as effective in fostering the development of responsibility and leadership in boys.

All these trends point to the conclusion that the "risks" experienced by each sex during the process of socialization tend to be somewhat different at different social class levels. Thus the danger of over-protection for girls is especially great in lower class families, but lower in upper middle class because of the decreased likelihood of over-protection. Analogously, boys are in greater danger of suffering from inadequate discipline and support in lower middle than in upper middle class. But the upper middle class boy, unlike the girl, exchanges one hazard for another. Since at this upper level the more potent "psychological" techniques of discipline are likely to be employed with both sexes, the boy presumably now too runs the risk of being "oversocialized," of losing some of his capacity for independent aggressive accomplishment.

Accordingly, if our line of reasoning is correct, we should expect a changing pattern of sex differences at successive socio-economic levels. Specifically, aspects of effective psychological functioning favoring girls should be most pronounced in the upper middle class; those favoring boys in the lower middle. A recent analysis of some of our data bears out this expectation. Girls excel boys on such variables as *responsibility* and *social acceptance* primarily at the higher socio-economic levels. In contrast, boys surpass girls on such traits as *leadership, level of aspiration,* and *competitiveness* almost exclusively in the lower middle class. Indeed, with a rise in a family's social position, the differences tend to reverse themselves with girls now excelling boys.[3]

Trends in Personality Development: A First Approximation

The implications for our original line of inquiry are clear. We are suggesting that the "love-oriented" socialization techniques, which over the past twenty-five years have been employed in increasing degree by American middle class families, may have negative as well as constructive aspects. While fostering the internalization of adult standards and the development of socialized behavior, they may also have the effect of undermining capacities for initiative and independence, particularly in boys. Males exposed to this "modern" pattern of child rearing might be expected to differ from their counterparts of a quarter century ago in being somewhat more conforming and anxious, less enterprising and self-sufficient, and, in general, possessing more of the virtues and liabilities commonly associated with feminine character structure.[4]

At long last, then, our strategy of inference has led us to a first major conclusion. The term "major" is appropriate since the conclusion takes as its points of departure and return four of the secular trends which served as the impetus for our inquiry. Specifically, through a series of empirical links and theoretical extrapolations, we have arrived at an estimate of the effects on children of the tendency of successive generations of parents to become progressively more permissive, to express affection more freely, to utilize "psychological" techniques of discipline, and, by moving in these directions, to narrow the gap between the social classes in their patterns of child rearing.

Family Structure and Personality Development

But one other secular trend remains to be considered: what of the changing pattern of parental role differentiation during the first three decades of the century? If our extrapolation is correct, the balance of power within the family has continued to shift with fathers yielding parental authority to mothers and taking on some of the nurturant and affectional functions traditionally associated with the maternal role. Again we have no direct evidence of the effects of such secular changes on successive generations of children, and must look for leads to analogous data on contemporaneous relationships.

We may begin by considering the contribution of each parent to the socialization process we have examined thus far. Our data indicate that it is primarily mothers who tend to employ "love-oriented" techniques of discipline and fathers who rely on more direct methods like physical punishment. The above statement must be qualified, however, by reference to the sex of the child, for it is only in relation to boys that fathers use direct punishment more than mothers. More generally, . . . the results reveal a tendency for each parent to be somewhat more active, firm, and demanding with a child of the same sex, more lenient and indulgent with a child of the opposite sex . . . . The reversal is most complete with respect to discipline, with fathers being stricter with boys, mothers with girls. In the spheres of affection and protectiveness, there is no actual shift in preference, but the tendency to be especially warm and solicitous with girls is much more pronounced among fathers than among mothers. In fact, generally speaking, it is the father who is more likely to treat children of the two sexes differently (Bronfenbrenner, 1960).

Consistent with this pattern of results, it is primarily the behavior of fathers that accounts for the differential effects of parental behavior on the two sexes and for the individual differences within each sex. In other words, it is paternal authority and affection that tend especially to be salutary for sons but detrimental for daughters. But as might be anticipated from what we already know, these trends are pronounced only in the lower middle class; with a rise in the family's social status, both parents tend to have similar effects on their children, both within and across sexes. Such a trend is entirely to be expected since parental role differentiation tends to decrease markedly as one ascends the socio-economic ladder. It is almost exclusively in lower middle class homes that fathers are more strict with boys and mothers with girls. To the extent that direct discipline is employed in upper middle class families, it tends to be exercised by both parents equally. Here again we see a parallelism between shifts in parental behavior across time and social class in the direction of forms (in this instance of family structure) favored by the upper middle class group.

What kinds of children, then, can we expect to develop in families in which the father plays a predominantly affectionate role, and a relatively low level of discipline is exercised equally by both parents? A tentative answer to this question is supplied by a preliminary analysis of our data in which the relation between parental role structure and adolescent behavior was examined with controls for the family's social class position. The results of this analysis are summarized as follows: . . . Both responsibility and leadership are fostered by the relatively greater salience of the parent of the same sex . . . . Boys tend to be more responsible when the father rather than the mother is the principal disciplinarian; girls are more dependable when the mother is the major authority figure . . . . In short, boys thrive in a patriarchal context, girls in a matriarchal . . . . The most dependent and least dependable adolescents describe family arrangements that are neither patriarchal nor matriarchal, but equalitarian. To state the issue in more provocative form, our data suggest that the democratic family, which for so many years has been held up and aspired to as a model by professionals and enlightened laymen, tends to produce young people who "do not take initiative," "look to others for direction and decision," and "cannot be counted on to fulfill obligations" (Bronfenbrenner, 1960).

In the wake of so sweeping a conclusion, it is important to call attention to the tentative, if not tenuous character of our findings. The results were based on a single study employing crude questionnaire methods and rating scales. Also, our interpretation is limited by the somewhat "attenuated" character of most of the families classified as patriarchal or matriarchal in our sample. Extreme concentrations of power in one or another parent were comparatively rare. Had they been more frequent, we suspect the data would have shown that such extreme asymmetrical patterns of authority were detrimental rather than salutary for effective psychological development, perhaps even more disorganizing than equalitarian forms.

Nevertheless, our findings do find some peripheral support in the work of others. A number of investigations, for example, point to the special importance of the father in the socialization of boys (Bandura and Walters, 1959; Mussen and Distler, 1959). Further corroborative evidence appears in the growing series of studies of effects of paternal absence (Bach, 1946; Sears, Pintler and Sears, 1946; Lynn and Sawrey, 1959; Tiller, 1958). The absence of the father apparently not only affects the behavior of the child directly but also influences the mother in the direction of greater over-protectiveness. The effect of both these tendencies is especially critical for male children; boys from father-absent homes tend to be markedly more submissive and dependent. Studies dealing explicitly with the influence of parental role structure in intact families are few and far between. Papanek (1957), in an unpublished doctoral dissertation, reports greater sex-role differentiation among children from homes in which the parental roles were differentiated. And in a carefully controlled study, Kohn and Clausen (1956) find that "schizophrenic patients more frequently than normal persons report that their mothers played a very strong authority role and the father a very weak authority role." Finally, what might best be called complementary evidence for our inferences regarding trends in family structure and their effects comes from the work of Miller, Swanson, and their associates (1958; 1960) on the differing patterns of behavior exhibited by families from *bureaucratic* and *entrepreneurial* work settings. These investigators argue that the entrepreneurial-bureaucratic dichotomy represents a new cleavage in American social structure that cuts across and overrides social class influences and carries with it its own characteristic patterns of family structure and socialization. Thus one investigation (Gold and Slater, 1958) contrasts the exercise of power in families of husbands employed in two kinds of job situations: a) those working in large organizations with three or more levels of supervision; b) those self-employed or working in small organizations with few levels of supervision. With appropriate controls for social class, equalitarian families were found more frequently in the bureaucratic groups; patriarchal and, to a lesser extent, matriarchal in the entrepreneurial setting. Another study (Miller and Swanson, 1958) shows that, in line with Miller and Swanson's hypotheses, parents from these same two groups tend to favor rather different ends and means of socialization, with entrepreneurial families putting considerably more emphasis on the development of independence and mastery and on the use of "psychological" techniques of discipline. These differences appear at both upper and lower middle class levels but are less pronounced in higher socio-economic strata. It is Miller and Swanson's belief, however, that the trend is toward the bureaucratic way of life, with its less structured patterns of family organization and child rearing. The evidence we have cited on secular changes in family structure and the inferences we have drawn regarding their possible effects on personality development are on the whole consistent with their views.

Looking Forward

If Miller and Swanson are correct in the prediction that America is moving toward a bureaucratic society that emphasizes, to put it colloquially, "getting along" rather than "getting ahead," then presumably we can look forward to ever increasing numbers of equalitarian families who, in turn, will produce successive generations of ever more adaptable but unaggressive "organization men." But recent signs do not all point in this direction. In our review of secular trends in child rearing practices we detected in the data from the more recent studies a slowing up in the headlong rush toward greater permissiveness and toward reliance on indirect methods of discipline. We pointed out also that if the most recent editions of well-thumbed guidebooks on child care are as reliable harbingers of the future as they have been in the past, we can anticipate something of a return to the more explicit discipline techniques of an earlier era. Perhaps the most important forces, however, acting to redirect both the aims and methods of child rearing in America emanate from behind the Iron Curtain. With the firing of the first Sputnik, Achievement began to replace Adjustment as the highest goal of the American way of life. We have become concerned—perhaps even obsessed—with "education for excellence" and the maximal utilization of our intellectual resources. Already, ability grouping, and the guidance counsellor who is its prophet, have moved down from the junior high to the elementary school, and parents can be counted on to do their part in preparing their youngsters for survival in the new competitive world of applications and achievement tests.

But if a new trend in parental behavior is to develop, it must do so in the context of changes already under way. And if the focus of parental authority is shifting from husband to wife, then perhaps we should anticipate that pressures for achievement will be imposed primarily by mothers rather than fathers. Moreover, the mother's continuing strong emotional investment in the child should provide her with a powerful lever for evoking desired performance. It is noteworthy in this connection that recent studies of the familial origins of need-achievement point to the matriarchy as the optimal context for development of the motive to excel (Strodtbeck, 1958; Rosen and D'Andrade, 1959).

The prospect of a society in which socialization techniques are directed toward maximizing achievement drive is not altogether a pleasant one. As a number of investigators have shown (Baldwin, Kalhorn and Breese, 1945; Baldwin, 1948; Haggard, 1957; Winterbottom, 1958; Rosen and D'Andrade, 1959), high achievement motivation appears to flourish in a family atmosphere of "cold democracy" in which initial high levels of maternal involvement are followed by pressures for independence and accomplishment.[5] Nor does the product of this process give ground for reassurance. True, children from achievement-oriented homes excel in planfulness and performance, but they are also more aggressive, tense, domineering, and cruel (Baldwin, Kalhorn and Breese, 1945; Baldwin, 1948; Haggard, 1957). It would appear that education for excellence if pursued single-mindedly may entail some sobering social costs.

But by now we are in danger of having stretched our chain of inference beyond the strength of its weakest link. Our speculative analysis has become far more speculative than analytic and to pursue it further would bring us past the bounds of science into the realms of science fiction. In concluding our discussion, we would re-emphasize that speculations should, by their very nature, be held suspect. It is for good reason that, like "damn Yankees" they too carry their almost inseparable sobriquets: speculations are either "idle" or "wild." Given the scientific and social importance of the issues we have raised, we would dismiss the first of these labels out of hand, but the second cannot be disposed of so easily. Like the impetuous child, the "wild" speculation responds best to the sobering influence of friendly but firm discipline, in this instance from the hand of the behavioral scientist. As we look ahead to the next twenty-five years of human socialization, let us hope that the "optimal levels" of involvement and discipline can be achieved not only by the parent who is unavoidably engaged in the process, but also by the scientist who attempts to understand its working, and who—also unavoidably—contributes to shaping its course.

NOTES

1. This paper draws heavily on results from a program of research being conducted by the author in collaboration with Edward C. Devereux and George J. Suci. The contribution of these colleagues to facts and ideas presented in this paper is gratefully acknowledged. The research program is supported in part with grants from the National Science Foundation and the National Institutes of Health.

2. For a summary of findings on social class differences in children's behavior and personality characteristics, see Mussen, P. H., and Conger, J. J., *Child Development and Personality.* New York: Harper, 1956.

3. These shifts in sex difference with a rise in class status are significant at the 5% level of confidence (one-tailed test).

4. Strikingly similar conclusions were reached almost fifteen years ago in a provocative essay by Arnold Green ("The Middle Class Male Child and Neurosis," *American Sociological Review,* 1946, 11, 31–41). With little to go on beyond scattered clinical observations and impressions,

Green was able to detect many of the same trends which we have begun to discern in more recent systematic empirical data.

5. Cold democracy under female administration appears to foster the development of achievement not only in the home but in the classroom as well. In a review of research on teaching effectivenes, Ackerman reports that teachers most successful in bringing about gains in achievement score for their pupils were judged "least considerate," while those thought friendly and congenial were least effective. (Ackerman, W. I., "Teacher Competence and Pupil Change," *Harvard Educational Review,* 1954, 24, 273–289.)

REFERENCES

1. Bach, G. R., "Father-Fantasies and Father-Typing in Father-Separated Children," *Child Development,* 1946, 17, 63–79.
2. Baldwin, A. L., Kalhorn, J., and Breese, F. H., "The Appraisal of Parent Behavior," *Psychological Monographs,* 1945, 58, No. 3 (Whole No. 268).
3. Baldwin, A. L., "Socialization and the Parent-Child Relationship," *Child Development,* 1948, 19, 127–136.
4. Bandura, A., and Walters, R. H., *Adolescent Aggression.* New York: Ronald Press, 1959.
5. Bronfenbrenner, U., "Socialization and Social Class Through Time and Space," in Maccoby, E., Newcomb, T. M., and Hartley, E. L., *Readings in Social Psychology.* New York: Holt, 1958, pp. 400–425.
6. Bronfenbrenner, U., "Some Familial Antecedents of Responsibility and Leadership in Adolescents," in Petrullo, L., and Bass, B. M., *Leadership and Interpersonal Behavior,* New York: Holt, Rinehart, and Winston, 1961.
7. Bronson, W. C., Katten, E. S., and Livson, N., "Patterns of Authority and Affection in Two Generations," *Journal of Abnormal and Social Psychology,* 1959, 58, pp. 143–152.
8. Gold, M., and Slater, C., "Office, Factory, Store—and Family: A Study of Integration Setting," *American Sociological Review,* 1959, 23, 64–74.
9. Haggard, E. A., "Socialization, Personality, and Academic Achievement in Gifted Children," *The School Review,* 1957, 65, 388–414.
10. Kohn, M. L., and Clausen, J. A., "Parental Authority Behavior and Schizophrenia," *American Journal of Orthopsychiatry,* 1956, 26, 297–313.
11. Kohn, M. L., "Social Class and Parental Values," *American Journal of Sociology,* 1959, 44, 337–351.
12. Lynn, D. B., and Sawrey, W. L., "The Effects of Father-Absence on Norwegian Boys and Girls," *Journal of Abnormal and Social Psychology,* 1959, 59, 258–262.
13. Miller, D. R., and Swanson, G. E., *The Changing American Parent.* New York, John Wiley, 1958.
14. Miller, D. R., and Swanson, G. E., *Inner Conflict and Defense,* New York: Holt, 1960.

15. Mussen, P., and Distler, L., "Masculinity, Identification, and Father-Son Relationships," *Journal of Abnormal and Social Psychology*, 1959, 59, 350–356.
16. Papanek, M., *Authority and Interpersonal Relations in the Family*. Unpublished doctoral dissertation on file at the Radcliffe College Library, 1957.
17. Rosen, B. L., and D'Andrade, R., "The Psychosocial Origins of Achievement Motivation," *Sociometry*, 1959, 22, 185–217.
18. Schachter, S., *The Psychology of Affiliation*. Stanford, California; Stanford University Press, 1959.
19. Sears, R. R., Pintler, M. H., and Sears, P. S., "Effects of Father-Separation on Preschool Children's Doll Play Aggression," *Child Development*, 1946, 17, 219–243.
20. Sears, R. R., Maccoby, Eleanor, and Levin, M., *Patterns of Child Rearing*. Evanston, Illinois: Row, Peterson, 1957.
21. Strodtbeck, F. L., "Family Interaction, Values, and Achievement" in McClelland, D. C., Baldwin, A. L., Bronfenbrenner, U., and Strodtbeck, F. L., *Talent and Society*. Princeton, New Jersey: Van Nostrand, 1958, pp. 135–194.
22. Tiller, P. O., "Father-Absence and Personality Development of Children in Sailor Families," *Nordisk Psykologis Monograph Series*, 1958, 9.
23. Winterbottom, M. R., "The Relation of Need Achievement to Learning Experiences in Independence and Mastery," in Atkinson, J. W., *Motives in Fantasy, Action, and Society*. Princeton, New Jersey: Van Nostrand, 1958, pp. 453–494.

1 7

A Century of Declining Paternal Authority*

by J. M. Mogey

A century ago Frédéric Le Play set forth the results he had obtained by systematic participant observation of family life in a book called *The Working Men of Europe.*[1] In this and in his subsequent writings on social reform,[2] he formulated the proposition that harmony in the family and in the society depended upon the appearance in the community of a particular type of family. This he called *La famille souche*, describing it in part from his field notes and in part as an ideal type.

* Paper read at the Annual Meeting, American Sociological Society, Washington, D.C., September, 1955.

Reprinted from *Marriage and Family Living*, 19 (August 1957), pp. 234–239, by permission of the author and the National Council on Family Relations.

The *stem family,* as the term is usually translated into English, is a form of extended family; and when it permeates the society, Le Play believed that it allows the best personalities, a group of people whom he spoke of as the natural hierarchy of ability and virtue, to control the positions where decisions are made in the family, in the workshops, and in the council chambers. The central characteristic of the stem family is the authority of the father, and the essence of his authority is his ability to bequeath the family possessions in one piece to his successor. Under the conditions of Western society this would always be one of the sons, and Le Play was sure that in France the chosen son would be the one best fitted to succeed and to carry on the family traditions.

Le Play put forward the hypothesis that social and family harmony depended upon the existence of paternal authority within the social structure of the stem family. In societies characterized by a family type that did not vest such authority in the father, and that lacked a mechanism for the transmission of the family property and traditions, he foresaw only social strife and individual misery. He called this type the unstable family. In it the parents do not teach traditional ways to the children, and as a consequence both the family and the society lack stability and continuity. The unstable family led frequently to divorce or desertion, while the stem family encouraged family stability through its preparation of the children to go out into the world or to succeed to the family inheritance.

The purpose of this paper is to propose that the role of the father in the family is a most important factor in family stability. It traces by means of a few historical examples the course of paternal authority over the past century; this part of the paper shows that as the legal and customary authority of the father declined, so has the number of broken families increased. The connection is not necessarily causal; and even if the factual position can be admitted, the correlation cannot be tested in any precise way. With Le Play, however, the paper agrees only in the emphasis it lays on the role of the father. His identification of paternal authority of a traditionalist type as the important factor in the stability of the family and in the harmony of the community goes too far. In the concluding section, the concept of paternal authority is redefined so that it has meaning for relations within the small closed family group of today. This suggests the hypothesis that in the nuclear family participation by the father counts for more towards family stability than a strict, legal, traditional type of authority behavior.

The Authority of the Husband
Before 1855

In drawing together the threads of the English common law in 1765, Blackstone stated that in marriage a woman dissolved her legal personality in that of her husband, losing her rights to own property or to enter into contracts. The power thus given to the husband marks the high point in paternal authority. French and German law were a little more liberal; the prerevolutionary code of Russia, on the other hand, said that the power of the husband in his family was "unlimited." [3] This type of legal thinking was carried to America and influenced decisions of the courts here, though custom soon became more liberal than in Europe.

The early novel reflected this state of affairs; English writers before 1860 accepted the authoritarian father as the pivot of the family. None of the literary reviewers of this period questioned this assumption. From Thackeray to Trollope, father figures were depicted as possessed naturally of authority and responsibility. Abuses of this power were frequently objected to, not the need for it. Within the family the hierarchy of members ran father, eldest son, his heir, other sons, then mother, daughters, and finally servants of long standing. A certain social distance was always maintained between the patriarchal father and the rest of the family group.[4] Such power in the hands of the husband served a serious social purpose. Although in origin probably connected with religious and with feudal thinking on social structure, it nonetheless rewarded the man for restrictions imposed upon his freedom of action and so by encouraging family life promoted social stability.

The experience of countries in times of crisis gives ample evidence of the importance of the "social cement," as Le Play might have called it, provided by the authority of the husband.

Changes in the Role of the Husband
During the Past Century

In 1789, the French revolutionaries looked on the family as too much identified with the older traditional institutions of the aristocracy and the church. An early law freed marriage from social constraints and made divorce as easy as the entry into marriage. To encourage youth to adopt the ideals of the Revolution a law of 1790 withdrew the power of the father to discipline them; a proposal of Danton and Robespierre to take all children away from their parents and bring them up as wards of the state was talked about but never acted upon.

The consequences of this marriage legislation astounded the new tribunals. In the days following the Terror, Paris became a city of license. Returning upper and middle class refugees were horrified at the reversal of customs. Fathers disappeared from whole sections of society, abandoning their wives and children; divorce at the will of one party, free love, illegitimacy, and juvenile crime were commonplace. By the year 1797, one divorce for every three marriages had become the rule. No country had up to this time seen such a transformation in familial habits. To say that the sole cause of all these changes was the alteration in the authority of the father would be going too far; but in the general loosening of political, religious, and customary controls, changes in the behavior of fathers were very striking.

For the lawyers drafting the *Code Civil* under Napoleon such alterations in family behavior served as a dramatic warning. Under this code divorce became more difficult, the rights of married women were reduced, and the legitimatizing function of marriage for the children was re-introduced.[5]

In a similar fashion during the Russian revolution the Bolsheviks stated that marriage was a purely personal affair of no interest to other parties and declared the family an obsolete, bourgeois survival. By 1926, chaos over desertions and divorces forced the state to re-introduce the civil registration of marriages. A new temper prevailed by 1936, when the family was said to be a social unit whose permanence and harmony were essential to the survival of the country. Measures to strengthen the family unit, to protect the mother and children against arbitrary divorce, and to enforce alimony payments were passed in 1936 and again in 1946.[6]

In the course of the past century, too, slower and more far-reaching alterations of the relative power of men and women in the family have taken place. The legal status of a wife has improved through appeals to equity; and she may now hold property, enter into contracts, and in other legal matters act as if she were a *feme sole*.

The entry of married women into the labor force, so that they acquire a money income independent of their husband, is another indication of decline in paternal power, for, as we shall see, a wife with her own income is less subject to her husband. In former times women worked alongside their menfolk in field and workshop but under their direction and without an independent income. Technological changes which have transformed women's work within the house and the smaller family have released them for gainful employment.[7] The continuing lowly status of housework, associated as it still is with such terms of abuse as "scullion" and "slut," should also be remembered when the entry of married women into the labor force is being considered. Over the past two decades the increase in the total number of women in the United States and the United Kingdom who are married has been very rapid, in itself an important pointer whose significance is considered later; the proportion of married women earning a wage has gone up even faster.[8]

Similarly the maintenance of traditional paternal authority over the children has become more difficult over the same period. Schools soon take them out of the family, and in addition in a changing society the skills of fathers become less and less useful to the sons. Such a society places little value upon continuity of tradition, and in this respect Le Play saw correctly the functions of the stem family in ensuring the continuity of family tradition.

This historical sketch will perhaps suffice to mark the mileposts by which in the course of the past century the patriarchal type of father, blessed with full legal power over his wife, children, and material possessions, gradually lost this position.

The purpose of this paper is not to investigate economic or other causes for this social change. It is rather to pursue the implications of it for family stability. The other roles of the father, in particular his role in socialization of the children, are not directly considered.

The Functions of Paternal Authority

Of all the roles in the family, fatherhood is the most social. It has been called the weak link in the chains of interaction that form the group.[9] The power and status of the husband and father in the past may be regarded as the minimum essential to make sure that most fathers carried out their responsibilities. In some societies the functions of fatherhood in giving the society legitimate offspring outweighed the expectations of love or pleasure in the marital relationship. "Here's to our wives and sweethearts, and may they never meet," expresses the attitude. The legal and customary responsibility of the man for the support of a wife and the desire for legitimate heirs to continue the family name kept the family stable, not love or affection.

Two recent studies of authority within the family underline this point. In 1940, Komarovsky examined the effects of long-term unemployment on the authority of the husband. Her material refers to fifty-nine relief-receiving families which had held together in spite of the husband having no job. In only 24 per cent of the households had the authority of the husband declined: almost all of this decline can be connected with lack of a job. It is striking that in three-quarters of the unemployed families which held together the husband played his full role.[10] Other writers mention the escape of adolescents from the paternal family during depression, marking families which have not remained together.[11] An analogous wandering about the countryside by bands of adolescents has always accompanied war and revolution in Europe. It appears from this that some power of cohesion still belongs to the husband who is playing his full part in the home. His integration into the economic institutions would appear desirable but not essential for the exercise of this function. Parsons has recently argued in a deductive fashion that integration of the husband with the occupational hierarchy is essential and a characteristic feature of the modern social system.[12] There need be no conflict between these two writers, provided that Parsons is considered to be elaborating conditions for the majority, and not for the whole population.

The importance of occupation on the distribution of power between husband and wife is also emphasized by a recent study in Paris, France. In 1950 three hundred marriages, partly working class and partly middle class, were studied. In households where the husband is a manual worker (*ouvrier*) 77 per cent of the wives had control of the family budget; at the other end of the scale, among the rich upper bourgeois, 95 per cent of husbands control the budget. In other social classes control of family purchases is variable. In homes where the husband is a non-manual worker, 50 per cent of husbands select family friends and 29 per cent even choose, independently of the wife, the place where the family shall spend its annual holiday. Equivalent evidences of paternal authority are strong among the upper bourgeois. The power and authority of the husband in contemporary France, therefore, varies by social class. A major part of this variation may be explained by considering the wife as an independent wage earner. In all classes wives who were at home were more frequently under the domination of their husbands than wives who had a job.[13] It will be remembered that desertion has always been more frequent among the working class.[14] It is in those sections that women are more often at work and most often earn as much as the men. Consequently if, as Parsons believes, the firm integration of the father into the wage earning structure is essential to the development of the typical family interaction pattern, then within families such as these where husband and wife are not clearly distinguished in earning ability, deviant behavior will most likely occur.

An examination of what practicing fathers say about their role is particularly relevant at this point. Most social psychological investigations have been interested in socialization rather than family stability. Many studies since the original one of 1936[15] have investigated the effects of an authoritarian father on the children. These are not being considered at the moment. A sample of eighty-five fathers, mostly lower middle class New Yorkers, is available to speak directly on the role of the father in the family. Fathers saw themselves as: (1) guide and teacher to the children, (2) economic provider, (3) the source of authority, (4) companion to the wife, (5) an active agent in child rearing, (6) maintainer of family unity, (7) disciplinarian. Family unity was mentioned specifically by 42 per cent of the fathers but if everyone who verbalized about the "together" aspect of the marriage was counted, almost all would be included. The range and number of activities with which fathers were engaged came as a surprise to the investigator.[16] In a re-study of war-separated families made after the man had returned, Elder also found the fathers doing much more than expected within the house. Only two out of fifty-four fathers had never played with the children, one third normally participated in washing and feeding them, and most surprising of all, half of the children had been to visit father at work. The affectional aspect of this activity is also given; two thirds said that they enjoyed being fathers and only 15 per cent thought that motherhood was the more enjoyable role.[17]

Seen against our historical information, these empirical studies, though the number of subjects involved is extremely small, show the concept of fatherhood to be the most rapidly changing role in the modern family. Some indication of the extent of this movement can be gathered from public opinion polls. These show the image of the father as that of an active, sharing helper, although actual behavior often falls short of this ideal.[18] The direction of the change is clearly towards the greater participation of the man in all the tasks of the household. Paternal authority of the jural type, backed up by the mores as well as the law and assigning to the husband full responsibility for family stability, is gone. In its place there has been a tendency to recognize the equalitarian family based on companionship. These studies and polls document a more active state of affairs.

Fatherhood and the Family

There are two schools of thought which seek to explain these developments in the family. One points to the evident loss of functions of the family; and it is true that in former times family members had a more direct responsibility for, among other things, their food, their clothes, and their amusements than the family today. A second interpretation of the same data however sees in this process the emergence of the nuclear family as a distinctive social group from the less definite sort of early family. In the course of acquiring a clear identity within the structure of modern society, the nuclear family, from this standpoint, has gathered to itself a specialized set of functions. The proponents of this explanation distinguish carefully between the *disintegration* of the family group which a loss of functions would seem to indicate and the *disorganization* of the group as it redefines its objectives.[19] In support of this standpoint the association of an open family structure with a closed and localized community should be noticed; the relatively closed nuclear family has in its turn associations with the open community of today. These hypotheses about the correspondence between family type and community structure require further work before they can be accepted without reservation.

Whether the changes in family living that are undoubtedly taking place should be interpreted as disintegration or as disorganization is relevant to the argument of this paper only in that the redefinition of the importance of the father falls more easily into the organization type of explanation than into the loss of function explanation. The basic contention of the argument thus far is that the key to family stability in the isolated nuclear family lies in the way in which the role of father is played. This in turn must be judged in the light of the expectations that surround the position.

All the evidence available points to an increase in the participation of fathers in the activities of the household over the past two decades. As the working week becomes shorter, the occupancy of single family houses, house ownership and house repairing more general, the word *companionship* becomes too passive a word to describe the relations between a man and his family. This newer father behavior is best described as participation, the re-integration of fathers into the conspicuous consumption as well as the child rearing sides of family life. And in a family unit where, over and above marital and mother-child relations, there also exists harmonious father-child relations, stability should ensue. Research will have to test this sort of proposition, though some support can be found in recent happenings.

Movements in the national social statistics may be interpreted as evidence of the appearance of considerable numbers of such stable marriages. In the past generation there has been in all countries of the West, and particularly in the United States, an increase in the proportion of the population marrying. In many countries the average age at marriage has also decreased. The increase in the marriage rate has been shown to be greater in the urban areas, among the educated, and among employees. The educated, urban, white collar worker is the bearer of this cultural change in family formation. The *baby boom,* another new feature of the population history of these countries, is concentrated among this section of the population, too. The two are undoubtedly connected, though the degree of correlation has not yet been worked out. In the educated, urban, white collar families such an increase in births must be desired by both partners since these are the people skilled in the practice of birth control.[20] A change in the position of the husband from a rigorous insistence on responsibility with its concomitant of social distance to a more active participation in domestic routines helps to explain these new developments.

An additional phenomenon, which an increasing involvement of fathers in family activities also helps to explain, is the present decline in the divorce rate. No comparable figures on this are available for the countries of the West but the trend in the United States has been well marked. Since 1946, when the divorce rate reached the highest point on record of 17.8 per thousand married females, it has fallen continuously to 10.3 in 1950 and to 9.9 in 1953.[21] If the hypothesis that the increasing involvement of the father in the intimate daily affairs of the family leads to family stability is correct, the divorce rate should continue to decline for some years to come. Such a prediction is based upon the belief that this change in the rate does not represent merely a variation on the long-term trend towards increasing divorce but that it is a reflection of the emergence within the population of a considerable core of stable families. Their stability rests upon a new base, the redefinition of the father role. At present largely confined to the urban prototype family, this new stability is expected to spread to other social classes in the community and in consequence to bring with it a continuing fall in the divorce rate.

NOTES

1. Frédéric Le Play, *Les Ouvriers Européens,* Paris: 1855, 1 vol. in folio.
2. F. Le Play, *La Réforme Sociale en France,* 1864. *L'organisation de la Famille,* 1870; *La Paix Sociale Aprés le Désastre,* 1871; *La Correspondance Sociale,* 1872; *La Constitution d'Angleterre,* 1875; *La Réforme en Europe et le Salut en France,* 1876; *Le Programme des Unions de la Paix Sociale,* 1876; *Les Ouvriers Européens,* 2ᵉ edition, 6 vols., 1877; *La Méthode Sociale,* 1879; *La Question Sociale,* 1879; *Les Ouvriers des Deux Mondes,* 1879, Tours: Bibliotheque de la Science Sociale, Alfred Mame et fils. English translations: Governeur Emerson, *The Organisation of Labour,* Philadelphia: Claxton, Remson and Haffelfinger, 1872; C. C. Zimmerman and M. E. Frampton, *Family and Society,* New York: D. Van Nostrand Co., 1937, includes a translation of part of volume 1 of *Les Ouvriers Européens,* 2nd edition.
3. Rudolph Schlesinger, *The Family in the U.S.S.R.,* London: Routledge, 1949, p. 266.
4. David K. Bruner, "Family Life in Early Victorian Prose Fiction." Abstract of a thesis, Urbana, Ill.: University of Illinois, 1941.
5. Robert Prigent (ed.), "Renouveau des Idées sur la Famille," *Institut National des Études Démographiques, Cahier no. 18,* Paris: Presses Universitaires de France, 1954, pp. 50–58.
6. Schlesinger, *op. cit.,* pp. 227, 269
7. W. F. Ogburn and M. F. Nimkoff, *Technology and the Changing Family,* New York: Houghton Mifflin, 1955.
8. *International Labour Review,* 63, Geneva: International Labour Office, 1951, pp. 677–697; 69, 1954, pp. 47–59.
9. Kingsley Davis, *Human Society,* New York: The Macmillan Co., 1949, p. 400.
10. Mirra Komarovsky, *The Unemployed Man and His Family,* New York: Dryden Press, 1940.
11. Ruth S. Cavan, *The American Family,* New York: Thomas Y. Crowell, 1953, pp. 10–15.
12. Talcott Parsons and R. F. Bales, *Family, Socialization and Interaction,* Glencoe: The Free Press, 1955, pp. 10–15.
13. Pierre Fougeyrollas, "Prédominance du Mari ou de la Femme Dans le Menage," *Population, Revue Trimestrielle,* 6 (1951), Paris: Institut National D'Études Démographiques, pp. 83–102.
14. Statistics on desertion are poor. Ogburn has estimated that in 1940 the number of separated couples was 1.5 million, or as many as those divorced. *American Journal of Sociology,* 49 (1944), p. 317. Desertion has been given as the principal cause, outranking death and incapacity, for payments to children under public assistance law. Paolo Contini, "Maintenance Obligations," *California Law Review,* 41 (1953), p. 107. An international commission has been working since 1926 on the problems of the maintenance of family payments by husbands who now live in another country; this category includes soldiers. United Nations Economic and Social Council, Session 17, Agenda item 17, *Annexes.*
15. Max Horkheimer, editor, *Studien über Autorität und Familie,* Paris, 1936. Translated by A. Lissance, New York: State Dept. of Social Welfare and Dept. of Social Science, Columbia University, 1937.

16. Ruth J. Tasch, "The Role of the Father in the Family," *Journal of Experimental Education,* 20 (June, 1952), pp. 319–361.
17. Rachel-Ann Elder, quoted in Reuben Hill, *Families under Stress,* New York: Harper and Bros., 1949, pp. 44–49.
18. Hadley Cantril, editor, *Public Opinion 1935–46,* Princeton: Princeton University Press, 1951.
19. Réné Koenig, *Materialen sur Soziologie der Familie,* Berne, 1946. Also: "L'hyperorganisation de la Famille," *Cahiers Internationaux de Sociologie,* 9 (1950), Paris: Editions du Seuil, pp. 42–56.
20. John Hajnal, "Age at Marriage and Proportions Marrying," *Population Studies,* 7 (1953), pp. 111–138. Hajnal, "Differential Changes in Marriage Patterns," *American Sociological Review,* 19 (1954), pp. 148–154. Hajnal, "Analysis of Changes in Marriage Patterns by Economic Groups," *American Sociological Review,* 19 (1954), pp. 295–302. Nelson N. Foote, "Changes in American Marrying Patterns," *Eugenics Quarterly,* 1 (1954), pp. 254–260.
21. U. S. Vital Statistics, *Special Reports,* 42 (June, 1955), p. 45.

18

The Outside Substitute for the Family

by Herma H. Kay

For some time social scientists have been calling attention to the changing nature of the American family. Some have discussed the problem in terms of a loss of function within the family. Thus Ogburn[1] listed in 1938 seven functions originally performed by the family (economic, status-giving, educational, religious, recreational, protective, and affectional) and concluded that "at least six of the seven family functions have been reduced as family activities in recent times,"[2] while only the seventh, the affectional function, remains vigorous. In 1949 Murdock[3] isolated four functions of the nuclear family—sexual, economic, reproductive, and educational—and found that the family as thus defined is a universal human social grouping, a conclusion that has since been disputed.[4] Even this limited definition of the family's functions has not escaped the challenge of changed conditions. Both the anthropologist Linton[5] and the sociologist Par-

Reprinted from Seymour Farber, P. Mustacchi, and Roger H. L. Wilson, *Man and Civilizaton* (New York: McGraw-Hill Book Company, 1965), pp. 3–14, by permission of the author and publisher. Copyright © 1965, McGraw-Hill, Inc.

sons[6] have reduced the functions of the modern nuclear family to two: to socialize children and to provide psychological and emotional security for adults.[7] Neither Linton nor Parsons views this specialization of the family with undue alarm. Indeed, both have separately concluded that the nuclear family is needed to perform these two essential functions for society and that it will survive to fulfill them. The loss of other functions is expressly viewed by Parsons as a transitional stage in family development leading to a basic change in family structure.[8]

A social change so basic that it produces a different structure in the American family must also be basic enough to be reflected in the American legal system because the law constantly deals with cases that test the limits of, and set the boundaries for, social institutions. The hypothesis that the customs and values highly prized by a people are reflected sooner or later in its legal system is neither original nor startling. The converse, that values and customs that have lost their cultural significance will be dropped from the legal system either formally, by repeal or reversal, or informally, by nonenforcement, is similarly commonplace. The interesting result of these propositions, however, is to "regard and study the law simply as a great anthropological document," as Oliver Wendell Holmes suggested a good many years ago. Perhaps by turning to American family law, tracing the recent history of changes in that law that have resulted in a reorganization of the legal structure of the family, and then looking for the lines of current development that may lead to still further changes in the future, we may gain some insights that will be useful to behavioral scientists working with the family.

The legal materials[9] indicate that the structure of the family in Anglo-American law has changed since the beginning of the nineteenth century from a patrilineal authority system to a bilateral system based on equality of the spouses. Because the law deals by and large with individuals instead of groups, the legal image of the common-law pre-nineteenth-century family must be pieced together by examining two of the diadic relationships within the nuclear family: first, the relationship between husband and wife and, second, the relationship between parent and child.

The common law defined the husband-wife relationship by suspending the legal personality of the wife. Prior to her marriage, a single woman had the same rights with respect to property, contracts, and capacity to use the courts as did a man. But upon her marriage, as Blackstone puts it, "the husband and wife are one person in law: that is, the very being or legal existence of the woman is suspended during the marriage, or at least is incorporated and consolidated into that of the husband." [10] This principle is often stated colloquially another way: At common law, the husband and wife were one, and that one was the husband. The ramifications of this doctrine were many and varied. In the first place, and generally speaking, the wife lost ownership of her personal property and control of her real property. Simply by virtue of the marriage, the husband became the owner of his wife's possessory personal property. He was entitled to its possession during his life and on his death it passed to his estate. The wife was, however, permitted to keep her "paraphernalia," that is, her clothing, jewels, and articles of convenience suitable to her rank after her husband's death, provided his creditors did not require them for the payment of his debts. The husband was also entitled to his wife's "choses in action," including her stocks and bonds, bills of exchange, debts owed to her, and her rights of action at law if he took active steps to reduce them to his possession intending to make them his own. Finally, although the husband did not own the wife's real property, he was entitled to the use of her lands during the marriage. If a child was born to the couple alive and capable of inheriting the wife's land, then the husband was entitled to the use of the land during his life as tenant by the curtesy. The wife, acting alone, had no power to sell or transfer her land.

A second consequence of the wife's loss of legal personality was her inability to make contracts and use the courts. Her contracts were absolutely void, and she was not bound by them unless her husband had been banished from the realm, had left voluntarily, or had been imprisoned for a term of years. Moreover, she could not sue or be sued in a court of law unless her husband was joined with her as a party.

A third consequence of the legal unity of husband and wife was that the husband was liable for his wife's torts (but not her voluntary crimes). Because husband and wife were one legal person, they could not sue each other for damages for wrongful acts committed by one of them against the person of the other.

In addition to positive legal disabilities, the common law emphasized the wife's inferior legal position negatively by denying her the right to recover damages in two situations where that right was granted to the husband. If there was a common accident in which both spouses were injured and rendered incapable of marital intercourse, the husband would have had an action for the loss of consortium but the wife would not. And if the wife was enticed away from the husband by a third party, he would have had an action for the alienation of her affections, but similar relief would not have been available to her under like circumstances.

Finally, the husband had the power to choose the family domicile and its mode of living. He had the duty of supporting his wife, and he could select the means and place at which his duty should be performed. The wife's unreasonable refusal to follow the husband wherever he chose to go constituted desertion.

The husband's paternal authority over his children was another illustration of his legal primacy over his wife. The parent-child relationship at common law was really a father-child relationship. The mother's rights were subordinate to those of her husband, and in many cases her rights arose only if his had been terminated by death. During his life, the father had virtually an absolute right to the custody and control of his minor children, and upon his death he could appoint for the child a guardian whose right to custody was recognized as superior to that of the mother. If he did not appoint a guardian, the mother succeeded to his parental rights.

Other aspects of the father-child relationship at common law illustrated the paternal structure of the family. Thus, the father was entitled to his child's services, and he could demand that the child work for him without pay. If the child worked for an outsider, the father was entitled to his earnings. Partly because of this paternal ownership of the child's services and earnings, the father's rights in his child were stated by the California Supreme Court in 1900 [11] to come within the constitutional provisions for the protection of property. The father's duty to support his children, however, was held in England and some American states to be only a moral obligation not directly enforceable by the child. If the father refused to provide for his child, the poor laws authorized the municipal authorities to do so and then demand reimbursement from the father to the extent of his ability. The father could disinherit the child by will, and the child was unable to obtain a support order against the father's estate. In contrast to the father's absolute right to the child's earnings, however, he had no rights at all to the child's other property.

The immunity from suit for wrongful acts that obtained between husband and wife also extended to parent and child, but the reason was different. There was no theoretical merging of the child's legal personality with that of his parent. Instead, the child's inability to sue the father for torts was based on an unwillingness to permit such a direct challenge to the father's authority in the home. For torts committed against the child by outsiders, however, the father had a right to recover damages just as he could recover for injuries to his horse or cow.

Finally, the parent had the right to punish his child in a reasonable manner—a right that even the common law never gave the husband over his wife's person. This power to correct the child could be delegated to the child's teacher or other persons filling a parental role for the child.

The development of American family law from 1850 to the present is virtually synonymous with the history of the emergence of the married woman as a legal personality. In general, the disabilities of marriage imposed upon her by the common law have been removed by legislation or judicial opinion while her rights as a mother have become equal, if not superior, to those of her husband as a father. The first major reform was legislative: beginning with Mississippi in 1839, every state enacted statutes known as Married Women's Acts to alleviate the harsh property rules of the common law. By and large, the statutes provide that real and personal property owned by a woman at the time of her marriage remains her separate property, and that all property acquired by her after marriage, including her earnings, becomes her separate property. In California and the other six states that follow the civil-law system of marital property, the earnings of both husband and wife are community property.[12] Although it was not until 1951 that a married woman in California was permitted to manage and control her own earnings,[13] she has had the right to prevent her husband from giving away the community personal property since 1891 [14] and from conveying the community real property since 1917.[15] Furthermore, partly as a result of judicial interpretation of the Married Women's Acts, the wife is now permitted to resort to the courts as freely as an unmarried woman, and her husband no longer need be joined with her as a party to the action.

Married women may now contract freely with their husbands as well as with outsiders, but, generally speaking, the husband is not liable for his wife's contract debts unless he has agreed, expressly or impliedly, to meet her obligations. On the other hand, the Married Women's Acts did not terminate the husband's duty to support his wife. Thus, when she contracts for food, clothing, home furnishings, and the like, called "necessaries" by the law, he is liable for the reasonable value of the articles supplied to the family.

Removal of the doctrine of spousal immunity from tort—the rule that since the spouses are one person in law they cannot sue each other for personal wrongs—has largely been a judicial task. Like other judicial reforms, it has proceeded slowly. The 1962 California case, called by a delightful quirk of circumstance *Self v. Self*,[16] that abolished the doctrine for this state was able to cite in its support only eighteen other states that had also done away with the prohibition. Indeed, one of those states had seen its judiciary promptly reversed by the legislature, which reenacted the common-law rule.

Many states have abolished the husband's actions for alienation of affections and loss of consortium, thus ending the common-law discrimination against the wife. The recent California case law on loss of consortium illustrates the change in judicial attitude toward the husband's position in the family. In 1958 a wife sued to recover for the loss of consortium arising from an injury to her husband when the taxicab in which he was riding collided with a train. The trial court in effect held that she had no cause of action, and the Supreme Court upheld the judgment, stating that if the common-law rule was to be changed, the legislature should change it.[17] But in 1960, when a husband sued to recover for the loss of his wife's consortium, the Supreme Court reversed a judgment in his favor based on the common-law rule, stating that "drawing a distinction between spouses on the ground that the husband, unlike the wife, had a right of recovery at common law would be extremely inequitable and, further, would ignore the fact that recognition of his right was based upon the wife's subservient position in the marriage relationship whereas, under present-day law, spouses are generally regarded as equals." [18]

The husband still retains his titular position as head of the family and his right to choose a reasonable domicile for the family. But a growing body of cases declaring that it is unreasonable for the husband to expect his wife to share their home with his mother perhaps indicates the law's preference for equality between the spouses in the family group.[19]

The recent history of the development of parent-child law again indicates the mother's strengthened legal position in the family. In nearly all states the mother's right to custody of her children has been made equal to that of the father. In some states, as in California, the statutes expressly give the mother preference where the child is very young if the parents are otherwise equally qualified to care for the child.[20] California balances this preference for the mother, however, by preferring the father "if the child is of an age to require education and preparation for labor and business." [21] The California statute declaring that mother and father are equally entitled to the child's services and earnings[22] is typical of other state laws, as is the provision that neither parent may appoint a guardian for the child without the consent of the other.[23]

This enlargement of the mother's rights, however, has so far simply meant that the common-law paternal property right in the child has now become a parental property right. The child himself still occupies nearly the same position he held at common law. The major exceptions to that statement are found in the support laws. The child's legal right to support from both his parents is now recognized, and in some cases he may compel support from his parents' estate. This last right, however, is not well established as yet, and the parental power to disinherit the child is undiminished.

Another exception in California law dealing with the child's earnings illustrates a growing protection of the child against the parent. Hollywood has frequently employed child actors whose salaries at common law would have been the property of their parents. But because minors, like married women, were not bound by their contracts at common law, they could repudiate contracts of employment at will. After several bad experiences, the Hollywood studios secured legislation providing that a minor's contracts for the performance of artistic or creative services could not be repudiated if approved by a court.[24] The statute also provides, however, that the court may withhold approval of the contract until the child's parent or guardian agrees to set aside not more than one-half of the child's earnings for the child's benefit.[25] Thus, the parents of child actors are effectively prevented from exploiting their children for their own profit, even though the California law still states unqualifiedly that the child's earnings are the property of his parents.

This brief survey of the family-law materials indicates a shift from a patriarchal family structure to one in which the spouses are more nearly equal as between themselves but dominant in their legal relations with their children. There are indications, however, that the future path of legal development will be directed toward the emergence of the child as a person in his own right. Thus, in child-custody cases, the prevailing standard for awarding custody is the best interests of the child. If one of the parties seeking custody is a parent, however, and the opposing party is a nonparent, the best interests of the child are presumed to be satisfied by granting custody to the parent unless he is demonstrably unfit to rear the child. Since "unfitness" has come to mean moral unfitness, the presumption in favor of the parent is rarely overcome. Some movement to abolish this so-called "dominant parental right doctrine" in the law of custody can be detected among judges and practicing lawyers.[26] If this were done, facts bearing on the child's needs would be considered first rather than facts establishing the good or bad character of the parent. The child would thus be treated less like the property of his parents and more like an individual.

Although we have been discussing family law, it is interesting to note that the law nowhere defines a family. As we have seen, family problems have been viewed as husband-wife or parent-child problems. The last legal development I wish to discuss today is the growing movement to treat the family as a unit and its problems as group problems. This idea grew out of experience with the juvenile court and its philosophy of protecting and rehabilitating children instead of punishing them. Thus, in California, when a child is referred to the juvenile court for the commission of an act which, had it been committed by an adult, would have been a crime, there is no trial by jury in an adversary setting to determine guilt and assess a penalty, as there would be in an adult criminal case. For example, if a minor is picked up by the police for stealing a car and sent to juvenile hall, the probation officer will secure a social study of the child, his family, and his background. The probation officer then may file a petition on behalf of the minor—not one adverse to him—setting forth the facts that indicate that the minor has stolen the car and thus comes within the juvenile court's jurisdiction. At a hearing before the juvenile court judge where the minor and his parents may be represented by counsel, a determination whether the minor comes within the court's jurisdiction is made. If the determination is in the affirmative, the court considers the social study and decides whether to place the child with a family of good character, in a foster home, a child-care institution, a public agency organized to care for children, or a county juvenile home, ranch, camp, or forestry camp. Throughout the proceedings and the subsequent treatment, the emphasis is on helping the child to become a valuable member of society.

The conclusion drawn from the juvenile court experience by some who have worked with it is that the problems there encountered are family problems. The notion of establishing a family court, with jurisdiction over all affairs of the family, has begun to emerge. Thus, the family court would handle cases involving consent to child marriages, annulment of marriage, divorce and alimony, judicial separation, child support, paternity, child custody, adoption, and juvenile court matters. The court would be assisted by a staff of social workers, psychologists, psychiatrists, and doctors. Information gathered about the court's "clients" would be kept in one place and be made available to the court either in the form of testimony by the social worker or a written report.

It has been suggested that the family court, like the juvenile court, should be freed from the hostility of the adversary process, particularly in divorce and child-custody cases. In counseling sessions with staff specialists an atmosphere of seeking the best interests of the family can be established. But if attempts at reconciliation or settlement fail, the parties are relegated to the more hostile atmosphere of the courtroom. This situation cannot be remedied unless the notion of fault in divorce is eliminated. Briefly, the point is that in legal theory divorces are granted to an innocent spouse as relief from the wrong committed by the guilty spouse. In most states no divorce can be granted unless the fault of the defendant and the innocence of the plaintiff are proved. It goes without saying that divorces are usually the "fault" of both spouses. And it is an open secret that when the parties agree to disagree they can avoid this legal doctrine by the simple expedient of the uncontested divorce. Against this background, a leading California case[27] permitted the granting of divorces to both spouses, thus holding both parties guilty, and pointed out that society would be better served by encouraging both husband and wife to speak freely so that their interests can be evaluated in an atmosphere of truth rather than falsehood.

The law's growing emphasis on the individuality of the persons who make up the nuclear family on the one hand and its tendency to treat their specific problems as group problems on the other seem basically sound. If the family structure is firm, the transfer of family functions to other institutions need not be of undue concern. Indeed, the law itself has reflected to some extent the loss of family functions. Thus, a recent California case held that parents could not remove their children from the public schools for education at home unless the parent acting as teacher held the proper state credentials for instruction in each course the child received at home.[28] Zoning ordinances prohibit the carrying on of certain business activities in residential districts. Although clothing can still be made in the home, it is doubtful whether cotton can be grown in the back yard. The important point to be made, however, is not what the family has lost but rather what the family can become. We have seen that the law is beginning to provide a foundation for the building of a family relationship that considers the needs of each person on a substantially equal basis as well as the interaction of each with the others. I do not know whether the conclusion logically follows from these materials that the family is necessary. I think it does follow, however, that the family is alive and healthy, and given that, and human optimism, I think the family will survive.

NOTES

1. William F. Ogburn, "The Changing Functions of the Family," in Robert F. Winch (ed.), *Selected Studies in Marriage and the Family,* New York, Holt, Rinehart and Winston, Inc., 1953, pp. 74–80.
2. *Ibid.,* p. 75.
3. George P. Murdock, *Social Structure,* New York, The Macmillan Company, 1949, pp. 1–13.
4. Melford E. Spiro, "Is the Family Universal?—The Israeli Case," in Norman W. Bell and Ezra F. Vogel (eds.), *A Modern Introduction to the Family,* New York, The Free Press of Glencoe, 1960, pp. 64–75. E. Kathleen Gough, "Is the Family Universal?—The Nayar Case," in *ibid.,* pp. 76–92. William N. Stephens, *The Family in Cross-cultural Perspective,* New York, Holt, Rinehart and Winston, Inc., 1963, pp. 12–32.
5. Ralph Linton, "The Natural History of the Family," in Ruth N. Anshen (ed.), *The Family: Its Function and Destiny,* New York, Harper & Row, Publishers, Incorporated, 1959.
6. Talcott Parsons and Robert F. Bales, *Family, Socialization and Interaction Process,* New York, The Free Press of Glencoe, 1955.
7. Linton speaks of "satisfying the psychological needs of the individuals who enter the marital relationship" (*op. cit.,* p. 49), while Parsons' phrase is "stabilization of the adult personalities of the population of the society" (*op. cit.,* pp. 16–17).
8. Parsons and Bales, *op. cit.,* p. 9.
9 Unless otherwise noted, the legal materials on which this paper is based are summarized in Joseph W. Madden, *Handbook of the Law of Persons and Domestic Relations,* St. Paul, Minn., West Publishing Company, 1931. See also Henry H. Foster, Jr., "Family Law in a Changing Society," in F. James Davis et al. (eds.), *Society and the Law,* New York, The Free Press of Glencoe, 1962, pp. 227–263; and Karl N. Llewellyn, "Behind the Law of Divorce," in *Selected Essays on Family Law,* Association of American Law Schools, Brooklyn, N.Y., The Foundation Press, Inc., 1950, pp. 27–96.
10. 1 Blackstone, *Commentaries on the Law of England,* 442; 2 Id. 433.
11. *In re Campbell,* 130 Cal. 380, 62 Pac. 613 (1900).
12. California Civil Code §§ 162, 163, 164.
13. California Civil Code §161c.
14. California Civil Code §172.
15. California Civil Code §172a.
16. *Self v. Self,* 58 Cal.2d 683, 376 P.2d 65, 26 Cal. Rptr. 97 (1962). See

also the companion case, *Klein v. Klein,* 58 Cal.2d 692, 376 P.2d 70, 26 Cal. Rptr. 102 (1962).

17. *Deshotel v. Atchison, T. & S.F. Ry. Co.,* 50 Cal.2d 664, 328 P.2d 449 (1958).
18. *West v. City of San Diego,* 54 Cal.2d 469, 477, 353 P.2d 929, 6 Cal. Rptr. 289 (1960).
19. See Anno., Acts or omissions of spouse causing other spouse to leave home as desertion for former, 19 A.L.R.2d 1428, 1456–1458 (1951).
20. California Civil Code §138.
21. *Ibid.*
22. California Civil Code §197.
23. California Probate Code §1403.
24. California Civil Code §36.
25. California Civil Code §§36.1, 36.2.
26. See, e.g., Justice Shauer's dissenting opinions, concurred in by Chief Justice Gibson, in *Roche v. Roche,* 25 Cal.2d 141, 152 P.2d 999 (1944) and *Stewart v. Stewart,* 41 Cal.2d 447, 260 P.2d 44 (1953); Henry M. Fain, "Custody of Children," in 1 *The California Family Lawyer,* Berkeley, Calif., Committee on Continuing Education of the Bar, 1961, pp. 587–589.
27. *DeBurgh v. DeBurgh,* 39 Cal.2d 858, 250 P.2d 598 (1952).
28. *In re Shinn,* 195 Cal. App.2d 683, 16 Cal. Rptr. 165 (1961).

19

The Changing Family in a Changing Society

by J. Milton Yinger

This presentation is primarily concerned with exploration of the ways in which family patterns are modified by the social setting in which they are found. By considering some of the forces affecting the whole kinship system, we may be able to formulate a helpful interpretation of the place of the family in a mobile, urban society.

Changes in family patterns are not necessarily either happy or unhappy facts. Among students of the family there is a strong tendency to lament most changes, sometimes with the implication that the family seems to be dying out altogether. We need to draw a distinction between "the family" and particular family systems. When a student of government traces the changes in the forms through which

Reprinted from *Social Casework,* 40 (October 1959), pp. 419–428, by permission of the author and *Social Casework.*

political power is expressed, he does not contend that government is disappearing. Economic patterns can change, through many stages, from subsistence operations in isolated villages to complex interdependent processes binding together several nations. We may applaud or lament the facts, but we are not likely to say that economic institutions are disappearing. When we study the family or religion, however, we are more likely to equate change with deterioration or even disappearance. We are more likely to be concerned with form than with function. This attitude is unfortunate, in my judgment, because it impedes the understanding of what is actually happening.

Students of the family have contributed to the confusion, both because they have allowed their own values to intrude into their interpretations, and because they have done little to bring family studies into the framework of systematic theories. Only very recently has this situation begun to change. In the last several years, the primarily descriptive and practical approach to family studies has been supplemented to some degree by a number of attempts to relate family patterns to social structure. Some of the ablest theorists (Parsons, Davis, Murdock, and Goode, for example) are involved in this effort.

It would be a mistake to think of this development as unrelated to the activities of a family service agency. Firm scientific knowledge about the ways in which a family system affects and is affected by the society of which it is a part can greatly strengthen the work of the clinician, especially in his long-range planning. Knowledge of culture and subculture, of role definitions and role conflicts, of socialization and the forces that impede it can be of great value to the practitioner. A recent comparative study, for example, demonstrates that as the woman's contribution to subsistence goes up, the economic aspects of marriage change—from a dowry system, to minor gift exchange, to bride-price.[1] This fact may seem to be far removed from any problem likely to be faced by a family counselor. But who can doubt that the dramatic change in the place of women in the economics of the family in the last twenty-five years has produced some new forces of great significance for family stability? Perhaps what we need is more basic research to identify the underlying principles involved.

Influence of Social Institutions

The central proposition of contemporary family theory is scarcely new or startling. It is that the family cannot be understood as an isolated phenomenon. It must be seen in the context of the economic and political institutions, the religious influences, the population facts of the society of which it is a part. It is not by chance that a static agricultural society will emphasize the extended family, will often permit or encourage plural marriage, and will give to parents the power to make choices of partners for their children. Such elements as these fit into a stable social structure, just as emphasis on the conjugal family, romantic love, and separate households is likely to characterize urban, mobile societies. Powerful forces create the kind of family system to be found in a particular setting. If the identity of these forces can be discovered, a family agency can work to maintain or secure the desirable elements. It seems likely, for example, that a still further shrinking of the importance of the extended family is inevitable in the United States. The nuclear family maintains or even increases its significance, but other aspects of the kinship system become weaker. "This means that the family has become a more specialized agency than before, probably more specialized than it has been in any previously known society." [2]

This shift does not make the family any less important. Indeed, its central functions remain. Granted the long period of helplessness of the human infant, the fact that man is a "culture-bearing animal" and requires, therefore, a long period of training; granted the need for a process for placing individuals in their various positions in society—to name only a few of the functions of the family—we can see its fundamental place in all societies. Revolutionary movements sometimes try to destroy the family in order to break the continuity of generations that ties a population to its past traditions. But before long every such movement—in the Soviet Union for example—begins to re-emphasize the importance of the family. On the basis of the evidence of the 1920's it seemed wholly unlikely that by 1940 leaders of Russia would be declaring that the family is the foundation of the state; but that is what happened. (Neither family nor state withered away.)

To stress the vitality of the family is not to contend that there are no serious strains. In a society that is changing as rapidly as is our own, almost every aspect of family life is subject to severe disturbance. We can see very clearly the way in which a family system is affected by its social setting if we look at the various levels of interaction in a family and note the ways in which they are changing. In a sense, the urban industrial revolution through which the United States has been passing for the last century has been breaking up established family structures, unwittingly and slowly, just as other kinds of revolutions do in a more explicit fashion. Culturally established attitudes toward the extended circle of kinfolk, toward the proper roles of men and women, and toward the training of children are being drastically revised. It will doubtless be two or three more generations before our society evolves a family pattern that fits into a mobile, urban, democratic situation. This type of family pattern, after all, is a major social invention—and like most complicated inventions, the early models are pretty crude, and sometimes don't work at all.

Role Expectations

Stable societies train most of their members to accept a particular role definition of what a good husband and a good wife are supposed to be. They also train each person to expect and want the characteristics in the other person which the other has been socialized to exhibit. There is little role ambiguity, either within an individual or between individuals. That this is often not the case in the United States, any member of the staff of a family agency can quickly testify. Our cultural heroes associated with romance are almost all glamorous, handsome, rich, and poised. If this has not become the established cultural definition of the good mate, at least such an image has mingled with older notions of domesticity. Most American men may feel most at ease with "the girl next door," but they have been half-trained to expect a little of the Marguerite Higgins career pattern, with a dash of Brigitte Bardot. Not only is this a difficult combination to find, but it is not at all clear that many men would be really ready to accept it as the appropriate role for their wives if they should find it. Moreover, the girls themselves are taught different role patterns that are at least partially mutually exclusive. To say that many women are taught two roles—one involving a career and the other the older wife-and-mother image—is an oversimplification, but it points to the ambiguity in cultural training. There is probably nothing inevitably contradictory about these different patterns, but our society has only partially invented the ways of institutionalizing their blending into a more complicated but unified single role. Until this blending is accomplished, both men and women will feel the strain.

In an interesting study, Mirra Komarovsky reports the feelings of role ambiguity among 153 young women whom she interviewed.

Almost half of them, under the constraints of the older role conception, had "played dumb" on dates, concealed some honor, or pretended ignorance on some subject, playing down some skill "in obedience to the unwritten law that men must possess these skills to a superior degree. At the same time, in other areas of life, social pressures were being exerted upon these women to 'play to win,' to compete to the utmost of their abilities. . . ." [3]

The difficulties associated with role ambiguity in our society are increased by the fact that, in mobile society, young men and women with different role expectations are more likely now than formerly to meet, to court, and to marry. A romantic ideal that holds that love alone counts makes it a little bit indecent to worry about such things as common values, interests, and role definitions; love should override any such minor separating facts. This is not to imply that romantic love is an American invention. William Goode has shown recently that it is found in a very large number of societies, if not in all, but it is much more hedged about by social controls in some than in others. In a society in which marriage has most of the elements of a governmental treaty and an economic contract between large family groups, one is not likely to find anything quite so capricious as romance determining who shall be marriage partners. By such various devices as child marriage, specific definition of potential mates in terms of their group membership, enforced physical separation of adolescents, or strong chaperonage, various societies keep romantic love at a minimum as the determining fact in mate selection.[4] Only in a society where isolated married couples, relatively unrelated to wider circles of kinfolk, are the primary family structure, can romantic love be permitted to operate as freely as it does in the United States. And even here it runs into the stubborn fact that successful marriage requires many shared values and role expectations, that love cannot conquer everything. Too often one of the persons concerned has discovered that the little plan to reform and remake the partner, once he has been caught, proves to be impossible—partly because the partner probably started out with the same hope of doing the reforming. It is better to get a good match to start with.

And even a good match is not without problems, for we demand so much more of marriage than is true in many societies. As Kurt Lewin pointed out, a husband wants his wife to be—at the same time —sweetheart, comrade, housewife, mother, manager of his income, perhaps co-supporter of the family, representative to the community, and so forth. A wife expects her husband to be sweetheart, comrade, support of the family, father, caretaker of the house, serious but care-free, a good provider but romantically reckless. Most of us are not so versatile. Moreover, the specialization of urban life tends to create differences in values and needs between husband and wife. In a rural society, marriage partners are influenced by more of the same forces, they often work side by side, they change together. In the city, a large share of the work life and even of the recreation of husband and wife is likely to involve the partner scarcely at all. The man, be-cause of wider contacts and greater mobility, is likely to change more; the wife, with a more restricted range of activity, retains more of her earlier perspectives and values. As *Fortune* magazine once put it, she has stayed home literally and figuratively. A couple that was well mated at the beginning of marriage may be faced with important dif-ferences in desire and outlook on life after ten or fifteen years. Even if there is no long-run drifting apart, the differences in schedule and routine create different needs, let us say at the end of the day. The wife is ready for some adult contacts and a little variety; she wants to go out. The husband has *been* out. Our contemporary family pat-terns have only partially begun to deal with the need for "mutual mobility" of husband and wife through the years and mutual interests and schedules through the days.

Child-Training Methods

The aspect of family life that has been most intensively studied is doubtless the relations between parents and children. Here is a prob-lem on which the psychologist and psychiatrist have a great deal to offer, but a sociological point of view may also be of some value. Child-training methods, to an important degree, are cultural facts; but they vary among classes and other groups, and they change through time—in our society with quite amazing speed. In stable societies, there is no question about how one should respond to his children. The rules are in the folkways and they have been largely internalized through the slow process of learning. But in our time, parent-child relations have become problematic. A young mother can-not turn to her mother for guidance, for they probably live a thousand miles apart—or some equivalent distance in cultural training and inclination. The federal Children's Bureau or the redoubtable Dr. Spock takes over as a grandmother substitute.

Having become self-conscious about our child-training methods, we have also become uncertain and at least slightly anxious. How many of us have felt dismay at the practices we used with our first or second child, in the name of "scientific management," only to discover that the authorities on whom we depended had reversed themselves a little later. Fortunately, children are resilient and survive most of our efforts to make them civilized. What we are witnessing is the development of child-training methods appropriate to the roles and experiences of an urban, changing, democratic society. The pendulum swings are testimony to the difficulty of working out new methods. The strains and conflicts are sometimes severe, but failure to redefine roles and methods of training in a society that has experienced so much change would impose even more severe strains.

In their recent study, Daniel Miller and Guy Swanson have described the child-training methods of earlier days and then studied, by careful interviews with 582 Detroit-area mothers, the range of methods today.[5] The observation that stands out is that parents, for the most part unaware of the choices they are making, treat their children in such a way as to try to prepare them for the kind of adult existence they are likely to face. In sociological terms, child-training methods are part of a complex social system; they both reflect and support economic, political, religious, and stratification facts. If important aspects of the system change, and there are not significant adjustments in the ways in which we socialize our children, the family can be the sources of serious mal-preparation.

It can well be argued, for example, that changes in the economy which have taken the father away from the home for the greater part of the day have left many boys without adequate adult male models. We tend to compound the difficulty by having boys taught primarily by women teachers in the early years. There are many subtle implications to this which we cannot explore here, but it seems reasonable to suppose that some of the difficulties of boys and male adolescents are associated with this shift in patterns of interaction. The resulting behavior seems sometimes to be the essence of anarchy; or it may be an effort on the part of boys who are uncertain of their own manhood—for they have not been helped to learn what it is to be a man—to overcome their own inner doubts. The problem is not made easier by the fact that girls grow up a year or two sooner, placing their age-mates among the boys in inferior positions. The over-compensation that often results is not a very graceful response, but its sources in the social structure are not difficult to find.

In comparison of the advice by the authors of *Infant Care* (issued by the Children's Bureau) in the 1914 edition with that given in 1942 and 1945, Martha Wolfenstein shows the extent to which new methods redefine the parental role. It is almost as if we were seeking to sweep away any vestiges of the personalities that resulted from the earlier methods in order to develop people adjusted to an "other-directed" world, ready to take their places as "organization men," skilled at the soft sell. The swing of the pendulum was doubtless much wider in the books of advice than it was in practice, but there is little doubt that in the course of a generation, significant changes occurred. In 1914, the parent was told that the child is endowed with strong and dangerous impulses. The child rebels fiercely if blocked but, since the impulses may easily grow beyond control and may wreck the child for life, he must be blocked. Mechanical restraints to prevent him from exploring his body or sucking his thumb were described. By the 1940's these fierce pleasures became unimportant incidents to be treated casually.[6]

Should a baby be picked up when he cries? Only if he has "real" needs the early authorities agreed—if he is ill or hungry or has the proverbial pin sticking in him—otherwise let him cry. John Watson set the tone for much of this. In 1914, he wrote:

> There is a sensible way of treating children. Treat them as though they were young adults. Dress them, bathe them with care and circumspection. Let your behavior always be objective and kindly firm. Never hug and kiss them, never let them sit in your lap. If you must, kiss them once on the forehead when they say good night. Shake hands with them in the morning. Given them a pat on the head if they have made an extraordinarily good job of a difficult task. . . .
>
> If you expected a dog to grow up and be useful as a watch dog, a bird dog, a fox hound, useful for anything except a lap dog, you wouldn't dare treat it the way you treat your child. . . .[7]

Thirty years later, however, the advice was quite different: babies need lots of attention; this is just as important as food and the absence of pain; the need is just as real. Play with your child; enjoy him; teach him the pleasures of human association.

When Vincent studied the methods of infant discipline recommended by three women's magazines, he found amazing shifts from one period to another. In 1890, 100 per cent of the articles recommended flexible scheduling. In the next thirty years this rule began to be supplanted by the advice that schedules should be fixed, that the child should be allowed to cry it out if he demanded attention when he was "not supposed to." By 1920, 100 per cent of all the articles took this position. But soon that advice began to be supplanted so that, by 1948, 100 per cent of all the articles recommended self-regulated schedules for the child.[8]

I doubt very much that such diversity of advice is best explained as a series of fads or the caprices of specialists who have built their ideas on too little evidence. What we see are the agents of a society struggling to rework the child-training methods they have received, in the face of overwhelming changes in the kinds of experience that individuals face. The kind of training that might equip one to deal effectively with life on a frontier—the creation, perhaps, of a tough self-sufficiency and individualism—might be a real handicap in a society of enormous bureaucracies, where one must feel at home with strangers, able to work with the team and to sell himself. I am not suggesting that millions of parents have developed this insight into an articulate philosophy. The simple fact is that in their own experience they have found that certain tendencies helped them to respond to situations they met; other tendencies made life awkward. Gradually this insight is woven into the patterns of interaction between parents and children.

Parent-Child Relationships

It is significant that Miller and Swanson found important differences between what they called individuated and entrepreneurial parents and the welfare-bureaucratic parents. By these terms they are drawing a distinction between those who earn their living in jobs that are "sharply affected by the risks and vicissitudes of the market place," and those who work in large, bureaucratic structures within which they have specialized tasks but no major risk-taking decisions to make. They described the transition from a society in which a large proportion of workers were independent farmers, craftsmen, or businessmen, to one in which the great majority of workers—from unskilled to professional —are part of large organizations over which they have little control. In the new situation, the need is not so much for boldness as for togetherness.

For students of the family the most interesting aspect of the Miller and Swanson book is the effort to see if this shift has affected parent-child relationships. On the basis of a wealth of material, the authors demonstrate some interesting trends that cut across class lines and religious lines (although these also affect family interaction of course). ". . . the parental practices that we believe are becoming conspicuous since 1940 look as if they were peculiarly in harmony with the values and ideas—with the way of life—of a new middle-class person whose numbers are rapidly increasing." [9]

An earlier emphasis on self-denial, rugged independence, and the postponement of satisfactions is fading most rapidly in those families, whatever their class or religion, who are part of the large bureaucratic structures so prevalent in our cities. Although Miller and Swanson do not use Riesman's[10] terms, they present good evidence to support the idea that the prevailing advice (if not practice) of forty years ago was the kind likely to produce an inner-directed person, one who could hold his own in "the jungle," as Upton Sinclair called the city. Both knowingly and unwittingly parents tended to train their children for life in a sea of strangers, to make them able to postpone, to save, to plan, to look after themselves without much dependence on the groups to which they belonged.

In recent years, however, more and more parents have begun to experience the need for close co-operation in large organizations. Many have moved away from the rapidly changing areas of cities to the less anonymous suburbs. They have felt the shift from an emphasis on production to a stress on consumption of goods, as the economy lifted large numbers above the subsistence level. Not surprisingly, the advice and, at least in some measure, the practice of parents have shifted. They have become more permissive. Parents are more likely today to be unhappy over signs that their children do not fit into the group than over signs of lack of individual accomplishment. Everywhere we hear the lament that schools have deteriorated in the last quarter of a century. In my judgment, the changes that have occurred are a manifestation of the kind of preparation for life that children experience on every hand. Every man is a salesman in our society, whether he be a business man, a minister, or a politician. If a choice has to be made between a capacity for smooth human relationships and an excellence that might be accompanied by a few "knobby" characteristics that cut one off from his fellows, better far, say most of the voices of our society, to choose the former.

I am not at all certain that the details of this shift from individualism to togetherness are correctly described—nor even that in the last analysis the thesis defended by Riesman, by Miller and Swanson, and others is correct. I do believe, however, that recent studies make clear how thoroughly a family system is embedded in the whole society, how it responds to changes therein and can be understood only in its total social context.

There is no better way to describe how deeply the experiences of the child within the family shape his adult tendencies and values than to make some comparative analyses. It is not possible, however, to do so within the limits of this presentation. I should like merely to mention a comparative approach made in an interesting study by Martha Wolfenstein, "French Parents Take Their Children to the Park." Although we shall have to leave unanswered the question of the representative quality of her observations, they seem to harmonize well with other studies of France. Wolfenstein notes how the mother or nurse trains the child to feelings of privacy, self-sufficiency, restraint. While the American child is being taught to share and to play in groups of children his own age, the French child is kept within the family circle, playing only with his own toys, and avoiding contact, pleasant or aggressive, with the children around him. There are arguments, of course, but they are primarily verbal, restrained from developing into fights by the stock parental injunction, "Disputez, mais ne vous battez pas." There is a seriousness about childhood in France that contrasts sharply with the widely held idea in America that childhood is primarily a time for fun. Our children will grow up soon enough, many American parents feel—time enough then for them to take on serious obligations. But many French parents make serious business even of the play that their children carry on. It is not enough to ride the carrousel because it is fun. The sign in the Luxembourg Gardens proclaims: "Chevaux Hygieniques. Jeu gymnastique pour les enfants developpant la force et la souplesse." [11]

What we see in this description is a somewhat extreme form of what Miller and Swanson called entrepreneurial family training. Undoubtedly there are wide variations in France. Perhaps some one of us can get a foundation grant to sit in the parks of Paris to see if more permissive child-training methods are developing, and if so, among whom. It would be important to discover whether such shifts have affected the famed ability of French adults to enjoy life. This ability, although probably exaggerated by the American's stereotype of the Frenchman, can scarcely be doubted. It stems from a well-disciplined childhood that both taught the restraints necessary to the achievement of many satisfactions and created a sense that one has earned the right to enjoy life as an adult without feelings of guilt because one is not working hard enough or is indulging himself too much. The stern training that characterized, and still characterizes, many

American families did not seem to produce this same result. In this difference we see again how a family system is intricately tied to the whole society.

Sibling Interaction

A sociological point of view can also contribute something to the understanding of the interaction among the children within a family. The position, "eldest child," for example, may have some aspects that are shared everywhere. Much more clearly, however, it is a position within a particular society, with specified role requirements and privileges, and with certain kinds of personality consequences for those who hold that position. It is one thing to be the eldest child in a society which emphasizes primogeniture, or in the context of an extended family system where there are, so to speak, many fathers and mothers. It is something else in a small, urban, democratic family which draws many of its traditions from an extended family pattern, but places its members in new relationships.

The result, until new role definitions can be worked out, is often a great deal of strain, particularly for the eldest child. Our present family structures are ill-equipped to help him struggle with the jealousy that almost inevitably hits him when a younger brother or sister arrives. Our democratic traditions even lead us to deny that it exists or to declare that it is the result of individual wilfulness, deserving only censure. In fact, however, our small, child-centered families seem almost designed to create a problem of jealousy. The first child is not only much loved but also the only loved. Then along comes a noisy competitor who manages to command a great deal of mother's time and even to be rewarded by attention for doing the very things that he, the older child, is now being punished for. If the latter wakes in the middle of the night and cries, his mother may well shout to him to go back to sleep; if baby wakes, mother gets up and soothes him. If the older child dirties himself he may well be sharply reprimanded or punished; but baby is patiently cleaned and cooed over. It's enough to make a body angry. To a two- or three-year-old, the whole affair is a basic injustice, and he is scarcely equipped to respond to it philosophically. He opposes the newcomer directly or indirectly, frequently with the result that he is punished for hurting baby—which only confirms his suspicions that this strange child that his mother has brought home is the cause of all his troubles. After a little while he gives up hope that the competitor is a temporary visitor, and turns to other strategies to win reassurance. He demands things selfishly, seeking for a sign that he is still loved; he is "bad," by mother's definitions, in order to test her; he regresses, hoping that by acting like a baby he can win the same attention.

Whether this is a small problem, easily smoothed over after a few years, or a basic fact in the personality formation of the individuals involved depends on the warmth and expressiveness of the parents, the presence of other adults, the comparative talents of the children, and many other factors—but there seem to be few situations in our small urban families where jealousy does not arise to some extent. Most first children experience a struggle for several years during which time they are likely to exhibit selfishness, antagonism to other children, and failure to use their full capacities. These should not be seen as fixed traits, but as tendencies, which become more or less inflexible depending upon how the situation is handled within the family and community. In fact, the tendencies vary day by day, even hour by hour, as every parent knows who has felt the peace of having only one child in the house while the others are visiting friends. Nor are the tendencies necessarily fixed at a four- or an eight-year-old level. The unexpressed sense of injustice may be a factor in the later achievements of the eldest, who often demonstrates a capacity for responsible work and for understanding.

There are, of course, many other aspects of sibling interaction. By this brief reference to the jealousy problem I have been trying only to illustrate how changes in the family structure (in this case, a decrease in the importance of the extended family and a reduction in size of the immediate family) create new kinds of influences within the group. By being aware of such developments, a society may be better prepared to devise forms of interaction to deal with them.

The Lack of Normal Family Patterns

To the student of social structure, some of the most interesting aspects of family life are related, not to the kind of redefinition of roles that we have been discussing, but to the appearance of situations where a viable family system is almost lacking. In such a setting we see all too clearly the significance of the family for personality formation, for socialization—in short as an agent for the creation of adults able to live in the society around them and able to achieve personal satisfactions.

We are well aware of the extent to which family inadequacy is related to personality disorder, to prejudice, and to delinquency. The need for repression and projection that looms so large among the mentally disturbed can often be traced to a neglectful and cruel home, a setting in which self-acceptance is difficult to achieve. The most intense prejudices are frequently the displaced hostility generated in a frustrating family situation. In commenting on the life histories of prejudiced adults, Selma Hirsh writes:

> It is startling to see how often the anger expressed by the prejudiced adult turned out to be nearly as old as he was himself. Usually he had acquired it in the first years of his life when he was forced to learn the most difficult lessons life has to teach long before he could understand them. He had learned too early, for example, that instincts are not always for expression, that love is not necessarily reciprocal, that promises are not always fulfilled, nor punishments always just. Usually these were the first things he had learned, and since he had no other reassuring experiences to cushion him against the shock of their discovery, they had served for him as a lasting introduction to the ways of the world.[12]

The same constellation of ego-alienating and hostility-creating conditions may, of course, lead to delinquency. We speak more cautiously about the causes of delinquency than we did a few years ago. The influence of broken homes, of class status of the family, of neighborhood patterns is not so simple as it once seemed. The value of a home in reducing delinquency is exaggerated by the official statistics, since two children committing the same violation, one with a home, the other without, are often given different sentences. One may be sent home, the other given a police record. In his recent study, Nye found somewhat more delinquency from broken than from non-broken homes, but he wisely notes the need for more careful study of families that have been internally split without a formal break. He found a small but non-significant relationship between the employment of the mother and child delinquency.[13] Such a finding only accents the need for more study to isolate the conditions under which the changing patterns of women working affect family structure.

Although one must speak with caution, because of the intricate network of forces relating an individual to a family and a family to a community, few of us would doubt that many of the trends in our cities today are creating areas in which normal family patterns are very rare. The population of the large cities has been expanding by about 400,000 per year for the last several years, while housing for about 250,000 per year has been built. Since approximately that same amount of housing has been removed, our cities have been getting vastly more crowded. The 400,000 have to be absorbed somehow into a constant amount of housing.[14] The results are well known to all of us: division of houses into apartments, break-up of apartments into one-room units, absorption of additional families into already over-crowded quarters. As Morton Grodzins asks: "How does a mother keep her teen-age son off the streets if an entire family must eat, sleep and live in a single room? What utility can be found in sobriety among a society of drinkers and a block of taverns?" [15] We are talking about the richest nation in the world in the richest period of its history. This may be "the affluent society," but we are not even holding our own in creating a physical setting within which stable family life is possible.

Even the urban renewal programs are sometimes destructive of the lines of communication, the social groups, the political organizations of an area. The result is *anomie*—normlessness, except as the residents improvise a culture of their own. This often takes the form of a gang, whose style of life has recently been described as sub-cultural, but which might more appropriately be thought of as contra-cultural— as a contrast conception by means of which confused and relatively powerless persons try to create a set of values that will place them on top, at the same time that it makes their lowly status unimportant in terms of dominant values.

Conclusion

On many aspects of family analysis there are large areas of disagree-ment. On this basic fact, however, I imagine that all will agree: the family is, to a vital degree, the creature of its environment. Whenever value confusion, physical blight, and inadequate institutions are the rule, the family will be weak. Whenever social change imposes new requirements and new potentialities, but when revised role-definitions have not yet been worked out, intra-family tensions will mount. A family agency, which has an enormous job simply to work with some of the results of these forces, may nevertheless gain by stepping back from the job occasionally to see the family as part of the whole society.

We in the United States have not yet completed the shift from life in small, face-to-face, stable communities to life in the city. We are confronted with many cultural lags, not least of all in family matters. It is to such groups as family service agencies that we must look for the leadership and skill necessary not only for the amelioration of problems but also for the imaginative rebuilding of a family equipped for a changing society. If the short-run aim is to help families manage and reduce the tensions they carry, the long-run aim must be to prevent tensions from reaching an unmanageable level. To this end we must study the family in its total social context.

NOTES

1. Dwight Heath, "Sexual Division of Labor and Cross-Cultural Research," *Social Forces,* Vol. 38, No. 1 (1958), pp. 77–79.
2. Talcott Parsons and Robert F. Bales, *Family—Socialization, and Interaction Process,* Free Press, Glencoe, Ill., 1955, p. 9.
3. Mirra Komarovsky, "Cultural Contradictions and Sex Roles," *American Journal of Sociology,* Vol. 52, No. 3 (1946), p. 187.
4. William J. Goode, in Merton, Broom, and Cottrell, *Sociology Today,* Basic Books, New York, 1959, pp. 178–196. "The Theoretical Importance of Love," *American Sociological Review,* Vol. 24, No. 1 (1959), pp. 38–47.
5. Daniel Miller and Guy Swanson, *The Changing American Parent,* John Wiley and Sons, New York, 1958.
6. Martha Wolfenstein, "The Emergence of Fun Morality," *Journal of Social Issues,* Vol. VII, No. 4 (1951), pp. 15–25.
7. John Watson, *Psychological Care of Infant and Child,* 1914, pp. 81–82.
8. Clark Vincent, "Trends in Infant Care Ideas," *Child Development,* Vol. 22, No. 3 (1951), pp. 199–209.
9. Miller and Swanson, *op. cit.,* pp. 30–31.
10. David Riesman, *The Lonely Crowd,* Yale University Press, New Haven, 1950.
11. Martha Wolfenstein, in Mead and Wolfenstein, *Childhood in Contemporary Cultures,* University of Chicago Press, Chicago, 1955.
12. Selma Hirsh, *The Fears Men Live By,* Harper and Bros., New York, 1955, p. 110.
13. Francis Ivan Nye, *Family Relationships and Delinquent Behavior,* John Wiley and Sons, New York, 1958.
14. Editors of Fortune, *The Exploding Metropolis,* Doubleday, New York, 1958, p. 101.
15. Morton Grodzins, "The New Shame of Cities," *Confluence,* Spring, 1958, p. 40.

PART III

Forecasts & Predictions

Introduction

Man, individually and collectively, has always taken an acute interest in the control of his destiny. Buffeted by the impersonal forces of history, he has sought an understanding, however dim, of the interplay between events and personal experiences. In this sense, change has always been problematic, for change alters the interconnection between societal forces and individual biographies. As technological change has accelerated, especially since the turn of the century, the attempts to control the targets and consequences of alterations have become of critical importance. With the increasing realization that fate need not be impersonal, attention has turned to the problem of consciously planning change. The importance of this endeavor is all the more crucial since any given future change will affect not only an ever greater proportion of individuals but also will have an impact of an intersocietal nature in many cases.

In explaining current relationships and extrapolating to future events, the social sciences, each concerned with certain sets of social factors and social behavior, occupy a central position. It should be understood, however, that the social-scientific disciplines are not manifestly suited to the demands of this role. Essentially, the veracity of prediction and forecasting rests on numerous contingencies. Infrequently repeated phenomena, the presence of unanticipated conditions and factors, the degree of complexity involved in processes, and the time factor itself all vitiate the accuracy of our estimates of the future. It is hardly surprising, therefore, that many social-scientific forecasts (as well as those of astrologers) possess the character of "broken-clock predictions," for, as a French proverb has it, even the broken clock is right twice a day. Given the quantity of predictions, on the basis of probability, some will be accurate. Yet, within the analytical and methodological confines of the social sciences, sensitization to significant, influencing properties and trends enhances the accuracy of the probabilistic statements that may be made.

Forecasting alterations in the family, of course, is not new. Considerable attention was given the task by early philosophers, and particularly by nineteenth-century writers. But only since the 1930s have such efforts gained significantly in their rigorousness and objectivity. Because of the nature of the social values imputed to the family, however, subjective evaluations of familial change still abound. In addition, disagreement about the causes of these alterations, as we have seen, is common. One result has been that contradictory analyses, forecasts, and predictions are proliferous. In this respect, the selections contained in Part III are not exceptional.

In selection 20, Robert Parke, Jr., and Paul C. Glick, confining their analysis to a consideration of demographic characteristics, present a detailed portrait of selected demographic patterns. Noting the prevailing patterns of marriage and the family, they project some of the probable changes in these configurations to 1985. Basically, the authors predict: a decline in teen-age marriages, a reduction in the frequency of widowhood and an improvement in survival rates, a relative decline in the frequency of divorce, and some decline in the average size of families. They also point to major increases in the proportions of unmarried individuals maintaining their own households.

F. Ivan Nye (selection 21), examining various facets of the family and change, proposes that the concept of value, a frequently employed analytical concept, is far too broad for use in the study of change. Of greater heuristic utility, he suggests, are the subconcepts of instrumental value and intrinsic value. Change, it is maintained, occurs most rapidly and with the least resistance in properties that are instrumentally valued. Increasingly, more normative family behavior is accorded instrumental importance. As this occurs, innumerable latent consequences emerge. With regard to employment opportunities, for instance, it is probable that as equalization is approached the divorce rate will increase, child-care functions will be transferred to other agencies, the birth rate will continue to decline, and the marriage age for girls will probably increase.

Attributing the decline in the intrinsic valuation of family life to the loss of functions, increased mobility, the emphasis on achieved status, and the dominance of materialistic values, Charles W. Hobart (selection 22) argues that the resulting value conflict has brought about a decline in commitment to familial norms. Characterizing the modern family as a loosely knit group, confused and alienated, he contends that institutionally today's family is rapidly weakening. Even the residual functions of socialization and companionship are losing significance. Some trends suggest, though, that a value revolution is imminent, a revolution that Hobart sees as imperative for the preservation of the humanistic family. The future family, then, will be one with less explicit structure, comprised of highly individuated persons, emphasizing their intrinsic worth. Child rearing and the provision of positive affect, under these circumstances, will take on new dimensions. Expanded leisure time, above all, will permit more intense familial commitments and enhance the meaningfulness of these interpersonal relationships.

Responding to Hobart's interpretation, selection 23 (the editor) questions the viability of functional losses, increased mobility, the decline in ascribed relationships, and the ascendancy of materialistic values as causes of familial change. Examining recent evidence pertaining to these phenomena, it would appear that their role in altering the family and familial commitments is secondary. The decline in commitments to the family, if such a decline exists, seems to emerge from our orientation to tangible rewards. Due to the dominance of the economic institutional sphere and its interpenetration with other institutions, we are socialized in reward-seeking behavior that is difficult to compartmentalize and confine in other social relationships. Inevitably, premarital and marital relationships are affected. Our current dilemma, as a result, is how to alter the present character of familial rewards, which are largely affective in nature, to complement those provided in other institutionalized relationships. The solution to this dilemma, it is suggested, appears to lie in increased interdependence with the economic sphere, not in a revolution of societal values.

Selection 24, evaluating different methods of projecting future alterations, suggests that the portrayal of the family as a disintegrating institution without functional significance is unjustified. Delineating four methods of projection, Reuben Hill indicates that, despite inherent weaknesses and limitations in each approach, the use of these methods points to the continuance of a flourishing institution. All projections denote an accelerated upgrading in the amenities, increased flexibility in family organization, and improvement in planning and decision-making competence. Although all of these trends may appear to be systematically functional for the family, Hill cautions that the family's resiliency in a changing social order should not be taken for granted.

Clark E. Vincent (selection 25) argues that an industrialized society necessitates, in actuality, a highly adaptable and loosely organized family system.[1] Historically speaking, the survival of our family system, in view of its alteration of functions and the presence of rapid societal change, is a consequence of this flexibility. Given this condition, the family mediates between society's changing requirements and individuals. Through its strategic socialization function, the family institution is thus able either to impede or to further change initiated by external sources. In so doing, however, the family itself is frequently altered, for overadaptation is a common response to the internal and external expectations with which it is confronted. In the main, adaptation and flexibility are eufunctional, but with the multiplicity of demands made and adapted to, the "spongia" quality has dysfunctional aspects. By implication, future alterations in the family depend on its degree of adaptiveness, the number of societal demands placed upon it, and its continued lack of institutional organization.

Focusing explicitly on the relationship between the family and the economy, as manifested in the occupational structure, selection 26 by Robert Rapoport and Rhona Rapoport explores the proposition that work and family continue to become differentiated. It is suggested that as critical transitions in work and family roles are approached (such as making a career choice and getting married), task accomplishment in one area profoundly affects the other. Hence, work and marriage may not be as differentiated as commonly supposed.[2] Moreover, when transitions in the two spheres are concurrent, conflicts and stresses need not be multiplied. Task accomplishment in one area may have beneficial consequences in the other sphere. Increasingly, the authors point out, transitions in work and family relations are simultaneous. This permits a wider range of possibilities in the choice of both work and spouse. At the same time, there is greater latitude in organizing family life in relation to the prescriptions of jobs. What this ultimately means for the individuals involved is that personality will play an increasing role in the organization of one's family and career.

In selection 27, Lee G. Burchinal examines some of the general changes in urban-family patterns, the emerging prototype of the urban family, and present rural-urban differences in patterns. On this basis (and the premise that rural-family patterns follow those in urban areas), he extrapolates to the future and discusses possible alterations in the rural family. In particular, the convergence of rural-urban patterns seems imminent. Both family types are moving toward moderate size and similar fertility rates, family decision making does not appear to be very different, the networks of kinship ties are quite similar, and the differential in levels of education is declining. One of the most notable differences remaining between the two types concerns the norms governing marital and familial relationships. The diffusion of urban norms to rural families seems to pose the most severe adaptive problems in the changing milieu.

Reviewing various accomplishments in the field of biological research, the late Meyer F. Nimkoff (selection 28) discusses their implications for family behavior. He advances the notion that the discoveries in human biology will have a far greater impact on the family than future technological developments. Perhaps the most significant in this regard is the accumulation of knowledge pertaining to reproduction and the subsequent development of effective contraceptive means. Rapid advances also have been made in sex control, and, in some measure, in the control of sex characteristics and in alleviating the biological problems of aging. Further achievements in these areas depend on two factors—the amount of accumulated knowledge concerning them and the social demand for them. Nimkoff predicts that the greatest changes will take place in controlling the process of aging and in contraceptive control, each profoundly affecting the social psychology of the family.

Barrington Moore, Jr., in the final selection, forcefully argues that the family, seen in an evolutionary frame of reference, is possibly an obsolete institution. Focusing on some of the traditional functions of the family, such as socialization and the fulfillment of personality and affectional needs, Moore seriously questions the necessity of their being confined to this group.[3] Alternative institutional environments, he contends, may fulfill these tasks with greater efficiency and with a great deal less degradation of the individuals involved. Leaving aside the question of whether such an alteration in institutional arrangements is probable, this selection suggests we should give greater consideration to weighing the consequences of various alternatives.

If we are to assume a constant state of flux in the family institution, as seems warranted from the foregoing analyses, a crucial question is:

To what extent may the changing family preserve existing patterns of the social order? For the most part, sociologists have emphasized that a family system, regardless of variability in structure and function from one society to another, is essentially a conservative force in society. Through its functional focus on the socialization of the young, continuity and order are maintained over the generations. But if in the future we are confronted with an acceleration of structural alterations, reaching the revolutionary proportions predicted by some analysts, will the family be able to maintain its function of conservation? For example, the present tension between conservation and change, dramatically revealed in the problematic character of the socialization process, suggests increased difficulties in this regard. Rewards for the purveyance of traditions appear to be less certain and the generational lag between the initiation of change and subsequent modification, less extensive. And with the increased interdependence of the multipartite society comes ramified consequences, especially of a latent sort. As modifications occur in one segment of society, they are likely to trigger reactions and alterations in other sectors completely unforeseen as following from the initial changes.

One answer is that kinship groups, as some of the selections in Part I illustrate, maintain an unexpected viability in the face of continued societal alterations. While bilateral kin do not exercise pervasive control over the nuclear unit, they provide support, primarily affective in nature, that contributes to the maintenance of tradition. Various other societal conditions, pointed out in several selections in Part II, also operate in the direction of stability.[4] Thus, for example, the stratification system with its inherent vested interests serves as a point of continuity in a state of uncertain but constant change.

Another basis for maintenance, albeit an evolving one, is the fact that the family makes only the most expedient modifications and adaptations to a changing society. These changes, as brought out at several points in this section, are not sufficient to alter radically the rewards for preservative activities. Ideal behavioral patterns, although widely departed from, change less rapidly than actual behavior. While it may be true that the usual becomes the expected in a normative system, the time and generational lags between the adoption of actual patterns as the right modes of behavior indicate the existence of an inextricable, conservative force.

This simply means that, while change is an intrinsic part of a family system, elements of stability are always manifest. It does not follow, however, that all aspects of the family are subject to the same forces of change and stability or that these forces are felt with the same intensity. Some relationships are strongly buttressed by tradition, while others are subject to considerable strains and profoundly influenced by other societal patterns. To answer fully the question concerning the balance between alterations and order, it is necessary to specify those aspects of the family to be considered and those social forces that are applicable to such relationships. At this juncture, the full answer is still forthcoming.

NOTES

1. William Goode, *World Revolution and Family Patterns* (New York: Free Press, 1963), notes that most cultures, under the impetus of industrialization, are moving toward some variant of the conjugal system, a system that is presumably more adaptable.
2. Based on ethnographic data, a relationship has been noted between such economic factors as subsistence patterns and the amount of family property and family type. See Meyer F. Nimkoff and Russell Middleton, "Types of Family and Types of Economy," *American Journal of Sociology*, 66 (November 1960), pp. 215–225.
3. The Israeli kibbutz is again a case in point where a substantial part of the socialization process has been taken from the family. Other evidence suggests that child rearing by other than biological parents is not uncommon. See Beatrice B. Whiting (ed.), *Six Cultures: Studies in Child Rearing* (New York: John Wiley, 1963). Even in the cases cited in Whiting's book, the parents retain responsibility in providing for the emotional needs of their children. In fact, Ira L. Reiss claims that the provision of affection or "nuturant socialization" is the one universal function of the family; see Reiss, "The Universality of the Family: A Conceptual Analysis," *Journal of Marriage and the Family,* 27 (November 1965), pp. 443–453.
4. For a cross-national comparison of the factors influencing consistency in generational family ideology, see Glen H. Elder, Jr., "Role Relations, Sociocultural Environments, and Autocratic Family Ideology," *Sociometry,* 28 (June 1965), pp. 173–196.

20

Prospective Changes in Marriage and the Family*

by Robert Parke, Jr. & Paul C. Glick

Trends in Marriage and Stability of Marriage

Consideration of prospective changes in American families can begin with no more appropriate issue than what is happening to the age at marriage. This subject is of interest in its own right, partly because of concern over the number of teen-age marriages. In addition, the age at marriage significantly influences events in the middle and late stages of the family life cycle; it determines, in part, the age at which the wife's responsibilities for child-care have declined to the point where she is free to seek full-time employment and the probability that she and her husband will survive to enjoy life together after the husband retires.

Increasing Similarity of Marriage Ages

For several years Americans have married at an exceptionally young average age for an industrial society. Furthermore, American women marry men who are more nearly their own ages than is generally true elsewhere.[1]

* This is a slightly revised version of a paper prepared for presentation to the annual meetings of the American Sociological Association, Miami Beach, Florida, August 29 to September 1, 1966. Tabulation of part of the data in this paper was made possible by funds provided by the U.S. Public Health Service (Research Grant CH-00075, formerly GM-08262) to the American Public Health Association for a series of monographs on vital and health statistics.

This paper focuses on data for the total population; marriage patterns by race were the subject of a companion paper, entitled "Marital Status of the Nonwhite Population in 1970," by Daniel O. Price, in the same session of the 1966 A.S.A. meetings.

Reprinted from *Journal of Marriage and the Family*, 29 (May 1967), pp. 249–256, by permission of the authors and the National Council on Family Relations.

One of the striking features of recent trends in American marriage is the extent to which marriage patterns are becoming standardized.

First, nearly everyone gets married nowadays. The projections shown in Table 2 suggest that as few as three percent of the men and women now in their late twenties may enter middle age without having married. These proportions are one-third of the corresponding proportions actually experienced by persons who are now in late middle age.

Second, to a greater extent than before, young persons are getting married at about the same age. The reduction in the age at marriage has been accompanied by a compressing of marriages into a narrower age range than before. This is shown in Figure 1 and Table 1. Among the ever-married men now in late middle age, about eight years elapsed between the age by which the first one-fourth of the men had married and the age by which three-fourths had married. For men who are now in their late twenties, the corresponding figure is expected to be about five years. That is to say, even after the younger group of men have been exposed to another two decades of first marriage experience, the interquartile range of age at first marriage for this group is expected to be only about two-thirds of that for the older men. A corresponding trend has occurred among women. The interquartile range of age at first marriage experienced by the women who are now in late middle age was about seven years. This is expected to contract to about four years by the time the women who are now in their late twenties reach middle age.

Third, women are marrying men who are closer to their own ages. This observation is suggested by the declining difference between the median ages at first marriage for men and women shown in Table 1 and is confirmed by data from the 1960 Census, which showed the median difference between the age of the husband and the age of the wife for married couples in which both partners were married only once. Husbands over 55 years old in 1960 were 3.6 years older than their wives, on the average; while husbands under 35 were only 1.9 years older on the average. Forty-two percent of the older husbands were at least five years older than their wives, as compared with only 17 percent of the younger husbands.[2]

Marriage Age and Joint Survival

The lessening of the difference between the ages of the husband and wife causes a significant improvement in the chances of joint survival

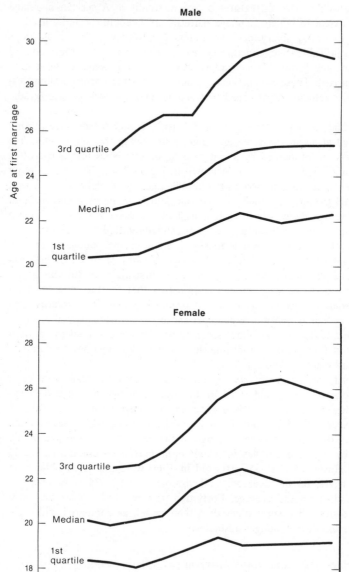

Figure 1
Median and Quartile Ages at First Marriage,
by Age in 1966 and Sex

Source: Table 1.

TABLE 1
Median and Quartile Ages at First Marriage, by Age in 1966 and Sex, for the United States: March, 1966*

AGE IN 1966	Male				Female			
	FIRST QUARTILE	SECOND QUARTILE (MEDIAN)	THIRD QUARTILE	INTERQUARTILE RANGE (YEARS)	FIRST QUARTILE	SECOND QUARTILE (MEDIAN)	THIRD QUARTILE	INTERQUARTILE RANGE (YEARS)
20–24	20.4†	—	—	—	18.4	20.2†	—	—
25–29	20.5	22.5	25.1‡	4.6	18.3	20.0	22.5	4.2
30–34	20.6	22.9	26.1	5.5	18.1	20.2	22.7	4.6
35–39	21.0	23.3	26.8	5.8	18.5	20.4	23.2	4.7
40–44	21.4	23.7	26.8	5.4	19.0	21.5	24.3	5.3
45–49	22.0	24.7	28.2	6.2	19.5	22.1	25.5	6.0
50–54	22.4	25.2	29.3	7.4	19.1	22.4	26.2	7.1
55–64	22.0	25.3	29.9	7.9	19.1	21.9	26.5	7.4
65–74	22.3	25.3	29.3	7.0	19.2	21.9	25.7	6.5

* *Note:* Based on data by single years of age in Table 2. Percent ultimately marrying used to calculate these values is percent first married before age 45 shown in Table 2. *Source:* Based on answers to March, 1966 Current Population Survey question on date of first marriage. The data cover the population of the United States, except for members of the armed forces living in barracks and similar quarters, who are not included in the survey.

† Experience during age 20 based on data for persons 21 to 24 years old in 1966.

‡ Experience during age 25 based on data for persons 26 to 29 years old in 1966.

of the married couple. Under mortality conditions prevailing in 1960, a woman who was married at age 20 to a man four years her senior ran a 42-percent chance of being widowed before age 65, assuming that she survived to that age. If she married a man only two years older than herself, her chances of widowhood before reaching 65 would be only 37 percent, and, if her husband were the same age as she, her chances of widowhood would be only 33 percent.

The joint survival of a married couple depends, of course, on a number of factors besides the difference between their ages. The foregoing figures assume no divorce, a fact which would not affect the interpretation if there is no fundamental change in the trend of the divorce rate; and the foregoing figures assume constant mortality conditions, whereas mortality conditions will likely change somewhat though probably not enough to negate the points being made. Nor do they take into account the effect of separation and desertion on the population of married couples; but, as indicated below, there seems actually to be a real likelihood that desertions will diminish, assuming that the educational and economic levels of the population improve over time.

However, the net effect of these factors over the past ten years has been such as to suggest substantial future increases in the proportion of persons living with their spouses in late middle age and in old age. For example, 64 percent of all women 55 to 64 years old were married and living with their (first or subsequent) husbands in 1965. According to experimental projections, the corresponding figure may increase eight points to 72 percent by 1985. The smaller increase of about three points that is projected for women over 65 nonetheless represents a substantial relative improvement over the current level of 34 percent in this age range.

Decline in Teen-Age Marriages

The public concern over the number of teen-age marriages has arisen because of the notorious instability of these marriages. The 1960 Census showed that, among the men who first married at age 18 during the period five to 15 years prior to the census, the first marriage was not intact at the time of the census in about 21 percent of the cases. This was twice as high as the proportion of not intact first marriages among men who first married at ages 23 to 24. A similar relationship was evident in the data for females.[3] (Nearly all such persons with first marriage not intact were divorced, separated, or remarried at the time of the census.)

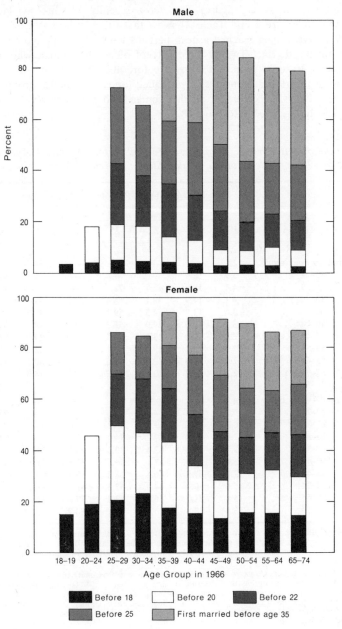

Figure 2
Percent of All Persons Who First Married Before
Specified Age, by Age in 1966 and Sex

Source: Table 2.

Actually, however, figures that have recently become available (shown in Figure 2 and Table 2) show that the marriage rate among very young women reached a peak perhaps ten to 15 years ago and is now on the decline. Twenty-three percent of all the women who are currently 30 to 34 years old married before age 18. The rate of early teen-age marriages is successively smaller for each younger group of women. Only 15 percent of all the women who are currently 18 and 19 years old married before age 18.

TABLE 2

Percent of All Persons Who First Married Before Specified Age, by Age in 1966 and Sex, for the United States: March, 1966*

AGE IN 1966	Percent of All Persons in Age Group Who First Married Before Age—						
	18	20	22	25	30	35	45†
Male							
18 and 19 year olds	2.9	—	—	—	—	—	—
20–24	3.9	18.4	—	—	—	—	94.7
25–29	4.4	18.5	42.5	72.2	—	—	96.7
30–34	4.1	17.9	38.1	65.4	84.0	—	95.3
35–39	3.6	13.8	34.3	59.3	81.1	88.7	93.6
40–44	3.3	12.0	29.9	58.3	81.3	88.3	93.1
45–49	2.2	8.8	23.3	49.5	79.7	89.5	94.1
50–54	2.5	8.4	19.7	43.5	71.1	83.9	90.7
55–64	2.6	9.6	22.5	42.6	67.1	80.1	89.1
65–74	2.1	8.7	20.1	41.8	69.0	78.8	87.8
Female							
18 and 19 year olds	14.7	—	—	—	—	—	—
20–24	19.1	45.6	—	—	—	—	95.5
25–29	20.3	48.8	69.1	85.2	—	—	97.2
30–34	22.9	46.7	67.2	84.0	92.8	—	97.1
35–39	17.1	42.9	63.4	80.3	90.5	93.7	95.9
40–44	15.0	33.0	53.1	76.1	87.8	91.6	95.0
45–49	12.8	27.8	46.4	68.3	85.4	91.0	94.1
50–54	15.6	30.1	44.0	63.6	81.2	88.7	93.0
55–64	15.4	31.7	46.3	62.2	77.6	84.8	90.7
65–74	13.5	28.8	45.3	64.2	80.7	85.8	89.6

* *Source:* Based on answers to March, 1966 Current Population Survey question on date of first marriage. The data cover the population of the United States, except for members of the armed forces living in barracks and similar quarters, who are not included in the survey.

† For persons under 45 years old in 1966, the percent first married by age 45 was projected on the assumption that the rate of first marriage per 1,000 single persons between the current age and age 45 will be the same as observed between corresponding ages among persons 45 to 49 years old in 1966. See John Hajnal, "Age at Marriage and Proportions Marrying," *Population Studies,* 7:2 (November, 1953), p. 115, for method of calculation.

Extremely young age at marriage has never been very widespread among men. Thus, the proportion of men who married before age 18 appears to have been no greater than four percent for any of the age groups shown. Even so, the percent of very young marriages among men who are now in their late twenties was twice as high as it was among men now in their forties, and there is evidence of a recent downturn in this percent among men who are now in their late teens.

This may or may not portend a downturn in the percent of all men who marry under age 20, which rose in recent years from nine percent for the men who are now in their late forties to a stable level of around 18 percent for the men who are now under 35.

The recent downward trend in teen-age marriages among women may be in part a response to the changing ratio of males to females in the marriageable ages. If so, this has interesting implications for the pattern of age at marriage in the next few years.

The "Marriage Squeeze"

Because of past changes in the annual number of births and because women marry men who are two or three years their senior, on the average, there has been, in the past few years, a drop in the number of males per 100 females in the main marrying ages. By the main marrying ages, the authors mean those between the first and third quartile ages at first marriage according to recent experience, or approximately ages 18 to 22 for females and 20 to 24 for males.

In the early 1950's there were, in the average year, about 104 males per 100 females in the main marrying ages. In the late 1950's this ratio had dropped to 99 per 100, and in the early 1960's it was only 94. In the latter half of the 1960's, it will average only about 93 and will subsequently return to 99 per 100 in the early 1970's.[4]

These figures describe, in broad terms, the "marriage squeeze" that has resulted from the fact that the girls born in the postwar baby boom have come of age (for purposes of marriage) sooner than the boys.

Generally speaking, the squeeze can be resolved in any or all of several ways: by the boys marrying for the first time at younger ages or by the girls marrying for the first time at older ages or marrying older widowed and divorced men or older single men who might not otherwise have married. Or it is possible that more girls will ultimately not marry at all.

Any of these ways out of the squeeze involves a sequence of changes in age at marriage and in the difference between the ages of the husband and wife. The evidence so far available suggests that, in the first half of the 1960's, the marriage squeeze was resolved in large part by changes in the marriage patterns of the women and not by alteration of the trend of ages at first marriage for men. The data in Figures 1 and 2 show no acceleration in the downward trend of male ages at first marriage. This fact may be construed as implying that, up to now, the young men have been successfully warding off any pressure from the mounting numbers of marriageable young women.

The marriage squeeze will continue for perhaps a decade. If the pattern of ages for men at marriage from 1965 to 1975 is like that observed in the first half of the 1960's, then about a million women will have to postpone getting married (Table 3). This figure represents

TABLE 3

*Test Projections of Marriages in the United States: 1965 to 1985 * (In Millions)*

Period (Beginning and Ending July 1)	Total Marriages in Period, Assuming Continuation of 1959 to 1964 Rates for:		Difference
	MALES	FEMALES	
1965–1970	9.3	9.9	.6
1970–1975	10.7	11.2	.5
1975–1980	11.9	12.3	.4
1980–1985	12.6	12.7	.1

* *Source:* See text.

the difference between (a) the number of women who would get married if marriages followed the rates observed for females from 1959 to 1964 and (b) the number who would marry if the number of marriages were governed by the observed marriage rates for males. If such a postponement occurred, it would force the lifetime age at first marriage up about one-third of a year for the women who enter the marriage ages during this period. Such an increase would represent a continuation of the rise in the female age at first marriage that has been observed since the late 1950's.[5]

Of course, in the next few years the tide may turn so that the women, rather than the men, will have their way. Thus, if the girls persuade the boys to marry prematurely, by the standards of recent years, there will be more marriages and more young husbands than otherwise.

More Marriages Remaining Intact

The preceding discussion already suggested the extent to which marital dissolution due to widowhood will be reduced by recent reductions in the difference between the ages of the husband and wife. Additional changes toward more marriages remaining intact may be expected as a natural result of the anticipated continuation in the upgrading of the population with respect to income inasmuch as separation and divorce are less extensive among the affluent than among the poor.[6]

Hollywood to the contrary notwithstanding, statistics from the 1960 Census provide further confirmation of the fact that stability of marriage is a condition that is shared less by the lower-status segments of the population than by the rest.

TABLE 4

Persons Per Household and Family in the United States, 1940 to 1966, and Test Projections for 1985 *

	Persons per Household			Persons per Family		
YEAR	ALL AGES	UNDER 18	18 AND OVER	ALL AGES	UNDER 18	18 AND OVER
1940	3.7	1.1	2.5	3.8	1.2	2.5
1950	3.4	1.1	2.3	3.5	1.2	2.4
1960	3.3	1.2	2.1	3.7	1.4	2.3
1966	3.3	1.2	2.1	3.7	1.4	2.3
1985	3.1	1.1	1.9	3.5	1.4	2.2

* *Source:* See text.

The special reports of the 1960 Census on *Marital Status* and *Age at First Marriage* devoted much attention to social and economic analysis of the patterns of marriage and dissolution of marriage among men 45 to 54 years old, a group that has reached its peak earning capacity and among whom few additional first marriages will occur. There were one and a half million ever-married white men in this age group with incomes of less than $3,000, and more than two million with incomes of $10,000 or more. Fully 29 percent of the poor men, but only 16 percent of the affluent men, were no longer living with their first wives at the time of the census. The corresponding relationship was even more striking among nonwhites than it was for whites.[7] These differences are too great to be attributed solely to socioeconomic differences in the proportion of men whose wives have died. It follows that these differences reflect, in part, socioeconomic differences in divorce and separation.[8] Barring a rise in the divorce rate or major changes in the pattern of divorce and separation by socioeconomic status, the reduction of poverty should result in a substantial long-term improvement in the average stability of marriages.

This expectation is expressed with slight reservations in view of the increases over the past few years in the percent of the population who are divorced. A recent Census Bureau report shows the following age-standardized percentages of divorced persons in the population 14 years old and over:[9]

YEAR	MALE	FEMALE
1966	2.2	3.1
1965	2.2	2.9
1960	1.9	2.6
1955	1.8	2.3

However, these increases do not necessarily imply the existence of a rising divorce rate, nor is there independent evidence of such. A stable divorce rate may produce an increasing accumulation of divorced persons in the population unless remarriage is universal and instantaneous. This it is not, although remarriage rates for divorced persons are high. Glick estimated that about three-fourths of the persons who were divorced from 1943 to 1948 had remarried by 1948.[10]

Family Size and Living Arrangements

Reference has been made to estimated future marriages and changes in the marital status of the population. These projections, and the ones to follow, are test calculations that have been produced in the course of work at the Bureau of the Census toward the preparation of a new set of household and family projections. These projections have been prepared in order to examine the effect of various assumptions on estimates for the future. They do not constitute official projections of the Bureau of the Census. They do represent a few among a variety of plausible or instructive ways of expressing the implications that recent trends may have for the future.

The family structure of the future is studied here by means of statistics on anticipated trends in the living arrangements of the population. In these figures, marriages have been projected by assuming that the marriage rates of 1959 to 1964 will continue and by imposing the condition that the number of marriages will be the average of the number projected separately for men and women. It is assumed further that the living arrangements of the population (as measured by percent living in families, percent maintaining their own households, etc.) will continue to change at the same rate at which they changed from 1957 to 1964. The population assumed in these projections is the Census Bureau's Series B. The results of one set of such assumptions are set forth in Tables 4 and 5.

Adults Per Household Declining

These results indicate a continued decline in the average number of adults per household and family and little change in the average number of children.[11] The figures express the average size of households and families in terms of the number of persons living together at any one point in time. The 1966 figures on children, for instance, refer to the average number now living in the household or family and not to the number born. Furthermore, the numbers of households and families include those with no children as well as those with children.

The 1985 estimate of 2.2 adults per family is very close to a minimum average. It is subject to substantial further reduction only by further reducing the number of offspring over the age of 17 who live with their parents. The average number of adults per family cannot fall much below two, since nearly nine out of ten families include a husband and wife.

The average size of household declines a small amount in the test projections; however, the relative decline is slightly greater than that for the average family size. The average size of household is smaller to begin with because it takes into account persons who live alone and maintain their own home. This average is subject to greater potential decline than the average family size, because there are still many people who potentially might set up housekeeping by themselves who have not yet done so. Moreover, there is a strong prospect for further household formation from this source if the projections in Table 5 prove to be well founded.

Increasing Headship Among Individuals

In 1965 about 78 percent of the married couples and individuals who might have maintained their own household were actually doing so. An *individual* who might maintain his own household is defined, for present purposes, as anyone 20 years old and over who is not "married with spouse present" and is not an inmate of an institution. The category includes heads of broken families, persons living alone, adult children and relatives in the home, lodgers, and other persons who live with a relative or share the living accommodations of someone else, and persons in rooming houses and other group quarters.

TABLE 5

*Percent of Married Couples and Individuals
with Their Own Households, for the United States, 1965,
and Test Projections for 1985**

| | Percent with Own Household | | |
Type of Unit and Year	TOTAL, AGE 20 AND OVER	20 TO 64	65 AND OVER
Married couples and individuals			
1965	78	78	79
1985	86	84	90
Married couples			
1965	98	98	98
1985	99	99	99
Individuals†			
1965	51	45	66
1985	64	56	84

* *Source:* See text.
† All persons except married, spouse present, and inmates of institutions.

No substantial increase in the number of separate households can result from an increase in the propensity of married couples to maintain their own households, since 98 percent already do so. However, only half the eligible individuals were maintaining their own households in 1965. Recent trends suggest that this figure may rise to two-thirds of the eligible individuals by 1985. The increase anticipated among individuals at age 65 and over is fairly striking, rising as it does from 66 to 84 percent of the eligibles. Medicare and other social programs may cause this to rise even further by making it possible for higher proportions of aged relatives who now share the homes of children to be self-sustaining or to remove themselves from the population of eligibles, as here defined, by entering a nursing home.

Conclusion

A review of recent trends in marriage and family statistics provides a basis for the following expectations, if one keeps in mind the foregoing qualifications:

1. Persons now in their late twenties and their early thirties are more likely to marry at some time in their lives than any other group on record.

2. The rate of teen-age marriage, which is now on the decline, will continue to go down for a while, then level off.

3. The relative oversupply of young women will tend to produce a further rise in the next ten years in the age at which women marry for the first time.

4. The compression of marriages into a narrow age range will cause marriage and household formation to be somewhat more responsive than before to changes in the number of past births from which the marrying population comes.

5. Over and above any general decline in mortality, the declines in the difference between the ages of the husband and wife will reduce the frequency of widowhood and increase the proportion of couples who survive jointly to retirement age.

6. Declines in the relative frequency of divorce and separation should result to the extent that there are reductions in poverty and general improvements in the socioeconomic status of the population.

7. The small average size of American families (in terms of related persons sharing the same living quarters) will not change very much, but the average number of adult members may come very close to a minimum size. Greater changes are likely to develop only if there are major changes in the average number of children in the home.

8. Nearly all married couples now maintain their own households. In addition, there is a good prospect that within the next 20 years five out of every six aged individuals not in institutions will keep house on their own, and more than half the adult individuals of other ages will do so.

In closing, it is acknowledged that here and there the observations presented have gone a step or two beyond the projections. Furthermore, the future patterns could actually veer off in new directions not anticipated in the projections. However, there is reason to expect that further development of the program for preparing marriage and family projections, and improvements in the data available, will make it possible to reduce the area of uncertainty and to provide prompt corrections of future readings so as to bring them in line with current developments.

NOTES

1. Based on comparisons of average age at first marriage for males and females. Except as noted, "marriage" in this paper refers to first marriage; in recent years about four-fifths of all marriages in the United States have been first marriages. For comparative data on the United States and selected European countries, see John Hajnal, "Age at Marriage and Proportions Marrying," *Population Studies,* 7:2 (November, 1953), pp. 119 and 120, Tables 5 and 6. In addition, several recent volumes of the United Nations *Demographic Yearbook* have included comparative statistics on marital status and on number of marriages, by age.

2. See *1960 Census of Population,* Final Report PC(2)-4E, *Marital Status,* Table 9, p. 151. To be sure, the younger men have had less opportunity than the older men to marry women who are five or more years younger than themselves. This is true even though the foregoing figures exclude second and later marriages. The biasing effect of this fact on the foregoing comparison is, however, probably compensated in large part by the fact that, by the time of the census, the marriages of the older men had been subject to years of selective attrition through divorce and widowhood with the result that the proportion of the older couples in which the husband was much older than the wife would have been much smaller than it was in the marriages of the original cohort. The facts in the paragraph following illustrate the faster than normal attrition by death of those couples in which the husband is considerably older than the wife. For evidence of a similar effect attributable to divorce, see Thomas P. Monahan, "Does Age at Marriage Matter in Divorce?" *Social Forces,* 32:1 (October, 1953), pp. 81–87.

3. See *1960 Census of Population,* Final Report PC(2)-4D. *Age at First Marriage,* Table 10.

4. Data for 1950 to 1964 were based on the U.S. Bureau of the Census, *Current Population Reports,* Series P-25, Nos. 311 and 314. Data for 1965 to 1974 were derived, on the assumption of no mortality or net immigration, from population estimates by single years of age for 1965 shown in Series P-25, No. 286.

5. The difference between the figures in the first two columns of Table 3 continues to 1975–1980, even though the sex ratio in the main ages at marriage returns to near balance in the early 1970's. This is in part because the ratio of men to women in selected ages does not adequately describe the relative availability of marriageable men and women of all ages and, in part, because marriage patterns over a period of years

affect the proportions of single persons in ways that are not taken account of in ratios that include all persons regardless of marital status. However, the apparent discrepancy is being made the subject of further study.

6. Furthermore, to the extent that poverty and unfavorable health conditions are deterrents to initial marriage or remarriage, the reduction of poverty and the improvement of health conditions in the future should increase the proportion who marry and the proportion who remarry. Available statistics on the relationship between socioeconomic status, health, and marriage are discussed in a monograph in preparation by Hugh Carter and Paul C. Glick, *Marriage and Divorce: A Social and Economic Study,* forthcoming.

7. The data are set forth in *1960 Census of Population,* Final Report PC(2)-4E, *op. cit.,* Table 6.

8. To assert the contrary is to imply extraordinary socioeconomic differences in the mortality of the wives. Suppose that 4.6 percent of the affluent white men were widowed. (This is an average figure based on white female mortality between ages 22 and 47 as given in 1950 life tables.) Subtracting this figure from the 16.2 percent who were not living with their first wives leaves 11.6 percent as the estimate of unstable marriages. If it be asserted that the same rate of instability characterized the marriage of the poor men, then the implied widowhood rate among these men is given by

$$28.7 - 11.6 = 17.1$$

where 28.7 is the percent of ever-married poor men not living with their first wives. The implied mortality of the poor wives is, therefore, nearly four times that assumed for the affluent wives. The present writers know of no reason to believe such a figure. The ratio of death rates among wives of the poor to those among wives of the affluent is more likely to be on the order of two to one according to the findings of Hauser and Kitagawa as reported in the *Washington Post,* July 10, 1966, page M3.

9. *Current Population Reports,* Series P-20, No. 159.

10. Paul C. Glick, "First Marriages and Remarriages," *American Sociological Review,* 14:6 (December, 1949), p. 733.

11. A household is all the occupants of a housing unit and may consist of one person living alone, a family and any lodgers, a few persons sharing an apartment, etc. A family consists of two or more related persons living in the same household.

2 1

Values, Family, and a Changing Society*

by F. Ivan Nye

The writer has felt that value is a key concept for understanding human behavior, whether it be on the individual, family, or societal level. On the societal level, if the value system of other nations could be adequately understood, international communications would be greatly facilitated, and one source of conflict removed. At the family level, if an adequate measure of the values relevant to the family could be constructed and spouses could be matched with respect to those values, conflict in marriage could be reduced, perhaps greatly.

The writer's continuing interest in values received a strong impetus three years ago when he had the pleasure of attending a national workshop of family life specialists. The conference theme was values in family life. At that interesting conference, a number of participants stated that the major task of action agencies is *to change* the values of families, while others deplored the fact that family values are changing, and still others felt that family values had not changed and would not change.

On that occasion it seemed that the two principal groups, those attempting to change family values and those who were attempting to prevent them from changing, were, in part, talking past each other. One of the exponents of change, for example, wanted to increase the value that rural parents place on the education of their children. Those opposing change of family values probably would not have been opposed to this but were probably thinking of other types of values, such as the decline in the feeling of responsibility of children for the care of aged parents.

* This article is a revised version of the Presidential Address, presented at the Annual Meeting of the National Council on Family Relations, Minneapolis, Minnesota, October 29, 1966. Work was conducted under Project 1792 of the College of Agriculture's Research Center of Washington State University, supported by a grant from the Welfare Administration, Department of Health, Education, and Welfare.

Reprinted from *Journal of Marriage and the Family,* 29 (May 1967), pp. 241–248, by permission of the author and the National Council on Family Relations.

It is suggested, therefore, that the word "value" conjures up a variety of images in the minds of people who employ or hear the term and that within this variety of meanings there are two that are conceptually different. These will be referred to as "instrumental" and "intrinsic" values.

What Is Meant by Values?[1]

Before proceeding to two major categories of values, the writer feels that it is only fair to communicate the general image of values in his mind. By value, he means a high-level abstraction which encompasses a whole category of objects, feelings, and/or experiences. Thus, if one says that he places a high value on education, he means more than the fact that he wants each of his children to earn at least a bachelor's degree. He means that he places a high value on all kinds of educational experiences and, other matters being equal, feels that the more education, the better. He is likely to support bond issues for new school facilities, scholarships for capable needy students, Operation Headstart, and any other program which appears to hold a good possibility for broadening educational opportunity or increasing the amount of education that citizens of this and other countries can obtain. Finally, it means that he will welcome and seek opportunities for continuing his own education in almost any way possible. Thus, to value something is to have a diffuse desire for a whole class of objects, feelings, and/or experiences either for oneself, for others, or for both.

To the writer, value has one other very important meaning, and that is its hierarchical characteristic. A person desires one class of objects or experiences more than another. Some of the pacifists have said, "Better Red than dead." Their opposites have replied, "Better dead than Red." Both have eloquently expressed the hierarchy of their values with respect to war and communism. The image, then, in the mind of the speaker with reference to values has two aspects: It is a desire for a broad category of objects, feelings, or experiences (or, if a negative value, a wish to avoid these); and it explicitly or implicitly involves a ranking of such categories. Values can be held for oneself, for special categories of others, for the society, or for mankind as a whole.[2] Likewise they are held by individuals, groups, societies, and perhaps by mankind.

Values and Closely Related Concepts

When one examines a concept, it is necessary not only to say what one means but also what one does not mean; that is, to distinguish it from closely related concepts, in this instance, goal, norm, and attitude.

It is not difficult to distinguish value from goal, the latter being a specific object or event within a broader category of objects that are valued. Thus, one with a high value on economic security sets a goal of $10,000 for his savings account.

The distinction from norm is considerably more difficult. A norm is a pattern of expected behavior, deviations from which result in sanctions against the individual. Normative behavior is rewarded, although less obviously than deviation from norms is punished. Is normative behavior positively valued? Clearly it is. Therefore, norms have a value aspect. Is the opposite true—that values per se are subject to sanctions? The answer appears to be no. For example, one may place a high value on travel, but, if he does not, no one will punish him for it. Furthermore, values are mental phenomena rather than behavior, and one cannot be punished for what he thinks. Thus, there is an adequate distinction between values and norms in that norms are behavior patterns, while values are mental phenomenon; and deviation from norms results in sanctions, whereas holding a set of values does not.[3]

The distinction between values and attitudes is perhaps the most difficult of all. Instead of saying that one places a high value on education, one can say he is favorable toward education and mean some of the same things.[4] However, attitude does not specifically indicate how the hierarchal relationship of this class of experiences compares with another, for example, health. One can say that he places a higher value on a stimulating job than he does on job security. This is an awkward statement if one tries to substitute attitude for value. In this perspective, value largely includes the content of attitude but adds the hierarchal arrangement of properties into those that are more desired or more disliked.[5]

Instrumental Values

It is evident that the concept of value is broad and multidimensional. In order to be useful in any specific context, it must be broken into component concepts. If one is to employ it as an aspect of family change, he is well advised to specify it in terms of classes of properties whose desirability changes with changes in other institutions or in other family properties, in contrast with those whose desirability changes little, if at all.[6] In order to specify this dimension of values, two subconcepts will be employed, "instrumental value" and "intrinsic value."

By instrumental value, the writer means the desirability which becomes attached to an object, experience, or event because the property has become identified as necessary or effective in producing an outcome desired by the individual or the society. As an example, again consider the value currently placed on education. Why is education receiving ever increasing financial support and stressed ever more strongly by societal leaders? Industry needs educated workers, most educated men can obtain steady employment, educated men earn more money, and so on. Educated people are better prepared, it is believed, to act intelligently as citizens. In each instance, education is valued not intrinsically, but because it is seen (with considerable accuracy) as instrumental in preventing individual and social problems or in achieving some desired goals.

To shift attention for a moment to an example of family behavior, there is considerable negative value attached to very early marriage— say 16 or younger for girls and 18 or younger for boys. What goes on here? Are the pleasures and satisfactions of marriage to be denied to people because they are young? Is society prejudiced against youth? The writer believes not, but the dissolution rate of marriages increases 50 percent with each two-year decrease in the age of the bride if one starts with brides in the 20–22-year category. Thus, negative value attaches to very early marriages because of the outcomes, namely,· marital dissolution, unhappiness of the spouses, and, frequently, economic dependency of the wife and children.

Intrinsic Values[7]

If instrumental value is that which attaches itself to properties that become identified with the successful attainment of certain ends, then how shall intrinsic values be viewed? First, it should be recorded that the writer decided to employ this term after considering several alternatives. "Ultimate values" was considered but seemed to have some religious or mystical connotations. "Outcome values" seemed to be too limited and suggest a mechanical connection with some determinant. "Terminal values" was attractive intellectually, but one colleague observed that she associated it with funerals! By contrast, "intrinsic" means exactly what is to be discussed here—objects, events, and experiences that are valued for their own sake without reference to still other consequences which flow from them. Only a few examples of intrinsic values will be offered. For one reason, the writer does not know very much about them! However, some nebulous ideas which are not necessarily original will be offered. Life itself is a cornerpiece among intrinsic values, and the writer is inclined to put freedom from continuous pain and major physical disability and chronic illness with it. Autonomy—to be free to choose one's activities, residence, friends, and ideas—is another. Some intrinsic values are better stated negatively, such as to be free of severe mental illness or chronic fear and anxiety. Finally, to love and be loved are such values. It is evident even from this short list that as individuals or societies pursue and realize one of these values, they are likely to deliberately or unknowingly forego others. But, despite the difficulty of identifying intrinsic values and the inevitability of some conflict among them, they provide criteria by which behavior patterns possessing instrumental value will be assessed.

What Is Instrumental, What Intrinsic?

To this point the attempt has been made to distinguish two types of values, instrumental and intrinsic, and it has been proposed that the values differ in terms of social change. Instrumental values change as new social inventions provide more efficient arrangements for achieving goals or as alterations in other segments of the society result in the increase or decrease of the value of a given object or social practice. For example, education is more widely valued now than it was 50 years ago. However, if these concepts are to be worthwhile, it must be possible not only to distinguish them at the conceptual level but, with some reliability, to assign given values to the instrumental or intrinsic category. This need not mean that the property be entirely one or the other. The current high value on education has been assigned to the instrumental category, and the writer believes it can be defended as primarily instrumental. Some value, however, is placed on knowledge for its own sake; it is better to be informed than ignorant, most would agree. As the attempt is made to define an aspect of the family in terms of its instrumental or intrinsic value, it should be remembered that, for some people or in some part, the property may have one or the other value aspect.

One phenomenon of family life presently and always in the news is that of sexual intercourse between unmarried persons. A negative value has been assigned to this behavior, or, to phrase it differently, a high value has been placed on chastity. The predominant value here appears to be instrumental. Society as an acting unity and most groups and individuals within it see "premarital intercourse" as likely to produce illegitimate children, forced early marriages (many of which end in divorce and economic dependency), and a variety of insecurity and anxiety feelings. Those who favor it bestow *positive* instrumental value, seeing it as correlated with mental health, a more sane choice of marital partners, and less hostile relationships between the sexes. However, what apparently is a minority of society's members place an intrinsic value—negative or positive—on sexual intercourse between unmarried persons. A few (probably more women than men and probably more ministers than social scientists) take the view that sexual relationships between persons not married are intrinsically wrong— that they violate the will of the Deity or that in some metaphysical sense they are wrong, regardless of the consequences which typically flow from them. On the other extreme are a few who maintain that sexual intercourse (including between persons not married to each other) is intrinsically good. One of our members has secured a unique spot for himself among family authors with a single expression—"Sex is fun and more sex is more fun." [8]

It has been suggested that for most Americans the practice of sexual intercourse between persons not married has an instrumental, negative value. It is usually opposed because of the costs of the outcomes both to individuals and society.

For another, but less emotionally charged, example, two generations ago a high value was placed on obedience of children to the rules and wishes of parents. In more remote epochs a child could be put to death for disobedience. What was so important about being obedient? First, in large families order must be maintained with minimum effort. Many tasks—unpleasant and/or boring—had to be performed by children, and this could be achieved only through strict obedience. In old age the parent had to depend on the child for sustenance. Finally, the world was a simple one, not yet changing rapidly, in which the parent was qualified to instruct the young in all aspects of social behavior. What has happened to the high value on child obedience? It has declined radically. In fact, the educated parent is likely to look askance at the entirely obedient child as one who has been brainwashed or intimidated. Why has this radical change occurred? The answer appears to lie in the changed social world.

No longer is the large family dominant with an overriding need to maintain order with minimum expenditure of time; no longer is the child's labor crucial; no longer will the parent be dependent on his children in old age; no longer is the world composed of a few unskilled or semiskilled occupations and predictable social relations; no longer is social control, imposed from without, a sufficient guide for the individual. Now, in a world which is complex and changing rapidly, unquestioning obedience is not an appropriate guide. Instead, self-controls within the individual and the ability to choose are crucial. Now a world exists in which each individual is more free to pursue his own tastes and interests, if he knows their essence. Gone then is the value on strict obedience to parents, never to return unless society itself should reverse its course and return to a more simple, undifferentiated, and static state more typical of early periods in the history of advanced societies. In place of strict obedience are generalized values on respecting the rights of others and of earning one's way in the world—values presumably more instrumental in achieving goals in the society of today and what is envisioned as that of tomorrow. Obedience to parents had a high instrumental value only a short time ago, but major changes both within the family and in the other social institutions have left this practice meaningless. It has been seen that when the practice outlasted its utility it was quickly abandoned, with the only tears shed by those who ascribed intrinsic rather than instrumental value to it or who continued to think in terms of past decades when it was highly utilitarian.

Another current family complex which may be instrumental in terms of one intrinsic value but may block the realization of another[9] is the value on strong families or on "strengthening families." Sociologically, a strong family is one that takes precedence over the goals, values, and interests of its group members. The image conjured up is of families that share tasks, play together, pray together, and sacrifice individual needs and interests for those of other members of the family. How does this realize intrinsic values? Its essence seems to be a socioeconomic security system for family members, which guarantees the minimum needs for companionship and material needs. Furthermore, it makes few, if any, demands on the society as a whole, since it attempts to take care of its physical and psychological cripples without outside assistance.

The strong family is instrumental in realizing the security values of family members, but at what cost? Society provides innumerable cases of older children who give up higher education to take unskilled jobs to support a mother and younger siblings or a daughter who foregoes marriage to care for an invalid parent. The contemporary family provides innumerable cases of a wife who bakes in the sun or is devoured by mosquitoes while the husband seeks an elusive trout. The strong family often takes its pound of flesh from family members in terms of sacrificed individual goals, interests, recreation, and social relationships outside the family. In an economically poor society, a strong family provides protections and minimum security which may not be available in any other way. In a prosperous one in which there is considerable provision for individual security from the state, "strengthening the family" must be evaluated not only in terms of what it *provides for* but in what it may *take from* family members.[10]

To return to the negative value on sexual intercourse between unmarried persons, the formal and informal proscriptions against sex outside marriage have been instrumental in reducing several negatively valued outcomes, such as illegitimacy, forced marriages, and subsequent personal unhappiness and social problems. The societal rules and social pressures against intercourse between the unmarried have always blocked or severely restricted some experiences and feelings which appear to be intrinsically valued. Among these are freedom of the individual (in this specific instance, freedom to enter into this intimate relationship with the other sex) and opportunities to satisfy needs for love and emotional security. These experiences and feelings of intrinsic value have been ignored insofar as the society and most groups within it are concerned.

Recently, however, more permissive, sympathetic and supportive attitudes have become prevalent in American society. This permissiveness seems attributable in part to the new contraceptive devices. The evidence is strong that premarital sexual intercourse has increased, partly as a consequence of these new attitudes. The result, however, has not been a lessening of, but an increase in, the personal and social problems—especially unwanted pregnancies—always associated with intercourse between the unmarried. The causal chain seems to go this way: increased value on experiences associated with sex outside marriage, lessened negative values on consequences of intercourse, more intercourse outside marriage, more premarital pregnancies and associated personal and social problems. Notably lacking from this chain is any more effective use of contraceptive devices by the unmarried.

The greater tolerance for intercourse among the unmarried has *not* taken the form of social action to make sterility pills readily accessible to unmarried women. In the writer's state, at least, these pills are still on medical prescription which is generally limited to married women. The single woman who wishes to guard against a possible pregnancy must take some married woman into her confidence in order to obtain help.

Perhaps the seeming lack of congruence between increased tolerance of intercourse among the unmarried and the continued denial of the effective means of preventing unwanted pregnancies lies in the nature of the instrumental value held by a majority of the members of the society. It does not appear to the majority as a positive value, but as a weakened or diluted negative one. Most would hesitate to advise a teen-age person to make sexual intercourse outside of marriage a continuous part of his life, especially if the teen-ager were a girl. If the young are determined to do so as a result of their own decision, most professional persons are likely to be supportive rather than punitive if adolescents get into trouble. It is only a small, although sometimes vocal, group of either professionals or lay persons ready to crusade for change in the social structure which would make regular sexual intercourse between the unmarried an accepted and expected aspect of American life. Lifting of the taboos on the possession of the means of contraception by unmarried women may come, but if so it is more likely in the context of minimizing the negative consequences of sexual intercourse rather than implementing the positive values in which it may be instrumental.

Another value that has changed so much that it is now recognized only with difficulty is the care of aged parents by their children. In preindustrial societies this provision for the care of the aged and infirm is a major reason for a high value on large families, especially on having one or more sons. In American society, legislation establishing Social Security, later supplemented by additional business and state retirement systems, marked the turning point. Now one deems himself unfortunate if he becomes dependent on his children for support, and the motivation for having large families so that one's children will care for one in his old age has almost disappeared. The value placed on filial responsibility for aged parents has changed dramatically within a single generation. That it had a high value and an important place in family values is a matter of record (and it still has a high value in preindustrial societies). Its sudden alteration with the creation of society-wide retirement systems provides a dramatic illustration of the effects of change in one institution on the norms of another.

Are All Values on Family Structure Instrumental?

Five examples of instrumentally valued family properties have been offered: negative value on early marriage, strict obedience to parents, "strong families," negatively valued intercourse among the unmarried, and care of aged parents by their children. The broader question is whether *all* customary practices in family life—whether incorporated into the legal structure or enforced only by social pressure—are more realistically viewed as means to ends rather than ends in themselves?

The question must have two answers. Perhaps for most lay people and a few professionals the answer will be "no." For example, they will say that it is intrinsically right for one woman to be married to one man (at least, at one time) or that sexual life be limited to persons who are married to each other. Just as clearly, the social scientist must answer "yes"; although he may feel he needs at least two hours to explain and qualify this reply! The anthropologists have provided the key information that the essential functions of the family clustered about child care and socialization can be achieved within *an infinite variety* of family structures or even that other institutional groups can be constructed, as in the kibbutz, largely to take over these central family functions.[11]

Perceived Instrumentality and Social Change

One might imagine for a moment that society viewed the normative patterns of family life as social inventions and that each family practice was viewed favorably only because it was effective in realizing one or more intrinsic values. More specifically, one might consider what it means in terms of changing family life whether, for example, he places a negative value on sexual intercourse among the unmarried because it is likely to lead to an undesired pregnancy or because such relationships are intrinsically wrong? It is evident that patterns of family behavior will change much more rapidly if they are seen as currently useful than if they are viewed as the only acceptable pattern.

The fact that social structure, including family structure, appears to the social scientist as instrumental in serving the intrinsic needs of individuals does not imply that drastic changes in family norms are imminent, but, if enough of the power structure in a society perceives family structure as possessing instrumental rather than intrinsic value, it is probable that certain limited changes in family structure are likely to be undertaken more readily. For example, the question has been raised whether day-care centers should be provided as needed from public funds. If the matter is viewed in terms of how individual and societal needs are served, it probably would be adopted; but, if one places an intrinsic value on children being always under the care of their own mothers, it would certainly be rejected.

This raises an important issue which cannot be pursued here: whether family members must *personally* perform the tasks for which they are responsible or whether it is only necessary that they see that the tasks are performed. Will society accept the competent baby-sitter or well-appointed day-care center as *an entirely acceptable* substitute for personal care and supervision by the mother? Can specialized agencies assume the central functions performed by families just as specialized agencies perform most other tasks in an industrialized society?

Latent Consequences of Social Change

The judgment that a given aspect of family behavior is valued only because its consequences are productive of the realization of other values does not in itself lead to any conclusions about whether it should be preserved or replaced. Those who would replace it must present not only a case that the alternative is even more efficient for realizing a given value but also reasonable assurance that its latent or unanticipated consequences do not increase the difficulty of realizing other values. For example, consider a decision which must be made now concerning vocational counseling of girls.

Traditionally, girls have been counseled into teaching, nursing, secretarial work, and the like, where they faced little competition from men and where the demands of the job were viewed as more or less compatible with those of marriage. They have been counseled away from careers in research, politics, and as executives in the business world. Now equality of opportunity has been legislated, and considerable efforts are being expended to interest women in professional, managerial, and executive positions. There is no physical or legal reason why women should not have careers equal to those of men. However, *if* women are to obtain the necessary interests and training, parents and counselors must accept and stimulate the interests of girls in mathematics and the physical sciences as much as in the humanities, education, and home economics. If this occurs, in the next generation girls will have a range of occupational choices which is as broad and varied as that for men. To have more occupations to choose from and to hold positions of more influence and which are better paid all point to the realization of certain intrinsic values for women. Why then might parents and counselors hesitate in choosing real occupational equality for women?

The issue lies in several probable, latent consequences of this change including the following:

1. In an increasing number of families the principal or only provider will be the wife, with the husband in some instances becoming the housekeeper in the family in a complete reversal of roles.
2. The divorce rate is likely to increase as the wife's occupation makes more demands on her time, requires her to travel, and leads to her financial independence.
3. Nurseries and day-care centers will increasingly care for children as the number of full-time homemakers decreases.
4. The sexual lives of women are likely to more nearly approximate those of men as women travel more and become less economically dependent on men.
5. The birth rate is likely to continue to decline as interesting and rewarding alternatives to rearing children develop.
6. The age of girls at marriage is likely to increase as the completion of education becomes more obviously useful to them.

If the above latent consequences are more likely than not to follow upon counseling girls into a full range of careers (and the writer believes they are), then the social scientist and practitioner may well weigh the matter carefully. Furthermore, this example is probably not unrepresentative of the complexity of latent consequences which are likely to accompany any major social change. This is not to say that social change should not take place or that it should not in some instances be speeded by practitioners and scientists, but it does suggest that the most careful attention be devoted to latent consequences. To fail to weigh the latent consequences is, it seems to the writer, irresponsible.

Conclusions

The attempt has been made to clarify the concept of value. It has been proposed that the concept is too broad for use in specific contexts and that, if we are interested in a changing society and its family structure, we need to specify subconcepts which explain both types of values—those that change along with other changes in society and those that change little, if at all. Thus, the subconcept "instrumental value" has been employed for the worth that is attached to some object, practice, or other property which has been established as an effective means toward the realization of some other value.[12] The subconcept "intrinsic value" is worth attached to a property for its own sake, ignoring it as a causal agent in a chain that continues beyond it. Any given property may possess both instrumental and intrinsic value, although presumably one is dominant, as in the currently high value—both instrumental and intrinsic—placed on education.

Individuals and groups within a society may differ on their beliefs of whether a given family property is instrumentally or intrinsically valuable. This issue must be resolved by the society before legal change can occur. If a property is viewed as instrumentally valuable, it falls within the matters viewed rationally and is subject to change as modifications prove or promise to prove more efficient. Properties viewed as intrinsically valuable will be protected and change in them resisted.

It appears evident that an era is imminent in which more normative family behavior will come to be viewed by the society as instrumentally valued only. This is illustrated by Margaret Mead's provocative article, "Marriage in Two Steps," [13] which requires that each person marry twice before he can become a parent. She is contending that the form of marriage is of instrumental value whereas the personality of the child who is conceived is of intrinsic value.

As the objectivity of science illuminates more and more family practices and as more rapid changes occur in other institutions, a faster rate of change of family norms is inevitable. It is particularly incumbent on behavioral scientists and practitioners to be alert to the latent consequences of family change. For example, the society cannot simply decide that adolescents should immediately be able to satisfy their sex needs at will. It would be inundated with a flood of illegitimate children. The behavioral scientists and practitioners should be able to anticipate such not-so-latent consequences. A hazard to such ability is the "expert's" own needs and desires which he can easily confuse with the best interests of society. Finally, even under the most favorable circumstances, one may be unable to anticipate some of the consequences of change in family behavior patterns. It is perhaps just as well then that, at the present stage of knowledge, professionals are not called on to be the final arbiters of family practices. However, they will have a part in shaping the family's patterns of behavior and a part in speeding or slowing family change.

There is nothing immutable about the specific definition of positions and roles in the family or in its customary patterns of interaction. However, many will be quick to seize on this fact to propose that family rules—formal or informal—be suspended in favor of their own immediate goals and gratifications. Of course, the practitioner and scientist must be aware of the variety and complexity of the latent consequence which is likely to accompany any important changes in the relationships of men, women, and children in the family; but it is not sufficient for professionals to be concerned with the latent consequences of family change. If a society is to become a truly competent and mature one, at least a broad segment of its members must be able and willing to be concerned likewise.

If the writer could make one general wish for the society of the future, it would be that society could view social structure as instrumental and, thus freed from the dead hand of traditional practice, objectively weigh the changes that from time to time need to be made if the family and other social institutions are to function more effectively. The emancipation from tradition must depend on societal foresight in anticipating the consequences likely to flow from change and, in the light of such probable consequences, in maintaining those restraints on the short-run desires of individuals which may be required so that the rights of others are taken into account and the necessary and important tasks of society are performed. This level of objectivity and understanding is not characteristic of American society of 1967; but, if family research, teaching and counseling move ahead at an increasing tempo, perhaps it will be more characteristic of 1977 or, if not, then of 1987.

There is little doubt that the institution of the family is *here to stay,* not because this basic unit of social structure is valuable per se, but because it is instrumental in maintaining life itself, in shaping the infant into the person, and in providing for the security and affectional needs of people of all ages. In fact, the family is so central to the fulfillment of several intrinsic values, that it is anticipated that the family will become an even more competent instrument for meeting human needs and, as a consequence, will become more highly and generally valued throughout society in that fascinating and ever more rapidly changing world of tomorrow.

NOTES

1. For a more detailed discussion, see William Wilson and F. Ivan Nye, "Methodological Problems in the Empirical Study of Values," Agricultural Experiment Station Bulletin No. 672, Washington State University, Pullman, 1966.
2. There are several ideas of values that will specifically be left to others. Ideals of "true" or "false" values are outside the realm of behavioral science. The present view of values is also unable to deal with the notion that some people have no values. Everyone apparently has general categories of objects or experiences which he desires, and he has some notion of those which he desires most.
3. Wilson and Nye, *op. cit.*
4. Morris has shown that it is possible to combine value with attitude and other related concepts into an idea of "preferential behavior." Charles W. Morris, *Signs, Language and Behavior,* New York: Prentice-Hall, Inc., 1965. This treatment leads to an even broader concept, whereas it is our position that more specific ones are required for most theoretical or research purposes.
5. It may be possible to add one additional distinction. Becker suggests that "in most instances in the social sciences, the word is used only in those cases where an action interactive relationship exists between needs, attitudes and desires on one hand and objects on the other hand. In contrast, one may have an attitude toward something in which he has not experienced intimate contact. Howard Becker, "Value," in *A Dictionary of the Social Sciences,* ed. by Julius Gould and William L. Kolb, New York, The United Nations Education, Scientific and Cultural Organization, 1964, p. 743.
6. Hereafter "property" is employed as a general term to include such specific terms as objects, experiences, and events and will be employed interchangeably with them.
7. The concept is inspired by John Dewey, *Theory of Valuation,* International Encyclopedia of United Science, Volume II, No. 4, 1939. However, the term is employed here in a very different context from its use by Dewey.
8. Albert Ellis, *Sex Without Guilt,* New York: Lyle Stuart, 1958.

9. Here we could readily substitute the concepts "functional" and "dys-functional."
10. The extent of sacrifice depends, in part, on the extent to which family members embrace common values and share the same interests.
11. Melford E. Spiro, *Kibbutz: Venture in Utopia*, New York: Schocken Books, 1963.
12. It should be pointed out that practices possessing instrumental value may do so because they are efficient in realizing another instrumental value. However, at some point it appears necessary that the chain lead to a property accorded intrinsic value.
13. Margaret Mead, "Marriage in Two Steps," *Redbook Magazine*, July, 1966.

2 2

Commitment, Value Conflict and the Future of the American Family

by Charles W. Hobart

There are many attempts to characterize the nature of modern society: the affluent society, the other-directed society, the managerial society, the mass society, the expert society, the pluralistic society, the achieving society, the insane society. Most of these characterizations share at least one underlying assumption, that as a society we tread where man has never trod before, that there are qualitative differences between our society and earlier ones which make extrapolation on the basis of earlier societal experience unreliable at best, and often completely invalid.

One consequence is that the continued utility of many features fundamental to earlier societies becomes problematic. Examples include the segregation of sex roles, homogeneity of culture, widespread status ascription. It is both important and difficult to speculate about what further structural modifications may be in the offing. So long as an institution provides functions prerequisite to the survival of any human social system we must think in terms not of the disappearance of the institution but of the evolution of functional alternatives.

Reprinted from *Marriage and Family Living*, 25 (November 1963), pp. 405–412, by permission of the author and the National Council on Family Relations.

It is in this context that the following discussion of the future of
the family is set. This paper deals first with the argument that the
family as we know it is becoming obsolete, and with some recent
changes in social structure which are contributing to this apparent
obsolescence. Second, there is a discussion of value conflicts and of
future societal development given continued pre-eminence of materialistic values. Finally, there is consideration of bases for anticipating
a value revolution which would facilitate renewed commitment to
family relationships.

There is no need to cite the varied evidence which seems to suggest
the progressive obsolescence of the family as we know it. Some maintain that the family, no longer an economic necessity, is an inefficient,
artificial, arbitrary, outmoded structuring of relationships. Barrington
Moore, in his provocative "Thoughts of the Future of the Family"
protests such "obsolete and barbaric features" as "the obligation to
give affection as a duty to a particular set of persons on account of
the accident of birth," "the exploitation of socially sanctioned demands
for gratitude, when the existing social situation no longer generates
any genuine feeling of warmth." [1] Moore concludes that "one fine day
human society may realize that the part-time family, already a prominent part of our social landscape, has undergone a qualitative transformation into a system of mechanized and bureaucratized child
rearing" since "an institutional environment can be . . . warmer
than a family torn by obligations its members resent." [2]

In contradiction to this position, it is the thesis of this paper that
though the family is from some value perspectives an outdated structural unit, defined in terms of responsibility and commitment it remains a necessary condition for the development and expression of
humanity. Furthermore, if it in fact is such a necessary condition,
concern for its effective survival should help to shape the course of the
future development of society.

It must be admitted that the family is undergoing changes, both
within itself and in relation to the rest of society which tend significantly to weaken its solidarity. At least four of these changes may be
mentioned: (1) loss of functions; (2) increased personal mobility
within society; (3) the decline of status ascription and the increase in
status achievement; and (4) the ascendency of materialistic values.

1. In regard to loss of family functions, note that not only has the
emergence of separate and distinct institutions accomplished the functional depletion of the once omnifunctional family, but active family
membership has become optional in our day. Social status placement

is primarily based on occupational achievement, rather than family ascription. There are now no imperious deterrents to a solitary family-alienated existence; all necessary services are available commercially. In fact, family responsibilities today distract and detract from single-minded pursuit of highly prized personal success in most occupations—scholarly, commercial, or professional.

Americans *are* getting married with greater frequency than ever before, a reflection, perhaps, of the increasing significance of companionship and emotional security within the family for people today. But if they marry for companionship and security, the high level of divorce rates[3] suggests that Americans seek divorce when they fail to attain these goals.

2. The rate of spatial mobility of Americans today is remarkable: in the last decade one half of all families in the States have moved every five years. Some consequences of this unprecedented movement have been (1) increase in the number and variety of readjustments which a family must make; (2) radical loss of support of the family by neighborhood, friendship, and kinship primary groups; and (3) weakened discouragement of separation and divorce by these groups. Thus increased mobility may be seen as (1) precipitating more crises and adjustment difficulties within the family, (2) stripping the family of external supports at the very time of heightened stress, and (3) weakening the opposition to traditionally disapproved means of resolving difficulties, such as divorce.

Since mobility involves physical removal from the informal controls exercised by primary groups, Howard S. Becker's conceptualization of commitment becomes relevant to this discussion. Becker conceives of commitment as an act, consciously or unconsciously accomplished, whereby a person involves additional interests of his ("side bets") directly in action he is engaged in, which were originally extraneous to this action. Becker emphasizes that the process is relative to the values or valuables of the person.[4] I am emphasizing its relativity to the importance of the reference groups in whose eyes he stands to gain or lose on his "side bets."

In Becker's terms, then, commitment in marriage was once strengthened by making side bets involving staking one's reputation on one's trustworthiness, loyalty, fidelity in marriage. These bets were secured by the scrutiny of unchanging reference groups: close neighbors, fellow parishioners, occupational associates. The increasing speed of physical mobility as well as the growth of value confusion and of heterogeneous sub-cultures have tended to sharply depreciate the coin with which side bets to marital commitment were once made. This devaluation further weakens the stability of marriage.

3. Another trend in American society which appears to have a powerful potential for further weakening the family is suggested by the phrase "proliferation of associations," "personality market," "individuation." These suggest a growing contrast with the recent past when most close relationships of people were traditionally defined ascribed relationships with mate and children, with other kin, with neighbors, with fellow parishioners. Today, more and more relationships are achieved. They are "cultivated" in school, at work, in voluntary associations; they are promoted through friends and professional or business contacts.

The significant point is that rather than being ascribed, and thus traditionally defined and delimited, relationships are now more often achieved and thus more idiosyncratic and potentially boundless. Herein lies their threat to the family, for they, like many other aspects of contemporary life, may readily infringe upon family claims, may alienate members from the family. Note that at one time only men, as sole bread winners of the family, were vulnerable to these possibilities, in work and voluntary association situations. Their colleagues in these situations were other men, thus posing no threat to devotion to the wife at home. But with the spectacular increase in the employment of married as well as unmarried women, both sexes are vulnerable, and increasingly their work and voluntary association relationships *may* endanger the marriage bond. With this bond under greater stress, the decline of the primary group discouragements to divorce becomes increasingly consequential.

The proliferation of achieved, and thus potentially unlimited relationships for both men and women is by no means exclusively dysfunctional. Restriction of "close" relationships to a small circle of sharply limited ascribed relationships tends to be delimiting as far as growth of the person is concerned. Mead and others have demonstrated that the personality is a social product, and personality growth can occur only in relationships. Hence a small circle of ascribed relationships tends to be stultifying in at least three ways. In the first place, since the limits of an ascribed relationship are traditionally defined in terms of convention and appropriateness, the personality potential in an ascribed relationship is far more limited than in the more open, uncircumscribed achieved relationship. Second, since the circle of ascribed relationships is more homogeneous than the range of possible achieved relationships, the latter may awaken a broader range of latent potentialities within the person. Third, the circle of ascribed relationships may soon be rather thoroughly explored and exhausted, especially given geographical immobility, early in life. By contrast, the opportunities for new achieved relationships may last until death and may be limited only by the activity and involvement of the person. Thus it seems that the increase in proportion of achieved relationships is a necessary condition for actualization of more human potential in society.

I noted above that any achieved relationship, particularly a cross sex one, may jeopardize the marriage bond and perhaps parental responsibilties. Yet, given extensive and rapid spatial and vertical mobility, almost all relationships tend to be shifting sand, lacking in dependability and security, providing no basis on which to build a life. The very impermanence of these manifold relationships heightens the need for *some* relationships which are dependable; which can be, invariably, counted on; which will not be weakened or destroyed by the incessant moving about of people. Such secure relationships can only be found, given the structural peculiarities for our society today, within the family. Actualization of this security within the family depends upon commitment, a commitment symbolized in the phrase "in sickness and in health, for better or for worse, for richer or for poorer, til death do you part."

4. A final source of instability within the family is the value confusion which appears to be one of the hallmarks of our age. The crucial significance of values depends upon the fact that man is a being who must *live* his life since it is not lived for him by imperious drives or instincts, as Fromm says.[5] Man, thus emancipated from the security of nature's control, needs human community to humanize him and to structure his choice between the alternatives which confront him. The basis for choice is a set of values, generated in society, in terms of which choice priorities may be assigned.

One linkage between values and the family lies in the fact that the original unit of human community and the universal humanizing unit of all societies is the family. It is in the family that many of the most important values, bases for choice, are learned. The family not only transmits values; it is predicated on, and in fact symbolizes some of the distinctively "human" values: tenderness, love, concern, loyalty.

Man's capacity for consistent and responsible action depends on his being able to orient himself and to act on the basis of commitment to values; thus a certain level of value consistency is important. But a prominent feature of American society today is a pervasive value conflict. The family depends upon and symbolizes "inefficient values" of being, knowing, caring, loving, unconditionally commiting oneself. These values are incompatible with the urban industrial values of production, achievement, exchange, quantification, efficiency, success. Simultaneous unlimited commitment to people—in love and concern—and to achievement, success, prosperity, is impossible. The resultant tension in a society which pays uncritical lip-service to both sets of values, is disruptive and potentially incapacitating. It tends toward resolution, in favor of the "inhuman" urban values. Fromm has noted that as a society we tend to *love things,* and *use people,* rather than the reverse. And Whyte has remarked that the "organization men" he interviewed seemed to prefer to sacrifice success in marriage to career success, if forced to choose between them.

This value confusion is, of course, a source of instability within the American family. A family presumes unlimited commitment between family members: "til death do you part" between husband and wife, "all we can do for the kids" on the part of parents toward children. But the priority of these love and concern values is directly challenged by success and achievement values which may imply that status symbols are more important than babies; that what a child *achieves* is more important than what he *is;* that what we *own* is more important than what we *are.* Thus the stage is set for conflict between a success oriented husband and a child-people welfare oriented wife, or for a rather inhuman family which values things over people, and which may raise children who have difficulty living down this experience of worthlessness.

The question may be raised whether what one does versus what one is are polar characteristics, or is not what one does a part of what one is? Purely logically the latter is of course true. But social psychologically speaking there are significant differences in the way these two value emphases influence the process and consequences of parent-child interaction. Briefly, parents who emphasize *doing* respond to their children in terms of conditional love, and the child comes to feel that he is unacceptable unless he conforms, and also unless he meets certain "production quotas." By contrast, parents who emphasize *being* respond to their children in terms of unconditional love, and their children come to feel that they are intrinsically acceptable and love worthy. Successful performance is thus a matter of much more anxious preoccupation for the former than for the latter ideal type of child.

This review of some changes in family and society—loss of functions, increased mobility, increased status achievement, and ascendancy of materialistic values—has pointed out that some of these changes have functional as well as dysfunctional consequences. What are the likely prospects for the future? Which way will the value conflict be resolved? What are the preconditions, the prospects, and the probable consequences of more explicit self-conscious commitment to the family?

Let us look first at some further consequences of the value predicament in our society today. Consider the emerging character type in America. Torn from family commitments by the demands of urban living—dedication to efficiency, success, etc., modern man is often alienated from himself and from others.[6] To escape the anxious awareness of his inability to express his humanity and to relate to others through his role as a functionary in a bureaucratic system, he is tempted to identify with the system, becoming, in Mills' terms, a "cheerful robot."[7] In Riesman's terms he is the "other-directed,"[8] forever adapting to the demands of the situation, of the people at hand; in Fromm's terms he is the "personality package," an exchangeable commodity to be sold for success.[9]

The ecology of the American city likewise reflects this value pattern and has important consequences for the family. Most cities can be characterized as central places for the merchandizing of goods and credits. They are the center of great webs of communication and transportation through which our economy of exchange functions. The natural areas of the city are determined by land values: the allocation of people and facilities is in accord with who can pay. Thus it is not for the family that the city functions, and it is not in accord with the values foundational to the family that people and facilities are located. Because the city is not a livable habitat for family units, families have fled to the suburbs. Here children can play, but here too, mothers are often stranded, driven to distraction by childish babbling from which there is no escape, and fathers are missing, early and late, commuting.

From an institutional perspective the family is weakening, and again our value confusion is involved. No longer a necessary economic unit, the family continues to provide for the socialization of children and for companionship. Yet even in these two remaining areas the family is losing significance. Children have more and more been turned over to schools, and, in some instances, nursery schools and Sunday schools, for a major portion of their socialization, as parents occupy themselves with other activities. More significant than the time turned over to such institutional socialization of children is the responsibility that parents more than willingly relinquish or do not recognize as theirs. There appears to be little concern in America today that the shaping of a human life, a human personality, a future of happiness or hell, which is best accomplished in a primary group, is turned over ever earlier and for longer periods to secondary, impersonal, social, agencies. In these agencies children can only be "handled" and manipulated in groups, rather than cared for as individuals.

Leisure time is used by some to cultivate companionship with wife and children. But for many it appears that what time is spent together is seldom spent primarily in *being* together, but rather in *doing* simultaneously: watching T.V., going someplace, being entertained. Leisure is thus often an escape from the tension of urban life which pulls people in different directions, a distraction from "the great emptiness."[10]

The family persists because people want and need the family. The problem is that, having often lost the family in its meaningful sense as a primary commitment, people want a fantasy; they compulsively seek security. They get disillusionment.[11] Pulled apart by the value conflict of our society they want both personal loving involvement and social efficient achievement, and often they can commit themselves to neither. Thus straddling both ways of life, they can only distract themselves from their predicament.

This admittedly pessimistic overview forces us to confront a further question. What kind of a *future* is in store for our society? Will time tolerate the tension of values, will it tolerate the embarrassing persistence of the family? Some current trends suggest the resolution of the tension in favor of materialistic urban values which place a premium on man, the efficient doer.

To be more explicit, the character type of the future, according to some, will be the true functionary, the "cheerful robot." "Human engineering" seems determined to insuring that man is socialized into this mold, his human anxieties conditioned out. The power structure of the society will be even more centralized than the current structure. The city will rid itself of remaining small shops and other lingering evidences of human sentiment, so that where there is now variety and diversity, there will be functional monotony. With the rapid increase in urban population there is the prospect that the inefficiency of suburban living will be eliminated and people will be housed in compact apartments or even in some collective arrangement.

The family as we know it will be eliminated from this society, Moore has suggested,[12] and Skinner, in *Walden II* [13] agrees.[14] Children, housed separately, will not endanger the efficiency of adult activity. They will not be left to the haphazard care of their accidental parents but will be socialized by behavioral conditioning experts. Couples will have no use for life-long commitments and will often tend to go their separate ways. Each man for himself by himself will escape into the mass of interchangeable associates. Such is the vision of the future that some foresee.

But it seems undeniable that such a future would, in one sense, mean the end of human society. Human society is not an automatic process as are subhuman spheres of life. There is reason to believe that man, *as we know him,* has to care enough to carry on,[15] and to care enough he has to have a reason; life has to have some meaning. Without at least the illusion, the vision, of human ends that today's contradiction of values yet provides man, what would keep him going? Thus it seems impossible to conceive of the future of man in the above terms. Something more or less than man might emerge to carry on something more or less than human society, but such speculation is best left to science fiction writers.

But while the inhuman potential in current trends is not only sobering but frightening, the *human* possibilities are also unparalleled. An alternative future depends upon a value revolution in American society —not just the emergence of an unambiguous value hierarchy, but a displacement of the now pre-eminent success, efficiency, productivity, prosperity values by the more human oriented being, knowing, caring, loving values. This revolution is in fact overdue; it is prerequisite to our continued societal survival. It is heralded by Winston White's provocative discussion *Beyond Conformity* which maintains that we are even now undergoing "a shift from emphasis on the development of economic resources to the development of human resources—particularly the capacities of personalities." [16] A society of scarcity must encourage productivity and efficiency upon pain of greater scarcity, poverty and starvation. But in an affluent society, plagued not by *underproduction* but by *underconsumption,* production-increasing values *are in fact dysfunctional,* aggravating the chronic overproduction problem. In the affluent society, the implementation of "human" values is not only possible as it is not in a society of scarcity, it is also functional in the sense of diverting initiative and energy from the productive sphere, where they threaten to aggravate existing over-production, to other areas where they may serve to free people to be more themselves.

A key to this value change lies in renewed commitment to the family and in thus re-establishing the centrality of the commitment to inefficient, human values which the family relationship symbolizes. There are some who would try to solve the problems of our heterogeneous society in terms of restructuring (Fromm's work communities for example), of eliminating structurally some of the diversity and complexity of our society. But this is the kind of shortsightedness that tries to move forward by moving backward. To look wistfully at the beauty and relative simplicity of the rigidly structured life in a primitive society without at the same time realizing that our human potentialities are greater than would be realized in such a society is the kind of irresponsibility that evades the task at hand. This is the most significant point made in *Beyond Conformity*. White sees human personality as emancipated from ascriptive ties in contemporary society. Since man is no longer *determined* automatically by family, church, or occupation, greater individuality of personality is possible. In the absence of automatic structural determinants, man is "indeed, forced to be free," to become more individualistic.[17]

It follows from this that the family of the future must not be defined in terms of more structure, but in terms of less explicit structure. It must at once be flexible enough for increasingly individuated people, yet a stable basic unit for human life. The family as a commitment implies freedom in the definition of the marital relationship in order to meet the demands of the particular way of life of the two people involved. For its members, family relationships should be a part of a larger pattern of meaningful, involving relationships. Only thus, individually defined and not exclusive, can the family tie avoid being a trapping, arbitrarily binding, stultifying commitment for its members. Defined in this way, the family would be a sustaining, liberating, and humanizing influence since it would invest life in modern society with context, continuity, and direction. As a commitment, a limiting choice, an orienting value complex, it would permit a decisive stance in the urban sea of alternatives, not an artificial reduction of the alternatives.

Are there any alternative side bet possibilities in our day to shore up the marriage commitment, which have not suffered the erosion of effectiveness noted earlier in contemporary society? I think that the answer is yes. It is an answer which is not only compatible with, but dependent on the fact that since *doing* is inescapably becoming less important in contemporary society than *being*, husbands and wives are increasingly chosen because of the persons that they *are*, rather than what they can *do*. Increasingly mates may be known deeply and loved for what they are. To know and love the person in this way is to feel for and care for the person. Love in this sense, then, involves the inadvertent side bet of deeply feeling with and for and caring about this person. A risking of the marriage vows involves immediate apprehension of the pain this causes my mate, as my own pain. My empathy with and ego involvement with my mate guarantees a "side bet penalty" which is likely to be heavier than the attractiveness of what I stand to gain from my breach of commitment.

Here is a basis for a new, deeper commitment to the family, in so far as couple members dare to invest themselves to this extent, in each other. And in this deeper commitment, more of meaning in life would be discovered in the experience of human values, the intrinsic values of being, becoming, knowing and being known, caring and being cared for, in contrast to the values of doing and achieving. And out of this profound experiencing of human values might come the basis for the slow revolution in values which would further facilitate deeper commitment to the family, and in time the reorientation of contemporary society.

The implications of such a changed significance of the family and such a value revolution for future society are many. The character type which could emerge in this kind of family setting would be neither the chameleon-like, other-directed nor the rigid, artificially dogmatic inner-directed, to use Riesman's terms. Instead there could emerge the autonomous individual who is able to see and consciously choose between the alternatives; who knows himself and can express himself in decisive, directed action; who retains his sense of identity discovered *beyond* role, in the various roles he must play. Not merely functioning, having sold his soul "true believer" fashion, not living oblivious of alternatives, he could consciously exercise the greatest sense of freedom and responsibility that man has ever known; he could live Winston White's vision.[18]

With renewed emphasis on *being* rather than on *doing,* the family and the concern with human relationships which it symbolizes could once again be an organizing principle in society. With less emphasis on over-efficiency our society could significantly cut down the length of the working day. Such a work schedule would make possible an enriched home life. While older children were in school both men and women could work, if they chose, and thus perhaps develop specialized interests. The specialization of their work could be balanced by the vocations of homemaking and greater involvement in parenthood for both men and women, and by the opportunity to develop other interests in their leisure time. A shorter work day would mean that children could once again be socialized more within the family primary group. The school could accomplish its distinctive function of transmitting knowledge in half a day, leaving the humanization responsibility to the home. Here the inefficient process of growing up could take place in a context where there is time for each child, and where each child is valued and known as an individual. In the home children need not be collectively handled, regimented and manipulated as they must be at school, but might be better freed to become, to find themselves, to develop their unique potentials.

In addition to assuming the responsibility for socializing children, such a family could provide meaningful and sustaining relationships which are a prerequisite to open, undefended, loving relationships with others. As I noted above, it is inevitable that most relationships in an urban society will be time-bound, that the demands of complex and highly mobile living will pull people apart, but the family can offer the element of permanence which other relationships cannot. And thus safeguarded by their family-centered security against being left unbearably alone when the hour of separation came, people could dare to invest themselves in a number of invaluable but often short term relationships whose dissolution would otherwise be unbearable. Increased leisure time would enable individuals to develop these relationships both within and without the family.

The question arises, could people really bear to spend more time with their families than they now do? To this a number of things can be said. In the first place, people presumably would not have the same need that they do today to escape the emptiness of shallow, family-togetherness by constantly doing or being with different people. Time spent together could be on a more meaningful level than it can now be. Secondly, time would also be spent in other meaningful, involving relationships with non-family members which would mean that the family would not seem a trap and would not degenerate into a stagnating aggregate of individuals. The family would lose the compulsive exclusive security which makes it dull for those who spend most of their leisure time with their family and dare not do otherwise. Assuming a commitment of family members to each other more profound than any based merely on exclusion or external structure, family members could tolerate an element of genuine insecurity in their relationships which would not have to be evaded and would keep the relationship from being static and dull.

Finally young people, no longer stranded, disoriented, alienated from parents—as they often are now when neither adolescents nor parents know each other—would not have to escape compulsively, haphazardly into marriage. They could postpone marriage until they knew what they wanted, needed, and were entering into.

There are a few shreds of evidence that the American family may in fact be evolving in the direction advocated in this paper. Hilsdale, in a rather sensitive interviewing study, sought to discover whether subjects entered marriage with an absolute commitment to marriage, or merely a commitment to trial of marriage. He found that 80 percent entered with an absolute commitment. This commitment was, significantly, associated with an "almost total absence of starry-eyed Hollywood-type 'romantic love.'" [19] Another finding of this study was the preoccupation of his subjects with communication: they felt that their marriage would last "because we can talk to each other, because we can discuss our problems together." [20] Hilsdale terms this faith "magical," but it can also be seen as a reaction to the fact that in an increasingly impersonal society, people cannot talk with each other. In this light it appears as both awareness by people of their need to really communicate with another, and a commitment to safeguard this highly valued and important aspect of the marriage relationship. Moreover, there is evidence that communication is related to marital adjustment.[21]

In this paper I have argued that if an affluent society is to survive, it must undergo a value revolution which will make what we have called human values pre-eminent over production values. Such a society-wide evaluation would eliminate a major source of the compromised commitment, of the value conflict between and within the family members, and of the inadequate and distorting socialization of children, which exist in the American family today. There seems to be reason for hoping that such a value revolution may come out of the changing pattern of husband-wife relationship. If this should continue such that the family were restructured along the lines suggested by these values, people could find the security and sustenance which they need, but often cannot find, in today's world. The nature of contemporary urban society makes this increasingly necessary for a number of reasons. Earlier alternative bases of family solidarity are disappearing, and thus commitment is an increasingly crucial bond. Increasingly, the family is the only security base available to man today. Where a commitment-based family security is dependably available to man, he will have a basis for relating fearlessly to the greater varieties of people available to him in a society organized in terms of achieved statuses, deepening and enriching himself and others in the process.

NOTES

1. Barrington Moore, "Thoughts on the Future of the Family," in Maurice R. Stein, Arthur J. Vidich and David M. White, Eds., *Identity and Anxiety*, Glencoe, Ill.: The Free Press, 1960, pp. 393–94.
2. *Ibid.*, p. 401.
3. See, for example, U.S. Bureau of the Census, *Statistical Abstract of the United States*, Washington, D.C., 1961, p. 48.
4. Howard S. Becker, "Notes on the Concept of Commitment," *American Journal of Sociology*, 66 (July, 1960) p. 35.
5. Erich Fromm, *The Same Society*, New York: Holt, Rinehart, and Winston, 1960, p. 24.
6. A few recent titles in the growing literature on alienation in modern man include: *American Journal of Psychoanalysis*, A Symposium on Alienation and the Search for Identity, Vol. 21, no. 2, 1961; Eric and Mary Josephson, *Man Alone*, Alienation in Modern Society, New York: Dell Publishing Co., 1962; Robert Nisbet, *The Quest for Community*, New York: Oxford University Press, 1953; Fritz Pappenheim, *The Alienation of Modern Man*, New York: Monthly Review Press, 1959; Maurice Stein, *The Eclipse of Community*, Princeton: Princeton University Press, 1960; Maurice Stein, Arthur Vidich and David White, Eds., *Identity and Anxiety; Survival of the Person in Mass Society*, Glencoe, Ill.: Free Press, 1960; Allen Wheelis, *The Quest for Identity*, New York: W. W. Norton, 1958.
7. C. Wright Mills, *The Sociological Imagination*, New York: Oxford University Press, 1959, p. 171.
8. David Riesman, Nathan Glazer, Reuel Denny, *The Lonely Crowd*, New York: Doubleday Anchor Books, 1956.
9. Erich Fromm, *The Art of Loving*, New York: Harper and Bros., 1956, p. 3.
10. Robert MacIver, "The Great Emptiness," in Eric Larrabee and Rolf Meyersohn, Eds., *Mass Leisure*, Glencoe, Illinois: The Free Press, 1958, pp. 118–122.
11. Charles W. Hobart, "Disillusionment in Marriage and Romanticism," *Marriage and Family Living*, Vol. 20 (May, 1958), pp. 156–162.
12. Barrington Moore, *op. cit.*
13. B. F. Skinner, *Walden Two*, New York: The Macmillan Co., 1948.
14. But note that evolution of child handling procedures in the Jewish communal Kibbutzim is in the direction of granting parents more access to their children and permitting children to spend more time in their parents' apartments. John Bowlby, *Maternal Care and Mental Health*, Geneva: World Health Organization, 1952, pp. 42-43.
15. William H. R. Rivers, "The Psychological Factor," in W. H. R. Rivers, ed., *Essays on the Depopulation of Melanesia*, Cambridge, England: The University Press, 1922.
16. Winston White, *Beyond Conformity*, New York: The Free Press of Glencoe, Ill., 1961, p. 162.
17. *Ibid.*, p. 164.
18. Winston White, *op. cit.*

19. Paul Hilsdale, "Marriage as a Personal Existential Commitment," *Marriage and Family Living,* 24 (May, 1962), p. 142.
20. *Ibid.,* p. 143.
21. Charles W. Hobart and William J. Kausner, "Some Social Interactional Correlates of Marital Role Disagreement and Marital Adjustment," *Marriage and Family Living,* 21 (Aug., 1959), p. 263.

2 3

The Future of the Family Revisited

by John N. Edwards

Familial change and institutional interpenetration are subjects which have attracted the continued but sporadic attention of sociologists and social scientists.[1] For the most part observers of the family, in essence, have considered the interchange between various institutional sectors and the family a one-sided affair. Familial change is perceived, in other words, as resulting from social changes in other institutional spheres with few, if any, reciprocal effects. A considerable amount of evidence has been and can be marshalled to substantiate this interpretation. Yet, one of the consequences of adopting this prevailing view is that it has frequently resulted in the formulation of a unifactorial "theory" or in the development of a theory of such a general nature that it has little heuristic and predictive utility. Ogburn and Nimkoff's[2] citation of technological innovations as the determinants of functional losses typifies the unifactorial approach, while Burgess'[3] suggestion that familial changes are the consequences of alterations in economic conditions and societal ideology is indicative of the level of abstraction with which change has been treated.

In addition to their predilection for unifactorial and highly general formulations, it has been noted that our earlier analysts of the family and social change were far from dispassionate observers. Either by implication or explicitly, the majority of writers during the 1940's took a stance on our perennial, theoretical antistrophe between persistence and change.[4] With few exceptions, social and family change was treated as a unique and disturbing occurrence. The views of

Reprinted from *Journal of Marriage and the Family,* 29 (August 1967), pp. 505–511, by permission of the National Council on Family Relations.

these sociologists were not only tainted with traditional nostalgia in the midst of generalized and rapid change but reflected an over-rigid model of society which was then current.

Despite an increased awareness of the limitations of prior discussions of changes in the American family, many of the issues recently have been raised anew. Hobart, in contending that the family serves as a humanizing influence in modern society, suggests four significant changes being undergone: functional losses, increased personal mobility, declining status ascription, and the continued ascendency of materialistic values.[5] Although there is a certain amount of confusion at times as to whether these are consequences or causes of change, all of these factors have been isolated as important explanatory variables by previous theorists of familial change. In combining these four factors, Hobart argues that they have led to a profound value predicament in which the primary commitment and meaning of the family are being lost. Material abundance and our present commitment to its expenditure, he maintains, threaten the centrality of "human" values and our prospects of "self-realization." Consequently, if the current trends persist, it is possible "that something more or less than man might emerge to carry on something more or less than human society." [6]

Within the limited compass of this paper, this interpretation of the variables will be examined and an attempt will be made to indicate, whenever appropriate, their limitations as explanations of change. In doing so, the efficacy of these variables as explanations of change, whether employed singly or in concert, will be evaluated. Secondly, an alternative interpretation of marriage and the family will be suggested as a base line for the development of future theories of change.

Variables of Familial Change

1. *Loss of Functions*

Hobart, in discussing the American family's loss of functions, points to the provision of companionship and emotional security as the basic function and reason for family formation today. Without question, many of the former functions such as economic production, education, protection, and recreation have been shifted to other institutional spheres or, at the very least, their content and form as they are carried out by the American family have been altered. Juxtaposed against this is evidence which suggests that the attractiveness of family formation has increased over the decades. However, Hobart's assertion that Americans seek divorce when they fail to attain a sufficient level of companionship and emotional security lacks empirical support. The precipitating influences in the initiation of divorce proceedings are, in fact, a matter of some debate. In making such an assertion, Hobart appears to be in accord with Ogburn that "the dilemma of the modern family is due to its loss of function" [7] and that family instability and disintegration are a consequence.

In the words of Barrington Moore, the American family today may have "obsolete and barbaric features," [8] but family units have persisted and the vast majority continue to persist despite the ongoing loss of functions. Durkheim's classic proposition concerning social differentiation is most suggestive in this connection. Increasing specialization and differentiation, concomitants of societal complexity, Durkheim contended, lead to an increment in interdependence.[9] This is no less true of familial functions than it is of the division of labor. Our present family system, organized around whatever tasks, is more highly interdependent with other institutional sectors than previously. Even the various totalitarian experiments with the eradication of family functions, including those of childrearing and socialization, tentatively suggest the ultimate functionality of the family in social maintenance, regardless of its specific structure and functions.[10] It thus would appear that the issue of functional losses as a source or indication of instability is a misleading one. It is indeed questionable if family instability (divorce and separation) can be eliminated or reduced however many or few functions the family performs. The issue for any theory of family change seems to be, rather, the identification of the specific direction of interdependence and the concomitants which accompany and lead to increased interdependence.

2. *Increased Personal Mobility*

The relatively high rate of spatial mobility within industrialized society, according to Hobart, affects the family in at least three ways: (1) it precipitates a larger amount of crises and adjustments, (2) it breaks the family from its external supports such as friendship and kinship groups, and (3) it weakens the proscriptions against divorce as a means of resolving family difficulties.[11] Increased personal or spatial mobility undoubtedly occasions the need for more adjustments. Generally such mobility is related to changes in work and, at times, to shifts in family status. The transitions attendant to these alterations are not to be underestimated. Yet, as the Rapoports indicate, conflicts and stresses are not necessarily multiplied by these transitions.[12] They may, in actuality, have desirable consequences. As a result of mobility, the functions of the family are by no means residual but become an inextricable background in the free choice of work and career. The prescriptions of work may allow, in turn, considerable latitude in the organization of family structure that was not formerly possible. The pursuit of higher education by women has enabled them to share occupational positions with their spouses and, in so doing, their involvement in the structuring of the family as well as in economic activities has been intensified.

The contention that the American family lacks external support during crisis periods is a corollary of the notion that the nuclear family is isolated in an urban situation. There are now a number of empirical indications which contradict or at least modify this view. Data from a Cleveland study, presented by Sussman, suggest that, in spite of extensive spatial mobility, nuclear families operate within a matrix of mutual kin assistance.[13] It is, in fact, during periods of crises that the aid of kin is most likely to be offered and accepted. Axelrod's research in Detroit indicates that relatives rather than non-relatives are the most important type of informal group association.[14] Babchuk and Bates, in a study of primary relations, also suggest that a large number of close friendships are maintained on a nonlocal and non-face-to-face basis.[15] On the whole, the evidence indicates that the high rate of annual movement by families has a relatively negligible effect on their external supports and does not, as often contended, weaken the informal controls of primary groups. It is patent that family transitions of one sort or another have always existed. The possibility that mobility as a crisis point in family life has merely superseded others is not to be discounted; but, if this is true, the impact of mobility on the family still remains to be demonstrated.

3. *Declining Ascribed Relationships*

In identifying the decline of traditionally defined or ascribed relationships as another element in the weakening of family bonds, Hobart concedes that the emphasis on achieved relationships fosters greater choice in establishing social relations. He argues, though, that the cross-sex contact, particularly in voluntary associations, subjects the marriage bond to greater stress.[16] To view voluntary organizations as potential agents for family dissolution is to oversimplify and distort the complexity of these organizations. Expressive voluntary groups (a dance club, for example) and those whose memberships are comprised of both sexes may serve to reinforce family relations. By their very nature, expressive associations are organized to supply immediate and personal gratification to their respective members. Their focus is, in other words, integrative at an individual level, while instrumental groups (such as the Chamber of Commerce) provide integration at a communal level. Particularly where expressive organizations are bisexual in composition, solidarity may be enhanced.[17]

It is, on the other hand, among those organizations which attract their constituencies from only one sex or the other that the probability of affiliation disturbing familial equilibrium is increased. In the one-sex groups, family members become geographically dispersed and may expend considerable amounts of time apart from one another. Even still, a number of relevant studies suggest that these are exceptional cases.[18] A sizeable proportion of the population are not affiliated with any type of voluntary association. Moreover, among those who do belong, their participation is neither extensive nor intensive. Americans, all folklore to the contrary, are not a nation of joiners, and it is thus difficult to perceive achieved relationships as a threat to family and marital solidarity.

In conceiving the proliferation of associations and achieved relationships as causes of dissolution and change, there is also an implicit assumption made about the nature of man. Basically, in positing cross-sex contact as a disruptive force, man is viewed as primarily a sexual being. Presumably, social control of the sexual drive is tenuous and exposure to the opposite sex is sufficient to deteriorate this control altogether. Since every society is interested in controlling sexual outlets to some extent, it is particularly imperative for an industrialized society which severely limits such outlets to segregate the sexes. This conception of man is not only incompatible with most sociological theories, but it is ultimately an untenable position. Even if we grant that adultery is a widespread experience, there remains the intricate, and as yet unaccomplished, task of sorting out extramarital involvement from other causes of instability.

4. *Ascendancy of Materialistic Values*

Materialistic values are seen as fundamentally incongruous with the more important values of the family; therefore, value confusion and instability result. The resolution of the present value confusion, Hobart notes, is doubly important for the family in that it is one of the basic socializing agents and it symbolizes many of the more fundamental humane values. Either human values must become preeminent in American society or the values of success, efficiency, and prosperity will continue to alter the family institution and eventually erode it. Hobart suggests, in this regard, that a value revolution is essential for continued societal survival. Such a revolution, he argues, cannot be a mere emergence of a consistent value hierarchy but must be a total displacement of our now-prevailing economic values. Although current trends appear to make such a revolution remote, the position set forth by Hobart is in essence optimistic. As a key to renewed commitment to marriage, he suggests that, increasingly, individuals in our affluent society are becoming more important for what they are, rather than for what they are capable of doing. Individuals are perceived and cared for in terms of their intrinsic value, rather than their extrinsic and utilitarian worth. Thus, despite the current prominence of utilitarian values, it is felt that the family is evolving in a new direction.[19]

The Family Today and Tomorrow

To this juncture, I have attempted to point out several limitations in invoking functional loss, spatial mobility, and the emphasis on achieved relationships as explanations for familial change. I should like, at this point, to offer an alternative interpretation of contemporary marriage and family living as a base line for further analysis, since it is quite apparent with the data now at hand that there is some measure of disagreement. Specific alternative explanatory variables of change will not be indicated; it is equally important in the formulation of any future theories of change, however, that we avoid stereotyping our present situation as we have done with the rural family of the past. In offering this admittedly tentative and sketchy analysis, Hobart's excellent example is followed by focusing on value orientations.

A basic underlying theme of American culture, Jules Henry has noted, is a preoccupation with pecuniary worth or value that is a consequence of what he terms "technological driveness." [20] Though our institutional structure is highly interdependent, the point is that our economic system and its values have become so pervasive that American life can be characterized as being driven by the constant creation of new wants and desires. Each new want—with considerable impetus from advertising—aids in the destruction of self-denial and impulse control, both virtues of a previous era. Where an economic system has no ceiling or production limits, all hesitation to indulgence must be overcome. And overcome it is, as witnessed by the tremendous growth of the advertising industry.

The preoccupation with pecuniary worth appears to be a necessary complement to a social system dominated by its economic institutional sphere. The nature of an economy of such a social system is that rewards must be transferable and negotiable; hence, the institutionalization of a monetary system. Whether one is selling the products of his labors or his personality and training, tangible rewards are mandatory. No doubt the efficacy of religious thought has suffered for this reason. Eternal damnation is not sufficiently definite, nor the prospect of heaven sufficiently imminent, to normatively persuade many who exist in a society where most rewards are quantified. Quantified rewards and our nearly obsessive concern with them are not identical with status achievement which other writers have cited as a crucial factor in the dissolution of the family. Status achievement may take many forms, of which the accumulation of monetary rewards is only one manifestation. The point is, rather, that the prospect of quantified rewards has become so pervasive in our society that it permeates virtually all social relationships including that between husband and wife and the progeny. The non-rewarding character of unlimited procreation has partially contributed to the diminution of that function and family size. To speak of "human obsolescence" and to consider the treatment accorded the elderly in our society are also evidence of the importance attached to tangibly rewarded behavior. In many instances it is not too much of an overstatement to consider as objects those that have not yet developed exchangeable resources (the young) and those who have exhausted theirs (the elderly). Even those occupying the middle ground, however, are not necessarily in an enviable position, for their relationships often lack all but a vestige of emotional interchange.

Insofar as marriage and the family are concerned, the first difficulties arising from this emphasis on pecuniary rewards are encountered in the dating process. The emergence of the rating and dating complex, Waller suggested, has fostered exploitative relationships in dating.[21] In such a relationship each partner attempts to maximize his or her returns with the least amount of concessions. Control and therefore the maximization of rewards are vested in that individual who has the least investment in the situation. Were it not a serious matter, it would be ironical that low commitment should be so highly rewarded.

Indeed it is significant and symptomatic of contemporary society that rewards from this type of relationship should be consciously and avidly pursued. The exploitative nature of dating, were it merely confined to dating, would be less problematic. Due to the lengthy dating period, ranging from the preteen years to the early twenties, this orientation becomes reinforced through repetition. It cannot fail, therefore, to have an impact on marital relationships, particularly in the first years of marriage, the period when couples are most vulnerable to divorce.

Marital relationships, ideally at least, are defined in our society as relationships involving mutual sacrifice, sharing, and giving. Magoun states in this regard: "Anyone going into marriage with the expectation of being thanked for bringing home the bacon—even against dismaying odds—or for shining the ancestral silver tea service till it glistens from the buffet in little pinwheels of light, is headed for heartache." [22] And heartache is precisely what a large proportion of marriages, not only those that terminate in divorce but also the so-called normal marriages, garner. With monotonous repetition we are conditioned, primarily as a result of the pervasiveness of our economic institutions, to react to situations in a manner designed to elicit rewards. When the potential of tangible rewards is absent, interaction tends to be halting and random. Through the conditioning of the economic system and the lengthy continuation of this basic orientation during the dating process, the newly married are grossly unprepared for the prescriptions of marriage.

Recent findings amply illustrate this trend. The marriages of what Cuber refers to as the "significant Americans" are predominantly utilitarian in nature. The partners of these marriages are primarily interested in what each derives from the relationship. There is little concern with mutual sacrifice and sharing other than that which is essential to the maintenance of the marital bond. Moreover, the types of rewards sought in these marriages are not psychic or emotional but those which enhance material security. In fact, these marriages are, as Cuber points out, characterized by continual conflict, passivity, and a lack of vitality. Only a minority of the marriages approximate the cultural ideal of an intimate, emotional attachment between partners that results in mutual concern and sharing; and it is these marriages which are most vulnerable to divorce. [23] Thus, it would appear that, like the devil, the family in contemporary, industrialized society must take the hindmost. As an institution it is unorganized and, therefore, lacks the influence that may be exercised by those institutions which are. Through necessity it must be flexible and adaptable; those that are not fail. [24]

A central proposition of functional analysis is that a change in one element of an integrated system leads to changes in other elements. The major impetus for social change in our society has been and continues to be our dynamic economic institutions, which seek to create ever new wants and markets for their products and services. Due to its decreasing size, the family's adaptability for change has kept pace. From many perspectives the various social alterations, such as the employment of women, have resulted in greater independence and increased potentialities for individual family members. In other respects, of course, the changes have been dysfunctional. As we have tried to indicate, the disparity that now exists between the ideal marriage and the real is considerable—just as considerable as it probably was in the past. Future alterations are of a high order of probability, particularly adjustments pertaining to the normative emphasis on material rewards and the affective character of marriage. Still, the desinence of the family appears to be a phantasm born of the anxiety accompanying rapid social change.

If, indeed, contemporary marriages are based more on what the marital partners *are* rather than what they *do* as Hobart suggests, the major disjunctive feature of current family life is that what individuals *are* is primarily reward-seeking organisms. This commitment to economic values is logically incompatible with the values of family life, but it is not a source of major dislocation or dissolution of the family group.

Given this condition, what future has our present family system? Earlier industrialization has relieved a major proportion of our female population from the more onerous activities associated with household management. In spite of the unprecedented opportunity for experimentation, women in general have found it to be a frustrating era. Either they have found a combination of childrearing and outside activities unrewarding or they have felt that the channels for careers remain severely limited. Ongoing social change with respect to career expansion has been marked, nonetheless, and it is highly probable that the tempo will be increased.

This may have major significance for future marital relationships. The tremendous expansiveness of the insurance industry signifies, to some at least, the import attached to the economic aspects of marriage. This is again highlighted by the frequency with which insurance enters into divorce suits. More importantly, it is clear that marriage for men is more desirable, if not perhaps more necessary, than it is for women. Bernard's study of remarriage adequately illustrates the greater dependence which men have on the marital relationship; women, especially those that are economically secure, are less likely to remarry.[25] With increased avenues for more satisfying gainful employment, women will be afforded an enhanced alternative to wedlock. The generalized societal expectations regarding the desirability of marriage for everyone is quite pervasive, to be sure. But marriage, to put it simply, has become a habit—a habit which many young women with attactive career alternatives are beginning to question, however.

Economic overabundance, it is submitted, in the long run will have a repressive effect on the rate of marriage. The recognition of alternatives to wedlock, as that concerning alternatives to premarital chastity, will not occasion sudden behavioral consequences. But change is overdue. When women, already imbued with the economic ethos, fully realize their equality in this sphere, much of the *raison d'etre* of marriage will no longer be present. This is not to say, it should be emphasized, that family formation will precipitously decline; it is merely contended that the consequences of our reward-seeking orientation will become more evident, and this will be reflected in the marriage rate. In other words, one of the present structural supports which buttresses the attractiveness of the marital relationship will cease to exist. Women will no longer find economic dependence a virtue and worthy byproduct of marriage, for, given the opportunity, they will succeed for themselves as ably as any male might.

Numerous other current trends support this contention. The availability of reliable contraceptive devices, the expectations regarding small family size, and the declining influence and authority of men all suggest that the supports for the marital bond are weakening. Educational opportunities for women and the impetus these provide for the pursuance of careers are another consideration. Universities and colleges will probably attract even larger numbers of women in the future, as they have done for each of the last seven decades. Although most of these women may anticipate marriage eventually, more equitable hiring practices and salaries guaranteed by the Civil Rights Act of 1964 will alter this to some extent. The current popularized literature on the single state also dramatizes the interest in alternatives to marriage.

As stated earlier, the family is not and is not likely to be a nonfunctional entity. The prominence of affective behavior in familial relationships as an ideal appears to be a central support for the continuance of these relationships. Still, just how important affective behavior will remain for individuals and how well these needs will be met in the family stand as primary issues in family research. It is illuminating that study after study to date has found that interaction among couples tends to be halting.[26] It is difficult to conceive of warm, intimate, and emotional relationships being maintained over time when vital interaction is almost non-existent. Perhaps even sporadic episodes of spontaneous communication are sufficient to sustain these relationships, but the accessibility of legal outlets suggests that, without these and other structural supports, many marriages will terminate in divorce.

Despite the many elements of organizational life that are incompatible with our more humane values, bureaucratic structures in many respects recognize the desirability of maintaining intimate familial relationships. W. H. Whyte has noted, in his inimitable analysis of bureaucracies, the attempt to integrate the wife into the organizational structure.[27] In many ways and in many corporations, of course, this is a defensive act. Even as a mechanism of defense, though, this maneuver implicitly recognizes the wife's role as a supportive agent. Regardless of corporate motivation, the attempted integration of wives into the system can have beneficial consequences for the family. Where such an attempt is not made, the abyss between the economic and family group is only widened. Naturally, from the viewpoint of many individuals, this is not an ideal solution. It is, nonetheless, an alternative—an alternative upon which improvement may be made and, in view of increasing societal bureaucratization, one which demands attention.

A man and woman marrying today can contemplate, in the majority of cases, over 40 years' duration of the relationship, encompassing over one-half of their lives. In a society in which group membership is extremely transitory, this represents a significant departure. Because of its duration and its small size, the individual has no greater opportunity in influencing the character and quality of a group.

What we are presently witnessing, moreover, is not a revolution of societal values or the demise and increased instability of the American family. Rather, given the current preeminence of economic orientations in our value system, the marital union and family are becoming more highly interdependent with the economic sphere. Cross-culturally and historically, the family, irrespective of its particular structure and functions, has been and is primarily an instrumental group from a societal perspective. It is not accidental, therefore, that marriage in most societies is based on considerations other than an affective and human orientation. That this is less true in the United States is not an indication of incipient instability but intimates that we are engaged in a radical experiment of familism. It is an experiment in which we are seeking to integrate a new individualism with the other more highly organized institutions. Insofar as our value orientations are dominated by economic values, marriages and family formation in the future are more likely to be based on reason rather than the impulse of habit.

NOTES

1. See, for example, William F. Ogburn, *Social Change,* New York: Viking Press, 1922; William F. Ogburn and Meyer F. Nimkoff, *Technology and the Changing Family,* New York: Houghton-Mifflin, 1955; Pitirim A. Sorokin, *The Crisis of Our Age,* New York: E. P. Dutton, 1941; Carle C. Zimmerman, *Family and Civilization,* New York: Harper and Brother, 1947; Margaret P. Redfield, "The American Family: Consensus and Freedom," *American Journal of Sociology,* 52 (November, 1946), pp. 175–183; Ernest Burgess, "The Family in a Changing Society," *American Journal of Sociology,* 53 (May, 1948), pp. 417–422; Lawrence K. Frank, "Social Change and the Family," *Annals of the American Academy of Political and Social Science,* 160 (March, 1932), pp. 94–102; Joseph K. Folsom, *The Family and Democratic Society,* New York: John Wiley and Sons, Inc., 1934; Ruth N. Anshen, "The Family in Transition" in *The Family: Its Function and Destiny,* ed. by Ruth N. Anshen, New York: Harper, 1959, pp. 3–19; Sidney M. Greenfield, "Industrialization and the Family in Sociological Theory," *American Journal of Sociology,* 67 (November, 1961), pp. 312–322; Meyer F. Nimkoff, "Biological Discoveries and the Future of the Family. A Reappraisal," *Social Forces,* 41 (December, 1962), pp. 121–127; and Reuben Hill, "The American Family of the Future," *Journal of Marriage and the Family,* 26 (February ,1964), pp. 20–28.
2. Ogburn and Nimkoff, *op. cit.*
3. Burgess, *op. cit.*
4. Sorokin and Zimmerman during this period were two outstanding proponents of the theme of family decay and deterioration.
5. Charles W. Hobart, "Commitment, Value Conflict and the Future of The American Family," *Marriage and Family Living,* 25 (November, 1963), pp. 405–412.
6. *Ibid.,* p. 409.
7. William F. Ogburn, "The Changing Functions of the Family," in *Selected Studies in Marriage and the Family,* ed. by Robert F. Winch, Robert McGinnis, and Herbert R. Barringer, New York: Holt, Rinehart, and Winston, 1962, pp. 159–163.
8. Barrington Moore, "Thoughts on the Future of the Family," in *Identity and Anxiety,* ed. by Maurice R. Stein, Arthur J. Vidich, and David M. White, New York: The Free Press, a division of the Macmillan Co., 1960, p. 394.
9. Emile Durkheim, *The Division of Labor in Society,* New York: The Free Press, a division of the Macmillan Co., 1947.
10. Nicholas S. Timasheff, "The Attempt to Abolish the Family in Russia," in *The Family,* ed. by Norman W. Bell and Ezra F. Vogel, New York:

The Free Press, a division of the Macmillan Co., 1960, pp. 55–63. Reiss has argued that Timasheff's interpretation of the Russian failure to eradicate the family may be based on a logical fallacy. See Ira L. Reiss, "The Universality of the Family: A Conceptual Analysis," *Journal of Marriage and the Family*, 27 (November, 1965), pp. 443–453.

11. Hobart, *op. cit.*, p. 406.
12. Robert Rapoport and Rhona Rapoport, "Work and Family in Contemporary Society," *American Sociological Review*, 30 (June, 1965), pp. 381-394.
13. Marvin B. Sussman, "The Isolated Nuclear Family: Fact or Fiction?" *Social Problems*, 6 (Spring, 1959), pp. 333–340. Similar findings based on New Haven, Connecticut, data are contained in Marvin B. Sussman, "The Help Pattern in the Middle-Class Family," *American Sociological Review*, 18 (February, 1953), pp. 22–28.
14. Morris Axelrod, "Urban Structure and Social Participation," *American Sociological Review*, 21 (February, 1956), pp. 13–18.
15. Nicholas Babchuk and Alan P. Bates, "The Primary Relations of Middle-Class Couples: A Study in Male Dominance," *American Sociological Review*, 28 (June, 1963), pp. 377–385.
16. Hobart, *op. cit.*, pp. 406–407.
17. The integrative impact of voluntary organizations is discussed at length in Nicholas Babchuk and John N. Edwards, "Voluntary Associations and the Integration Hypothesis," *Sociological Inquiry*, 35 (Spring, 1965), pp. 149–162.
18. For instance, see Charles Wright and Herbert Hyman, "Voluntary Association Memberships of American Adults: Evidence from National Sample Surveys," *American Sociological Review*, 23 (June, 1958), pp. 284–294; John Foskett, "Social Structure and Social Participation," *American Sociological Review*, 20 (August, 1955), pp. 431–438; Wendell Bell and Maryanne Force, "Urban Neighborhood Types and Participation in Formal Associations," *American Sociological Review*, 21 (February, 1956), pp. 25–34; and John Scott, Jr., "Membership and Participation in Voluntary Associations," *American Sociological Review*, 22 (June, 1957), pp. 315–326.
19. Hobart, *op. cit.*, pp. 407–412.
20. Jules Henry, *Culture Against Man*, New York: Random House, Inc., 1963.
21. Willard Waller and Reuben Hill, *The Family: A Dynamic Interpretation*, New York: Holt, Rinehart and Winston, 1951, pp. 131–157.
22. F. Alexander Magoun, *Love and Marriage*, New York: Harper and Brothers, 1956, p. 44.
23. John F. Cuber and Peggy B. Harroff, *The Significant Americans: A Study of Sexual Behavior Among the Affluent*, New York: Appleton-Century, 1965.
24. Clark E. Vincent, "Familia Spongia: The Adaptive Function," *Journal of Marriage and the Family*, 28 (February, 1966), pp. 29–36.
25. Jessie Bernard, *Remarriage*, New York: The Dryden Press, 1956, pp. 55, 62–63.
26. Robert S. Ort, "A Study of Role-Conflicts as Related to Happiness in Marriage," *Journal of Abnormal and Social Psychology*, 45 (October,

1950), pp. 691–699; Peter C. Pineo, "Disenchantment in the Later Years of Marriage," *Marriage and Family Living,* 23 (February, 1961), pp. 2–11; and Cuber and Haroff, *op. cit.*
27. William H. Whyte, Jr., *The Organization Man,* Garden City, New York: Doubleday and Company, Inc., 1957.

24

The American Family of the Future*

by Reuben Hill

Previewing what the American family of the future will be like necessitates something of a world perspective through acquaintance by study and personal observation with the similarities and differences in family patterns by class, ethnic background, and region in various countries of the world.

Although the structural forms of marriage and the family vary from society to society and within the regions and class strata of societies, the functions carried out by families show high similarities. Moreover, the trends in form and functioning appear very similar in all of the industrializing countries of the world. Household size, location of power in decision-making, marriage forms, age and sex roles, rules for residence, inheritance, and methods of reckoning kinship continue to show marked variations, although these differences too are narrowing. But the functional assignments of socializing, motivating, and restoring family members in what Parsons has termed the area of "tension management" appear common to each of the societies which the present author has studied. In none of these countries is the family regarded as functionless; indeed, it is highly visible as a flourishing institution in most of the world.

The author's point of view, therefore, is less one of despair about the contemporary family and more one of admiration and respect for its flexibility, its resilience, and its capacity for survival and growth in such varied social and cultural settings. The continued develop-

* Originally presented at the annual meeting of the National Council on Family Relations, Denver, Colorado, August 21–23, 1963.

Reprinted from *Journal of Marriage and the Family,* 26 (February 1964), pp. 20–28, by permission of the author and the National Council on Family Relations.

ment and elaboration of the family within the relatively affluent and beneficent environment of urban, industrial America hardly seems problematic. Certainly our society is far from the most hostile social and economic order yet encountered by marriage and family institutions. Moreover, when viewed historically as a phenomenon of Western civilization, more options are probably open to families today to experiment, invent, and innovate than in any previous epoch.

Four methods may be delineated for projecting the contemporary American family into the future: extrapolation from current family trends; inferences from differences among three generations of contemporary families; inferences from the impact of current inventions on the family; and inferences from the writings and researches of family specialists. This paper will attempt some projections using each of these methods and will close with a set of objectives for the American family of the future.

Extrapolation from Trends into the Future

Projection of current trends in marriage and the family into the future involves predictions in the following areas: trends with respect to proportion married (higher), age at marriage (younger), family size (larger), divorce and separation (higher), remarriage (higher), births out of wedlock (higher), premarital intercourse (higher), power structure (more equalitarian), division of tasks and responsibilities (more flexibility), communication, affectional patterns, delegation of family functions, childrearing beliefs (developmental), and policies and practices (permissive).

This method of projecting into the future is hazardous because some trends are short-term ones tied to the economic climate of prosperity that so affects marriage, birth, and divorce rates. To predict with some certainty, it would be necessary to specify what the state of the economy is going to be—maintenance of full employment, continued economic growth, or stabilized economy.

The projection method is also hazardous because many trends are not necessarily linear. Completed family size has been dropping for 250 years in the United States, and it continued to drop during the high baby boom of the 1940's and 1950's, but it has just turned the corner, with 1954 as the probable low point at 2.4 children. The cohort of women born from 1916–20 who close their reproductive cycle from 1960–64 have had 2.9 children, whereas the women born from 1931–37 have had or expect to have had 3.2 children by the time they reach age 45. Extrapolation into the future is difficult with 250 years of decline and a very recent upward turn. Will large families of six or more children be the rule 50 years from now? The trend in ideal family size suggests not; this trend indicates that families will have more nearly between three and four children, with 85 per cent of couples regarding this size as ideal. To take another trend, age at marriage for men has dropped from 26.1 in 1890 to 22.8 in 1960, but the decrease was ever so gradual from 1890 to 1950, with no drop during the Depression decade at all, and most of the drop was from 1940–50, with no decrease since 1950. Headlines to the contrary, age for women has not dropped in the past decade and has not varied more than one-half year in 40 years. Americans may be marrying at an age level that is unlikely to drop further, but linear extrapolation might lead to the suggestion of American men marrying at the ages men are married in India if the trend were carried forward in linear fashion. It is instructive to recall the startling projections made by Lewis Terman from his data about virginity at marriage:

> In contrast with the slow tempo of many cultural changes, the trend toward premarital sex experience is proceeding with extraordinary rapidity. . . . In the case of husbands the incidence of virginity at marriage is 50.6 per cent in the oldest group and only 13.6 per cent in the youngest. The corresponding drop for wives is from 86.5 per cent to 31.7 per cent. If the drop should continue at the average rate shown for those born since 1890, virginity at marriage will be close to the vanishing point for males born after 1930 and for females born after 1940. It is more likely that the rate of change will be somewhat retarded as the zero point is approached and that an occasional virgin will come to the marriage bed for a few decades beyond the dates indicated by the curves. It will be of no small interest to see how long the cultural ideal of virgin marriage will survive as a moral code after its observance has passed into history.[1]

Needless to say, empirical studies on the age groups born in the 1940's and thus predicted to be completely nonvirginal do not confirm Terman's predictions; the trends are not necessarily linear.

Power structure shifts are likewise difficult to extrapolate. Fewer families today are father-centered in decision-making; the trend is toward equalitarian patterns. A recent survey of several thousand families in Ohio and North Carolina finds roughly 50 per cent of families democratic-equalitarian with regard to parent-adolescent decision-making and only 34 per cent father-centered and autocratic-authoritarian. A representative sample of Detroit families suggests that 46 per cent are equalitarian, with about 22 per cent male dominant and 22 per cent female dominant. But as extrapolation proceeds, is the result to be 100 per cent equalitarians in the future? During most of their lives, children are relatively puny contributors to decision-making. Will not parents be authoritarian with respect to children into adolescence while being equalitarian with respect to husband-wife participation in decisions? Will equalitarian mean more shared decision-making or more segregation of decisions in which the wife makes most of the household and child-care decisions and the husband makes many of the financial decisions most of the time? A quick assessment indicates that this method of extrapolating on trends (which has failed in the past) would be an exciting but dangerous method to use in identifying the family of the future unless assumptions about the social and economic order were made crystal-clear and predictions were charted accordingly.

Projection from Generational Changes

A second method carries some of the same hazards but justifies attention; namely, the projection of changes perceived by studying three generations of the same family as the author and his colleagues have done in the metropolitan Minneapolis–St. Paul area. The method consists of examining the consistent differences which persist over three generations into the married-child generation—regarding the families of this latter generation as the best indications of what the American family of the future will be like. The sample studied consists of intact families linked through three generations and living within 50 miles of Minneapolis–St. Paul who were obtained from area probability samples of the metropolitan area. One hundred grandparent families (ages 60–80), 100 parent families (ages 40–60), and 100 married-children families (ages 20–30) survived five interviews extending over a year's period. These families are ecologically dispersed, distributed by social class and economic levels, but somewhat more stable residentially than comparable families without three-generation linkages.

A number of changes over the three generations are notable: In average years of schooling completed, each generation surpasses its predecessor by an impressive margin, especially in the case of husbands. The superiority in education of wives over their husbands has decreased with each generation (grandparents, eight vs. six, parents, 11 vs. nine, and married children, 12.4 vs. 12.6). No longer is the wife as likely to be the more educated and literate member of the family.

Age at marriage has declined from 25.8 for grandfather to 23.6 for son to 21.9 for grandson, and from 21 for grandmother to 19.9 for granddaughter, showing a smaller age gap between spouses in the newest generation, two years vs. five years.

The number of children born and their spacing is curvilinear, with the parent generation (married during the Depression) having progessively longer intervals between births, from 18 months to five years compared with intervals of more nearly two years for the grandparent and married-child generations. The grandparent generation closed its family at 5.2 children, with over a fourth bearing eight or more children. The last child was born after 15 years of marriage, which stretched childbearing over a long period. The parent generation closed its family at 3.5 children, with over half in the two and three child categories. Their last child was born after ten years of marriage, shortening the childbearing span by more than four years over the preceding generation. The married-child generation still has over 20 years of possible childbearing ahead but has already produced more than two-thirds the number of the parent generation, averaging 2.4 children to date. It will surpass the parent generation but will close its family earlier as a result of closer spacing in the early years.

Comparing the occupational careers of the three generations, the impression emerges of acceleration in upgrading in the youngest generation. The married-child generation starts below the parent generation in less skilled jobs at the beginning of its career, but once under way in their chosen vocation, within a few years after marriage, their rate of advancement is clearly faster than their parents' was during the corresponding phase of their careers. By contrast with both, the grandparent generation suffered the lowest start and the slowest movement upward over their entire working lives. In each successive generation, more of the wives have worked the first several years of marriage, and more have returned to work as their children have grown up. In the married-child generation, 60 per cent of wives are working in the first years of marriage as compared with 20 per cent of wives at the beginning of marriage in the parent generation, and although still in the childbearing period, 40 per cent of the wives in the married-child generation married six to ten years are employed. The impact of the working wife on level of income, home ownership, and acquisition of durable goods is enormous.

In all economic matters, the married-child generation appears destined to outstrip the previous generations based on the achievements of each generation during the first ten years of marriage. Eighty per cent of the married-child generation has already exceeded the grandparent generation by becoming homeowners, an achievement reached by that proportion of the parent generation only after 20 years of marriage. In acquisition of durable goods, the married-child generation has overtaken the grandparent generation and is at the point in its inventory where the parent generation was after 35 years of marriage. The same can be said for bathroom and bedroom spaces in the home and other amenities. This has not been done at the expense of protective insurances or retirement provisions, for the married-child generation is well along in the acquisition of a portfolio of insurances and investments. Over 50 per cent have retirement provisions over and beyond social security, and 95 per cent have life insurance. This generation starts its marriage with 82 per cent covered, which is higher than their grandparents ever reached and as high as their parents achieved after 30 years of marriage.

Nelson Foote,[2] in examining these findings, characterized the phenomenon of change over the generations as "acceleration"—not just linear upward movement, but changes occurring at an accelerated rate: upgrading in education, in occupational composition toward professionalization, in income, in employment of wives, in upgrading of housing and the durable goods inventory, and in progressive improvement in protective insurances and investments—all at an accelerated rate. Each generation has become more innovative, as is indicated by the receptiveness to adoption of new home products earlier in marriage.

Certain other differences may seem more relevant to the description of the family of the future since they refer to the family's value orientations, organization, and problem-solving behaviors. In value orientations, the study drew from Brim's Cognitive Value Scales,[3] which were ingeniously devised from proverbial-type statements about life in several dimensions: fatalism, impulsivity, pessimism, and time orientation. The two older generations are predominantly fatalistic, prudential, optimistic, and present- or past-oriented; whereas the married-child generation is the least fatalistic and is prudential, moderately optimistic, and oriented to the future rather than to the present or past. Using Blood's[4] scaling of Evelyn Duvall's typologies of ideologies about parenthood and childhood which he formed into a Developmental-Traditionalism Scale, the grandparents are clearly the most traditional of the three generations, averaging less than half developmental responses: the parent generation is more developmental, with several parents falling on the clearly developmental side of the scale. The married-child generation is, as might be expected, the most developmental of all, with the longest range and the highest average score. The higher education of the third generation and its greater accessibility to parent-education materials may account for its greater espousal of developmental beliefs.

In family organization, marked differences appear in the authority patterns, the division of labor, and the marital integration of families by generation. In authority patterns, the shift to equalitarian patterns is greatest from the grandparent to the parent generation, but it holds up in the married-child generation. In division of tasks, there is more sharing of tasks and less specialization in the married-child generation as well as less attention to the conventions about what is men's work and women's work. Eighty-three per cent of couples did some role crossing in this generation, compared to 60 per cent in the grandparent generation.

Consensus on family values improves, but role integration deteriorates by generation; marital communication is especially low in the grandparent generation where role integration is highest. In the observations in the joint interview with husband and wife, in which differences between the spouses were generated by posing difficult questions which they were expected to answer as a pair, the interviewers found a greater readiness to enter into conflict among the youngest generation. The parent generation was loath to enter into conflict and slow to express hostility toward one another but proved to be lower on achieved consensus on the issues raised. The pattern of the youngest generation was frequently one of identifying differences, engaging in conflict, and then locating a basis for agreement with one party undertaking to smooth over the differences and seeking to "save face." Altogether, the interviewers found the youngest generation the most colorful and interesting—the couples of this generation were both most likely to experience conflict and to express hostility, but they were also most likely to conclude with consensus and gestures of affection.

Finally, the planning and problem-solving performance of the three generations over the year's period of observation was studied. In each successive generation, the number of plans expressed was greater, the number of actions taken during the year greater, and the proportion of pre-planned actions greater. Here the differences may only reflect the stage in family development of the representatives of each generation. The married-child generation makes many plans and carries out many actions because it is in an expanding phase of need. What is interesting, however, is that the so-called "flighty" young generation is the most likely to pre-plan its purchases, its residential moves, and its other consumer actions, with 51 per cent of its actions during the year pre-planned compared with 44 per cent in the grandparent generation. Moreover, the components of rational decision-making are more faithfully met in the married-child generation than in its antecedents. That is, the child generation is more likely than the more seasoned generations to search for information outside the immediate family, to weigh satisfaction among alternatives, and to take into account long-term as well as short-term consequences.

Surely these data are adequate to demonstrate the possibilities of utilizing generational changes as the basis for capturing the American family of the future. From this analysis a picture emerges of increasing effectiveness, professional competence, and economic well-being, of greater courage in risk-taking accompanied by greater planning, of greater flexibility in family organization with greater communication and greater conflict between spouses. There is little evidence in this generation of the phenomenon of reaction-formation which is supposed to explain the turn to the right politically. This is a generation which has enjoyed the material amenities and has already chosen to elaborate the nonmaterial values of home and children. Their educational aspirations for their children are the highest of the generations.

The Impact of Inventions

The third method for capturing the future family involves speculation about the impact of inventions on the family. (With the imagination and skill of Meyer Nimkoff and his eminent colleague, the late W. F. Ogburn, whose work on inventions is now classic, this method might pay off.) The assumption here is that household conveniences designed to save time will have specified effects on family patterns. Among the many time-savers that have been invented and merchandised are the clothes dryer, the TV dinner and other kinds of processed foods, and automatic cookers. Then, to take up the time saved, time-fillers have been invented, such as television, now fully diffused among the entire population; hi-fi; do-it-yourself tools; and go-primitive-in-your-own-backyard-barbecuing types of inventions.

This particular method for identifying the future is exciting but hazardous, for the invention of time-savers results in increasing the quality of service but not in more leisure time, so that the sheer number of hours employed in housekeeping has not decreased markedly except for gainfully employed women who take advantage of these devices to save time. Inventions instead seem to increase the family's level of living before they reduce homemaking time: wearing a clean shirt daily instead of making it last three days is now the norm. There is also some evidence that families have turned away from the accumulation of durable time-savers, time-fillers, and comforts to make *children* the articles of consumption that they wish to enjoy. Some families have gone so far as to reject comforts and time-savers in order to live under simpler conditions.

Extrapolating to the family of the future by extending changes that inventions are intended to bring about may overstate the impact of these inventions. In the past we have overestimated the speed with which certain inventions would be merchandized and underestimated the toughness of the fabric of family habits. We probably overlooked the interaction between consumer and invention in shaping the use to which an invention is put.

The Family Specialist's Future Family

The fourth method for dealing in futures is most novel of all but may not provide any prediction regarding the American family of the future. This method starts with the fraternity of professionals engaged in marriage and family research and education. It asks what the future of the American family would be if the family inadvertently advocated through the choice of problems selected for research and for discussion in textbooks and classes were to be taken seriously by the whole country and used as a basis for upgrading American families. This method is dealt with last so that it may be pondered longer. As active agents in shaping the future of the American family by their writing, teaching, and counseling, what variety of family forms and functions are family professionals advocating?

A content analysis of the indexes of a number of marriage and family textbooks published this year has been compared by this writer with the emphases in the first marriage text, published thirty years ago. Examination has also been made of the research problems published in

Marriage and Family Living for the past five years for other evidences of current concerns. The table prepared by Nye and Bayer[5] showing the independent and dependent variables employed in marriage and family research from 1947–61 in 456 publications has been utilized. Finally, attention has been given to the properties which have been operationalized into scales and indexes and which Murray Straus has evaluated in his abstracts of family measurements.[6] The author has attempted to rephrase the most frequently mentioned concerns in the textbooks into miniature objectives which add up to major clusters. A parallel listing of research problems most frequently treated has also been made.

TABLE 1

A Ranking of Objectives for the American Family from Frequency of Attention in Textbooks and Research

First Marriage Textbook (1934)

I. Better understanding of sex and reproduction (33%)
Pregnancy and childbirth
Conception and contraception
Anatomy of sex
Psychology of sex
Menopause
Infertility
Homosexuality
Masturbation

II. Control of communicable diseases and inherited disabilities (18%)
Venereal diseases
Cancer, heart disease, diabetes, glaucoma
Hereditary disabilities, epilepsy, hemophilia, psychoses

III. Better functioning families (17%)
Parental competence in infant and child care and training
More equitable division of power and duties
Better family adjustment

IV. Better mate selection and screening of unmarriageables (17%)
Better use of courtship and engagement (avoid breach of promise suits)
Marriage not for everyone
Later age at marriage

V. More effective and companionable marriages (14%)

Better financial planning
Better adjusted marriages
More stability, less divorce
Better sex adjustment
Better use of honeymoon

Published Empirical Research, MFL, 1958–63

I. Better functioning families (45%)
Comparative family structures and their consequences in other
   societies
Correlates of effective family—size control
Correlates of different types of power structures
Causes and consequences of maternal employment
In-law and kinship interactions
Family structure and child adjustment
Consequences of different childrearing practices
Correlates of family integration
Developmental changes in the family over the life span

II. Improved preventive and remedial services (20%)
Techniques and consequences of marriage and family education
Methods and consequences of marriage and family counseling

III. More effective and companionable marriages (15%)
Correlates of marital satisfaction and adjustment
Correlates of marital communication and marital interaction
Correlates of types of sex role allocations
Consequences of sex role expectations and conflicts
Consequences of religious factors
Correlates of sex adjustment
Consequences of extramarital relations

IV. Better mate selection and screening of unmarriageables (15%)
Consequences of differences in timing of marriage, late mar-
   riage vs. early marriage
Dating patterns and consequences
Courtship progress
Experiments and controls in mate selection by class, religion,
   and ethnic groups
Correlates of romanticism
Controls and consequences of premarital sex behavior

V. Sex and sexuality (5%)
Sex deviation patterns
Sex attitudes

Sex drive
Conditions and properties of unwed mothers

Three 1963 Marriage Textbooks

I. Better mate selection (34%)
More realistic motives for marriage
Later age for marriage, maturity
Considerations of marriageability
Use of dating for developing competence in interpersonal relations
Use of engagement for testing compatibility
More mutuality in sex relations, less exploitation
Single high or single permissive standard for premarital sex
Homogamous over heterogamous combinations

II. More companionable and competent marriages (33%)
Better adjusted, happier, and more satisfied marriages (11%)
Less divorce, but remarriage acceptable
Maintenance of companionship in marriage
Better planning for contingencies, better decisions
Better preparation for pregnancy and parenthood
More constructive use of conflict
More use of marriage counseling and family-life education

III. Better functioning families (17%)
Greater competence in childrearing, more developmental views
More equitable division of power between sexes and ages
More mutuality and sharing of home tasks, less conformity to conventional sex roles
Improved in-law and kinship relations
More effective family-size control at optimum size

IV. Better understanding of sex and reproduction (14%)
Better information about:
Conception and contraception
Infertility and sterility
Techniques of coitus
Pregnancy and childbirth
Psychology of sex

Research Variables Operationalized into Scales and Indexes (Straus, *Family Measurement Abstracts,* 1963) 263 Measures

I. Family, parent-child, and child properties (52%)
Parent-child control and authority

        Parent-child adjustment
        Parent-child affection and support
        Parental activity with children
        Family integration
        Family solidarity
        Family adjustment
        Family authority or power
        Family division of duties
        Familism-individualism
        Traditional-developmental beliefs about parenthood and children
        Family-kinship interaction
        Parental attentiveness to children
        Family acceptance of community

II. Properties of the marriage (32%)
        Marital adjustment
        Marital agreement
        Marital authority
        Marital empathy
        Marital happiness
        Marital projection of agreement
        Marital tension
        Marital communication
        Marital community of interests

III. Properties of the premarital pair (16%)
        Romanticism
        Marital role expectations
        Engagement adjustment
        Courtship involvement and progress
        Conformity to moral codes

It can be seen that the research· problems treated are for the most part instrumental in type. Given the family objective, the research tells what the correlates are which will have to be manipulated to achieve the research objectives or tells the consequences of manipulating the dependent variables. Thus there are many items such as Correlates of Marital Adjustment, Consequences of Different Childrearing Practices, or Consequences of Premarital Sex Relations.

What does this method indicate about family workers' concerns and interests? The first marriage textbook put heaviest emphasis on Better Understanding of Sex and Reproduction (33%) and Control of Communicable Diseases and Inherited Disabilities (18%); 30 years later it is almost assumed that these objectives are achieved. Disease control, including venereal disease control, is absent from the 1963 texts, and virtually no research by family researchers treats it; hereditary issues are no longer problematic. Better Understanding of Sex and Reproduction is in last place in the 1963 texts, and the anatomy of sex and issues of masturbation, homosexuality, and the menopause are no longer seen as deserving of attention.

In 1963, in contrast, first place goes to a host of objectives under the cluster of Better Mate Selection (34%)—particularly to the screening out of unmarriageables, a preventive-type objective. Agreement seems to exist on the objectives of screening out immature personalities and slowing up couples with insufficient acquaintance or of incompatible backgrounds and temperaments; the effort seems directed at making it more difficult to enter marriage. Longer and more effective courtships and engagements are advocated for testing and previewing the marriage relationship. Exploitation in sex relations and in dating is deplored, and mutuality and companionship in dating and courtship are favored. But disagreement arises over whether a single code of high premarital sex morality or of permissiveness should be encouraged among young people today—some proof that Terman's prediction has not yet been achieved. Timing marriage after schooling has been completed is preferred, but the high quality of many college marriages and some high-school marriages necessitates the qualification, "It all depends. . . ." In general, marriage of people with similar backgrounds is advocated, but the success of many international, interethnic, and interfaith marriages, and the evidence that all marriages are to some degree "mixed marriages" are facts which temper this preference.

In second place, with very nearly as much attention in the 1963 texts as Better Mate Selection, is the cluster, More Companionable and Competent Marriages (33%). In 1934 the same cluster appeared in last place, but it won 14 per cent of the author's attention. The chief attention in this cluster is focused on better adjusted, more satisfied, and happier marriages. Whereas in 1934 this problem was seen as a function of good sex adjustment and psychological compatibility with good financial planning, in 1963 the researches cited include over two hundred different factors related at least once to good marriage adjustment. Nye and Bayer show 193 different analyses of the correlates of marital success. Indeed, marital success outnumbers any other dependent variable in their inventory. They state that if one were to join the analyses of dating success, courtship success, and marital success together, they would find that one-quarter of the analyses reported over the 14-year period deal with the success or failure of the marital relationship or the preliminary interaction preceding such success or failure. Surely this is one cluster of objectives—Better Adjusted Marriages— where family professionals hope to affect the family of the future.

The balance of the miniature objectives are highly related to marital adjustment, more companionship in marriage, and better preparation for pregnancy and parenthood. But there is some uncertainty among writers as to how much conflict is constructive for families. Although essential agreement exists on the values of family stability, divorce and remarriage have been regarded as a healthier alternative for spouses and even children to continued unhappy marriage if marriage counseling fails. Family-life education and marriage counseling are also openly fostered, and the implications of this trend for the future family are broad.

In 1934 a higher rank was given to the cluster of objectives, Better Functioning Families, than in 1963, although the frequency of mention is about identical (17%). The ideology preferred for parents is developmental, the policies and practices permissive, and the power structure equalitarian. A more flexible division of tasks, more mutuality and sharing of home tasks with interchangeability of men's and women's tasks appears to be advocated rather than conformity to conventional sex roles. The only moot questions in the objectives of this cluster have to do with timing of participation of children in decision-making and the severity of discipline for different age levels. Family-size control is treated in 1934 as a matter of sex knowledge involving the methods and techniques of contraception, but in 1963 it is treated as a family function to be mastered by arriving at agreement on number of children desired, spacing, and methods to be used. Some attention is given to conflicting beliefs of religious groups on the matter of methods.

In undertaking this content analysis of the 1963 textbooks, the author has been impressed by the research documentation which underpins the bulk of the treatment: the authors are selective of the problems they treat with an eye on the audience, but they are increasingly careful in their documentation of all generalizations. It is of interest, therefore, to see what differences are found between the listing of emphases in the marriage texts and in the research publications. Research emphases are less provincially limited to America than the textbooks which have been prepared for marriage and family classes. These researches permit the placing of American family patterns in cross-national perspective. The ranking of variables as important to study by researchers interchanges the clusters Improved Family Functions and Better Mate Selection, in comparison with the textbook writers. Some research problems studied are not given much attention in the textbooks: causes and consequences of maternal employment, family structure and child adjustment, family integration, methods and consequences of marriage and family counseling, consequences of extramarital sex relations, and conditions and characteristics of unwed mothers. The order with which research has been attentive to what is important to study puts heavy accent on issues which lend themselves to programs of upgrading families quite as well as to building a body of theory.

These materials have been scrutinized for the dependent variables most frequently chosen for study in research on the one hand, and the topic headings in leading texts on the other. There has been some hazard in doing this; namely, that neither researchers nor authors have said, "These are our goals for the family." They are implicit rather than explicit goals, goals identified through the selection of emphases in research and teaching. The yield of this study is both in its indications of new emergents and of things missing. In-law and kinship interaction concerns have emerged which were absent a decade ago— family and social network, family and neighborhood, and family and community studies. Other relationships have gone untouched: sibling relations, stepchild and stepparent relations, and analysis of one-parent families. Are all families intact, nuclear units of first marriages without horizontal relations between children?

Another question which arises is whether the several implied objectives are compatible: Are the goals for premarital pairs compatible with those for married pairs, and in turn for families and family-kin relations? Are there discontinuities in implied goals from one stage of development to the next? Are the goals of individuals, unvoiced in this series of researches, compatible with the goals for marriage and the family?

Conclusion

A rough summary follows of the properties and procedures which family-field professionals, according to their writings and researches, seem to want perpetuated in families of the future.

1. The mate-selection machinery should be reorganized to encourage

couples of reasonably similar backgrounds to meet and be tested for compatibility through a prolonged courtship and engagement.

2. Premarital sex relations should be no more intimate than the consciences of the couple can tolerate and the courting relation can sustain psychologically.

3. Premarital examinations, counseling, and education should help prepare the couple for marriage, postponing and returning to circulation those who are not ready.

4. The objectives of marriage should include the continued matching and stimulating of companionship, mutual understanding, common interests and joint activities, as well as building a system of planning and problem-solving.

5. With the coming of children and the activating of the parental roles, attention to family issues of needs of dependents competes with the needs in the marital relation for which preparation is indicated.

6. The chief objectives for the family phase can be listed as mastering the family tasks of each stage, including family-size control, physical maintenance, socialization, and gratification of emotional needs, and providing the motivation and morale necessary for the stimulation and development of personality potentials of all members.

7. To attain this high plane of family achievement, an effective group organization must be built and a competent family leadership must be trained. The accent in family organization should be on integrating objectives, good internal communication, clarity of role definitions, and patterns of problem-solving and decision-making. Leadership qualities needed stress interpersonal competence, of which autonomy, empathy, judgment, creativity, and self-mastery are highly relevant to marital and family success.

In projecting plans for NCFR during the next 25 years, recruitment of a membership increasingly sensitive to the needs and organizational properties of families is increasingly important. The day of taking the family for granted should be drawn to a close in America. Family specialists must consider what concerted effort they can make to help *all families* in a program of *family development,* which in a democratic society can be seen as a progressive upgrading of families comparable to urban development, economic development, and community development. Such a program is intended to be in contrast to the concepts of family adjustment or preservation of families which imply some restoration of the status quo. Families should be viewed as more than accommodating and adapting units; indeed, they should be seen as capable of transcending their present dimensions in realizing their goals and objectives, in growing and developing over time. The author advocates this program of family development not as a sentimental movement such as Americans mount on Mother's Day, which is more ritualistic than durable, nor as a militant movement European style, but as a sober recognition that only through a program of development can excellence be achieved in family living.

The capacity of families to take up the slack in the social order has limits which should not be tested by continued negligence. The tremendous resilience and recuperative strengths of families must be fostered and developed. The formulation of national policies which deal with America's millions of families as a precious national resource in social organization should be undertaken by this generation. This task will have the support of findings from hundreds of research studies and the approval of the great majority of families rearing children today.

NOTES

1. Lewis M. Terman, *Psychological Factors in Marital Happiness,* New York, McGraw-Hill, 1938, pp. 321–22.
2. Personal correspondence with the author.
3. See Appendix B in Orville G. Brim, Jr., *et. al., Personality and Decision Processes,* Stanford: Stanford University Press, 1962, pp. 309–12.
4. Robert O. Blood, Jr., *A Teacher's Manual For Use With Anticipating Your Marriage,* Glencoe, Illinois: Free Press, 1956, pp. 46–47.
5. F. Ivan Nye and Alan E. Bayer, "Some Recent Trends in Family Research," *Social Forces,* 41 (March, 1963), p. 294.
6. Murray A. Straus, "Measuring Families," in *Handbook on Marriage and The Family,* ed. by Harold T. Christensen, Chicago: Rand McNally, in press.

2 5

Familia Spongia: The Adaptive Function*

by Clark E. Vincent

The adaptive function is a vital but overlooked function of the family in all societies that are either highly industrialized or undergoing industrialization. This thesis, which the author is deliberately and provocatively writing to rather than attempting to test, could also be stated: The rapid and pervasive social changes associated with industrialization necessitate a family system that both structurally and functionally is highly adaptive externally to the demands of other social institutions and internally to the needs of its own members.

This thesis does not imply that the family is the cause or prime mover in social change. Nor does it imply that the adaptive function is performed exclusively by the family, or that the family is essentially passive in relation to other institutions. Other social institutions are deeply involved in social change, do respond to changing needs and demands of the family system; and the family system is selective in its adaptations. But the family, to a greater degree and more frequently than is true of the other major social institutions, facilitates social change by adapting its structure and activities to fit the changing needs of the society and other social institutions. A major reason for this is that the strategic socialization function of the family in preparing the individual for adult roles in the larger society is inseparable from the family's *mediation* function[1] whereby the changing requirements (demands, goals) of the society and its other social institutions are translated and incorporated into the ongoing socialization of both child and adult members of the family. A second reason is that the family as a social institution lacks an institutional spokesman or representative voice through which it might resist change.

In addressing this thesis the present paper is organized into four

* Presidential Address presented at the Annual Meeting of the National Council on Family Relations, Toronto, October 1965.

Reprinted from *Journal of Marriage and the Family,* 28 (February 1966), pp. 29–36, by permission of the author and the National Council on Family Relations.

parts. First is an abbreviated and highly selective review of some of the background issues and historical junctures in the literature on functions of the family. Second is a consideration of the adaptive function of the family in relation to the society and other social institutions. The third part considers the adaptive activities of the family in relation to its individual members and the fourth part raises the question of when adaptation becomes dysfunctional.

Background Issues and Historical Junctures

William F. Ogburn comes readily to mind when considering the functions of the family. His major interest in the processes of social change and his earlier writing on the impact of technology, inventions, and ideologies on the family provided the context for the massive empirical data he compiled in the late 1920's to emphasize the increasing transfer of economic, protective, recreational, educational, and religious activities from the family to outside agencies.[2] His initial and more cautious interpretation that these increases in outside-the-home activities were indices of decreases in the *traditional* functions of the family was replaced in his later writings by assertions about the family's loss of functions.[3]

Ogburn's initial interpretation was rarely given critical examination or tested in the textbooks and writings on the family in the 1930's and 1940's. Consequently, his observations and impressive statistical data concerning the decreases in the *traditional* (forms of) functions of the family became the basis or reference point for two widely held beliefs: (1) The family has lost many of its functions. (2) This loss of functions represents a decline (decay, disorganization) of the family.

Textbooks and journal articles published since the early 1930's have included a variety of data and illustrative materials interpreted to demonstrate that the family has lost many of its functions. Descriptions of an "ideal typical" pioneer or rural family needing only a few dollars a year for supplies it could not produce were contrasted with census data on, for example, the number of women in the labor force and the increasing number of restaurants, laundries, stores, etc., to show that the family was no longer a self-sustaining production unit economically. Loss of the educational function was illustrated with observations that sons were no longer apprenticed to their fathers, daughters learned cooking in home economics courses rather than at home, and the teaching hours and authority of the schools had increased constantly since the turn of the century. The loss of the protective function was illustrated with references to the duties of the policeman, truant officer, nurse, fireman, and the use of nursing homes and mental institutions. Support for the notion that the religious function was being transferred from the family was found, for example, in statistics reporting a decreasing proportion of families having daily devotions, reading the Bible, and saying grace before meals. In regard to recreational activities, it was noted that the family no longer produced its own recreation in the form of quilting parties, corn husking bees, and parlor games, and figures were given to show the marked increase in attendance at movies and spectator sports.

The Loss of Functions—A Myth?

It is interesting to speculate about what might have happened if students of the family: (a) had kept in mind Ogburn's central interest in social change, and (b) had emphasized that it was the traditional content and form of given functions, rather than functions *qua* functions, that were being performed decreasingly by the family.

Taking the latter possibility first, one can argue that in each case of a traditional function supposedly lost to the family as a social institution, the loss has in reality been but a *change in content and form.* For example, although the U.S. family is no longer an economic producing unit to the degree it was in the pioneer and rural America of several generations ago, it is an economic consuming unit. Is consumption by the family unit any less important an economic function in today's society than production by a family unit was in yesterday's society? To what degree does our current economy depend on the family *qua* family to "consume" houses, cars, boats, cereals, furniture, vacations, sterling silver, china, and pet food?

Similarly, one might argue that society is currently quite dependent on the family function of consuming recreation. It is quite possible (but almost impossible to measure) that today's family spends far more time not only in consuming but also in producing its own recreation than did the family of 50 or 100 years ago. Here we think not only of the multimillion dollar sales annually of croquet, ping-pong, and badminton sets, cameras and home movies, family card games and barbecue equipment, but also of the family's expenditures for and use of swimming pools, rumpus rooms, camping equipment, summer homes, boats, television and hi-fi sets, etc.

Similar arguments can be made in relation to the purported loss of the educational, religious, and protective functions. That fewer families, for example, say grace and have daily Bible reading today than 100 years ago (assuming this to be the case) does not demonstrate the loss of a religious function. For to omit grace before meals, nightly prayers, and daily Bible reading is one kind of religious instruction, albeit not the traditional kind. If the family has lost its educational and religious functions, why do the majority of children hold religious, political, and social class beliefs similar to those of their parents? Why are the asocial attitudes and immoral practices of the delinquent and the criminal traced to the family and not to the church? Why is it that the family in general and the parents in particular are considered to be key variables in determining how well and how far the child progresses in school? Why is the family, more so than the school system, blamed for dropouts? Did parents of 100, 50, or even 20 years ago spend as much time as today's parents do in helping and prodding their children with homework? Did the pioneer parents who withdrew their children from school to work on the farm perform more of an educational function than today's parents who save, borrow, and mortgage to provide 16-plus years of schooling for their children?

The foregoing questions and examples grossly oversimplify the arguments and beg the question on many issues involved. In fact, many of these questions and examples would be irrelevant if Ogburn and the earlier family textbook writers had emphasized that the family had lost, for example, an *economic production* function but gained an *economic consumption* function. Instead, however, they emphasized that the family had lost its *economic* function. (Similarly, they emphasized the loss of the religious, educational, protective, and recreational functions.) They thereby precluded analysis of changes in the family's economic function and set the stage for the subsequent equating of the loss of functions with the decline of the family. Thus, the foregoing questions remain relevant and are intended to provoke some students of the family to critically examine the myth of the family's loss of functions. Hopefully, such students will focus their attention more on the structural changes, the sharing of functions among social institutions, and the changing content and form of the functions of the family.

What might have happened if Ogburn's observations and data had not been taken out of the context of his general interest in social change and his specific interest in tracing the causes of changes in the family? Would the family textbooks and literature of the past three decades still have had a predominant emphasis on the declining importance of the family? Probably! Because, since the earliest writings available, changes occurring in the institution of the family have been used and interpreted to support either an optimistic or a pessimistic premise concerning social change, and the pessimists have consistently outnumbered the optimists. As Goode has noted in his sound criticism of the descriptions of the United States family of the past as a misleading stereotype of "the classical family of Western nostalgia," the same stereotype has been accepted as the baseline by those who view subsequent changes as progress as well as by those who interpret the subsequent changes as retrogression of the family.[4]

Ogburn's stature as a sociologist, his considerable ability in mining and compiling impressive empirical data, and his delineation and naming of broad categories of functions purportedly lost by the family all combined to make his writings an important juncture for the family literature of the past three decades. The issues involved are of long standing, however, and space permits only passing reference to the existence of a much earlier and voluminous literature in which the differences and/or changes in the structure and functions of the family were interpreted to support quite different "theories" of social change. Some earlier writers with an optimistic premise of unilinear progress made considerable use of the "voyage literature" and "social Darwinism" to try to demonstrate a progressive evolution of the family from "primitive" to "modern" forms and from promiscuity to monogamy.[5] Other earlier writers reflected a more pessimistic premise in attempting to show that changes from a previous form of social order represented decay, instability, or disorganization of the family.[6]

To move quickly and briefly from Ogburn to the present, it was noted earlier that the purported loss of functions by the family was interpreted in the majority of family textbooks written during the 1930's and early 1940's to be evidence, if not the cause, of the decay, disorganization, and deterioration of the family as a social institution. Sorokin wrote:

> The family as a sacred union of husband and wife, of parents and children will continue to disintegrate—the main socio-cultural functions of the family will further decrease until the family becomes a mere overnight parking place mainly for sex relationship.[7]

But Sorokin was not alone. John B. Watson in psychology and Carle Zimmerman and Ruth Anshen in sociology were only a few among the many writers in the 1930's and 1940's who not only assumed a decay or decline of the family, but (a) attempted to explain how that decline had come about and (b) posited that the family was the prime mover or first cause of social change.[8]

A More Optimistic Premise about Social Change

The assumption that the loss of functions was synonymous with a decline of the family began to share the limelight in the late 1940's with more optimistic interpretations. One interpretation, largely attributable to Burgess and Locke, emphasized that the changes in the family really represented progress in the form of a change from an institutional to a companionship orientation.[9] In the late 1950's and early 1960's, a generally more optimistic view of changes in the institution of the family gained support from a number of writers who still accepted the premise of a loss of functions but who argued that the remaining functions had become more important. Straus,[10] Kirkpatrick,[11] and Rodman[12] have noted the increasing variety of conceptual labels used to convey this more optimistic view of the changing nature of the American family. As an alternative to Burgess and Locke's "companionship family," Miller and Swanson[13] have proposed the "colleague family," and Farber has suggested the "permanent-availability model." [14]

Notable among the writers emphasizing that the remaining functions are more important is Parsons. His current interpretations, as Rodman has noted,[15] represent a much more optimistic position than he had taken earlier. In his more recent writings, Parsons has emphasized that changes occurring in the family involve gains as well as losses and that when functions are lost by a particular unit in society, that unit is freer to concentrate upon other functions. "When two functions, previously imbedded in the same structure, are subsequently performed by two newly differentiated structures, they can *both* be fulfilled more intensively and with a greater degree of freedom." [16] Parsons has also emphasized increasingly that the contemporary American family is differentiated and not disorganized. "The family is more specialized than before, but not in any general sense less important, because the society is dependent *more* exclusively on it for the performance of *certain* of its various functions." [17]

Goode has also supported a more optimistic interpretation of changes in the family by emphasizing its *mediating* function. The idea that the family is a mediator (buffer, strainer, funnel) between the individual and the larger society has been both implicit and explicit in the family textbooks for several decades, but Goode is the first (to this writer's knowledge) to base the strategic significance of the family specifically on its mediating function.[18]

The Adaptive Function and Society

The following discussion of the adaptive function of the family in relation to society and/or other social systems in that society is within the framework of what Mannheim called "relationism" [19] and what Goode and others have referred to as the "fit" between a given family system and the larger society.[20] Thus, the present discussion is not dependent on an "organic analogy," or on the idea that there is some inherent or ideal function that the family "ought to perform." [21]

Superficially, the adaptive function of the family has some sponge-like characteristics that are evidenced by the family's absorption of blame for most social problems (mental illness, delinquency, dropouts, alcoholism, suicide, crime, illegitimacy, etc.). And future studies of the scapegoat function within and among groups may have some applicability to the scapegoat function among social systems or institutions. Evidences of the family's adaptive function relevant to the present discussion may be illustrated with reference to the economic system.

Adaptation to the Economic System

The economic system of a highly industrialized society demands a mobile labor force as well as some professional, skilled, and semi-skilled personnel who will work on holidays, Sundays, and at night. When the company employing father decrees that father shall move to another city, furtherance of the company's objectives is made possible by the adaptiveness (willingly or grudgingly) of the entire family; collectively and individually, the family members uproot themselves, adapt to a new city and neighborhood, enter different schools, and make new friends.

The varieties of family adaptation required by particular occupations have been illustrated in a number of studies, such as the early one by W. F. Cottrell, "Of Time and the Railroader." [22] The family of the railroad engineer, fireman, conductor, or porter might celebrate Christmas on the 23rd or the 27th of December, as dictated by the railroad schedule. The reader can supply many examples of jobs in transportation, communication, entertainment, and various professional services which require considerable adaptiveness in the schedules and patterns of the families involved. William Foote Whyte,[23] among others, has described in some detail the degree to which the family and particularly the wives of management are required to adapt to the large corporation. Somewhat conversely, studies such as the one by Alvin W. Gouldner have shown how becoming a husband and father can influence the union leader's role performance on the job.[24]

The adaptation of the family to occupational demands and economic pressures also includes the pattern observed in the Appalachian area where employment is more readily obtained by wives and where thousands of husbands have adapted to the role of homemaker.

It is true that the family breadwinner has a choice, and that the family can be selective in its adaptation. The breadwinner can change jobs, but this becomes only a choice of the manner in which one adapts. Rarely is the worker able to refuse to adapt to the demands of a job or position and still retain that position without a future adaptation of his family to less security and income than might have been forthcoming.

The adaptations required of the family by the educational systems are both minor and major. The minor adaptations may be found in such areas as P.T.A. pressures for parental attendance at monthly meetings, increased homework and the expected supervision of such homework by parents, funds for daily lunches, lack of control over the use of personality and achievement test results, categorizing of rapid and slow learners, and split or double shifts. Major adaptations are related to the increases in the number of years, the costs, and the specialization of formal education that frequently necessitate heavy family indebtedness.

The Reproductive Function and Reciprocal Adaptation

That the educational, religious, and economic systems in society adapt to the family is most evident in regard to the reproductive function of the family. Educational and religious institutions have had to expand their facilities considerably as a result of the rise in the birth rate in the middle and late 1940's. The business world has adapted its advertising and merchandising to the crest of the population wave—the initial boom in infant foods, children's toys, clothes catering to teen-agers' tastes and influence on family buying habits, the increasing market in automobiles for the 16-21 year olds, the recent and current increase in sales of diamond rings and sterling silver, and the anticipated uptrend in housing for newlywed couples in the late 1960's.

At least three crucial points may be hypothesized concerning the reciprocal adaptation among various social systems: (1) Social institutions or systems other than the family adapt to the degree that such adaptation is in the interest of their respective goals. (2) If there is a conflict of interests or goals, it is the family which "gives in" and adapts. (3) The family adapts for lack of an alternative and in so doing serves the goals of other social systems and facilitates the survival of a society based on social change.

The plausibility of the first hypothesis is suggested by the fact that although the reproductive function would appear to be the one major function whereby the family "forces" adaptation from other social institutions, this is tolerated only to the degree that such adaptation furthers the ends or goals of the other institutions. The upswing in births in the 1940's was initially interpreted to represent more profits for business. In fact, the baby boom was equated with prosperity. The birth rate rise was also favorably viewed as meaning more potential converts for the churches, and higher wages and better job security for teachers, school administrators, and professors. However, in the late 1950's and early 1960's, the baby boom acquired another, almost opposite interpretation as the increasing number of teen-agers about to enter the labor market added to fears about the unemployment rate, and as high schools and colleges faced enrollments and building programs that necessitated sharp increases in tax monies. Equally, if not more important, has been the world-wide concern about depletion of natural resources and living space.

The subsequent and current concerted attack upon the problem of "conceptionitis," "birthquake," or "population explosion" provides a fascinating illustration of how even in regard to its traditional function of reproduction, the family adapts (gradually, and rarely through force) to the goals and interests of the society and of its other major social systems.

That it is the family system that gives in or adapts in cases of conflict of interests or goals was noted earlier in the discussion of the demands of the labor market, job position, and business corporation. The school system, the business world, and even church services are geared to time schedules that serve first the needs, interests, and efficiency of the school, the business, and the church. The family adapts its schedule accordingly. Even in times of war and armed conflict, the adaptations required of economic, educational, and religious institutions usually have some side-effects beneficial to those social institutions, whereas the family sacrifices most in the interests of winning the war.

That the family lacks an alternative to adaptation (although it may select among several patterns of adaptation) may be illustrated with reference to what Ogburn called the protective function. Within the past half decade, there has developed very rapidly a nationwide program to return mental patients to their families. Backed by multi-million dollars in federal funds, this program is intended to greatly reduce the number of patients in mental hospitals and institutions. Comprehensive community mental health centers will be built and staffed to provide outpatient, night-care, day-care and "half-way cottage" services. The family is expected to adapt to the return of its mentally ill or emotionally disturbed members, just as it was expected to adapt to the return of the parolee member of the family several decades ago. The family will also be expected to adapt to the intrusion of the mental health personnel concerned with the rehabilitation of the patient, just as it has adapted to the intrusion of the parole and probation officers, the judge of the juvenile court, and the social worker.

Why? Because the family has no realistic alternative. Given the mores of our society, how could the family maintain its ideological image if it refused to accept one of its members convalescing from mental illness or rehabilitating from crime or delinquency?

More importantly, who would be the spokesman for the family's refusal? The National Association for Mental Health has a powerful and effective lobby. The family has none. Almost every segment of the religious, educational, professional, recreational, political, and occupational worlds has strong and powerful spokesmen at local, state, and national levels. Each group of 20 physicians, 30 ministers, 40 school teachers, five manufacturers, or three union men in a given city can exert more influence and pressure directly or indirectly than can 5,000 families living in that same city.

Thus, no one asks: How will the family be affected by the return of a mentally ill member? What will double shifts at school do to the family? Will the regulations of ADC encourage husbands to desert the family? Will urban renewal disrupt the family and the network of extended family relationships? Would it be easier on the family to draft 45-year-old fathers for many service tasks prior to drafting 25-year-old fathers for those same tasks?

And even if such questions were asked, who would answer? The family system has no collective representative, no lobbyist, no official spokesman. Therefore, to observe that the family is the most adaptive of the several social systems in a rapidly changing society is perhaps only to recognize that it is the least organized.

Adaptation Within the Family

Adaptiveness would appear to be inversely related to the degree of organization and to the size or number of the group. The rigidity of the army, for example, is apparently positively related to its chain of command and its size. The size or number involved in what we refer to as the family system, however, tends to be the number in each individual family; and because the family system is *un*organized as a family system beyond each individual family, it is easily divided and its resistance conquered. Thus, in a given community, the organizational spokesmen for the teachers, the union, the clergy, or business can be and are heard and heeded much more clearly than are 50,000 *individual* families.

Its small numerical size and its lack of an organizational tie-in with all other families not only predisposes the individual family to adapt to the needs and demands of the other social systems, but facilitates its adaptation to the needs of its individual members. The highly individualized needs of each of 40 persons cannot possibly be heard or met to the same degree in the classroom, factory, office, or church as within the respective families of those 40 persons.

Much of the lament about the impersonalization, alienation, or dehumanization of human beings in the multiversity, factory, corporation, hospital, or large urban church obscures the lack of an alternative. The same individuals who may privately bemoan the *a*personal cashier in the supermarket, the tight-lipped teller in the bank, the hurried physician, the unavailable professor, or the uncommunicative dispenser of other professional services would strongly object to waiting in line for an extra hour while other customers and clients were being responded to warmly and personally on an individual basis. The Lilliputians, who thought that Gulliver's timepiece must be a God to require such frequent consultations, would justifiably infer that the citizens of highly industrialized societies not only worship but are governed and ruled by time. In such societies, the family becomes even more important as a flexible social unit wherein there is time and tolerance for expressing and acting out individual needs, and wherein being a few minutes late does not disrupt the production lines, board meetings, transportation schedules, and classroom lectures. The time-scheduling demands which a technological society makes of the individual are perhaps minor in comparison with its demands for productive output, self-discipline, and emotional control. In combination, these demands increase the importance of what Goode has phrased as the family "task of restoring the input-output emotional balance of individualism. . . ." [25]

Can a society undergo industrialization and/or remain highly industrialized without a family system that is highly adaptive to change, to the demands of other social systems or institutions, and to the needs of its individual members? Although a negative answer to this question was stated in positive form as a thesis at the beginning of this paper, the final answers will depend on considerable historical and cross-cultural research *in context*. Goode's recent work has provided some invaluable bench marks for such research. His comparative analysis of the family systems in quite disparate cultures provides sound support for the idea that ". . . we are witnessing a remarkable phenomenon: The development of similar family behavior and values among much of the world's population." [26]

Eufunctional or Dysfunctional?

The thesis of the present paper represents only one selected facet of Goode's much broader inquiry concerning whether and why there is an increasing world-wide similarity in family behavior and values. Thus far, our attempts to illustrate the merits of this thesis have interpreted the family's adaptiveness to other social systems and to its own members as predominately eufunctional. Is the adaptive function of the family at times dysfunctional? And if so, dysfunctional at what point? for whom? and in relation to what purposes?

One example of dysfunctional adaptation is provided by the Aid to Dependent Children (ADC) program. In adapting to the early regulations of ADC, an unknown proportion of fathers deserted their families, or perhaps in collusion with their wives simply disappeared from public view, to enable their wives and children to qualify for ADC funds. Current awareness that the early regulations may have encouraged such desertions, and the belief that such families need a father present (or the premise that an unemployed father in the home is better than no father or a series of adult males) have resulted in much discussion and some revisions of the regulations. Similarly, the family's adaptiveness (for lack of an alternative) to urban renewal may prove in some instances to have ill-served the interests of either the families forced to move or the city planners and taxpayers.

The fact that these two examples pertain to lower-income families illustrates the variability in the degree and form of adaptive activities among the family systems of various socio-economic and ethnic groups. In the United States, for example, it has been postulated that the nuclear family system of the middle class is more likely to manipulate the extended family, whereas the lower- and the upper-class family systems are more likely to be manipulated by or to adapt to the extended family.[27]

An example or illustration which cuts across class lines is to be found in the internal adaptiveness of the family to its teen-age members. When familial adaptation to the needs and wants of its teen-age members reaches the point or degree where parental control is lost, such degree of adaptation becomes dysfunctional within the context of the socialization function of the family. That parental control is frequently lost or tenuously held at best is not surprising when we consider that: (a) a sizable proportion of the current generation of teen-agers was reared via a permissive philosophy that equated wants with needs; (b) teen-agers are highly organized in their selective translations to parents about what the teen-age peer group is allowed to do by other parents; and (c) parents are remarkably *un*organized in their resistance to teen-agers' demands and expectations.

Again, the reader will be able to supply many examples of both external and internal adaptations of the family which he or she regards as dysfunctional. The more difficult task is to make explicit: dysfunctional for whom and for what goal? To return the mental patient to the family may well serve the goals of reducing the inpatient load of mental hospitals, save the taxpayers money, and prove highly therapeutic for the patient. But will it also have some dysfunctional aspects for the family and society?[28] Will the family still be able to permit the emotional blow-offs and to provide the relaxation and the emotional input needed daily by its "well" members whose output, tight schedules, and emotional control will continue to be expected in the office, factory, and schoolroom?

The foregoing is not intended as an argument against the gradual return of emotionally disturbed, aged, or infirm persons to their families. It is simply a further attempt to illustrate: (a) that the adaptive function of the family system is crucial in any society characterized by rapid social change, (b) that the adaptive family system of our industrial era generally is *un*organized and unrepresented beyond each individual family, and (c) that it, therefore, is predisposed to being overloaded with or overadaptive to the demands and expectations with which it is confronted, internally and externally.[29]

The author's thesis remains that an industrialized society characterized by rapid social change necessitates a highly adaptive family system. This adaptiveness of the family will be interpreted by some as evidence of weakness and by others as evidence of strength. Those who view it as weakness may point to the family's loss of power and authority, while those who interpret its adaptability as strength may see the dependence of the larger social system on the flexibility of the family and see the family's adaptive function as crucial to its socialization and mediation functions. The family's internal adaptiveness may well prove to be a key variable in socializing the child for the flexibility needed in future adult roles within a rapidly changing society.

NOTES

1. William J. Goode, *The Family*, Englewood Cliffs, N.J.: Prentice-Hall, 1964, p. 2.
2. See William F. Ogburn, *Social Change*, New York: Viking Press, 1922; and "The Changing Family," *Publications of the American Sociological Society*, 23 (1929), pp. 124–133; and William F. Ogburn and Clark Tibbitts, "The Family and its Functions," Chap. 13 in *Recent Social Trends in the United States*, New York: McGraw-Hill, 1933.
3. William F. Ogburn, "The Changing Family," *The Family*, XIX (1938), pp. 139–143; W. F. Ogburn and M. F. Nimkoff, *Technology and the Changing Family*, New York: Houghton-Mifflin, 1955, pp. 15, 45–48, 129–130, 244–247.
4. William J. Goode, *World Revolution and Family Patterns*, Glencoe, Ill.: Free Press, 1963, Chap. 1.
5. See, for example, Franz C. Muller-Lyer, *The Family*, New York: Alfred A. Knopf, 1931; and Herbert Spencer, *Principles of Sociology*, New York: Appleton-Century, 1897, Vol. I, pp. 653, 681–683.
6. For a cogent review of the major "Traditionalists" and "Philosophical Conservatives" who reacted to the individualism of the French Revolution legislation with efforts to strengthen the family and reconstitute the *ancien regime*, see Robert A. Nisbet, *The Quest for Community: A Study in the Ethics of Freedom and Order*, New York: Oxford U. Press, 1953.
7. Pitirim A. Sorokin: *Social and Cultural Dynamics*, 1937, Vol. V, p. 776; and *The Crisis of Our Age*, New York: E. P. Dutton, 1941, p. 187.
8. Carle C. Zimmerman, *Family and Civilization*, New York: Harper &

Bros., 1947, pp. IX, 782–783, 802 ff.; *The Family: Its Function and Destiny,* ed. by Ruth N. Anshen, New York: Harper, 1949, p. 4.

9. Ernest W. Burgess and Harvey J. Locke, *The Family: From Institution to Companionship,* New York: American Book Co., 1945.

10. Murray A. Straus, "Conjugal Power Structure and Adolescent Personality," *Marriage and Family Living,* 24:1 (February 1962), pp. 17–25.

11. Clifford Kirkpatrick, "Housewife and Woman? The Best of Both Worlds?" in *Man and Civilization: The Family's Search for Survival,* ed. by S. M. Farber, P. Mustacchi, and R. H. L. Wilson, New York: McGraw-Hill, 1963, pp. 136–152.

12. Hyman Rodman, "Introduction" to Chap. 8, "The Changing American Family," in *Marriage, Family and Society: A Reader,* ed. by Hyman Rodman, New York: Random House, 1965, pp. 249–258.

13. Daniel R. Miller and Guy E. Swanson, *The Changing American Parent,* New York: John Wiley, 1958, pp. 198–202.

14. Bernard Farber, *Family: Organization and Interaction,* San Francisco: Chandler Publishing Co., 1964.

15. Hyman Rodman, "Talcott Parsons' View of the Changing American Family," in *Marriage, Family and Society: A Reader, op. cit.,* pp. 262–286.

16. Talcott Parsons, "The Point of View of the Author," in *The Social Theories of Talcott Parsons,* ed. by Max Black, Englewood Cliffs, N.J.: Prentice-Hall, 1961, p. 129.

17. Talcott Parsons and Robert Bales, *Family, Socialization and Interaction Process,* Glencoe, Ill.: Free Press, 1955, pp. 10–11.

18. Goode, *The Family, op. cit.,* p. 2.

19. Karl Mannheim, *Ideology and Utopia,* New York: Harcourt, Brace & Co., 1957, p. 86.

20. Goode, *World Revolution and Family Patterns, op. cit.,* pp. 10–26.

21. For a critical review of some of the historic, methodologic, and theoretic issues involved in "functionalism," see *Functionalism in the Social Sciences,* ed. by Don Martindale, Philadelphia: American Academy of Political and Social Science, Monograph 5, 1965.

22. W. F. Cottrell, "Of Time and the Railroader," *American Sociological Review,* IV (April 1939), pp. 190–198.

23. William F. Whyte, Jr.: "The Wives of Management," *Fortune,* October 1951; and "The Corporation and the Wife," *Fortune,* November 1951.

24. Alvin W. Gouldner, "Attitudes of 'Progressive' Trade Union Leaders," *American Journal of Sociology,* 52 (March 1947), pp. 389–392.

25. Goode, *World Revolution and Family Patterns, op. cit.,* p. 14.

26. *Ibid.,* p. 1.

27. See Marvin B. Sussman and Lee Burchinal, "Kin Family Network: Unheralded Structure in Current Conceptualizations of Family Functioning," *Marriage and Family Living,* 24 (August 1962), pp. 231–240; Eugene Litwak: "Geographic Mobility and Extended Family Cohesion," *American Sociological Review,* 25 (June 1960), pp. 385–394; and "Occupational Mobility and Extended Family Cohesion," *American Sociological Review,* 25 (February 1960), pp. 9–21.

28. Some of the contraindications and possible dysfunctional aspects of returning the patient to the family are discussed and relevant literature is cited in Clark E. Vincent, "The Family in Health and Illness,"

Annals of the American Academy of Political and Social Science, 346 (March 1963), pp. 109–116.

29. Lee Rainwater has commented on this predisposition to overloading as a concomitant of individualism and of how the family unit is perceived as secondary to the roles of its individual members in other social systems. "The [family] internal adaptation process presumably is guided by the demands that family members bring home based on their involvement with other institutions—career, teen-age peer group, school, etc. The family is seen by each particular institution as an extension of the person who has a role in that institution—business sees the executive's family as an extension of him in his executive role, the school sees the pupil's family as an extension of the pupil in his learning role, etc. Because of the value placed on individual achievement and gratification, the individual often identifies more with the demands of the secondary institution in which he has a role than he does with a solitary family." (Personal communication to the author.)

2 6

Work and Family in Contemporary Society*

by Robert Rapoport & Rhona Rapoport

In traditional societies, work and family structures tend to be linked as parts of an integrated cultural whole sustained by a complex web of social controls, so that the relations between work and family life

* The original draft of this paper was written while the authors were visitors at the Tavistock Institute of Human Relations, London, 1963. Thanks are extended to the staff of the Tavistock Clinic and Institute, and particularly to Eric Trist and Fred Emery for their stimulation and support. The part of the study most directly related to the family research stems from a project directed by Rhona Rapoport as part of the Unit headed by Dr. Gerald Caplan at Harvard (formerly the Community Mental Health Program of the Harvard School of Public Health, now the Laboratory of Community Psychiatry of the Harvard Medical School) under a grant from the U.S. Public Health Service, NIMH Grant #MH-03442. Thanks are due to Gerald Caplan for his consistent support and encouragement. Robert Rapoport was supported while at the Tavistock Institute by a Social Science Research Council Faculty Research Grant, and gathered some of the data on which the paper is based while supported by a Research Professorship at Northeastern University and working as a member of a study group of the Committee on Space supported by a NASA grant to the American Academy of Arts and Sciences. A draft of this paper was presented at the Eastern Sociological Association Meetings in Boston, 1964. In revising that draft, critical comments from Marc Fried were most helpful.

Reprinted from *American Sociological Review,* 30 (June 1965), pp. 381–394, by permission of the authors and The American Sociological Association.

in any individual case are primarily a matter of degree of conformity to a dominant cultural norm. In contemporary urban society, life patterns tend to be segmented and norms are heterogeneous, but the relations between work and family life are not unstructured, i.e., an infinite variety of arrangements, subject only to the individual's wishes, does not exist. Cultural, social-structural and personal regularities interact to determine the ways in which work and family life affect one another. Our concern here is to detect some of these regularities. We propose to do so by studying a *process* whereby the structure of interrelationship is established rather than by attempting to sort out the permutations and combinations of structures characterizing work-family relations.

The process we have in mind is that of *task accomplishment*. We are concerned specifically with the intrinsic stimuli presented to individuals at critical role transitions in the life cycle. We suggest that certain tasks are inherent in each such transition, and that the pattern of dealing with them affects subsequent structuring of work-family interrelations.[1]

After considering some of the prevailing theoretical issues implicit or explicit in the relevant professional literature, we shall apply the task-accomplishment framework to *one* critical life-cycle role transition —the formation of the conjugal family unit through marriage—in *one* occupational group—professional technologists at the point of completing their university training.

Current Issues of Work-Family Interrelations

The relations between work and family life have seldom been studied explicitly, for specialists in family sociology, kinship, industrial sociology and occupational psychology have tended to treat each of these areas as a relatively closed subsystem. It is as though family structure, organization, and functioning depended entirely on factors associated with the family and the individual personalities within it, while the organization and functioning of work groups could be explained exclusively in terms of the work situation.[2]

Those who have considered the relations between these two spheres of life have generally been concerned with one or more of the following theoretical points:

1. *Family and work have become increasingly differentiated* in our society, due to the specialization of work roles and the importance of universalistic norms in contemporary society.

2. *Work and family roles vary in their relative salience* in the lives of their incumbents. In general the professions require the strongest commitment of their incumbents and therefore potentially compete most with family roles for emotional involvement. Salience of work as a positive area of personal commitment tends to decline as one descends in the social class hierarchy.

3. *Work and family modes of interaction tend to be isomorphic;* they affect each other in such a way as to induce similar structural patterns in both spheres. Heteromorphism also occurs frequently, however, particularly in occupations that lack salience or are highly threatening for their incumbents.

4. *The life-cycle stage affects relations between work and family life.* The situation at the beginning of marriage, for example, differs from what it is at the time of rearing small children, and at an early point in the work career, from what it is at retirement. Furthermore, whether a critical transition in one sphere (e.g., marriage) precedes, coincides with or follows a critical event in the other (e.g., graduation from college) also affects relations between family life and work.

The differentiation of work from family roles has long been recognized as fundamental to the evolution of contemporary society. At the simplest levels of social organization, the division of labor that held for work closely paralleled that of the family. The primitive band, for instance, was both food-producing and consumption unit, and its members tended to be kin. Curle describes the situation associated with the ideal-typical tribal society:

Among the most primitive peoples . . . life is all of a piece. It is not split, as it is for a vast majority of the habitants of Western Europe and America, into what one does to earn a living—called work—and what one does during the rest of the time.[3]

Thus, activities in both spheres are subject to the same over-arching cultural beliefs and values, and the significance of an event or object in one sphere is comprehensible only with reference to the other sphere as well. Firth expresses this notion well with reference to the value of a cow in African tribal cultures:

The value of a cow in African culture cannot be reckoned by what its yield of milk, flesh, hide, horns, etc., will bring on the market, but to this must be added the noneconomic values of their importance as displays of wealth, their part in initiating or marrying a son, their place in ritual sacrifice.[4]

These tightly integrated and pervasive norms and values accompany a relatively rudimentary division of labor. Under these conditions (characterized by Durkheim as *solidarité mécanique*), everyone did pretty much what everyone else did. Major social segments based on the differentiation of productive economic roles developed only after a series of technological revolutions made possible large concentrations of people, storage of predictable food supplies, etc.

Because more diversified normative patterns tended to develop in various segments of society associated with this differentiation of occupational roles, family structure was necessarily affected. But the logic of modern industrial enterprise called for separation of familial considerations from those of the industrial undertaking. Weber, among others, called attention to this as one of the essential conditions for the formal rationality of capital accounting in any modern productive enterprise. He notes, among other factors, the importance of "The most complete possible separation of the enterprise and its conditions of success or failure from the household or private budgetary unit and its property interests." [5] Smelser has analyzed the actual process of differentiation in some detail, elucidating some of the changes in the English textile industry in the 18th and 19th centuries that led to enduring structural changes in relations between work and family life.[6] Initially weaving and associated tasks were performed by family members in the service of family subsistence. As textile production had increasingly to be geared to a cash market and to compete with similar operations elsewhere, problems of efficiency became more salient, which encouraged specialization of function and the selection of specialists according to competence rather than traditional kinship duties and obligations *vis à vis* the entrepreneur. Entrepreneurial success came increasingly to depend on assigning specific jobs to the most competent individuals available, regardless of sentimental or familial connections.

Throughout this overall development, however, one kind of enterprise has succeeded partly because family members have special commitments and loyalties to one another. Under favorable conditions some family firms have flourished throughout the industrial revolution and in various national-cultural settings. And among the executives of large corporations, work and family life are intermingled to a degree reminiscent of pre-industrial revolution times, not only in the great family firms of Europe (whose astonishing growth since World War II contradicts predictions based on the notion that family involvement in industrial management is disadvantageous), but in the U.S. as well. If

Whyte's observations are accurate, advancement in a large firm often hinges on the way an individual's wife behaves and on her attitudes and values.[7] Industrial management is susceptible to the wife's influence, for she may influence her husband's orientation to problems of human relations, and his willingness to work late hours, to move his household, and so on, depends partly on her attitudes and aspirations.

These examples suggest that family-work differentiation has not proceeded to its ultimate, logical limit. Indeed, contemporary observations of work-family relations indicate that several countervailing trends or forces have interfered with complete segregation of work from family life. For one thing, more women are being formally educated than in the past, and more of them are entering the full range of occupational positions. Though wives are no longer as economically dependent on their husbands as formerly, they now more often share with them certain interests and role dilemmas. At the same time, in the complex urban setting, the force of corporate primary groups based on extended kinship, neighborhood or age has diminished. One consequence has been an intensification of involvement in the nuclear family and its activities. Together, these trends have produced a new, more egalitarian kind of marital relationship. Women and men have access to similar educational, economic and associated opportunities. Diffusion of role definitions has not only permitted wives to take on many roles traditionally reserved for men, but also made it possible for men to perform and gain gratification from certain traditionally feminine activities. Zweig notes, in his observations on changing work-family relations among British workers, that even in this relatively conservative segment of British society men are increasingly engaged in hitherto unthinkable activities, like changing baby's diapers.[8] Indeed, one might say that a "second revolution" in marital relations is going on, and that it is intimately associated with the attempt to work out new solutions to the issues of occupational and household role definitions. This second revolution is no longer focussed, as the first one was, on the issue of giving women access to the traditional masculine occupational privileges, but on reallocating familial and occupational roles on the basis of skills and interests, using sex-correlated elements where appropriate, but not necessarily according to conventional constraints.[9]

The relative *salience* of work and family life varies according to the type of work involved. At one extreme are the professions, whose historical model, that of the clergyman with his divine "calling," is still preserved in the celibate Roman Catholic priesthood. The roles of artist, statesman, athlete and scientist, like those of doctor, lawyer, and clergyman, illustrate the higher levels of commitment to work expected in the professions. Oeser and Hammond, who gave systematic attention to the salience, or "potency" of work in the individual's life space, found in Australia that considerations of work had much greater weight among middle-class than among working-class individuals.[10] Numerous other findings and observations about the relation between attitude toward work and class position lead to similar conclusions.

The public image of professional work tends to assume that family requirements are inherently incompatible with those of work. For instance, when the former British cabinet minister, Maudling, was being considered in 1963 as a possible successor to Macmillan, it was said that he was too happily married to make a good Prime Minister.[11] The British railway engineer, Brunel, once said (for professionals generally), "My work is my only true wife." [12] This is not to say that active professional life is *necessarily* incompatible with a happy marriage, only that sources of potential conflict increase. New potentialities for deepening the complementary basis of the marriage also arise, as reflected in the Shavian image of the Webbs ("two typewriters beating as one"), or in the public image of the Franklin Roosevelts.

Thus, work assumes its maximal personal meaning for individuals when the occupational role is highly individualized, notably among the professions. Other high-status occupations, e.g., executives in large corporations, demand a similar primacy of commitment, with perhaps somewhat less scope for individualized participation than the "free" professions, but with other incentives for a high degree of involvement. Where especially gratifying incentives do not exist, as in the lower-status occupations, work has less salience, or it may take on negative significance, with different kinds of repercussions on family life.

While relative salience is probably the single most important factor in the patterns individuals develop to integrate work with familial role demands, others exist that are less closely related to occupational prestige. Thus, the requirement that an individual frequently relocate his residence may pertain to a migrant laborer or to a space-age technologist; extensive traveling may be expected of a hobo, a salesman or a physician; job insecurity may threaten an unskilled laborer or a highly specialized technician whose specialty is becoming obsolescent; competitiveness may characterize a Madison Avenue advertising firm, a criminal gang, or an academic department. All of these occupational characteristics affect familial role relationships, and we shall consider a few of them illustratively in the context of "isomorphism" between work and family life.

A number of statements in the literature support the impression that a general tendency toward isomorphism, or similarity of behavior patterning, exists between the major life spheres. Oeser and Hammond state the proposition in a psychological framework: "The breadwinner's pattern of relations in both regions (work and family) is likely to have much the same form because in both cases his behavior will depend upon his beliefs and expectations about his 'self' and others." [13] Inkeles argues from a social structural vantage point that individuals who are treated with dignity at work will tend to treat their families with dignity—i.e., isomorphically.[14] Raymond Smith has evidence indicating that the structured instabilities of West Indian family life constitute a response to the instabilities of the male occupational situation.[15] Rapoport and Laumann interpret their finding that conjugal decision-making among the more science-oriented technologists is organized on a "joint" basis more often than it is among the "hardware" types partly in terms of the diffusion of universalistic norms associated with the life of science.[16] Miller and Swanson, concentrating on socialization, observe that entrepreneurially employed individuals encourage individualistic behavior in their child-rearing practices, and Aberle and Naegele observe in a middle-class suburb that fathers tend to evaluate their children's behavior in terms of the aggressiveness and competitiveness expected in the occupational world, despite their view that the two spheres should be kept quite distinct from one another.[17]

On the other hand, tendencies toward heteromorphism have also been observed. For those in occupations that induce boredom or alienation C. Wright Mills characterized the situation as follows: "Each day men sell little pieces of themselves in order to try to buy them back each night and weekend with the coin of fun." [18] Dubin suggests that the kind of compensatory tendency characteristic of the factory situation, in which mechanization has robbed the manual worker of the sense of ego-involvement that craftsmen formerly found in work, has led workers to develop an interest in domestic activities.[19]

It is not only boring or alienating situations that stimulate heteromorphic complementarities, however. Dennis, Henriques and Slaughter describe an English coal-mining village in which the men are deeply involved in their work and have considerable autonomy on the job. The danger of the underground work encourages a propensity for mutual protection, taking the form of co-operation in crises, strong union organization, and intense peer group camaraderie during weekend "pub crawls." Miners expect their wives to feed them and look after them when they are out of the tense mine situation, but to be as undemanding as possible. Hence, the family structure emphasizes the subservience of the wife and the segregation of most of the spouses' activities, particularly in leisure hours, during which the men affirm their solidarity and seek release from the tensions of work.[20]

The same tendency toward heteromorphism also occurs when the occupational role does not involve interpersonal relations reproduceable in other spheres—e.g., deep sea divers, astronauts, racing car drivers—and in other occupations, reproducing the occupational role at home is possible but grossly unconventional. The film "Cheaper by the Dozen" caricatured an industrial time-study man who organized his family according to his own prescriptions for the workplace. Presumably there are soldiers who organize their families like platoons, computer technicians who program their families as they do their machines, and boxers who use physical violence at home. The evidence suggests, however, that complementarity is often practiced, and the general human tendency is to segregate spheres of involvement and behave differently according to context.[21] And in situations where alienation from work is accompanied by a search for compensatory gratifications, the tendency toward heteromorphism is strengthened.

In general, the issues associated with isomorphism between work and family patterns are not satisfactorily conceptualized in the literature. A number of variables, properly separated for analytic handling, are dealt with as though similar issues of psychodynamics and social-system functioning were involved, but individualism-collectivism, stability-instability, dignity-degradation, involvement-alienation, the fit between values and behavior, and other polarities are probably differently arrayed under different circumstances. For example, alienation from work might be associated in one situation with an increase in domesticity while in another it might be associated with withdrawal or discord in marital relations and increased peer-group activities. Intervening variables, such as cultural norms for marital roles, competitiveness in the work situation, and so on must be taken into account to improve the utility of the isomorphism concept.[22]

Finally, *life cycle stage* must be considered in generalizing about work-family relations. When two university students, both majoring in electrical engineering, marry while at college, role differentiation in their early marriage stage is likely to be minimal. Following the birth of their first child, the role differentiation is likely to increase, particularly if the husband is establishing himself in a new job or a course of graduate studies critical for his career.[23] The salience of the work for the man in this stage is very high, while his wife's involvement is likely to be diverted into familial roles, at least temporarily. But this degree of salience is not life-long, in most cases. At retirement, for example, the man must detach himself from the specific occupational involvements that hitherto engaged him and reapportion his involvements and interests.[24]

Another life cycle phenomenon to consider is the fact that each sphere, work and family, has its own sequence of stages, and that critical role transitions may be scheduled as between the two spheres. To some extent timing the critical transition points is within the control of individuals, though traditionally, in Western society, it has been considered appropriate to deal with one's early, identity-establishing occupational transitions before marriage. Until recently, professionals who deferred occupational entry longest married later than other occupational groups.[25] This supports the theory that the critical issues around identity (which, for many men and women, are closely tied up with occupation) naturally precede critical issues associated with psycho-social intimacy.[26] A similar view has been supported in several more overtly moral arguments. To show that marriage of college students should be discouraged, for example, early marriage has been said to interfere with studies, to exploit the wife, to reflect an immature choice that will produce later incompatibility, and so on. Research on the recent increase in marriages among college students, however, has indicated that the early marriers tend to be more mature, to be better academic performers, and to display fewer indications of marital disruption, than the students who were single or married after graduating from college.[27] The outcome of such marriages probably depends on the partners' ability to handle the situations confronting them at this point in their respective life cycles, rather than on the order in which they schedule the events. Obviously, more complex notions of identity and intimacy are necessary than those derived from a simple assignment of one or another institution to one or another psychological crisis. The framework we present here is one approach to the solution of such problems.

The Task Framework

The central question here has to do with the principles that govern choice among the many possible arrangements for dealing with the issues of the salience of work, isomorphism of work-family relations, scheduling transitions in the life cycle, and the form and degree of integration between work and family life generally. We believe that it is useful to concentrate on "critical" points of major role transition, when the structural elements of both personality and social system are in a somewhat "fluid" state, and new structures are in the process of being established. These structures, according to our view, are the resultants not simply of traditional socio-cultural prescriptions or of personal needs, but of the complex interplay among these in a given field of forces. The field of forces varies among different individuals at different points in their lives. We propose the variable "task accomplishment" to encompass the resultant effect of elements on all levels that individuals mobilize to deal with new situations. We conceive each status-transition situation as presenting a specific complex of *tasks,* from which the work-family structure emerges.

The changes attendant on critical status transitions—marriage, death, adolescence, and so on—have long been emphasized in both sociological and psychological theory. In his classical work, Van Gennep[28] highlighted the very wide prevalence of "rites of passage," or ceremonies that help individuals pass over a threshold, leaving one form of social participation to enter a new one. The social relevance of these rituals has recently been elaborated further by Gluckman and other British anthropologists.[29] The personal functions of the ritual activity associated with these transitions may be considered both restitutive—as in Freud's notion of the "work of mourning"—and defensive against the anxiety engendered by leaving the familiar and security-giving conditions of the preceding stage and facing the threats and challenges of new situations.[30]

Earlier writers in the field of family research saw marriage as an important transition, but they aimed to relate antecedent factors to subsequent marital success or failure.[31] Our interest is in understanding marriage as a transition process, a process more or less by-passed in earlier analysis.[32] By seeking to understand the relation between critical task accomplishment and outcome, we stress the couple's adaptability in shaping whatever resources they brought to the marriage in their new situation (in contrast to an orientation emphasizing the determinacy of prior factors). Couples enter marriage with certain advantages or handicaps and cope with the tasks of making the transition with varying degrees of effectiveness or creativity. In the end, their success is determined by their skill in coping with these tasks, rather than being immutably set by the factors constituting obstacles for them at the point of transition.

Despite the fact that previously defined conventional patterns for coping with the major life cycle transitions are no longer adequate in a heterogeneous and rapidly changing society, we expect to find that individuals combine personal and social structural elements to form *patterns* of task accomplishment.[33] In the quest for these emergent patterns of behavior, our central question is: Under what conditions is task accomplishment maximally functional? That is, when is it consistent with the individual's established personality needs, with the needs and expectations of others whose roles are reciprocal with his in this particular sphere of behavior, and with requirements in other spheres of life?

Factors allowing or inhibiting a maximally functional resolution include personality, early experience, and sociocultural elements, as well as a situational factor presenting, on the one hand, intrinsic tasks to be faced and adapted to, and, on the other hand, uncertainties due to the absence of adequate behavioral models. The lack of prior models is stressful, but it also provides new opportunities for creativity. The potentials are further enhanced by the fact that at critical role transitions not only do new situations arise, but new persons—wives, colleagues, etc.,—enter in reciprocal roles, and these people are likely to be working at new forms of adaptation too. The adaptive solutions to tasks presented at these times may either confirm prior patterns, further crystallizing them in the personalities and behavior of the individuals concerned, or encourage growth and development. But in either case we assume that the period of heightened susceptibility is relatively brief; new patterns are crystallized within a few weeks after the critical transition period of intensive involvements.[34]

Simultaneous Status Transitions: Graduation and Marriage

When two critical transitions in the life cycle must be accomplished simultaneously, as, for example, when an individual marries at about the same time that he graduates from college, each behavioral structure is in a condition of maximum fluidity; at this point they have the greatest mutual influence. To investigate this influence, we studied couples who were undergoing these transitions simultaneously, and our preliminary findings illustrate the postulated utility of the task framework. In other words, we have studied the process of work-family interaction when a transition point in the occupational sphere —graduation—coincides with a transition in the family sphere—mar-

TABLE 1

Critical Transition Tasks for Early Career and Family

	Phase I	
	Career: Training	Family: Engagement[36]
PERSONAL TASKS	1. Accomplishing the tasks set by the curriculum at a satisfactory level of proficiency 2. Paying the financial costs of training 3. Deferring gratifications that require an income and a full occupational role, for whatever time the training period takes	1. Accepting the emotional responsibilities of marriage 2. Accepting the material responsibilities of marriage 3. Developing a pattern of gratification compatible with the partner's expectations and needs
INTERPERSONAL TASKS	1. Accepting the teacher's authority 2. Working out satisfactory arrangements to meet other obligations (e.g., to parents) 3. Competing with peers in the same training situation	1. Establishing an identity as a couple. 2. Developing a mutually satisfactory sexual adjustment for the engagement period 3. Developing a mutually satisfactory orientation to family planning 4. Establishing a mutually satisfactory mode of communication 5. Establishing satisfactory relations with others 6. Developing a mutually satisfactory work pattern 7. Developing a mutually satisfactory leisure pattern 8. Developing a mutually satisfactory plan for the wedding and early marriage 9. Establishing a mutually satisfactory decision-making pattern

PERSONAL TASKS	1. Gathering information about available alternatives 2. Deciding among actual offers	1. Learning to participate in an intimate sexual relationship 2. Learning to live in close association with the spouse
INTERPERSONAL TASKS	1. Undergoing job interviews in such a manner as to satisfy the prospective employers that one is technically competent 2. Undergoing interviews in such a manner as to satisfy prospective employers that one is personally acceptable	1. Developing mutually satisfactory sexual relations 2. Developing a mutually satisfactory shared experience as a basis for the later marital relationship

PERSONAL TASKS	1. Developing a rhythm of life geared to the world of work 2. Adapting one's performance to the multiple criteria for good job performance, to which the skills learned in the training phase must be accommodated 3. Broadening the range of tasks dealt with in the course of one's work to suit the expectations of the work role 4. Developing gratifying leisure activities 5. Developing a self-image consistent with new status	1. Helping to establish the home base 2. Accommodating daily living patterns to the marital situation 3. Developing further sexual competence 4. Developing an appropriate commitment to the marriage 5. Developing a self-concept congruent with one's marital role
INTERPERSONAL TASKS	1. Accommodating oneself to relations with peers on the job 2. Accommodating oneself to the authority structure of the job 3. Developing commitment to work and loyalty to the organization and to one's professional reference groups	1. Cooperating with spouse to set up the home base 2. Developing a mutually satisfactory network of external relations 3. Developing an internal organization for managing domestic routines 4. Developing mutual esteem and a positive orientation to the marriage

riage, for a specific type of occupation, namely the professional engineer.

Occupations vary tremendously in the degree to which choices made have enduring, and to some extent irrevocable, consequences. Some occupations are entered casually with little intention on the part of incumbents to form a life-long commitment, while others involve the expectation of life-long commitment once the occupation is entered. Some are entered early, some later, after various stages of prior experience or preparation. Some involve an expected progression of stages of advancement toward a remote peak position, while others are relatively undifferentiated, the individual expecting simply to "hold a job" until death or retirement.[35] The professional career, with its preparatory stages prior to formal entry, its high degree of expected commitment, and its anticipated sequence of stages of advancement, bears the greatest structural and psychological resemblance to the family, and for this reason we chose in the first instance to examine professional engineers.

Our restriction to a single stage in the life cycle and to a single occupational type simplifies our analysis as well as providing symmetry, but another restriction reduces symmetry in the interest of concentrating on the more prevalent situation. Our sample consists of couples in which the husband was entering a professional career, while the women are distributed randomly in this regard.

From exploratory interviews in depth with a dozen couples undergoing the twin transitions, we have developed an initial formulation of tasks inherent in these status transitions. For convenience of presentation we have listed them together in parallel fashion, but they do not necessarily coincide in this timing and sequence in all situations. (See Table 1.) In each sphere, we distinguish personal tasks, or those involving an individual's personality, from interpersonal tasks that involve his marital partner or his colleagues at work. The three phases are more clearly indicated in our data on the marriage transition (where marriage, honeymoon and establishment of a neolocal residence are institutionalized) than for the career, where there are wider ranges of variation.

In each of these phases, the patterns set up in one sphere must be accommodated in some degree to the requirements of the other sphere. Thus, during the early marriage phase, family-building tasks must proceed in the context of some effort to establish or maintain an economic base for the family. For a majority, this means the husband's job, though it may also involve the wife. Relatively few couples have no need to work at all. Similarly, in the early career-establishment phase, married individuals must to some degree accommodate the demands of the work situation to domestic life. Patterns of accommodating work to family needs and developing a family life in the context of a career are the resultants of the task-accomplishment process with which we are now concerned.

A survey of 1954 graduates of three technical universities indicates that the wife's religion is related to career line choices.[37] The graduate's own religion is not significantly correlated with mobility, but those with Catholic or Jewish wives were less likely to move about geographically. Graduates with Catholic wives had less intense a general professional orientation, even on a local basis; within the profession such individuals are found more frequently in the lower technical or managerial jobs. The lower-level career type is associated with a conventional family structure in which the division of labor is based on highly differentiated sex roles rather than on the more "joint" organization of shared activities and decision-making characteristic of graduates who express a stronger commitment to professional values and a greater tendency to seek science-oriented (research or academic) positions.

The following specimen case from our intensive interview series involves the socio-cultural features just described, but the outcome deviates from the modal one in our sample. Not only does it illustrate relations among patterns of career, marital and individual functioning, but it shows how the "task" framework permits us to explain a wider range of variant patterns.

Task Accomplishment as an Independent Variable in a Variant Case

Rosalie was the only child in an urban Jewish family possessing considerable wealth and many cultural interests. Relations within her family of orientation, however, were somewhat strained, and one of her own goals was to achieve a warm and happy family life. Elmer, on the other hand, grew up in a large, very warm and tight-knit small-town Protestant family and was, from childhood, a "typical" American boy in his interests. He was athletic, loved to tinker with automobiles, considered being a mechanic but in view of his aptitude responded to the scholarships that enabled him to attend a technical university.

During Elmer's career in the university, he "shopped around" in various courses and programs, but his grades and summer job experiences in his first two years confirmed his basically "hardware" orientation to technological studies. He performed at an "average" level of academic accomplishment, a level made relatively easy for him by his natural aptitudes. The reason he gave for not doing better was that he didn't feel that the commitment required to get top grades was worth it in terms of his other values: an easier pace of life and maintenance of social relationships including dating relationships. He was confident that he would do well as an engineer without taxing himself unduly during his university years, that he was learning enough to be conversant with the relevant fields, and that he could qualify for a wide range of technical jobs in his field, increasing his specialized knowledge on his own when he found out what a specific job required. At the university, Elmer's professors were aware that he was meeting the requirements of the program relatively easily, but not making the extra effort needed for outstanding performance. He got on well with his peers and belonged to a fraternity. Here again, others felt that he took life relatively easily, doing enough to get through comfortably but not placing himself under undue strain. His summer job experiences confirmed his technical skills, and he knew by the end of the second summer that he could already perform many of the role requirements of professional engineers, but that his problem would be to find a career line that would do more than provide a source of income. He did not seek more challenging professional interests, but rather greater personal meaning in his extra-professional activities. After he became engaged to Rosalie, who was a student in a neighboring university, he began to participate in the more cosmopolitan and humanistic world of her interests.

Rosalie, a student of social work, was intensely preoccupied with the need to find socially significant meaning in her life and activities. She was dedicated to various welfare interests and to such causes as the civil liberties movement. While she did not value the accumulation of money as a goal in itself, she had wide-ranging interests' and would eventually require a fairly high living standard. Unlike the modal Jewish wife in our survey, however, she was familistic without being "local." She was willing to go anywhere so long as there was a chance for her to do good works.

During their engagement, Elmer and Rosalie discussed various issues of family life and actually rehearsed possible future joint involvements when Elmer took summer jobs associated with social work agencies. He applied some of his technical skills to automobile maintenance and various odd jobs, while she worked at apprentice social-work tasks. He experienced gratification not only from the technical application of his skills, but from doing something worthwhile, and jointly with Rosalie. He began to think of career possibilities that would cultivate the rewards he experienced in this type of situation. Thus, these summer experiences, followed through in his junior and senior years at the university, gave Elmer and Rosalie a basis for working out a possible pattern of life together and at the same time allowed him to reconsider his own career plans, the issues of which were becoming acute as his graduation approached. During their engagement, they frequently visited each other's families and worked out satisfactory relations all around, resolving such issues as religious participation and so on.

By the time of graduation, when the critical issues of job choice were at hand, Rosalie and Elmer had worked out together the following plan. He would take a job in the airplane company that had given him scholarships throughout his educational career. Although he was not under pressure to repay this as a debt, he did feel a moral obligation he wished to discharge, "all other things being equal." The fact that they had a plant nearby would allow her to finish her training and together they could continue to consolidate their position as a family and to visit both families of orientation. His prospective job was neither too abstract for his training nor too "purely hardware" to interest him. He was sure that the job would satisfy many of his technical requirements, which he had spelled out quite explicitly to himself and explored in detail with company representatives and through company visits, as well as his financial requirements. He was less certain, however, that it would satisfy his growing interest in doing something worthwhile for humanity and in working with people over problems with which they personally were concerned.

In discussing future phases of their work-family development, Elmer and Rosalie planned to consider mutually acceptable alternatives. They felt that they would be less interested in living locally, as time went on, but would go wherever the best situation, that is, a satisfactory job for Elmer, was available; welfare work was more or less universally available for her. From Elmer's point of view, however, the enthusiasm that she had generated for good causes made him more interested in finding something in which they could both participate. He mentioned as one alternative a career in teaching. Perhaps they would put in a period with the Peace Corps. Their wedding took place in his home town and church. Afterwards, their honeymoon was assisted financially by her parents. Their physical intimacy, which was satisfactory for both, seemed to be cemented by the idealistic goals that they re-emphasized as binding them together and over-riding their differences in background. On the job he was popular with colleagues and considered intelligent and competent by his employers. Though only average at the university, his performance was more than adequate in the industrial setting, and he was considered stable professional material for an orderly advance through technical and perhaps managerial promotion within the firm.

Elmer missed a feeling of fulfillment in this kind of work, however, and as he had half expected prior to entering the job, he began actively to entertain the idea of changing his career line. At our last contact with them, they had decided to make joint application to the Peace Corps. Following this experience, he resolved to enter teaching, probably in secondary-school science. He and Rosalie were planning a family life in which both would work, and in which the pursuit of their interests and values would prevail over attachments to locality and extended family contacts.

In Phase I, both Elmer and Rosalie were involved in career as well as engagement tasks. Each accomplished satisfactorily the tasks set by the curriculum; neither had difficulties with the financial task. They both pursued their career training without pressure and attained much personal gratification from their courtship; they accepted university requirements and competed with their peers while maintaining good interpersonal relations, and both sustained satisfactory relations with their families. During their engagement, each developed a responsible economic orientation and an appropriate pattern, in terms of each other's norms, of gratification in an intense emotional relationship. Their family-planning and communications patterns were mutually satisfactory, and they established satisfactory relations with others, including their parental families; they planned successfully for the wedding and its immediate aftermath.

In his relations with Rosalie at this time, Elmer's values and personality underwent considerable development. His previously covert conflict between a conventional technical career and a more humanistic one became overt. In choosing his first job, he had a number of attractive options; he chose to remain with the firm that had financed his training. Although this did not satisfy his humanistic goals it did offer the characteristics he desired in a technical job. In the job he performed satisfactorily but was personally dissatisfied because his work activities did not further his humanistic goals. As his wife entered the critical transition of graduation, a new family-work decision was precipitated, involving the resolution of conflicts between work and family life as well as his intrapersonal conflict.

This case indicates how the task-accomplishment framework supplements the traditional predictive analysis, relating antecedent variables like religion, social class, personality and value orientations to the outcome. We would hold that even if it were possible to introduce a wide range of other independent variables with known effects the task-accomplishment framework would still provide an important set of intervening variables, showing how the antecedent variables are interrelated in the specific situation of transition. For example, even if we could measure the personality dispositions of Elmer and Rosalie, to show that she was less committed to her parental family and values than the modal Jewish wife in our culture and that he was more sensitive to human problems than the modal engineer, several outcomes would still be possible. For example, Rosalie and Elmer could have been expected to settle close to his family, under which circumstances Rosalie might have used his family as a substitute basis for realizing the culturally valued familial ties that had been unsatisfactory in her own particular family background. Elmer might then have derived sufficient gratification of his humanistic interests through her work, through his leisure activities, or through management or personnel work. Other possibilities include those actually mentioned, e.g., the Peace Corps or teaching, new lines of endeavor that were of interest to both.

By closely analyzing their patterns of coping with status transitions, we have learned just how this couple dealt with their divergent backgrounds and values so as to find mutually acceptable solutions. The patterns of task accomplishment themselves helped to determine the outcome. For example, their efforts to share each other's interests as much as possible led to his taking a summer job in her sphere of interest rather than in the usual line of engineering summer jobs, an experience that contributed to a change in his conception of his capacities and career alternatives.

Conclusion

At critical transition points in work and family role systems, patterns of task accomplishment in one sphere affect those in the other. While the inter-system influence is probably maximal when individuals are undergoing transitions in both simultaneously, all points of status transition necessarily involve a process of readjustment, potentially affecting not only the specific behavioral spheres, but others linked to it. When transitions occur simultaneously in two spheres, conflicts and stresses are not necessarily multiplied. The concurrence of the challenges presented by the two sets of tasks may, under some circumstances, have mutually beneficial consequences, and coping with one set of challenges does not necessarily detract from performance on others. Mobilization of latent types and levels of involvement, perhaps hitherto impossible for the individual in question, may improve his capacity to make choices and to commit himself to a challenging performance level, rather than making him perform one set of tasks at the expense of the other. Task accomplishment in conformity to normative patterns for the group to which the individual belongs does not necessarily entail good psychological functioning, nor does task accomplishment in a variant pattern necessarily entail stressful consequences.

The problem of apportioning ego involvements, or "sub-identities," [38] is a vital one in contemporary society. On the one hand, a great variety of possible patterns are available, due to rapid social change and to the complexity of urban life. On the other hand, the traditional emphasis is so much on achievement, productivity, competence and similar values that men find it difficult to look elsewhere for self-fulfillment. But with the increase in shared activities, the family can play a new role in relation to the world of work. Family and work are no longer subject to a single overarching set of role prescriptions in an integrated cultural whole, nor are family functions as residual as they are when work is either overvalued or alienative, as it was in the era following the industrial revolution. Individuals now have a wider range of possibilities to consider in choosing both work and spouse, and greater freedom in organizing family life in relation to job requirements. Social prescriptions set broad limits of acceptability but family structure, both internally and in relation to work, is increasingly determined by the individuals' personality needs, their interpersonal "fit" and, as a derivative of these dimensions, their capacity to cope with the tasks specific to each phase of family life. Similarly, the career options open to individuals, particularly in the high-demand professions, are numerous enough to permit each person to develop a pattern of work participation according to his personality needs, his relations with others, and his capacity to cope with the tasks of career development at each phase. Fitting participation patterns in work and family together, like coping with the tasks posed within each sphere, is partly a matter of an individual style that emerges as the individuals meet each successive situation, rather than the outcome of conformity to or deviance from a preexisting normative pattern.

NOTES

1. Our psycho-social approach to critical role transitions has roots in both social science and psychiatry, and like-minded efforts are currently being made in Harvard's Laboratory of Community Psychiatry. For example, cf. Gerald Caplan, *An Approach to Community Mental Health,* New York: Grune and Stratton, 1961 and *Principles of Preventive Psychiatry,* New York: Basic Books, 1964. Based to some extent on the work of Erich Lindemann, "Symptomatology and Management of Acute Grief," *American Journal of Psychiatry,* 101 (1944), pp. 141–148, Caplan's work supports and is complementary to several basic social science research programs. Recent published work in the family research program includes the following: Rhona Rapoport, "Normal Crisis, Family Structure and Mental Health," *Family Process,* 2 (March, 1963), pp. 68–80; Rhona Rapoport, "The Transition from Engagement to Marriage," *Acta Sociologica,* 8 (1964), pp. 36–55; and Rhona Rapoport and Robert Rapoport, "New Light on the Honeymoon," *Human Relations,* 17 (1964), pp. 33–56.
2. Exceptions include Theodore Caplow's chapter on "Occupation and Family" in his *The Sociology of Work,* Minneapolis: University of Minnesota Press, 1954. Caplow is concerned on the one hand with the way in which a man's occupation locates his family in the social class system and, on the other hand, with the difficulties married women encounter in reconciling occupational and familial roles. Fitting together work and family life has long been seen as a "problem" for women but not for men. Here we concentrate on situations in which only the husband is employed, but our conceptualization would encompass the entire range of situations. A comparable precursor from the family vantage point is Robert Angell's *The Family Encounters the Depression,* New York: Charles Scribner's Sons, 1936. This book reflects a common tendency to see work-family interrelations as problematic when severe disturbance occurs in one sphere or the other. We concentrate on the processes of patterned interaction in "normal"

situations here, but our conceptualization applies as well to the more traumatic and unpredictable crises.

3. Adam Curle, "Incentives to Work: An Anthropological Appraisal," *Human Relations,* 2 (1949), pp. 41–47.

4. Raymond Firth, *Human Types,* London: Thomas Nelson, 1938. We do not mean to imply that cultural traits in the Western societies are not adumbrated with values and meanings from other spheres (e.g. in American society, the social and psychological significance of driving a large, late-model car) but that the *degree* of functional interdependence among the spheres tends to be less in Western than in tribal societies.

5. Max Weber, *The Theory of Social and Economic Organization* (trans. by A. M. Henderson and Talcott Parsons), London: Hodge, 1947.

6. Neil Smelser, *Social Change in the Industrial Revolution,* London: Routledge & Paul, 1959. William J. Goode notes in *The Family,* Englewood Cliffs, N.J.: Prentice Hall, 1964, that since World War II the leaders of countries wishing to facilitate industrialization have introduced legal changes, well ahead of public opinion, to create family patterns more compatible with the demands of urban and industrial life (p. 2). Also see William J. Goode, *World Revolution and Family Patterns,* New York: The Free Press, 1963, for an analysis of worldwide patterns of change in family life under the impact of technological change.

7. William H. Whyte, *The Organization Man,* New York: Simon and Schuster, 1956. Cf. Eugene Litwak, "Occupational Mobility and Extended Family Cohesion," *American Sociological Review,* 25 (February, 1960), for the resiliency of extended family relations under the impact of occupational mobility, and Harold Wilensky, "Work, Career and Social Integration," *International Social Science Journal,* 12 (1960), for an analysis of new trends of work-family relations.

8. Ferdynand Zweig, *The Worker in an Affluent Society,* London: Heinemann, 1961. Some of the forthcoming reports by Marc Fried and his colleagues dissect the variations in family structure associated with this process in an urban working-class neighborhood. Cf., for example, Marc Fried and Ellen Fitzgerald, "Structure in Marital Role Relationships: Role Interaction and Social Class Variations," Research Document #26, Center for Community Studies, Boston.

9. Alice Rossi's position, as set forth in "A Good Woman is Hard to Find," *Transaction,* 2 (November–December, 1964), is based on a sophisticated view of the possibilities for reciprocal realignment in marital roles at different points in the life cycle. An articulate specimen of the phenomenon itself is Robert Varga, in his "Dilemmas of a Househusband," *Saturday Review of Literature,* January 2, 1965, p. 100.

10. O. A. Oeser and S. B. Hammond, editors, *Social Structure and Personality in a City,* London: Routledge & Paul, 1954.

11. *The Observer,* London, June 1963.

12. Lionell Thomas Caswell Rolt, *Isambard Kingdom Brunel,* London: Grey Arrow, 1961.

13. Oeser and Hammond, *op. cit.,* p. 238.

14. Alex Inkeles, paper delivered before the Society for Applied Anthropology, San Juan, Puerto Rico, Spring 1964.
15. Raymond Smith, *The Negro Family in British Guiana,* London: Routledge & Paul, 1956.
16. Robert Rapoport and Edward O. Laumann, "Technologists in Mid-career: Factors Affecting Patterns of Ten-year Out Engineers and Scientists from Three Universities," in Robert Rapoport (ed.), *The Impact of Space Efforts on Communities and Selected Groups,* American Academy of Arts and Sciences, Committee on Space (in preparation).
17. Daniel Miller and Guy Swanson, *The Changing American Parent,* New York: John Wiley, 1958; David F. Aberle and Kaspar D. Naegele, "Middle-Class Fathers' Occupational Role and Attitudes Toward Children," *American Journal of Ortho-Psychiatry,* 22 (1952), pp. 366–378.
18. C. Wright Mills, cited by Stephen Cotgrove and Stanley Parker, "Work and Non-work," *New Society,* July 11, 1963, p. 16.
19. Robert Dubin, "Industrial Workers' Worlds," *Social Problems,* 3 (January, 1956), pp. 131–142.
20. Norman Dennis, Fernando Henriques and Clifford Slaughter, *Coal Is Our Life,* London: Eyre & Spottiswoode, 1956.
21. Parsons and Bales have argued that the tendency is nearly universal for families to assign "instrumental" activities to men and "affective" activities to women. To the extent that the husband's role is confined to articulating the family with the outside world of work, in which the instrumental mode is dominant, and the wife's to managing behavior within the family, the tendency is toward heteromorphic complementarity.
22. Marc Fried distinguishes between "role-determined" and "goal-determined" behavior patternings, a distinction useful in understanding the process of change and emergence of new structures where different segments of life are subjected to different kinds of influence. Marc Fried, "Social Problems and Psychopathology," GAP Symposium #10 (in press).
23. Robert Rapoport, Edward O. Laumann, and Theodore Ferdinand, "The Power of Choice: Critical Career Decisions of Senior Technologists, 1964," in Robert Rapoport (ed.), *op. cit.*
24. For a good statement of the general developmental framework, see Roy H. Rodgers, "Toward a Theory of Family Development," in the *Journal of Marriage and The Family,* 26 (August, 1964), pp. 262–270.
25. Robert Rapoport, "The Male's Occupation in Relation to His Decision to Marry," *Acta Sociologica,* 8 (1964), pp. 68–82.
26. Erik Erikson, *Identity and the Life Cycle,* New York: International Universities Press, 1959.
27. Rapoport, Laumann, and Ferdinand, *op. cit.* N. Medalia in his unpublished paper, "Explaining the Increase in College Student Marriage: Some Observations on an Institutionalization Crisis," points to some of the problems that prevent general recognition of positive elements in the situation. The picture may differ somewhat for secondary schools. Cf. Lee G. Burchinal, "Research on Young Marriages: Implications for Family Life Education," *The Family Life Coordinator,*

8 (September, 1960), and Joel Moss, "Teen-age Marriage: Cross-national Trends and Sociological Factors in the Decision of When to Marry," *Acta Sociologica,* 8 (1964), pp. 98–117.

28. Arnold Van Gennep, *The Rites of Passage,* Chicago: University of Chicago Press, 1960.

29. Max Gluckman (ed.), *Essays on the Ritual of Social Relations,* Manchester: Manchester University Press, 1962.

30. Cf. Isabel Menzies, "A Case Study in the Functioning of Social Systems as a Defense Against Anxiety," *Human Relations,* 13 (1960), pp. 95–122, reprinted as Tavistock Pamphlet No. 3, 1961.

31. E.g., the classic work of Ernest Burgess and Paul Wallin, *Engagement and Marriage,* Chicago: Lippincott, 1953.

32. Some of the recent work of Reuben Hill and his colleagues reflects an orientation similar in many respects to ours. For their use of the task concept see, for example, Evelyn Duvall and Reuben Hill, *When You Marry,* Boston: Heath, 1945, and Evelyn Duvall, *Family Development,* New York: Lippincott, 1962. The work of Erikson, *op. cit.;* Lindemann, *op. cit.;* and Caplan, *op. cit.,* has been most directly relevant to ours. The concept of fluidity and the potentialities at this point for intervention are examined by Gerald Caplan in "Patterns of Parental Response to the Crisis of Premature Birth: A Preliminary Approach to Modifying Mental Health Outcome," *Psychiatry,* 23 (1960), pp. 365–374. Personality growth potentials in such experiences have been emphasized by psychologists like Robert White, Robert J. Havighurst, Nevitt Sanford, and Abraham Maslow.

33. The term "task" may seem to imply some notion of hard work and an unpleasant or chore-like quality. This is not what is meant. The process of task accomplishment may be automatic, pleasurable or painful, depending on the situations and persons involved. By "task" we mean only that issues must be joined and the necessary energy expended to shift orientation and behavior patterns as the expectations encountered in the new status require.

34. Psychiatrists interested in preventive intervention at points of maximal fluidity have judged that the period of effective flux, or "crisis," tends to be about two months: see Lindemann, *op. cit.,* and Caplan, *op. cit.*

35. We owe thanks to David Riesman for some of these ideas, generated in informal discussion and to Everett C. Hughes, *Men and Their Work,* Glencoe, Ill.: The Free Press, 1958.

36. Rhona Rapoport, *op. cit.;* Rhona Rapoport and Robert Rapoport, *op. cit.,* 1964.

37. This survey, reported in Rapoport and Laumann, *op. cit.,* was conducted by mailing career questionnaires to all 1954 graduates of three technical universities representing a spectrum of technological types, in the northeastern region of the U.S. The case presented here was drawn from a sample of recent graduates of the same institutions.

38. Robert L. Kahn and R. P. French, "A Programmatic Approach to Studying the Industrial Environment and Mental Health," *The Journal of Social Issues,* 17 (July, 1962).

2 7

The Rural Family of the Future

by Lee G. Burchinal

While value-statements and idealized descriptions of the rural family
—particularly of the farm family—abound, until recently there has
been a dearth of research studies on rural or farm family patterns.
The rudiments of a body of research data on rural and farm family
relationships is represented by the recent reports by Brown (11, 12),*
Bauder (1), Wilkening (89–91), Straus (79–81), and Blood and
Wolfe (8). However, data from these and a few additional studies
provide only meager information on rural family structure and processes. The most systematic and comprehensive data related to family
patterns in the United States are derived from studies of white, urban,
middle-class, Protestant couples. In the absence of comparable data
for rural family patterns, descriptive data from this urban category of
American families may be useful in predicting and understanding
changes in rural family organization. Detailed consideration of this
premise led to the development of ten interrelated propositions which
form the framework of this [selection].

1. In the past century, the foundation of American society has
shifted from relatively isolated, self-sufficient rural communities with
an agricultural economy to metropolitan complexes with an industrial
economy.

2. The American family system, originating in the frontier era, was
shaped by and adapted to the rural environment. As a pattern maintenance system, it has been continuously adjusting to the demands of
urban ways of life, which are largely a function of the scientific,
technological, and industrial developments in our society.

---

* Numbers within parentheses refer to literature cited at the end of this [selec-
tion]. No attempt has been made to provide an exhaustive reference list; rather,
the most significant or typical references pertaining to a given point are cited.

Reprinted from James H. Copp (ed.), *Our Changing Rural Society: Perspectives
and Trends* (Ames, Iowa: Iowa State University Press, 1964), pp. 159–197, by
permission of the author and publisher.

3. In this process of change, the family system has most frequently been required to adapt to extrafamily requirements of change rather than to prompt extrafamily system changes. The family system is taken as a set of dependent variables whereas economic and other nonfamily social organization changes are taken as the independent variables in the change model.

4. A prototype of the emerging family system can be discerned in urban society. This family type, which has its modal representation among the college educated, professionally employed urban couples, is probably the best gauge of the direction of future change in the American family system.

5. Functionally important linkages connect rural society and the larger society. These linkages provide the bases for diffusion of knowledge, values, and behavioral patterns from one sector of society to another or from one region of the country to another.

6. It is assumed that most changes in the American family system have been developing in urban communities and have been diffusing to rural communities by means of the institutionalized and informal linkages between the rural and urban populations.

7. The six preceding propositions suggest that important data for understanding changes and for predicting future developments in rural family systems may be obtained by studying changes which have been occurring in the urban family system, especially those observable in the prototypal professional families.

8. The above premises are not meant to imply that changes in rural family patterns occur only through the diffusion of urban family patterns to the rural population. Endogenous changes in rural community organization and family patterns are associated with the continuing technological changes in American agriculture. The effects of agricultural technology are reflected in the higher levels of living and education for rural persons and in the specialization and professionalization of rural and farm occupational roles. In turn, these developments generally reinforce changes in rural family patterns induced by the diffusion of the developing urban family patterns.

9. Yet, changes in any system introduced by elements outside that system are selective. Simple analogies from urban to rural family systems with appropriate time lapse estimates are likely to be deceptive. The intrinsic relationship between the farm family and the farm firm conditions the nature of farm family patterns. Moreover, differences in rural and urban levels of living or in aspects of community organization such as education, health, and welfare facilities may differentially affect the functioning of families.

10. Therefore, some important differences may still exist between rural and urban family systems. It is important to assess available data to determine in what ways rural and urban family systems are most similar and in what ways they are most different. These data will be useful in predicting future directions of change in rural family systems and in assessing potential strengths and weaknesses of the rural family system for adapting to an urban, industrial, bureaucratic society.

The foregoing ten propositions provide an overview of this chapter. First, attention will be given to general changes in urban family patterns. Then, on the basis of these changes, an attempt will be made to characterize the prototype of the emerging urban family. Next, some inferences will be drawn regarding the present status of rural-urban differences in family patterns. Finally, the preceding data will serve as the basis for pointing out some problems and potentialities of the rural family system.

Emerging Patterns in the American Family System

In comparing early with contemporary American family relationships, a great number of transitions are apparent. In the following section, some of the most significant emerging patterns in the organization of American family life will be briefly delineated under ten headings. The presentation should be regarded as suggestive rather than exhaustive.[1]

1. *Enhanced Status of Women*

One of the most far-reaching social changes related to family organization in the United States has been the comparatively recent elevation in the status of women. Equal education for men and women, expansion in the frequency and range of employment opportunities for women, the decline of segregation of sexes in work roles, adoption of masculine dress by women, and a wider range of social contacts for women before and after marriage are just a few of the unmistakable signs of increasingly equal status for women and men. Furthermore, there is now a formidable basis for male-female equality under the law.

The results of this transition toward equality in male-female status include a trend away from the semipatriarchial authority patterns of the last century, the emergence of equalitarian dating and courtship patterns, and a consequent shift toward equalitarian and personality-centered marital relationships.

A powerful combination of factors operate to maintain equal status relations between the sexes, both before and after marriage. It is clear that the long-term increase in the status of women to approximate equality with men will be a prominent feature of American family organization in the foreseeable future.

2. Less Stereotyped Division of Tasks

A favorite generalization of family sociologists is the change from sex-linked division of labor in home and family activities to shared activities performed freely by either or both spouses. Some research (45) strongly supports these generalizations. Middle-class husbands have most freely accepted responsibility for family tasks. Also, middle-class spouses perceive more tasks as joint responsibilities than their lower status counterparts.

A different conclusion is reported by Blood and Wolfe (8). The division of labor in their sample of Detroit families coincided with the division of labor in the traditional rural family. The authors report, however, that the sexually differentiated roles of Detroit couples were not rooted in the "dead hand" of culture, but were a reflection of equity: roles were assigned on the basis of the amount of time, energy, and skill which each family member could contribute to the common family tasks.

Both studies agree in reporting that household division of labor is more likely to be based upon the interpersonal relationships of the couple than upon widely accepted cultural norms. General societal trends support the movement toward informality in household division of labor and spousal decision-making processes.

3. Changed Definition of Children

Children were an economic asset in the earlier, fertile, relatively self-sufficient rural family, but they occupied an inferior status position in their parent-oriented or father-centered family. A lowered birth rate was one of the adjustments of the family system to urbanization (52, p. 198). Reductions in fertility have been accompanied by an increased status for children vis-à-vis their parents and by dedication to corresponding modes of child rearing.

Changes in child-rearing techniques reflect the movement from formal parent-child relationships based upon differential status positions with clearly defined roles toward the informal, varied, and person-centered relations in the modern family. These changes are manifested in the greater use by both parents of "psychological" or "symbolic" techniques of discipline, greater permissiveness for child behavior, freer expression of affection, greater participation by children in family decision making, and more conscious attempts by parents to help children develop their intellectual, social, and emotional potentialities (10). These changes in family socialization patterns, actively promoted by family life educators, also receive increasing societal support.

4. *Increased Use of Person-Centered Criteria in Mate Selection*

The improvements in the level of living freed adolescents from the labor market, provided them with leisure time and, with the relatively equal sex standards which have been developing, created the conditions for contemporary dating and courtship patterns. One result has been an increase in the spatial mobility of youth and, with this, an opportunity for a wider choice among dating and potential marriage partners (20, 25). In this context of wider choice in prospective mates, mate selection standards based on love and companionate interests appear to be overcoming institutionalized endogamous norms such as those forbidding interfaith marriages (19, 20, 43, 84). It appears that norms of class endogamy have remained unchanged or, given the wider territorial range in mate selection, may even have become stronger (25).

5. *Increasing Permissiveness of Sex Norms*

A revolution in American sexual norms has occurred in the last half-century. There has been a socially sanctioned change in attitudes toward the rights of both men and women to attain enjoyable and satisfactory marital sex relations. Expectations for enjoyable sex relations at varying levels of involvement have carried over into dating and courtship relations. Premarital coital relations are still condemned, and the double sex standard is still openly tolerated, but all available data point to increases in nonmarital sexual activity. Given the emphasis on free selection of dating and courtship partners, affectionate and companionate personal relations, individualism, equality of male and female status, secularization of values, earlier ages for initial dating, and more serious emotional involvements at younger ages, the double sex standard has become less tenable and there are fewer societal supports for continence.

The Kinsey studies and other data indicate that the increase in premarital coital activity occurred during World War I and shortly thereafter. The change in female behavior was more marked than in male behavior. Present evidence suggests that the prevalence of premarital coital activity has remained relatively stable during the past several decades. However, rates of petting have increased notably since the 1920's (26, 55, 56, 73). This increase in petting may lead, in time, to an increase in the number of couples who will accept premarital coitus (73). The prediction that premarital coital rates will increase is based on the probable diffusion of the single standard, permissive-with-affection sex code evolving in American society. This code permits greater freedom, ultimately leading to nonmarital coitus, in person-centered relationships where a high degree of affection is present. Reiss argues that such a sex code is associated with the emerging male-female equality and the emerging individuated, companionate, affectional marriage system (73).

6. *Differentiation and Specialization in Family Functions*

Industrialization and consequent urbanization, plus geographical mobility, have decreased the importance of the extended family and have increased the significance of the nuclear family in the provision of services for its members. This movement from an extended family system to a nuclear family system and the resulting specialization of functions within the nuclear family system has led to the familiar portrayal of the "loss of functions" in the nuclear family organization. While it is true that the American family no longer represents a "little society" to its members, there are still certain generalized functions which the family system, now in its nuclear form, continues to provide for society in general. These include the reproduction of new members, child care, and important contributions to the socialization of children. The family also continues to provide tension management for its members, including the regulation of sexual behavior and the provision of affectional-companionate relations. Beyond these sexual, socializing, and maintenance functions, the family system retains the function of initial status ascription and provides a basis for the transfer of property.

Williams (92) and Bell and Vogel (7) approach the subject of specialization of functions within the family system by focusing on the interchanges between the family system and the other social systems. In this context, lists of functions which the nuclear family system is expected to fulfill become less relevant. The important foci become the nature of the systemic linkages between the family system and other social systems (including the roles, status, norms, and values involved), and the associations between intrafamily activities which are related to the systemic linkage roles and the activities performed in the systemic linkage roles. Of particular importance, are the systemic linkages between the family system and the economic or occupational systems.

General changes in society . . . require specialization in the family system and at the same time increase the importance of the nuclear family in providing adequate socialization, personality development, and tension-management experiences for its members. The importance of these functions of the family will likely increase, not diminish, as marital roles will likely be increasingly based on personally perceived satisfactions arising from interpersonal relations.

7. Reassertion of Kinship Ties and Family Continuity Patterns

Another widely accepted generalization in the family literature is that industrialization and urbanization are antithetical to close and continuous relationships among kin. Until recently sociologists have described the American family as primarily a simple conjugal system with no important kinship connections. Litwak (61, 62) has carefully analyzed several of the assumptions of the Parsonion model and has suggested an ideal type, the "modified extended" family, as appropriate for describing contemporary kinship patterns among urban nuclear families. The "modified extended" family differs from the "classical extended" family in that it does not demand territorial propinquity, occupational involvement, or nepotism, nor does it have a hierarchical authoritarian pattern. On the other hand, it differs from the isolated, nuclear family structure in that it does provide significant and continuing aid to the nuclear family.

Research in various metropolitan areas of the United States and England support the validity of the modified extended family system in urban social structures. These studies reveal a kin family system involving a network of mutual assistance, visiting, and socio-emotional support encompassing several generations.[2]

8. Professionalization of Marital and Parental Roles

Specialization in family functions has led to professionalization of parental and marital roles for both partners, but especially for the wife. Wives cannot rely upon their informally acquired "folk knowledge" as a basis for performing their roles. The knowledge necessary for performance of contemporary marital and parental roles must be rationalized and kept up to date. Coeducational classes on preparation for marriage and family life, in-service training as provided by the women's magazines, study, and discussion groups, and consultation with specialists at the medical clinic, nursery school, PTA meeting, or in the counseling office reflect the desire to prepare for, or seek help in, performing marital and parental roles.

9. Development of Programs to Increase the Well-Being of the American Family

At the turn of the century, most people had great respect for the institution called the family, yet they were reluctant to learn much about it. The family was taken for granted and was expected to cope automatically with whatever internal or external crises occurred (45). As the ban on discussion of family matters has been lifted and as the results of research and reflection have permeated the society, a wide variety of educational, counseling, judicial, and governmental programs have evolved to ameliorate problems associated with American family life. These programs will probably receive increased support and be staffed by increasingly competent persons in the future.

10. Interpersonal Criteria of Success and Stability of Marriage

The emerging norms for evaluating marriage and family relationships are based on the interpersonal needs and relationships of all family members. These norms impose far greater demands on family members than criteria based on economic interdependence or on legal and social obligations. The long-term increase in divorce rates represents a shift from the criterion of relative permanence, come what may, to the criteria of interpersonal relations, which permit divorce if the relationship between the spouses becomes intolerable.

Contrary to the beliefs of traditionalists, there are indications that the interpersonal criteria for evaluating marital and family relations are associated with increased stability in marriage. Marriage and re-marriage are at the height of their respective popularities. Divorce is not a rejection of marriage; rather it apparently represents an attempt to improve marital experiences. Divorce rates have declined from an all-time high in the late 1940's, are now fluctuating in a narrow range, and may be expected to remain at their present levels or to show a long-term, gradual decline, although they will probably never reach the low level of the late 1880's (34, 51).

Reasons for expecting a decline in divorce rates would include the emergence of socialization patterns which are oriented to the acquisition of interpersonal competence skills, opportunities for greater freedom in mate selection, the relative equality between men and women, greater flexibility in male and female roles, increased emphasis on sex satisfaction for both spouses, the desire for and satisfactions gained from child rearing, less puritanical attitudes toward deviations from chastity, increased levels of living, additional support for nuclear families through the revitalization of the kinship system, and the professionalization of marital and family roles—all of which are buttressed by private and public family service programs.

Another way of supporting the prediction of increased marital stability in the United States is to compare divorce rates among different segments of the population. As Foote (29) has pointed out, the standard assertion that urbanization and industrialization are inexorably destructive of family stability and solidarity is contradicted by the fact that the families of college educated, salaried, professional couples have a low divorce rate. Yet these families are the fullest beneficiaries of such aspects of industrialization and urbanization as the reliance upon science, spatial and social mobility, and emphasis on the welfare and freedom of the individual. The professional group is most liberal in its attitude toward divorce, is most equalitarian in its views on the employment of married women, and strongest in espousing equality of status and flexibility of roles between husbands and wives. And this group appears to be most cosmopolitan in its selection of marriage partners, least affected by propinquity, and closest in age at marriage.

At present, it seems that the voluntary commitment to marriage based upon companionship and mutual development, as found among the professional groups, is a stronger bond for marriage than functional economic interdependence and the social and legal sanctions which held traditional families together.

The Emerging Urban Prototype

Precise empirical data for documenting the characteristics of an emerging urban family organization are lacking. The currently offered typologies—traditional, companionate or colleague, for example—appear to be inadequate for conceptualizing urban family organization (35). For this reason, a neat typology cannot be used to summarize the current pattern of urban family organization or that of the urban professional class. Yet a prototype of urban family organization may be inferred from projections of past changes. This prototype is most clearly represented among families in the urban professional class and, in varying degrees, reflects the following characteristics: enhancement of the welfare, freedom, and personality of individual family members by means of family relationships; development of nuclear and extended family bonds based upon loyalty, affection, and companionship; maintenance of equalitarian relationships and a flexible family division of labor; differentiation in family and occupational roles resembling the colleague conceptualization of Miller and Swanson (68) or the mutually contingent careers idea of Foote (29); desire for children based on the opportunities for providing for the personality development of the children and the enrichment which the children bring to the couple; active pursuit and implementation of knowledge (professionalization) related to marital and family roles; use of person-centered criteria in dating, courtship, mate selection, and marriage; and tolerant views toward nonmarital sexual experiences.

It cannot be established when these prototypal patterns will become modal characteristics of urban families.[3] It is even less clear when and in what ways rural family organization will reflect these prototypal patterns. However, in terms of long-run developments, these prototypal patterns may be used as a point of departure for assessing circumstances which rural families will probably encounter as they continue to change under the joint impact of specialization through social and technological developments in the rural scene and of "modernization" of family patterns spreading from urban to rural communities.[4]

Changes in the Rural Family System

How have the changes described for the urban family system, and now emerging in a prototypal urban pattern, affected rural family organization? Adequate research data are not available to answer this question, but some tentative inferences, suggested as hypotheses, may be drawn from the available data. In the discussion which follows, overgeneralization and oversimplification cannot be avoided unless the results of available research were rigidly limited to the particular state, county, or community from which the samples were drawn. A broader canvass than this is needed for the presentation of tentative assessments of the relationships between rurality and family patterns. Therefore, in the present discussion, speculation has been granted a freer hand and careful limitations have not been placed on generalizations.

All empirical data consistently support the generalization that changes in rural family organization have followed those described for the urban family system. While this statement is hardly startling, the generalization is valuable as a perspective for predicting changes in rural family patterns. For instance, Brown's observations of changes in the organization of Kentucky mountain families (11, 12) indicate that changes in the family patterns of these relatively isolated people parallel, but lag about 50 years behind, those in the general society. If the relatively isolated, strongly kinship-oriented family of Beech Creek is undergoing many of the same changes as the family system in the wider society, but not as quickly, it is likely that family systems in less isolated rural areas will display even less difference from the emerging urban family pattern (1, 32, 54). Unfortunately, data are not available for systematic analysis of this proposition. But some indication of the narrowing gap in the family-related values and attitudes may be gleaned from a number of investigations.

Twenty-five years ago Beers observed that the patterns of New York farm families which he studied were becoming more like those of urban families. These farm families were smaller, less familistic, and the roles of parents and children were becoming more flexible, with a definite democratization in family status positions. The latter was best evidenced by the shared executive roles of the fathers and mothers, although these joint decision-making patterns appeared to be a function of the economic scale of the farm enterprise rather than the result of a democratic normative pattern (5).

The generalization of declining familism in the rural family system is supported by additional research (24). Several investigations of differences in opinions between rural and urban wives on problems related to marriage failed to reveal many striking differences (57, 76). While the foregoing data and portions of additional data which follow indicate that changes in rural family organization are following changes in urban family patterns, some differences may still exist between rural and urban family systems. Available descriptive data for comparable rural and urban family patterns may be organized under the following eight headings.

Rural-Urban Differences in Family Patterns

1. Family Decision-Making Patterns

Only small or nonsignificant differences in family decision-making patterns have been reported by two studies, each of which employed a different dichotomy for studying the relationship between rural-urbanism and family decision-making patterns. Blood and Wolfe compared farm and Detroit, Michigan, couples (8); Bock and Burchinal employed a farm-nonfarm distinction for Greene County, Iowa, families and applied controls for age and education levels (9). The absence of uncompromising paternal dominance patterns and evidence for husband-wife sharing of the executive role in farm families have also been reported in earlier research (5, 27).

The decision-making items in all of the preceding studies pertain to family interaction patterns which did not directly involve work or occupational roles. Research by Wilkening and Straus can be used to test the validity of the companionate model for farm operations decisions. This model is implied in most of the thinking and the action programs related to farm family and farm firm interrelationships. Husband–wife interaction in relation to decisions about farm operations is not a simple function of the status of either spouse or the complexity of the farming enterprise. Rather, the joint decision-making pattern appears to be a function of the extent to which farm family and farm firm decisions are viewed as having joint consequences for both the farming enterprise and the household (91). Wilkening further suggests that the roles played by husbands and wives in decision making are determined more by their perceptions of farm and household needs than by culturally determined patterns of interaction.

Under these conditions, wide variations in husbands' and wives' roles in decision making should be observed. The needs perceived by the couple may vary over time and interact in numerous ways with the degree of commercialization of the farm and the levels of aspiration of the farm operator and his wife. For instance, contrary to what might have been assumed to be the dominant interests of farm wives, Wilkening found that more farm wives than farm operators in one sample preferred purchases of farm items over purchases of household equipment (89).

Wilkening's social psychological frame of reference, including perceived needs and consequent interaction patterns of husbands and wives, is congruent with the general thesis emerging from Straus' investigations of farm family role differentiation. In his investigation of the wives' contributions to success in settlement in the Columbia Basin Project (80, 81), Straus found that wives in the high success group and wives in the low success group of settlers were not appreciably different in background characteristics or in their direct economic contributions to their respective families. Instead, the qualities which differentiated the two groups of wives were certain attitudes, values, and personality characteristics.

The wives in the high success group more frequently accepted the traditional pattern of male dominance in the economic area. They were more active in food preparation, less active in farm work roles (further evidence for a traditional sex-linked division of labor), were better adjusted psychologically, were more optimistic, and were more persevering than were the wives of the low success settlers. Straus draws an analogy between the wives of the high success group and the image of the successful corporation wife, suggesting that the differentiating factors between the wives in high and low success categories are those which "enable the wife to play a supportive and complimentary role in helping her husband meet the many decisions, difficulties, and frustrations which arise in developing a new farm" (81, p. 64).

In later research, Straus tested the relationship between the integrative, supportive wife role and the technological competence of her husband. The existence of the "wife role factor" in understanding the adoption of farm practices by the husband was demonstrated, but no causal relationship was implied (79).

Wilkening also studied relationships between adoption of farm practices and family-related variables (89, 90). No consistent relationship was found between the authoritarian role of the husband-father or between measures of familism or family integration and the farm operator's acceptance of changes in farm technology. Instead, roles and values of family organization centering around acquiring a good living, education for the children, security, recreation, and health were related to the acceptance of changes in farm technology.

2. Household Division of Labor

Blood and Wolfe found that farm and Detroit wives reported the same median number of sex-stereotyped household task allocations, five out of eight tasks (8). However, farm wives performed a consistently greater share of household roles than city wives and helped their husbands more frequently with their work. In the aggregate, about 70 per cent of the farm wives did more than half of the eight tasks all by themselves while only 39 per cent of the city wives handled as many tasks on their own.

Data related to husband-wife role differentiation for samples of farm and nonfarm families are also available for Greene County, Iowa. Age and educational level controls were used in all comparisons of items related to household tasks, child care tasks, and management of money tasks. In general, the farm and nonfarm wives described similar patterns of husband–wife role differentiation in the three areas tested (9).

3. Employment of Wives Outside the Home

Aside from the several comparisons already cited, farm and nonfarm or city wives appear to contribute to the economic welfare of their families in distinctively different ways. The comparison of economic functions of wives showed that farm wives more frequently made most of their dresses, prepared more baked goods, more frequently raised summer vegetables, and canned or froze more foods. The Detroit wife apparently looked more frequently to paid employment as her means of contributing to the family income and gaining whatever satisfactions work meant to her. Twenty-four per cent of the sample of the Detroit wives were employed compared with only nine per cent of the farm wives (8).

Comparisons of employment rates of farm and nonfarm wives in Greene County, Iowa, have the advantage of controlling for employment opportunities for the two populations of women living in the same county (17). In this county, approximately eight per cent of the farm wives included in a probability sample were employed off the farm in contrast to approximately 26 per cent of the nonfarm wives who were employed outside their homes. In each of three farm-nonfarm comparisons using controls for the educational level of the wives, a greater proportion of nonfarm wives were employed. Also, significantly greater proportions of the nonfarm wives were employed before their marriages and continued to work after marriage than the farm wives.

Data available from another survey in Cass County, Iowa, agreed with the Greene County results (17). Only about nine per cent of the wives in a random sample of Cass County farm families with children in school were employed, in comparison with 31 per cent of the nonfarm wives with children in school.

A general premise of this [selection], diffusion and acceptance of urban-developed values by rural persons, points to greater participation of farm wives in the nonfarm labor force. Questions frequently arise as to the "effects" of employment of married women on family variables. Because of the recent and expected long-term increases in employment of married women, a brief and highly generalized summary of research on relationships between maternal employment and family variables appears warranted.

A growing body of research based mainly on urban families, though including some studies based on farm families (2, 3, 17, 70, 74), indicates that family task patterns and spousal decision-making patterns are related to the employment status of the wife.[5] Among families where the wives are employed, husbands generally are more active in household task roles, but the data are not as clear in regard to alterations in the spousal balance of power which may be associated with the employment of wives. Some studies report that wives enhance their power vis-à-vis their husbands when they are employed, but Hoffman questions this conclusion. Her results led her to suggest that employment of wives does not affect family power relations directly, but only in interaction with the existing ideology and personality of the actors. Power relationships, unlike division of labor, are either too deeply interrelated with psychological components of the husband-wife relationship to respond readily to the impact of the wife's employment, or employment per se is too weak a variable to accomplish this change (48).

The most extensive data on employment of farm wives and associated patterns of spousal relationships are those reported by Bauder (2, 3).[6] Bauder found that employment of farm wives was associated with increased household task performance by farm husbands. Nonfarm employment of farm husbands had no apparent effect on the spousal division of labor. The most pronounced effects on the spousal division of labor occurred among farm families where both husband and wife were employed off the farm. For these families, household tasks were performed more frequently by the children or adults other than the parents, and when they were performed by one spouse, they were done by the person who had the most time or who happened to be available.

The same pattern was observed in relation to husband–wife decision-making patterns, although it was less marked than for the division of labor patterns. For instance, major punishment of children was typically a joint decision role between farm parents when neither was employed off the farm. It generally remained so when either the husband or wife worked, but when both were employed major punishment of children was less frequently reported as a joint decision responsibility. Instead, it was decided more frequently by either the father or mother, generally on the basis of who was available at the time.

A modest body of research pertaining to relations between employment of mothers and developmental characteristics of children has appeared in recent years. The usual assumption about the detrimental influence of employment of mothers on their children has not been supported by most of this research. In the most carefully designed studies, generally small, nonsignificant, or inconsistent differences in personality and social characteristics have been found between children and youth whose mothers have been employed and those whose mothers have not been employed: see the summaries by Burchinal (18) or Herzog (44).

Exceptions to these null differences between children whose mothers have been and have not been employed come from two studies based on samples of rural families. In these studies the results suggest that employment of rural mothers is associated with positive child development and family relations results. In three of five comparisons between younger children of employed and nonemployed mothers and in all five comparisons between similar groups of older children, Nolan and Tuttle (70) found differences favoring the children whose mothers had been employed. The comparisons were based on teachers' ratings on children's academic achievement, relations between ability and achievement, acceptance by peers, acceptance of the teacher's supervision, and evidence of home training.

In a study of rural and town families living in Washington, Roy found that "rural families in general benefited from the employment of the mother, in that the girls, and, in part, the boys, showed less delinquency, more affection, more fairness of discipline, more democracy and more cooperation in their families." (74, p. 349).

4. Satisfaction with Marriage and Family Relations

Some data show no differences between marital satisfaction levels of farm and nonfarm couples; other data suggest higher satisfaction levels among nonfarm couples; and with only relatively minor exceptions, no data of which the writer is aware suggest higher satisfaction levels among farm couples. In the aggregate, however, the data suggest that farm family living may produce lower levels of marital and personal satisfaction than nonfarm family living.

Null differences in marital satisfaction or happiness scores between farm and city wives were reported by Blood and Wolfe (8) and among farm, rural nonfarm, and small-town couples studied by Burchinal (15). Other data indicate that people living in metropolitan areas express greater marital happiness and less feelings of inadequacy than other persons, particularly rural persons (38, p. 229). Blood and Wolfe observed that the pattern of disagreement or complaints regarding marriage was similar for the farm and city families. Both samples of wives reported that companionship in doing things with their husbands was the most valuable aspect of marriage to them.

Blood and Wolfe found several differences related to marital relations between the samples of farm and Detroit families. Husbands' responses to their wives' troubles was one of these. Farm-reared husbands tended to be passive listeners, whether they still lived on farms or had moved to Detroit. Men still engaged in farming were more likely than city husbands to dismiss their wives' troubles. Their failure to help the wife in her crisis seems to correspond with their slight participation in household tasks (8, p. 209).

Another farm-Detroit marital relationship difference centered on satisfaction-with-love scores. Satisfaction with love was the only aspect of marriage in which Blood and Wolfe found a significant difference between farm and city wives. Farm wives were less satisfied in their love relationships with their husbands than city wives (8, p. 223). Further analysis of the wives' satisfaction-with-love scores, based on the sizes of communities in which the wives had spent most of their lives, suggested that family expressions of love and affection are most widely encouraged and practiced by persons with urban socialization experiences.

Other data suggest less satisfaction in marital and personal relations in farm families as compared with nonfarm families. In 1940, McVoy and Nelson found that farm women were more dissatisfied than village women in regard to a number of categories of family living, had lower social participation scores, displayed poorer general adjustment, and had poorer self-happiness ratings. When the samples of farm and village women were matched on several variables, the farm women still had significantly lower satisfaction scores, poorer general adjustment, and lower happiness scores (66). In a restudy of the farm and nonfarm populations in the same county ten years later, Taves found that although living conditions had improved markedly for both populations, and more so for the farm families, farm women still had lower family living satisfaction scores than village women (83).

Thorpe's investigation of farm and town family interaction patterns suggest that there was greater spousal companionship among the town couples than among the farm couples who were included in her Michigan samples (85). Town husbands and wives, in comparison with farm couples, spent more time together exclusive of other family members.

Results of two other studies suggest that interpersonal relations in farm or rural families are less often marked by affection than those in the urban families. Beers observed that the shared activities and group rituals of the New York farm families he studied were not ordinarily accompanied by overt demonstrations of affection. Traditions of restraint and habits of emotional control may have been vestiges of the earlier pioneer attitude of inner control (5, p. 596).

Indirect support for the view of less affectionate or companionate relations between farm husbands and wives comes from the study of rural-urban differences between young married women in Washington. The most striking rural-urban differences between the young married women with rural and urban socialization background was the much higher proportion of rural than urban women who considered sexual adjustment a major problem in marital happiness or unhappiness (57). The greater perception of sexual difficulties among the rural-reared married women may reflect less satisfactory spousal relations, which, in turn, may be based on socialization experiences which make it more difficult for rural-reared spouses than urban-reared spouses to develop satisfactory sex and love relationships. Otherwise, the Kinsey data suggest that only minor differences exist in the variety and frequency of sexual outlets among rural- and urban-reared males and females, although urban-reared persons were generally more active in most outlets (55, 56).

5. Divorce Proneness

All available data support the generalization that marital stability is higher among farm or rural couples than among urban couples (51, 52, 60, 64). All of the foregoing studies, though, suffer from a common limitation—the analyses were based upon current residence at the time of divorce. Information is not available regarding what proportion of urban divorces include persons who had a rural residence immediately prior to divorce. Undoubtedly, some relationship exists between divorce and migration from farm to urban areas. On the other hand, it is easy to overgeneralize the frequency of migration-linked divorces and, consequently, to underestimate the true magnitude of rural-urban differences in divorce rates. Some Iowa data suggest that the observed differences in rural and urban divorce rates are not spurious, even though urban divorce rates may be inflated as a consequence of separation, migration, and subsequent divorce (69).

Divorced farm men are not under the same necessity to migrate from the farm as divorced farm wives. Therefore, divorce ratios based upon men's occupational roles should provide a better estimate of rural-urban differences in divorce rates than those based on residence at the time of divorce. Monahan has provided divorce ratio data by occupational categories for Iowa males in 1953. The ratio of divorces per 1,000 employed farm laborers was 0.9 against 26.9 for other laborers; the divorce ratio for farm operators was 1.7 against 2.9 for owners and officials engaged in nonfarm occupations (69). Clearly, some combination of circumstances associated with farm socialization and farm living, especially for the lowest occupational status comparison, are reflected in these farm-nonfarm divorce ratio differences.

Goode has provided data which support the view of greater reluctance of persons with rural backgrounds to seek divorce. Respondents with rural backgrounds had the longest median duration of marriage, the longest period of serious consideration of divorce before filing and, when the divorces occurred, most frequently reported trauma associated with their divorces. Urban-reared wives were most different from rural-reared wives while the wives from small towns were intermediate in these respects (36).

6. Social Relationship Patterns

Numerous studies support the generalization that farm husbands and wives are less active in social organizations than nonfarm couples who live in the same areas served by the organizations. This generalization appears to have been true for at least three decades: see Leevy, data from 1935 to 1938 (58); McVoy and Nelson, 1940 (66); and Bock and Burchinal, 1958 (9). If farm couples do not participate as actively in social organizations as neighboring nonfarm couples, it could be hypothesized that farm couples have more active informal social relationship patterns, including visiting with relatives, than the nonfarm couples.

Two recent studies, conducted in the Midwest, provided tests of differences in kinship-related visiting and nonkinship-related visiting by farm and nonfarm couples. In Greene County, Iowa, farm and nonfarm families appeared equal in the total number of families or individuals with whom they regularly visited. But the farm families reported that a larger proportion of the families they visited were related to them while the nonfarm families reported that a larger proportion of the families they visited were unrelated to them. However, there appeared to be little difference between the farm and nonfarm families in the frequency of visiting related families. A large difference between farm and nonfarm families in the total frequency of visiting was observed because nonfarm families reported a greater frequency of visiting with nonrelated persons or families (9).

Key (53) failed to find a linear relationship between residence position along a rural-urban continuum and the degree of social participation of men and women in either their nuclear or extended families. Instead, he observed a U-shaped curve, with the low point at the village or small urban category and with the high points at the extremes—the rural sample, on the one hand, and the middle-sized city or metropolitan sample on the other hand.

To a limited degree, the results of these studies suggest that visiting patterns based on extended family relationships were stronger among rural than among the nonfarm or urban family members, but that the nonfarm or urban families visited nonrelated families more frequently. However, no controls were used for the presence of related families.

7. Child-Bearing and Child-Rearing Patterns

Historically, the farm family has been more fertile than the urban family, but the size of rural-urban difference in fertility rates has varied with general socioeconomic conditions in the United States. The effect in recent years has been toward a narrowing, but not a vanishing, fertility differential between rural and urban women (52, 63).[7]

Some fragmentary data from Blood and Wolfe (8) suggest a future similarity in farm and urban birth rates. They found that both farm and city wives wanted approximately four children and that two to four children was considered as the ideal family size.

What children mean to parents appears to have somewhat different meanings for the farm and city mothers in the Detroit area study. The ranking of criteria for defining what was good about having children was the same for the farm and city mothers, but the two groups of mothers gave differential emphasis to some of the good things about having children. For instance, city wives mentioned emotional satisfaction more often than farm wives. Farm wives were more apt to mention the companionship of the child, the belief that the presence of the child strengthened the home, and that children helped parents and provided security.

The meager data that are available on parent-child relationships in rural and urban families support the generalization that parent-child relationships are less satisfactory in rural and farm homes than in urban homes. In the early 1930's Burgess reported that parent-adolescent relationships were less satisfactory in rural than in city families (88). Researchers in Washington found that both urban-reared mothers and daughters more frequently rated their parental homes as very happy than did rural-reared mothers and daughters. The urban daughters more frequently than any other group came from very happy parental homes (76). The foregoing data from different time periods and from different parts of the country are buttressed by the results of a careful study by Nye. Nye found that children from Michigan city families enjoyed better parent-adolescent relationships than other children, and that parent-adolescent adjustment declined with increasing rurality. When family socioeconomic status was held constant, the differences were absent at the high socioeconomic level and, though diminished, were still evident in the medium and low levels (71).

8. Rural-Urban Differences in Preparation for Adult Roles

Recognition of the increased similarity in rural and urban socialization systems has led to the generalization that personality or value-related characteristics of rural and urban children or youth are not very different; or if differences currently exist, they will become smaller and even negligible in the future. A considerable body of data points to the opposite conclusion—that there are significant differences in the socialization experiences of rural and urban youth. These differences are shown in school achievement levels, occupational aspiration and achievement levels, value-orientations, and personality-related characteristics of rural and urban youth.[8]

Historically, rural males have had lower educational levels than urban males. This is still true for rural and urban populations in general and for current populations of rural and urban youth. Among persons 16 to 24 who were not enrolled in regular or special schools in October, 1959, the farm population showed the highest proportion who lacked a high school education, as well as the lowest proportion with some college (86). Furthermore, reports from farm, rural non-farm, and urban high school seniors about their college plans and the degree to which they realized their plans one year later point to the maintenance of a better educated urban-reared than rural-reared population. In the national sample of youth surveyed in 1959, the smallest proportion of high school seniors who planned to go to college came from farm homes, rural nonfarm youth were intermediate, and urban youth most frequently planned to go to college. Rates of college attendance one year later were highest for urban youth and lowest for farm youth (87).

Controls for intelligence levels, grade in school, socioeconomic status of family, and sex of child, tend to diminish rural-urban differences in educational aspiration, but do not entirely remove the differences (37, 67, 75). For instance, Sewell found that Wisconsin farm children, regardless of their sex, levels of intellectual ability, or family status levels, generally had lower educational aspirations than similar children from village homes and almost always had lower levels than comparable urban children (75). An intriguing result of this study was that the differences in the proportions of farm, village, and urban youth who reported college plans were greatest for the comparisons where least differences might have been expected, among high intelligence high socioeconomic status groups. It is these groups which should provide the greatest proportions of college students. Results from an investigation in Florida agree with those from Wisconsin. High school seniors from rural and urban communities were matched on intelligence levels. Larger proportions of urban white males than rural white males, at each of several intelligence levels, reported plans to attend college (67).

The fact that sizable differences existed among the educational aspirations of farm, rural nonfarm, and urban youth after controls for intelligence and status were applied indicates that these variables do not explain why rural youth lag behind urban youth in educational aspirations. Differences in the value given education by rural and urban persons probably provides a more adequate explanation of the educational aspiration and achievement differences between rural and urban youth. Results from some markedly different studies support this view.

First, the lack of emphasis on advanced education for rural youth relative to urban youth, as reflected in their educational aspiration or achievement levels, may be a vestige of the view that advanced education is unnecessary, even a luxury, for youth who plan to enter farming. Research in a number of states indicates that this view still persists (21). Generally, farm youth who plan to farm are less likely than any other category of youth to consider education beyond high school. The norm of lower educational attainment for farm youth planning to farm may also influence educational norms for rural nonfarm students in rural communities, thus lowering educational aspiration norms for rural youth as a whole in contrast to urban youth.

Second, in the October 1959 survey of rural and urban youth, there was evidence that attitudinal differences outweighed economic differences in the formation of the educational plans of rural and urban youth. The most important difference in reasons for not attending college given by farm and nonfarm persons was the higher proportion of farm males (45 per cent) than nonfarm males (30 per cent) who reported "no desire" to attend college. Smaller and generally negligible differences were found for other reasons, such as finances, marriage, military service, or employment (87).

Finally, parental encouragement of male high school seniors to attend college was reported considerably more frequently by a sample of urban than by a sample of rural nonfarm or farm boys in Iowa. Whether they planned to farm or to enter nonfarm careers, the farm boys least frequently reported definite parental encouragement to attend college, and urban boys most frequently reported definite parental encouragement to attend college (16). In all three residence samples (farm, rural nonfarm-small town, and urban) mothers were reported to have more frequently provided definite encouragement to attend college than were fathers.

Most studies agree in finding lower occupational aspiration levels, probably related to lower educational aspiration levels, among rural youth as compared with urban youth. The differences in occupational aspirations of rural-urban or farm-urban high school boys persist when intellectual levels or family socioeconomic levels have been controlled (37, 67). Among boys living in a highly industrialized area of Michigan, Haller found that the difference in occupational aspiration between farm and nonfarm youth was principally due to farm-reared boys who planned to farm (41). When the occupational aspiration levels of only the farm boys who planned nonfarm careers were compared with those of the nonfarm boys, nonsignificant differences in occupational aspirations were observed between the two groups of boys. Different results were found in an Iowa investigation (16). When the Iowa farm-reared boys who planned to enter the nonfarm jobs were compared with small-town and city boys, the occupational aspirational levels of the nonfarm-oriented farm-reared boys approximated those of the nonfarm and small-town boys, but both were lower than the occupational aspiration levels of the city boys.

Compared with the urban boys, the Iowa rural or small-town boys less frequently reported that their parents discussed the boys' occupational plans with them or were involved in the boys' occupational decision-making processes (16). Other data suggest high school boys planning to farm were less well informed about nonfarm job opportunities and training requirements, were more satisfied with their present sources and levels of occupational information, and were less actively seeking information about nonfarm job opportunities (39, 40).

Rural-urban differences in adolescent personality characteristics are another reflection of rural-urban differences in socialization experiences. Results of various studies of rural-urban differences in personality characteristics have presented all three possible conclusions: (a) better adjustment characteristics among rural as contrasted with urban youth (65, 78); (b) better personality adjustment characteristics among urban as contrasted with rural youth (42, 93); and (c) no difference between personality characteristics of rural and urban youth (14). The two most recent and probably most powerful studies support the second generalization.

The Minnesota study, based on more adequate samples than have been used previously and the use of more powerful personality diagnostic instruments, reported that farm and rural youth more frequently than urban youth expressed feelings of shyness, self-deprecation, and suspicion or distrust of others. Urban youth were more likely to rebel against authority, be less self-critical, and be less suspicious of the motives of others than rural adolescents (42).

Results of research in Michigan generally confirm those derived from the Minnesota comparisons. Wolff and Haller found that in comparison with village and rural nonfarm boys or urban boys, farm boys had the greatest indications of submissiveness, shyness, or withdrawal tendencies. The farm boys tended to be less willing to move away from their home communities and were less likely to believe that man has much control over events which influence his life. Urban boys scored highest on dominance, aggressiveness, self-confidence, and independent self-sufficiency. The urban boys took a more positive attitude toward moving and tended to believe man can have control of events which influence his life (93).

Other data from several studies indicate that important differences in general value-orientations exist between boys who planned to farm and those who planned to enter nonfarm careers. The boys who preferred to farm were more localistic in their orientations, had greater interest in physical or mechanical work, and had less interest in work requiring use or development of social relations (21).

Haller also has reported personality-related differences between farm youth who plan to farm and those who do not plan to farm. These differences followed the farm-nonfarm comparisons just presented. In comparison with boys who planned to farm, farm boys who did not plan to farm had greater emotional stability, greater independence and self-sufficiency, and a greater interest in people, or at least were less afraid of social relationships. The youth intending to enter nonfarm roles were more confident of themselves and their relations with others (39, 40). Additional differences between farm youth who plan to farm and those who plan nonfarm careers are discussed by Burchinal (21).

Evidence of possible differences in rural and urban socialization patterns is reflected in the comparisons of occupational achievement levels of farm-to-urban migrants and urban-reared males. Rural-reared persons who migrate to urban areas are generally found disproportionately in lower income or lower prestige occupations. For instance, in a recent study in Cedar Rapids, Iowa, farm-urban migrant males were underrepresented in the high status occupations and overrepresented in the low status occupations, as compared with two urban-reared control groups (22). Similar results were still observed after controls for age and education level were applied. The discovery that greater proportions of similarly aged and educated urban-reared men than farm-reared men were in middle or high status occupations was interpreted as indicating that factors other than years of formal education contributed to the greater occupational achievement among the urban-reared males. The "other factors" would very likely include differences in value-orientation and personality characteristics between the farm-reared and urban-reared men, such as those previously reviewed, as well as possible differences in the quality of the educational experiences of the rural-reared and urban-reared men who had equal years of formal education.

When the Cedar Rapids study was repeated in Des Moines, Iowa, less consistent results emerged (4). In the Des Moines study, the usual differences in occupational achievement of farm-to-urban migrant men as against urban-reared migrant men or men who were natives of Des Moines were found for the total samples. However, when the age and educational controls were applied to these samples, nonsignificant differences in occupational achievement levels were obtained among the three samples for all but the lowest level of education. For males having less than 12 years of education, the occupational achievement of farm-reared males was only slightly lower than that of urban natives, but both were lower than that of urban migrants.

The partially conflicting results of the two Iowa studies may be the result of numerous factors. First, there is the possibility that sampling error in each of the studies may account for the differences in the results between the two studies, but this is probably less important than other factors. More likely, the occupational structures of the two metropolitan areas serve to attract and retain workers having different levels of education and skills. Cedar Rapids has a wider diversification of light and heavy industry while Des Moines, being the state capital and an insurance office center, has a greater portion of its labor force in clerical and white collar employment.

Other studies of the occupational achievement of farm or rural-reared versus urban-reared men are limited in their information value because controls for age and education were not used (6, 31, 94).

Other data related to comparisons of social participation patterns of farm-urban migrants and other urban inhabitants suggest that farm- or rural-reared persons are less able to cope with the complexities and formal characteristics of urban life than urban-reared persons

(6, 31, 94). Rural migrants belonged to fewer formal organizations and participated less in the organizations to which they belonged. Farm migrants had the slowest rate of entry into the formal social structure of the city. The rural migrants, especially the wives, took part in fewer informal activities and tended to be less active politically than the urban migrants or the natives of the city. However, Zimmer found that given time, all migrant groups, including those having farm origins, eventually become similar to the natives in their social activity patterns (94).

Implications of Rural-Urban Differences and Changes in Rural Family Patterns

Consideration of *the* rural family, apart from comparisons of rural-urban differences in family patterns, requires a high and somewhat spurious level of generalization. Each population, rural and urban alike, involves great heterogeneity in racial, ethnic, and status characteristics. Most of the available research, however, is based on white, predominately Protestant, middle status families. If our interest is restricted to rural and urban populations from white, predominately Protestant, and middle status families, the foregoing data point to many implications for persons interested in rural family life, only a few of which can be handled in the present section. Partly for similar and partly for different reasons, rural and urban family organizations are becoming more alike.

Rising levels of education in the rural population will continue to contribute to the convergence of rural and urban family patterns. One of the conclusions of a recent national study of the mental health of the American people offers additional support for the view of rural-urban convergence in family patterns and personality characteristics. The researchers found that a "young, educated, male farmer is more like a young, educated, male New Yorker than either of these people is like his own father" (38, p. 230). This conclusion is based on young farm or rural and urban males having approximately equal levels of education and, consequently, approximately equal status. Some similarities in rural and urban family patterns apparently exist today despite educational and status differences between the two populations. Rural-urban differences in other family patterns are at least partly a reflection of variables associated with educational and status differences between the two populations. Brief examination of present similarities and differences in rural and urban family patterns, against the backdrop of rising educational levels in rural areas and the diffusion of urban norms, suggests some critical areas of change in rural family relationships.

Family and household decision-making patterns and role performances do not appear to be very different between the two populations. The revitalization of kinship ties among urban families, if the decay of this network of relationships ever occurred to the extent that some social theorists maintained, suggests that urban families are becoming more like the traditional rural families in this respect.

However, the rural family reflects some vestigial elements which still differentiate it from the urban family. The fact that the rural family is still more fertile than the urban family is not of pressing importance at the moment. Rural and urban family size will probably move toward the moderately sized family. This trend may be desirable. Some family sociologists believe the moderately sized family provides the best structure for meeting interpersonal needs and for contributing to the development of all family members.

The lower divorce rates among farm and rural couples is evidence for the greater retention among rural than urban persons of the value of marriage permanence despite personal evaluations of the marital relationship. The rural-urban divorce rate differential remains despite the fact that the rural population has a lower educational level, lower income, and a lower level of living than the urban population—conditions which should, if operating by themselves, produce higher divorce rates among rural couples than among urban couples. Also, the rural-urban divorce rate differential exists even though some data suggest less satisfactory family relationships among the farm and nonfarm families as compared with city families.

It is difficult to say whether the rural-urban differential in divorce rates will continue as the companionate, mutual development, and personal-centered norms for evaluating marital relations diffuse more widely in rural areas. It could be hypothesized that at present more rural and farm couples are willing to tolerate less satisfactory interpersonal relations in marriage than urban couples, but that rural wives, in particular, may be less willing to do so in the future. Continuing this conjectural mood, future farm wives may expect their husbands to be more responsive to their emotional needs and to be more companionate than currently. Rural and farm males will probably have to become more attentive to and skillful in the nuances of interpersonal relations and especially heterosexual relations, if they are to meet the expectations of their wives.

The possibility of changes in rural divorce rates or other family patterns, raises a number of theoretical questions. For example, by what mechanisms and through what channels do urban norms of marital stability or other family patterns diffuse to rural areas? By what mechanisms and through what roles will the processes continue? Is it through the occupationally linked roles of her husband? Or by means of the roles of the wife, her reading of the mass media, her awareness of the family educators' opinions, or perhaps through her employment and other extrafamily experiences? Do the children provide the basis for changes in parent-child relationships and perhaps even marital relationships as a result of their school and community experiences? The effects on rural family life may be very different depending on the status and role positions of the family members who introduce the ideas of change and how these interact with the particular status and role systems in the family. These are difficult and important research questions which need to be examined.

Consideration of alternative norms for evaluating marital relationships leads to what appear to be the most significant differences in rural and urban family patterns. These differences concern the role of companionate or affectionate relationships in family relationships, the importance of attempting to meet interpersonal needs of family members, and the emphasis put upon developing interpersonal competence skills among family members. The present ways in which urban families are structuring their marital relationships do not represent perfect models. However, the meager data which are available suggest that greater emphasis is being given to these matters among urban families, and apparently more satisfactory results are being attained by urban than by rural families.

The prototypal urban family patterns discussed earlier represent the development of family patterns which currently permit the greatest expression of companionship and affection in the family, recognize and attempt to meet interpersonal needs of family members, and attempt to enhance development of interpersonal competence skills. Family relationship patterns based on these norms reflect adjustments to the newly emerging and varied sex roles of American men and women. The decline in the segregation of sexes and in sex-stereotyped roles need not lead to reductions in masculinity or femininity. Instead, the potential satisfactions which may be achieved from heterosexual relationships have been conspicuously heightened. As Nelson Foote has put it: "The repertoire of masculine and feminine sexual roles has widened among most segments of our society. Many now enjoy experiences that once were the possession or prerogative of a few" (30, p. 329).

Present research suggests that the socialization experiences of urban youth as compared with those of rural youth are more likely to help the urban youth realize their potential heterosexual satisfactions. Now and in the future, success in marriage and family relationships will be related less to propinquity and homogamy patterns and will be increasingly related to the interpersonal competency of the spouses. The association between successful family relationships and the ability to develop companionate or colleague roles based on mutually enhancing love will increase in the future. Present social organization apparently gives an advantage to urban youth in preparing them for adult family roles based on these emerging norms. Consider, for instance, the following quote from Blood and Wolfe:

> Farmers and immigrants come from environments which give low priority to the expression of love and higher priority to the economic and other functional interdependencies of husband and wife. Love is an artistic creation which reaches its widest perfection in the sophisticated upper reaches of American society. It is a boon which a more leisurely, better-educated society has conferred upon its members. The progressive urbanization, acculturation, and education of the oncoming generation suggests there is likely to be correspondingly more expression of love in the future. (8, pp. 234–35.)

The social organization of both rural and urban segments of our populations can be changed to provide greater support for enhancing expressions of love and for contributing to human development. Present information indicates that the rural family will have to undergo more radical changes than urban families. Furthermore, the demands for adequate socialization of youth may be more exacting for rural than for urban families. Families in both populations have responsibilities for the personality development and tension management of family members. The greater demands placed on the rural family lie in the fact that rural families must prepare their children and youth for adult experiences in either the rapidly changing rural social systems, of which the parents and young people have considerable awareness, or in urban social systems, of which they are less well aware. And the preparation must not be for the family, occupational, and community systems as they are known today, but for the requirements of these systems 20 years or more from now.

Adaptation to the new interpersonal demands will not be easy. Also, rural families face certain handicaps as they attempt to cope with present changes and to reintegrate behavior around interpersonal norms. How can rural families and communities compensate for their present low level of education? The arts of human relationships and family living are probably best, though far from perfectly, practiced in what has been called the urban professional class. Yet the demands for successful functioning will increasingly require that these arts be practiced at all social levels in rural as well as urban society. In moving toward the prototypal norm, families in urban communities have the advantages of higher levels of education, assumed to be a rough index of general personal resources, and greater opportunities for help and support of all kinds than rural families. In general, rural communities have fewer educational and ameliorative agencies and specialists whose services can help prepare persons for professionalization in marriage and family roles and support them in these roles.[9]

On the other hand, rural and farm families have certain structural and functional strengths which can be used in meeting changes. For the farm family, there are certain stable, integrative factors built around attachment to the land and family development of resources through shared tasks and common enterprise. These factors do not insure family solidarity, nor by themselves do they automatically contribute to the development and maintenance of interpersonal relationships built upon affection, companionship, or mutual respect. However, these characteristics provide mechanisms for doing so, provided the parents perceive the value and importance of developing family and work interaction patterns which contribute to integrated personality development and enhancement of personal identity and interpersonal competence.

American families, rural and urban alike, have shown great ability to adjust to drastic changes in societal organization. Today, the family is in a better position than ever before to adjust to the amazing technological developments predicted for this particular age. This optimism is based upon the universality of the family, the past record of American society and American family organization in meeting changes and crises, and the development of a body of research about family functioning serving as the basis for educational and ameliorative programs designed to integrate and strengthen family life.

NOTES

1. Descriptions of the Colonial or pre-Civil War northern rural family systems are taken as the base points for descriptions of changes in American family patterns: see Sirjamaki (77) or Cavan (23). In his

discussion of the changing rural family, Hill distinguishes among several types of rural southern family patterns of which the yeoman-farmer pattern was dominant (46). Data for these ten points are drawn mainly from Foote (28), Hill (45), Ogburn and Nimkoff (72), and Sirjamaki (77).

2. For an extensive review of the literature on the isolated, nuclear American family and a theoretical critique, see Marvin B. Sussman and Lee G. Burchinal (82).

3. There may be alternate and competing patterns of family organization emerging among different social groupings in the United States. Only one set of patterns, assumed to be the most general, has been identified. Differences associated with racial and status characteristics are known to exist. Also, Lenski organizes a considerable body of data to suggest that differences in family organization patterns exist among socioreligious groupings, and that differences between white Protestants and Catholics may be increasing, not decreasing as generally assumed (59).

4. Olaf Larson uses "modernization" in place of the impact of "urbanization" to describe changes in rural family patterns which are probably related to urban value systems and the use of urban reference groups by rural persons.

5. Several reviews of the literature on relationships between maternal employment variables and child development and family relationship variables are available: see Herzog (44), Burchinal (18), and Hoffman (48, 49). The most recent significant research on the employed mother, motivations for work, development of children, marital relations, and other characteristics of the employed mothers are reported in a forthcoming book edited by Hoffman and Nye (50). See also the November, 1961, issue of *Marriage and Family Living*, Vol. 23, which contains eleven articles on "Women and Work."

6. See also Nolan and Tuttle (79), and for a report of the attitudes of rural homemakers toward employment of married women, see Glenn (33).

7. Loomis and Beegle also present some data on demographic differences between rural and urban families which are not treated in this paper (63, pp. 69–81).

8. For a more extensive discussion and summary of studies related to the occupational decision-making process of rural youth and rural-urban differences related to educational and occupational aspiration and achievement levels, see Burchinal, Haller, and Taves (21).

9. See (13) for the differences in medical facilities in rural and urban communities. It is assumed that these differentials also carry over in most educational, religious, and welfare agencies.

LITERATURE CITED

1. Bauder, W. W. "Characteristics of Families on Small Farms," Ky. Agr. Exp. Sta. Bul. 644, 1956.
2. ———. "Effect of Nonfarm Employment of Farm Wives on Farm

Family Living," paper given at the Rural Sociological Society meeting, Pa. State Univ., Aug., 1960.

3. ———. "Impact of Wife's Employment on Family Organization in Farm and Urban Families," paper given at the National Council of Family Relations meeting, Salt Lake City, Aug. 1961.

4. ———, and Burchinal, L. G. "Occupational Achievement of Rural-to-Urban Migrant Males in Comparison With Two Urban Control Groups," paper given at the American Sociological Association meeting, St. Louis, Sept. 1961.

5. Beers, H. W. "A Portrait of the Farm Family in Central New York State," *Amer. Sociol. Rev.*, 2:591–600, 1937.

6. ———, and Heflin, C. "Rural People in the City," Ky. Agr. Exp. Sta. Bul. 478, 1945.

7. Bell, N. W., and Vogel, E. F. "Toward a Framework for Functional Analysis of Family Behavior," in Bell, N. W., and Vogel, E. F., eds., *A Modern Introduction to the Family*, The Free Press, Glencoe, Ill., 1960, pp. 1–33.

8. Blood, R. O., and Wolfe, D. M. *Husbands and Wives*, The Free Press, Glencoe, Ill., 1960.

9. Bock, E. W., and Burchinal, L. G. "Comparisons of Spousal Relations, Community Participation and Kinship Relation Patterns Between Farm and Nonfarm Families," paper given at the Midwest Sociological Society meeting, Omaha, Apr. 1961.

10. Bronfenbrenner, U. "The Changing American Child," Reference Papers on Children and Youth, prepared for the 1960 White House Conference on Children and Youth, 1960, pp. 1–8.

11. Brown, J. S. "The Family Group in a Kentucky Mountain Farming Community," Ky. Agr. Exp. Sta. Bul. 588, 1952.

12. ———. "The Farm Family in a Kentucky Mountain Neighborhood," Ky. Agr. Exp. Sta. Bul. 587, 1952.

13. "Building America's Health," a report to the President by the President's Commission on the Health Needs of the Nation, Washington, D.C., 1952.

14. Burchinal, L. G., Hawkes, H. R., and Gardner, B. "Adjustment Characteristics of Rural and Urban Children," *Amer. Sociol. Rev.*, 22:81–87, 1957.

15. Burchinal, L. G. "Correlates of Marital Satisfaction for Rural Married Couples," *Rural Soc.*, 26:282–89, 1961.

16. ———. "Differences in Educational and Occupational Aspirations of Farm, Small-town, and City Boys," *Rural Soc.*, 26:107–21, 1961.

17. ———. "Factors Related to Employment of Wives in a Rural Iowa County," Iowa Agr. and Home Econ. Exp. Sta. Bul. 509, 1962.

18. ———. "Maternal Employment, Family Relations and Selected Personality, School-related and Social Development Characteristics of Children," Iowa Agr. and Home Econ. Exp. Sta. Res. Bul. 497, 1961.

19. ———, and Chancellor, L. "Ages at Marriage, Occupations of Grooms, and Interreligious Marriages," *Social Forces*, 40:348–54, 1962.

20. ———, and ———. "What About School-age Marriages?" *Iowa Farm Science*, 12:12–14, 1958.

21. ———, in collaboration with Haller, A. O., and Taves, M., for the

subcommittee on family and youth of the North Central States Rural
Sociology Committee: "Career Choices Among Rural Youth in a
Changing Society," Minn. Agr. Exp. Sta. Bul. 458, 1962.
22. ———, and Jacobson, P. "Occupational Achievement Differentials
Among Farm-Urban, Other Urban Migrant and Native Males," paper
given at the Midwest Sociological Society meeting, St. Louis, Apr.,
1960.
23. Cavan, R. The American Family, Crowell, 1953.
24. Cleland, C. B. "Familism in Rural Saskatchewan," Rural Soc., 20:249–
57, 1955.
25. Dinitz, S., Banks, F., and Pasamanick, B. "Mate Selection and Social
Class: Changes During the Past Quarter Century," Marriage and Family Living, 22:348–51, 1960.
26. Ehrmann, W. Premarital Dating Behavior, Holt, 1959.
27. Fitzsimmons, C., and Perkins, N. L. "Patterns of Family Relationships
in Fifty Farm Families," Rural Soc., 12:300–303, 1947.
28. Foote, N. N. "Changes in American Marriage Patterns and the Role
of Women," Eugenics Quart., 1:254–60, 1954.
29. ———. "Matching of Husband and Wife in Phases of Development,"
Transactions of the Third World Congress of Sociology, Internat.
Sociol. Assn., London, 1956, 4:24–34.
30. ———. "New Roles for Men and Women," Marriage and Family Living, 23:325–29, 1961.
31. Freedman, R., and Freedman, D. "Farm-reared Elements in the Nonfarm Population," Rural Soc., 21:50–61, 1956.
32. Gladden, J. W., and Christiansen, J. R. "Emergence of Urban Values in
Mining Families in Eastern Kentucky," Rural Soc., 21:135–39, 1956.
33. Glenn, H. M. "Attitudes of Women Regarding Gainful Employment of
Married Women," Jour. Home Econ., 51:247–52, 1959.
34. Glick, P. C. American Families, Wiley & Sons, 1957.
35. Gold, M., and Slater, C. "Office, Factory, Store and Family: A Study
of Integration Setting," Amer. Sociol. Rev., 23:64–74, 1958.
36. Goode, W. J. After Divorce, The Free Press, Glencoe, Ill., 1956.
37. Grigg, C. M., and Middleton, R. "Community of Orientation and Occupational Aspiration of Ninth Grade Students," Social Forces, 38:
303–8, 1960.
38. Gurin, G., Veroff, J., and Feld, S. Americans View Their Mental
Health, Basic Books, 1960.
39. Haller, A. O. "Planning to Farm: A Social Psychological Interpretation," Social Forces, 37:263–68, 1959.
40. ———. "The Occupational Achievement Process of Farm-reared Youth
in Urban-Industrial Society," Rural Soc., 25:321–33, 1960.
41. ———. "Research Problems on the Occupational Achievement Levels
of Farm-reared People," Rural Soc., 23:355–62, 1958.
42. Hathaway, S. R., Monachesi, E. D., and Young, L. A. "Rural-Urban
Adolescent Personality," Rural Soc., 24:331–46, 1959.
43. Heer, D. M. "The Trend of Interfaith Marriages in Canada: 1922–
1957," Amer. Sociol. Rev., 27:245–50, 1962.
44. Herzog, E. "Children of Working Mothers," Children's Bureau Publ.
No. 382–1960, Washington, D.C., 1960.
45. Hill, R. "The American Family Today," in Ginsberg, E., ed., The Na-

tion's Children. Part I: *The Family and Social Change,* Columbia Univ. Press, New York, 1960, pp. 76–104.

46. ———. "Family Patterns in the Changing South," *Transactions of the Third World Congress of Sociology,* Internat. Sociol. Assn., London, 1956, 4:127–45.

47. ———. A revision of Waller, W. *The Family,* Holt, Rinehart and Winston, 1951.

48. Hoffman, L. W. "Effects of the Employment of Mothers on Parental Power Relations and the Division of Household Tasks," *Marriage and Family Living,* 22:27–35, 1960.

49. ———. "Effects of Maternal Employment on the Child," *Child Development,* 32:187–97, 1961.

50. ———, and Nye, I. *The Employed Mother,* Rand McNally, 1963.

51. Jacobson, P. H., and Jacobson, P. F. *American Marriage and Divorce,* Rinehart, 1959.

52. Kenkel, W. F. *The Family in Perspective,* Appleton-Century-Crofts, 1960.

53. Key, W. H. "Rural-Urban Differences and the Family," *Sociol. Quart.,* 2:49–56, 1961.

54. Keyfitz, N. "A Factorial Arrangement of Comparisons of Family Size," *Amer. Jour. of Soc.,* 58:470–80, 1953.

55. Kinsey, A. C., Pomeroy, W. B., and Martin, C. E.: *Sexual Behavior in the Human Male,* W. B. Saunders, 1948.

56. Kinsey, A. C., *et al. Sexual Behavior in the Human Female,* W. B. Saunders, 1953.

57. Landis, P. H. "Two Generations of Rural and Urban Women Appraise Marital Happiness," Wash. Agr. Exp. Sta. Bul. 524, 1951.

58. Leevy, J. R. "Contrasts in Urban and Rural Family Life," *Amer. Sociol. Rev.,* 5:948–53, 1940.

59. Lenski, G. *The Religious Factor,* Doubleday, 1961.

60. Lillywhite, J. D. "Rural-Urban Differentials in Divorce," *Rural Soc.,* 17:348–55, 1952.

61. Litwak, E. "Geographic Mobility and Extended Family Cohesion," *Amer. Sociol. Rev.,* 25:385–94, 1960.

62. ———. "Occupational Mobility and Extended Family Cohesion," *Amer. Sociol. Rev.,* 25:9–21, 1960.

63. Loomis, C. P., and Beegle, J. A. *Rural Sociology: The Strategy of Change,* Prentice-Hall, 1957.

64. Mangus, A. R. "Marriage and Divorce in Ohio," *Rural Soc.,* 14:128–37, 1949.

65. ———. "Personality Adjustment of Rural and Urban Children," *Amer. Sociol. Rev.,* 13:566–75, 1948.

66. McVoy, E. C., and Nelson, L. "Satisfaction in Living: Farm Versus Village," Minn. Agr. Exp. Sta. Bul. 370, 1943.

67. Middleton, R., and Grigg, C. M. "Rural-Urban Differences in Aspirations," *Rural Soc.,* 24:347–54, 1959.

68. Miller, D. R., and Swanson, G. E. *The Changing American Parent,* Wiley & Sons, 1958.

69. Monahan, T. P. "Divorce by Occupational Level," *Marriage and Family Living,* 17:322–24, 1955.

70. Nolan, F. L., and Tuttle, D. H. "Certain Practices, Satisfactions, and

Difficulties in Families with Employed Homemakers," Pa. Agr. Exp. Sta. Bul. 655, 1959.
71. Nye, I. "Adolescent-Parent Adjustment—Rurality as a Variable," *Rural Soc.,* 15:334–39, 1950.
72. Ogburn, W. F., and Nimkoff, M. F. *Technology and the Changing Family,* Houghton-Mifflin, 1955.
73. Reiss, I. L. *Premarital Sexual Standards in America,* The Free Press, Glencoe, Ill., 1960.
74. Roy, P. "Maternal Employment and Adolescent Roles: Rural-Urban Differentials," *Marriage and Family Living,* 23:340–49, 1961.
75. Sewell, W. H. "Rural-Urban Differences in Educational Aspirations," paper given at the Amer. Sociol. Assn. meeting, New York, Aug., 1960.
76. Sheeley, A., Landis, P. H., and Davies, V. "Marital and Family Adjustment in Rural and Urban Families of Two Generations," Wash. Agr. Exp. Sta. Bul. 506, 1949.
77. Sirjamaki, J. *The American Family in the Twentieth Century,* Harvard Univ. Press, Cambridge, Mass., 1953.
78. Stott, L. H. "Some Environmental Factors in Relation to the Personality Adjustments of Rural Children," *Rural Soc.,* 10:394–403, 1945.
79. Straus, M. A. "Family Role Differentiation and Technological Change in Farming," *Rural Soc.,* 25:219–28, 1960.
80. ———. "Matching Farms and Families in the Columbia Basin Project," Wash. Agr. Exp. Sta. Bul. 588, 1958.
81. ———. "The Role of the Wife in the Settlement of the Columbia Basin Project," *Marriage and Family Living,* 20:59–64, 1958.
82. Sussman, M. B., and Burchinal, L. G. "Kin-Family Network; Unheralded Structure in Current Conceptionalizations of Family Functioning," *Marriage and Family Living,* 14:231–40, 1962; "Parental Aid to Married Children: Implications for Family Functioning," *Marriage and Family Living,* 14:320–32, 1962.
83. Taves, M. J. "Farm Versus Village Living: A Decade of Change," *Rural Soc.,* 17:47–55, 1952.
84. Thomas, J. L. "The Factor of Religion in the Selection of Marriage Mates," *Amer. Sociol. Rev.,* 16:487–91, 1951.
85. Thorpe, A. C. "Patterns of Family Interaction in Farm and Town Homes," Mich. Agr. Exp. Sta. Tech. Bul. 260, 1957.
86. U.S. Bureau of the Census. *Farm Population,* P-27, No. 27, 1960.
87. ———. "Educational Status, College Plans, and Occupational Status of Farm and Nonfarm Youths: Oct., 1959." *Farm Population.* P-27, No. 30, 1961.
88. White House Conference on Child Health and Protection. "The Adolescent in the Family." Report of the subcommittee on the function of house activities in the education of the child. E. W. Burgess, chairman. Appleton-Century-Crofts, 1934.
89. Wilkening, E. A. "Adoption of Improved Farm Practices as Related to Family Factors," Wis. Agr. Exp. Sta. Res. Bul. 183, 1953.
90. ———. "Change in Farm Technology as Related to Familism, Family Decision-making, and Family Integration," *Amer. Sociol. Rev.,* 19:29–37, 1954.
91. ———. "Joint Decision-making in Farm Families as a Function of Status and Role," *Amer. Sociol. Rev.,* 23:187–92, 1958.

92. Williams, R. *American Society,* 2nd ed., Knopf, 1960, pp. 39–86, 113–14, 520–27.
93. Wolff, C. E., and Haller, A. O. "Farm, Village, Rural Nonfarm, and Small Urban Differences in Selected Personality Orientations of 17-Year-Old Boys in Lenawee County, Michigan," paper given at the Rural Sociological Society meeting, Pa. State Univ., University Park, Aug. 1960. Later published as Haller, A. O., and Wolff, C. E. "Personality Orientations of Farm, Village, and Urban Boys," *Rural Soc.,* 27:275–93, 1962.
94. Zimmer, B. G. "Participation of Migrants in Urban Structures," *Amer. Sociol. Rev.,* 20:218–24, 1955.

2 8

Biological Discoveries and the Future of the Family: A Reappraisal*

by Meyer F. Nimkoff

A little over a decade ago, I advanced the thesis that discoveries in human biology are potentially more significant for the social psychological aspects of family life than are technological developments.[1] Biological discoveries are more proximate or direct in their influence on the family because they change the internal environment of man, —that is, man's constitution. Technological innovations change the external environment and only indirectly affect the internal environment.

This fact notwithstanding, social scientists have paid more attention to technological changes. They have done so in part presumably because technological changes are more visible, and up to now, have been more extensive than biological discoveries. But an additional reason is that, because of occupational bias, sociologists are not so familiar with developments in human biology and tend to overlook or underestimate the internal environment of man.

When, in 1950, I advanced the thesis I have stated, I took an inventory of several promising lines of development in the biochemistry

* Presidential Address, Southern Sociological Society, April 13, 1962, Louisville, Kentucky.

Reprinted from *Social Forces,* 41 (December 1962), pp. 121–127, by permission of Mrs. M. F. Nimkoff and the University of North Carolina Press.

of sex and reproduction. Now, a little over a decade later, it seems appropriate and worthwhile to take another inventory, to see what progress has been made and what we can learn about factors in social change, with special reference to the family.

In 1950, there was considerable interest in the prospect for a physiological means of contraception. In that year James Conant, former President of Harvard University, in an address before the American Chemical Society, predicted that in ten years an effective contraceptive would be developed which could be taken as a supplement to the diet. This prediction was accurate, and the contraceptive pill is now a reality. We can see now that his prophecy was based on accurate knowledge of two factors: the cultural base and the social demand. Conant correctly saw that there was a sufficient base of existing knowledge of the reproductive process to warrant optimism regarding the additional discovery that had to be made; and he correctly estimated the social demand for such a discovery. Absence of demand for an innovation is a retarding factor, as is the lack of a sufficient body of accumulated knowledge.

As to the demand for a more effective contraceptive, the social climate in recent decades has become more favorable because of the sexual revolution resulting from such influences as the increasing emancipation of women and the impact of the work of Freud and Kinsey and their followers. It is a far cry from the early days of stubborn opposition to birth control in the United States, highlighted by the arrest and jailing of Margaret Sanger, to the Planned Parenthood Clinics that now dot our land, the current widespread discussion of birth control in mass circulation journals, and the availability on our news stands of authoritative pocket books on birth control.

For some time, government in the United States has supported birth control, especially in the South at the state level although not yet at the federal level. But the national governments of other lands are backing such a program: Scandinavia for some time, England and Japan more recently, and India and Pakistan more recently still. The impetus in the Far East is the so-called population explosion, and in Europe, the extension of the democratic principle.

Also it may be surmised that the opposition from religious sources has been diminishing, not at the formal level but at the informal. The doctrines of the Roman Catholic Church regarding contraception may not change but there is evidence of diffusion of contraceptive practices among Catholics. It is perhaps symbolic that a prominent figure in the development of the steroid pill, Enovid, was Dr. John Rock, a Catholic.

The steroid pill is not the last word in physiological control of conception but only the first word. The reproduction cycle is complex and may be amenable to control at a number of stages of the cycle. An extensive program of research is underway, under such notable auspices as the Population Council. A realistic possibility in the future is a contraceptive vaccine which would provide immunity for an extended period of time. The immunity must, however, be reversible.

As to the social effects of the innovations in contraceptives, it may be noted that the improvements in contraception are mainly a matter of degree of control, safety, convenience, and economy. There are other choices open to potential users, some rooted in hoary tradition. Indeed, there is evidence that the reduction in the birth rate in Sweden in the 1930's was accomplished by the use of folk methods, without benefit of modern contraceptives. The import of these remarks is to indicate that where innovations are matters of degree of improvement, they will not—all things equal—have as much social impact or significance as where innovations introduce entirely new elements, where the choice is between all or nothing. Immunization against conception is in this regard vastly different from immunization against typhoid. It is important to note also that a variation in degree of control can have significant social consequences. An inexpensive, reversible contraceptive vaccine would of course greatly facilitate the attack of certain nations on their population problem. It would also not be without influence on marital relations.

Potentially more revolutionary in its social effects than an improved contraceptive would be the knowledge of how to control the sex of the child, for at present we have no substitute for such knowledge. As to demand for it, we have in many cultures a strong preference for males. One of my graduate students, from Iraq, tells me that in his country the displeasure over the birth of girls may be reflected in the names they are given, such as Unwanted One and Allah's Displeasure. So strong is the preference for males in some cultures that when the family lacks a male child, the problem is solved by adoption. Only a male heir can say the prayers for the departed, and such prayers are necessary for salvation. In the United States, parents may prefer boys, in part because boys—and not girls—preserve the family name, in which there may be pride. Margaret Mead [2] believes most American parents would like a balanced family of boys and girls but probably prefer that the first born be a boy. If so, they would welcome control over the sex of the child, if it could be had.

Even so, there is considerably less demand for sex control than for birth control, and this difference in demand is reflected in the appreciably small effort which scientists are making in the field of sex control. A decade ago a promising advance in our knowledge in this field was provided by Newton Harvey with his discovery of the fact that the X and Y chromosomes differed in the size and density. It has long been favored theory that the sex of the child depends on these chromosomes, a combination of X's producing a female and a combination of X and Y a male. Since the female sex cell consists only of X chromosomes, the sex of the child is determined by the father, on the basis of chance, depending on whether an X or Y chromosome of the spermatazoa combines with the X chromosome of the ovum. Harvey's discovery of a difference in size and density of the X and Y chromosomes led him to speculate that the two types of spermatazoa might be separated by a special centrifuge, roughly in the way in which cream is separated from milk. I checked with Professor Harvey some years later and learned that he had not continued his interest in this problem but had turned his attentions to a very different field, luminescence. Professor Harvey has since died and recent word from his widow, who is also a scientist of note, is to the effect that neither he nor she ever did anything more with the problem of sex control.

Since Harvey's studies, the X chromosome has been found to be three times larger than Y. Thus the human female cell is about 4 percent greater than the male in chromosome volume.[3] The female cell has a substantially richer genetic capacity than the male, and one may speculate as to whether this contributes to the female's greater longevity. The fact that the female generally outlives the male is an important reason why there are many more widows than widowers, with serious consequences for family life.

Some work has gone forward in this field on the part of persons interested in animal husbandry, where the demand for sex control has an economic or pecuniary value and where there are no mores to worry about. Knowledge gained in connection with experimental animals often has value for human beings. A promising technique of separating X and Y sperms, reported since my inventory of 1950, involves electrical charge. The control of sex ratio in rabbits by electrophoresis is based on the fact that Y sperms will migrate to the cathode and X sperms to the anode with approximately 80 percent accuracy, as determined from the sex of offspring. This process requires artificial insemination.[4] The same researcher comments on the work of others in which the migration of human sperm was noted under electrophoresis, but without progeny testing, for obvious practical reasons. Another process of separating X and Y chromosomes is counter steaming centrifugation. Used with the spermatozoa of bulls, it has led to an alteration in bovine sex ratio, apparently resulting from the differential destruction of X-bearing sperm in the process of centrifugation.[5]

The most exciting new report regarding control of human sex is that of Dr. Landrum Shettles, Columbia Presbyterian Medical Center, New York. He has discriminated two morphologically distinct groups of human spermatazoa, about equal in number, using a phase-contrast microscope. The differences, which include a contrast of smaller rounded heads and larger oval ones, are clearly discernible in a color photograph in the citation given below.[6] Although it is not yet possible to assign X and Y status to the sperm groups and thus identify them for artificial insemination, this seems a likely development in the near future.

When the identification and separation of X and Y spermatazoa is accomplished, artificial insemination will have to be utilized if sex control is to be achieved. This will pose a problem for the mores. Artificial insemination, a rather simple technical process, is now employed without objection in certain cases of sterility. But considerable opposition to artificial insemination exists where donors are involved. The moral problems in sex control are different from those in insemination with donors, and it will take time to work them out. Developments in biological science are often ahead of the mores. The period during which the moral issues are raised, debated, and settled, may be a rather lengthy period. Lacking a specific societal directive, the scientists may take the matter into their own hands and utilize the new skills if they are convinced that these procedures contribute to the health and happiness of their patients. Doctors tend to take an instrumental rather than an ethical view of scientific advances. This probably accounts for the number of inseminations utilizing donors—a number thought to be considerable although no accurate figure is available.

A decade ago, beginnings had been made in the preservation of human spermatazoa by freezing. Possible developments here are in the nature of the case limited, but improvements have been made in the decade in the conditions of preservation which increase the percentage of viable cells. A decade ago, physicians reported that they had inseminated three women using stored spermatazoa. Now, the same physicians report 20 such cases and indicate that no genetic defects have been detected in any of the cases, nor any health problems which can be ascribed to the inseminations.[7]

The knowledge of how to store human male germ cells brings somewhat closer to realization the dreams of the eugenists—somewhat closer, but not much. Still lacking is the knowledge of how to collect and preserve ova, a much more difficult problem. Even more important, we still do not know much about human heredity, what traits are desirable, and how they are carried and transmitted. If all the technical knowledge were available, there would still remain the question whether men and women in a democratic society would look with favor on relinquishing individual control over the process of reproduction in the interest of eugenic ideals.

The eugenic ideal may be remote, but the knowledge of how to preserve male spermatazoa, presumably indefinitely, has some immediate societal utility. It proves a safeguard where the sterilization of the male is practiced, should the couple at a later date wish to have children. In a nuclear age it offers insurance against the effects of irradiation, particularly in the case of men whose work exposes them to special risk.

No review of the biochemistry of sex and reproduction is complete without reference to the sex hormones. A decade ago it was possible to report a substantial body of knowledge in this field. A great deal of success was reported in modifying the secondary sexual characteristics of males and females. The increase in knowledge in this field has continued although no major break-through seems to have occurred. Doctors now recommend that steroid support be given when the individual reaches the climacteric.[8] This is not a panacea but is often beneficial. The administration of androgenic steroid to aged men has resulted in some restoration of muscle tone.[9] Female sex hormones, given to a group of women 75 years old, led to improvements in intellectual functions.[10] In another group, oral androgen improved memory on some tests.[11] On the negative side, treating pregnant women with progestins led to harmful masculinizing effects on 18 female babies. The experimenters recommend that such treatment be abandoned.[12]

The relative lack of major developments in the area of sex hormones, at least so far as hormonal therapy or practical aspects are concerned, is not perhaps so much the result of diminished attention to the problems of this field as it is to a scientific impasse. If I may digress, such impasses are not uncommon in natural science where many workers may labor hard and long on a problem without much success until someone comes up with a serendipitous discovery which opens up new possibilities. The phenomenon of the impasse is not to be confused with the problem of discontinuity, which is also a common factor affecting the pace of discovery. There are discontinuities as well as impasses in natural science, as I have shown in connection with the problem of controlling the sex of the child. But it is my impression that impasses are more common than discontinuities in natural science, and that discontinuities are more common than impasses in sociology. I am very much impressed by the discontinuities in research in the field of the family. I am struck by the fact that since the pioneer work of Burgess–Cottrell and Burgess–Wallin, there have been, except for Burgess' own continuing work, no major follow-up studies; so far as I can determine, no one else but E. Lowell Kelly has administered prediction schedules and then followed them through to see the extent to which the test actually did predict marital adjustment. Much the same thing has happened to Winch's theory of complementary needs in mate selection; that is, little has been done with it since his research was published although it is a promising and intriguing theory. Why there should be so much discontinuity in sociological research compared to biological research is an interesting question.

The final area of biological research to be reassessed pertains to geriatrics. Anyone reviewing this field must be impressed by the prodigious growth of interest in it. The literature in the decade is voluminous, and the amount of resources committed is very large. It is estimated that in 1960 the expenditure of over 16 billion dollars was administered by the Federal Government alone in providing services and benefits for older people.[13] Most of the amount involves income maintenance programs (old-age and survivors insurance, retirement systems, veterans compensation, and the like), requiring 19 of every 20 dollars. Such services are not the concern of this paper, but the scope of the economic programs is an indication of the social demand. Expenditures for health and medical care in the United States in 1958–59 mounted to 25.2 billion dollars, of which less than 5 percent was spent for research.[14] The fact that there is available an estimate of 16 billion dollars as the amount administered by the Federal Government in behalf of older people in 1960 is interesting in itself, for on inquiry to the Children's Bureau and the Women's Bureau I learned that no comparable estimates have been made as to federal expenditures for children and women. On April 9, 1962 the Children's Bureau celebrated its fiftieth birthday. The Women's Bureau was established later, in 1920. There is at present no comparable autonomous, independent bureau for the aged, but bills have been introduced in Congress to establish one. The aged are riding the wave of the future. If Ellen Key was right in calling the first half of the twentieth century the Children's Century, it may turn out to be appropriate to call the second half the Century of the Aged.

Why the increased accent on the health needs of the aged? For one thing, they constitute an increased proportion of our population. In 1940, there were 9 million persons in the United States 65 years old and over, comprising 6.9 percent of the total population. In 1960, the number exceeded 16.5 million, or 9.2 percent of the total. Incidentally, the average age of the aged population has increased. So also has the percentage of women among the aged, the figure being 55 in 1960. More important from the standpoint of political influence, the aged as a proportion of the voting population (21 years old and over) has increased from 10.7 in 1940 to 15.4 in 1960. This is a significant point when considering the shift in national interest from children to old people, for the aged are voters and the children are not.

Also affecting the shift in demand is the fact that the medical needs of the aged are paramount. The diseases of old age are many but the principal ones are the so-called degenerative diseases, mainly cancer, degeneration of the blood vessels, arthritis, and nervous and mental disorders. There are 900,000 deaths a year in the United States caused by cardiovascular disease; 260,000 deaths from cancer. Arthritis and rheumatism afflict 11 million, including an estimated 97 percent of persons over 60.[15] It is difficult, of course, to delimit the diseases of old age, for they extend downward into the earlier years and even into childhood.

The progress in the last decade in dealing with degenerative diseases has not been so impressive. There have been biological-medical advances pertaining to all stages of the life span, but the most notable progress has been made in coping with infections and nutritional disorders, having the greatest impact on the earlier years of life. Some saving of life of cancer patients has resulted from early detection and treatment, but there has not been a major break-through in the last decade comparable to the conquest of poliomyelitis. An extraordinarily comprehensive study of six years' duration has demonstrated that blood lipid elevation does precede heart attacks rather than the reverse. The association between serum cholesterol and the incidence of arterosclerosis has thus been established. But whether diet is a factor in control has not been established and is a medical policy taken on faith.[16] As to the third major disease of old age, steroid drugs reduce the pain of rheumatoid arthritis but offer no cure.

Although the biological gains in terms of specific cures have not been spectacular in the decade, the progress in other terms is not inconsiderable. For one thing, in general old people today are in better health than in the immediate past, which means they are more capable of being useful and are not so long an economic burden.[17] For another thing, the progress that is occurring in the biochemistry of man is at a basic, theoretical level which may not pay off in control immediately, or very soon, but offers great prospect for success in the future. The greatest achievement in scientific medicine in 1959 is said to have been made in the chemistry of genetics, pertaining to such discoveries as the synthesis of DNA and RNA.[18] DNA is the substance that controls vital activities in all living cells. It is found in the nuclei of cells and acts as a blueprint for making enzymes and other proteins. The DNA molecule consists of two long strands of atoms twisted together, resembling a spiral staircase. Between the strands, like steps in a staircase, are hundreds of smaller groups called bases. Only four types of bases have been found and their particular arrangement along the DNA molecule is believed to be the code containing the information on heredity. When a cell divides, DNA is duplicated so that both new cells receive a complete "set of instructions." [19] For the first time, in 1960, the exact spot affected by a mutation, or change in heredity, was pinpointed. The discovery was made in the tobacco mosaic virus, and the mutations were identified as tiny loops in molecules of DNA.[20]

The growing knowledge of the chemistry of the DNA, and the knowledge of the location of the genes that are involved in inherited disease combine to give an optimistic picture of the future of research in human heredity. With our current interest in man's chromosomes, mutations, and genes, a leading student of medical genetics has predicted that progress in that field will occur at a much faster rate than that at which the medicine of communicable diseases has advanced. To reach our present position in preventive medicine where so many diseases are virtually controlled, it has taken about one hundred years. According to Professor Kloepfer, it will take much less time before we reach a comparable position in the control of genetic disease.[21]

To conclude, our review of developments in the biochemistry of man during approximately the last decade shows great progress in birth control, promising although much slower achievement in sex control, an intermediate degree of control of sex characteristics via hormonal therapy and of the biological problems of aging. In all these fields, there is no major problem of opposition from the mores; rather, American society is favorable to most biological research. The uneven progress in the several areas is partly the result of uneven difficulty in coping with the problems involved and partly the result of uneven demand. The simplest scientific problem is that of birth control; somewhat more difficult from a theoretical standpoint is the problem of the control of the sex of the child; and much more complex are the problems of the control of aging and of sexual characteristics. As to social demand, that for control over the process of aging is probably greatest; that for an improved contraceptive is considerable; that for increased control over sex characteristics is less; and that for control over the sex of the child is least. The greatest control, then, has been achieved in contraception where the scientific problems are the simplest and the demand is great. For the long pull, however, the greater promise lies in fundamental research. It is intriguing to speculate upon what another review a decade hence may show as to the nature of the living cell and the location of the genes which control the constitution of man.

NOTES

1. M. F. Nimkoff, "Biological Discoveries and the Future of the Family," *American Journal of Sociology,* 58 (1951), pp. 20–26. Presidential Address, Eastern Sociological Society, Boston, April 22, 1950.
2. *Male and Female* (New York: William Morrow, 1949), p. 264.
3. J. H. Tjio and T. T. Puck, "The Somatic Chromosomes of Man," *Proceedings of the National Academy of Sciences* (December 1958), p. 1229.
4. M. J. Gordon, "Control of Sex Ratio in Rabbits by Electrophoresis of Spermatazoa," *Proceedings of the National Academy of Sciences,* 43 (1957), pp. 913–918.
5. P. E. Lindahl, "Separation of Bull Spermatazoa Carrying X- and Y-Chromosomes by Counter Steaming Centrifugation," *Nature,* 181 (1958) p. 784.
6. Robert Demarest, "Sperm Shape and Sex of Offspring," *What's New* (a trade journal of Abbott Laboratories, North Chicago, Illinois), number 225 (August–September 1961), pp. 2–3.
7. In correspondence of the writer with R. G. Bune, M.D., University Hospitals, University of Iowa, November 27, 1961.
8. William H. Masters (Washington U. School of Medicine, St. Louis, Mo.) and John W. Ballew, "The Third Sex," *Geriatrics,* 10 (1955), pp. 1–4.
9. The work of Dr. Gregory Pincus, Worcester Foundation for Experimental Biology, Shrewsbury, Mass., reported in *Science News Letter* (January 9, 1960), p. 19.
10. Bettye McDonald Caldwell, "An Evaluation of Psychological Effects of Sex Hormone Administration in Aged Women. II: Results of Therapy after Eighteen Months," *Journal of Gerontology,* 9 (1954), pp. 168–174.
11. V. A. Kral and B. T. Wigdor, "Androgen Effect on Senescent Memory Function," *Geriatrics,* 14 (July 1959), pp. 450–456.
12. Melvin M. Grumbach, Jacques R. Ducharme, and Ralph E. Moloshok,

"On the Fetal Masculinizing Action of Certain Oral Progestins," *Journal of Clinical Endocrinology & Metabolism,* 19 (11), pp. 1369–1380.

13. *Programs for Older People* (1960 Report to the President, Federal Council on Aging), p. 67.
14. Union Calendar No. 103. 87th Congress, 1st session. House Report no. 321, pp. 2–3.
15. *Research in Gerontology: Biological and Medical.* Reports and Guidelines from the White House Conference on Aging. Series Number 10. U. S. Department of Health, Education, and Welfare, Special Staff on Aging, Washington 25, D. C., August, 1961, p. 119.
16. *Ibid.,* p. 30, p. 90.
17. *Ibid.,* p. 20.
18. *Science News Letter* (January 16, 1960), p. 38.
19. *Science News Letter* (April 30, 1960).
20. *Science News Letter* (December 17, 1960), p. 407.
21. Dr. H. Warner Kloepfer, Professor of Medical Genetics, Tulane University Medical School, reported in *Science News Letter* (June 27, 1959), p. 403.

2 9

Thoughts on the Future of the Family

by Barrington Moore, Jr.

Among social scientists today it is almost axiomatic that the family is a universally necessary social institution and will remain such through any foreseeable future. Changes in its structure, to be sure, receive wide recognition. The major theme, however, in the appraisal American sociologists present is that the family is making up for lost economic functions by providing better emotional service. One work announces as its central thesis that "the family in historical times has been, and at present is, in transition from an institution to a companionship." In the past, the authors explain, the forces holding the family together were external, formal, and authoritarian, such as law, public opinion, and the authority of the father. Now, it is claimed, unity inheres in the mutual affection and comradeship of its members.[1] Another recent work by a leading American sociologist makes a simi-

Reprinted by permission of the author, Barrington Moore, Jr., *Political Power and Social Theory* (Cambridge, Mass.: Harvard University Press, copyright, 1958), pp. 160–178, by the President and Fellows of Harvard College.

lar point. The trend under industrialism, we are told, does not constitute a decline of the family as such, but mainly a decline of its importance in the performance of economic functions. Meanwhile, the
author tells us, the family has become a more specialized agency for
the performance of other functions, namely, the socialization of children and the stabilization of adult personalities. For this reason, the
author continues, social arrangements corresponding rather closely to
the modern family may be expected to remain with us indefinitely.[2]

In reading these and similar statements by American sociologists
about other aspects of American society, I have the uncomfortable
feeling that the authors, despite all their elaborate theories and technical research devices, are doing little more than projecting certain
middle-class hopes and ideals onto a refractory reality. If they just
looked a little more carefully at what was going on around them, I
think they might come to different conclusions. This is, of course, a
very difficult point to prove, though C. Wright Mills, in a brilliant essay, has shown how one area of American sociology, the study of
crime, is suffused with such preconceptions.[3] While personal observations have some value, one can always argue that a single observer is
biased. Here all I propose to do, therefore, is to raise certain questions
about the current sociological assessment of the family on the basis of
such evidence as has come my way rather casually. In addition, I
should like to set this evidence in the framework of an intellectual
tradition, represented, so far as the family is concerned, by Bertrand
Russell's *Marriage and Morals,* that sees the family in an evolutionary
perspective,[4] and raises the possibility that it may be an obsolete institution or become one before long. I would suggest then that conditions have arisen which, in many cases, prevent the family from
performing the social and psychological functions ascribed to it by modern sociologists. The same conditions may also make it possible for
the advanced industrial societies of the world to do away with the
family and substitute other social arrangements that impose fewer unnecessary and painful restrictions on humanity. Whether or not society
actually would take advantage of such an opportunity is, of course,
another question.

It may be best to begin with one observation that is not in itself
conclusive but at least opens the door to considering these possibilities.
In discussions of the family, one frequently encounters the argument
that Soviet experience demonstrates the necessity of this institution in
modern society. The Soviets, so the argument runs, were compelled
to adopt the family as a device to carry part of the burden of making

Soviet citizens, especially after they perceived the undesirable consequences of savage homeless children, largely the outcome of the Civil War. This explanation is probably an accurate one as far as it goes. But it needs to be filled out by at least two further considerations that greatly reduce its force as a general argument. In the first place, the Soviets, I think, adopted their conservative policy toward the family *faute de mieux*. That is to say, with their very limited resources, and with other more pressing objectives, they had no genuine alternatives. Steel mills had to be built before crèches, or at least before crèches on a large enough scale to make any real difference in regard to child care. In the meantime the services of the family, and especially of grandma (*babushka*), had to be called upon. In the second place, with the consolidation of the regime in the middle thirties, Soviet totalitarianism may have succeeded in capturing the family and subverting this institution to its own uses. At any rate the confidence and vigor with which the regime supported this institution from the early thirties onward suggests such an explanation. Thus the Soviet experience does not constitute by itself very strong evidence in favor of the "functional necessity" of the family.

If the Soviet case does not dispose of the possibility that the family may be obsolete, we may examine other considerations with greater confidence, and begin by widening our historical perspective. By now it is a familiar observation that the stricter Puritan ethics of productive work and productive sex have accomplished their historical purposes in the more advanced sections of the Western world. These developments have rendered other earlier elements of Western culture and society, such as slavery, quite obsolete, and constitute at least prima facie evidence for a similar argument concerning the family. Let us ask then to what extent may we regard the family as a repressive survival under the conditions of an advanced technology? And to what extent does the modern family perform the function of making human beings out of babies and small children either badly or not at all?

One of the most obviously obsolete features of the family is the obligation to give affection as a duty to a particular set of persons on account of the accident of birth. This is a true relic of barbarism. It is a survival from human prehistory, when kinship was the basic form of social organization. In early times it was expedient to organize the division of labor and affection in human society through real or imagined kinship bonds. As civilization became technically more advanced, there has been less and less of a tendency to allocate both labor and affection according to slots in a kinship system, and an increasing

tendency to award them on the basis of the actual qualities and capacities that the individual possesses.

Popular consciousness is at least dimly aware of the barbaric nature
of the duty of family affection and the pain it produces, as shown by
the familiar remark, "You can choose your friends, but you can't
choose your relatives." Even if partly concealed by ethical imperatives
with the weight of age-old traditions, the strain is nevertheless real and
visible. Children are often a burden to their parents. One absolutely
un-Bohemian couple I know agreed in the privacy of their own home
that if people ever talked to each other openly about the sufferings
brought on by raising a family today, the birth rate would drop to
zero. It is, of course, legitimate to wonder how widespread such sentiments are. But this couple is in no sense "abnormal." Furthermore, a
revealing remark like this made to a friend is worth more as evidence
than reams of scientific questionnaires subjected to elaborate statistical
analyses. Again, how many young couples, harassed by the problems
of getting started in life, have not wished that their parents could be
quietly and cheaply taken care of in some institution for the aged?
Such facts are readily accessible to anyone who listens to the conversa-
tions in his own home or among the neighbors.

The exploitation of socially sanctioned demands for gratitude, when
the existing social situation no longer generates any genuine feeling of
warmth, is a subtle and heavily tabooed result of this barbaric heritage.
It is also one of the most painful. Perhaps no feeling is more excruciat-
ing than the feeling that we ought to love a person whom we actually
detest. The Greek tragedians knew about the problem, but veiled it
under religion and mythology, perhaps because the men and women of
that time felt there was no escape. In the nineteenth century the theme
again became a dominant one in European literature, but with the
clear implication that the situation was unnecessary. Even these authors, Tolstoi, Samuel Butler, Strindberg, and Ibsen, in exposing the
horrors and hypocrisies of family life, wove most of their stories
around the marital relationship, where there is an element of free
choice in the partner selected. Kafka's little gem, *Das Urteil,* is a significant exception. With magnificent insight into the tragedy on both
sides, it treats the frustrations of a grown-up son forced to cherish a
helpless but domineering father. Henry James' short story, *Europe,* is
an effective treatment of the same relationship between a mother and
her daughters. Despite some blind spots and limitations, the artists, it
appears, have seen vital aspects of the family that have largely escaped
the sociologists.

In addition to these obsolete and barbaric features one can point to certain trends in modern society that have sharply reduced rather than increased the effectiveness of the home as an agency for bringing up children. In former times the family was a visibly coherent economic unit, as well as the group that served to produce and raise legitimate children. The father had definite and visible economic tasks, before the household became separated from the place of work. When the children could see what he did, the father had a role to be copied and envied. The source and justification of his authority was clear. Internal conflicts had to be resolved. This is much less the case now.

It is reasonably plain that today's children are much less willing than those of pre-industrial society to take their parents as models for conduct. Today they take them from the mass media and from gangs. Radio and television heroes, with their copies among neighborhood gangs, now play a vital part in the socialization process. Parents have an uphill and none too successful struggle against these sources. Like adult mobs, children's groups readily adopt the sensational, the cruel, and the most easily understood for their models and standards. These influences then corrupt and lower adult standards, as parents become increasingly afraid to assert their own authority for fear of turning out "maladjusted" children.*

The mass media have largely succeeded in battering down the walls of the social cell the family once constituted in the larger structure of society. Privacy has greatly diminished. Newspapers, radios, and television have very largely destroyed the flow of private communications within the family that were once the basis of socialization. Even meals are now much less of a family affair. Small children are frequently plumped down in front of the television set with their supper on a tray before them to keep them quiet. Since the family does less as a unit, genuine emotional ties among its members do not spring up so readily.[5] The advertising campaign for "togetherness" provides rather concrete evidence that family members would rather not be together.

The mother, at least in American society, is generally supposed to be the homemaker and the center of the family. Has she been able to take up the slack produced by the change in the father's role? Is she,

* It is sometimes claimed that the modern family still represents a bulwark against mass and totalitarian pressures. No doubt this is true in the best cases, those few where parents are still able to combine authority and affection. These are, however, mainly a relic of Victorian times. By and large it seems more likely that the family constitutes the "transmission belt" through which totalitarian pressures toward conformity are transmitted to the parents through the influence of the children.

perhaps, the happy person whose face smiles at us from every advertisement and whose arts justify the sociologists' case? A more accurate assessment may be that the wife suffers most in the modern middle-class family, because the demands our culture puts upon her are impossible to meet. As indicated by advertisements, fiction, and even the theories of sociologists, the wife is expected to be companion, confidante, and ever youthful mistress of her husband.

If the demands could be met, many wives might feel very happy in this fulfillment of their personality. The actual situation is very different. The father is out of the house all day and therefore can be neither overlord nor companion. With the father absent, radio and television provide the mother with a watery substitute for adult companionship. A young colleague told me recently that his wife leaves the radio on all day merely to hear the sound of a grown-up voice. The continual chatter of little children can be profoundly irritating, even to a naturally affectionate person. The absence of servants from nearly all American middle-class households brings the wife face to face with the brutalizing features of motherhood and housework. If she had the mentality of a peasant, she might be able to cope with them more easily. Then, however, she could not fulfill the decorative functions her husband expects. As it is now, diapers, dishes, and the state of the baby's bowels absorb the day's quota of energy. There is scarcely any strength left for sharing emotions and experiences with the husband, for which there is often no opportunity until the late hours of the evening. It is hardly a wonder that the psychiatrists' anterooms are crowded, or that both husband and wife seek escapes from psychological and sexual boredom, the cabin fever of the modern family. For the wife, either a job or an affair may serve equally well as a release from domesticity.

A further sign of the modern family's inadequacy in stabilizing the human personality may be seen in the troubled times of adolescence. This stage of growing up has been interpreted as a rejection of adult standards of responsibility and work by youngsters who are about to enter adult life. It seems to me that this period is more significantly one of pseudo-rebellion, when the youngsters copy what they see to be the real values of adult life instead of the professed ones. Even in the more extreme forms of youthful rebellion, relatively rare among respectable middle-class children, such as roaring around in noisy cars to drinking and seduction parties, the adolescents are aping actual adult behavior. Adolescents then do things they know many grown-ups do when the latter think they are escaping the observant eyes of the young.

A "hot-rod" is, after all, nothing but an immature Cadillac. Where the Cadillac is the symbol of success, what else could be expected? Adult standards too are made tolerable through commercialized eroticism that lures us on to greater efforts and greater consumption from every billboard and magazine cover. Thus the whole miasma of sexual and psychological boredom in the older generation, pseudo-rebellion and brutality in the younger one, is covered over by a sentimental and suggestive genre art based on commercial sentiment.

No doubt many will think that these lines paint too black a picture. Statistics could perhaps be accumulated to show that families such as the type sketched here are far from a representative cross-section of American middle-class life. Such facts, however, would not be relevant to the argument. As pointed out elsewhere in these essays, the representative character of certain types of social behavior is not necessarily relevant to estimates of current and future trends. This kind of statistical defense of the status quo represents that of a certain maiden's virtue by the claim, "After all, she is only a little bit pregnant."

To refute the appraisal offered in these pages it would be necessary to demonstrate that they misrepresent basic structural trends in the family in advanced industrial countries. The most important argument of this type that I have encountered asserts that the proportion of married people in the population has steadily risen while the proportion of single individuals has steadily dropped. Therefore, people obviously prefer family life to bachelorhood, and the gloomy picture sketched above must be nothing more than vaporings of sour-bellied intellectuals thrown on the dumpheap by the advance of American society.

Before discussing the question further, let us look at some of the relevant facts. The table below shows changes in the proportions of single, married, and divorced persons in the United States from the age of fourteen onward. The source, an authoritative and very recent statistical survey of the American family, has standardized the proportions for age, using the 1940 age distribution as a standard, in order to eliminate changes due merely to shifts in the age composition of our population, which would merely confuse the issue.[6]

The figures do show a rise in the proportion of married persons and a decline in the proportion of single ones. They also show that the proportion of married persons is overwhelmingly larger than the number of divorced ones. But the biggest change has been in the proportion of divorced people. For men it has risen ninefold since 1890 and for women more than fivefold. A bigger proportion of people are

Percentage Distribution of Persons 14 Years and over by Marital Status and Sex in the Civilian Population 1890–1954

	Male			Female		
YEAR	SINGLE	MARRIED	DIVORCED	SINGLE	MARRIED	DIVORCED
1954	28.4	66.7	1.8	22	65.8	2.2
1950	29.4	65.5	1.5	22.5	64.8	2.1
1940	34.8	59.7	1.2	27.6	59.5	1.6
1930	34.7	59.1	1.1	26.9	59.7	1.3
1890	36.7	57.9	0.2	27.8	57.7	0.4

married now than in 1890, but a *much* bigger proportion have abandoned the marital state. In the long run, the latter change might turn out to be the more important one.

Even the statistical evidence, in other words, does not uphold in a completely unambiguous manner the sociologists' argument for the family. Sometimes an attempt to save the case is made by interpreting the rise in divorce as something that allows greater freedom for the individual to choose marital partners on the basis of congeniality. Thereby divorce allegedly strengthens the family's function as a source of emotional support.[7] By talking about greater freedom for the individual in this fashion one has already taken a long step toward the opponents' view that marriage as such may be superfluous.

The point cannot be considered merely in the light of the facts as they exist now or have existed in the past. To do this in social questions is basically unscientific. Those who dismiss negative appraisals of the family with the crude observation that they reflect personal bias or mere "European decadence" deserve an equally crude reply: "So what if Americans prefer to get married! That simply shows how stupid they are."

Acrimony here unfortunately conceals a genuine issue. It is perfectly possible that conditions exist, perhaps even now, that permit better institutional arrangements than most people would be willing to accept. The word better, of course, implies a definite standard of judgment. One can debate such standards endlessly, and perhaps cannot reach agreement without at some point making arbitrary assumptions. I shall not enter this debate here except to say that any social institution is a bad one that imposes more suffering on people than is necessary when they have sufficient material resources and scientific knowledge to do away with this suffering. This standard, anthropologists tell us, is that not only of Western culture, but of all culture.[8]

What then are the prospects for the future? We need not take a completely determinist view. Indeed, the perceptions that both plain people and opinion makers have about the present enter in as a significant component among the forces shaping the future and thereby provide an entering wedge for rational adaptation.

Among those who accept a substantial part of the preceding image of the family as basically correct, one frequently hears the prescription that what American culture really needs is a higher evaluation of the social role of the housewife and of motherhood. The trouble with this prescription, I would suggest, is that it merely increases the element of self-deception already so prevalent in our culture. Under present conditions motherhood *is* frequently a degrading experience. There is nothing to be gained by concealing the facts in the manner of an advertising campaign designed to raise the prestige of a particular occupation. We would not think of trying to eliminate the hazards of coal mining in this way. Why should we try to do it with motherhood? If it is true that under present circumstances the experience of motherhood narrows and cramps the personality rather than promotes the development of its capacities, some other way will have to be found if it is to be a real solution.

The trend towards a continually more efficient technology and greater specialization, which dominates the rest of our culture, may conceivably provide an answer. In regard to the division of labor it is important to recall one widely known but neglected fact. In the past, whenever human beings have acquired sufficient resources and power, as among aristocracies, they have put the burden of child-rearing on other shoulders. Twenty years ago Ralph Linton pointed out that "aristocrats the world over . . . are reluctant to take care of their own children. Anyone who has had to take care of two or three infants simultaneously will understand why. This arduous business is turned over to slaves or servants. . . ."[9]

Since the decline of slavery, a basic trend in European society has been to transfer to machines more and more tasks formerly carried out by slaves. By and large, this change has been accompanied by the growth of large organizations to perform tasks formerly scattered among many small groups. This trend may well affect the family. Specialized human agencies, developing from such contemporary forms as the crèche, play school, and boarding school, might assume a much larger share of the burden of child rearing, a task that could in any case be greatly lightened by machinery for feeding and the removal of waste products. Can one sensibly argue that the technical ingenuity and resources required to solve this problem are greater than those necessary for nuclear warfare? Are we to regard as permanent and "natural" a civilization that develops its most advanced technology for killing people and leaves their replacement to the methods of the Stone Age?

Against this viewpoint it is usually argued that human infants require some minimum of human affection, even fondling, if they are to survive, and that therefore some form of the family is bound to remain. The premises may be correct, but the conclusion does not follow. A nurse can perform these tasks of giving affection and early socialization just as well as the parents, often better. The argument does not prove anything therefore about the inevitable necessity of the family.

At the same time this point of view does call attention to certain important problems. Industrial society is not likely to produce household nurses, or any form of "servant class" in abundance. On the other hand, as everyone knows who has been in a hospital, nurses in a bureaucratic setting have a strong tendency to treat persons under their care "by the book," without much regard for their individual tasks and requirements. This is a well-known trait of bureaucracy, which tends to treat people and situations alike in order to achieve precision and efficiency. Infants and small children on the contrary require individual attention. For some years they may need to feel that they are the center of the universe. How then can the characteristics of bureaucracy be brought in line with those of maternal affection?

Though this may be the most difficult problem facing any qualitative transformation of the family, it is not necessarily insoluble. In the first place, as Bertrand Russell points out, a good institutional environment may be better for the development of the human personality than a bad family one.[10] In the second place, an increase in the resources allocated to a bureaucratic organization can greatly increase its flexibility and capacity to satisfy variations in individual temperament. Any first-class hotel knows how to cope with this problem. In a few of the best ones in Europe the guest can have privacy and the illusion of being the center of the universe. Finally, one might legitimately expect that the persons who are drawn to serve in any such child-rearing institutions of the future would have more than the average amount of fondness for children, as well as general human warmth and kindliness. Under proper circumstances and management such institutions could give full scope to these benevolent sentiments.

Certain other considerations suggest an alternative that has at least the merit of being much more palatable to the vast majority of people today, since it is more in line with our deep-rooted cultural traditions. These considerations are essentially two. One is the possibility of some innate biological trait roughly resembling the "maternal instinct." The other lies in technological developments that might allow for wider dissemination of machinery to lighten household tasks and to take over the more routine aspects of child rearing. The dish-washing machine, laundromat, and, as a much more extreme device, the "Skinner box" represent prototypes of this technological development that could strengthen decentralized arrangements for rearing children.

I do not know what students of human physiology now believe about the maternal instinct. Common observation is enough to show that it cannot be an instinct like sex or hunger. There are many women who never become fond of children, or who soon cease to be fond of them. For them the institutional outlet just sketched would be the most satisfactory way of providing for their offspring. But for others, possibly the majority, the gestation period with its trials and burdens may be enough to create in the mother a desire to retain the infant under her care, after which she could become reluctant to give it up. If machinery were available to lighten child-rearing and household tasks on a far wider scale than is now the case, mothers might be able to satisfy the more positive desires of motherhood. One that seems to be quite important in the middle class is the desire to mold the child according to some ideal image, though it is now contradicted by fears of damaging the child that derive from superficial popularizations of Freud.

For the home to become again the place where human beings take the first important steps toward realizing their creative potentialities, parents would have to become willing once more to assert their authority. In turn this authority would have to acquire a rational and objective basis, freed of current attempts to revive religious taboos. Thus there would have to be a philosophical as well as a social revolution whose implications we cannot here pursue. One aspect, nevertheless, deserves to be stressed. Rational arguments can be given only to persons competent to understand them. For obvious reasons children are not able to absorb all rational arguments at once, though the present system of education undoubtedly postpones the development of this faculty where it does not destroy it altogether. Therefore parents will have to learn not to be afraid of saying to a child, "You are not old enough yet to understand why you have to do this. But you must do it anyway." The "progressive" family, where every decision turns into an incoherent and rancorous debate, actually contributes to reactionary tendencies in society by failing to equip the next generation with adequate standards of judgment.

There are, however, some grounds for doubting that this conservative solution will eventually prevail as the dominant one. The disappearance of the wider economic functions of the family would make it very difficult, and probably impossible, to restore the emotional atmosphere of a cooperative group in which the father has a respected authority. Furthermore, the bureaucratic division of labor has proved the most effective way of solving recurring and routine problems in other areas of life. Though a considerable part of the task of raising children is not routine, a very great portion is repetitive. For these reasons one may expect that semi-bureaucratic arrangements will continue to encroach on the traditional structure of the family. No doubt many individual variations, combinations, and compromises will remain for some time to come. Yet one fine day human society may realize that the part-time family, already a prominent part of our social landscape, has undergone a qualitative transformation into a system of mechanized and bureaucratized child rearing, cleansed of the standardized overtones these words now imply. As already pointed out, an institutional environment can be warm and supporting, often warmer than a family torn by obligations its members resent.

Such a state of affairs, if it comes at all, is well over the visible horizon now. Quite possibly it may never come at all. If it does come, there is not the slightest guarantee that it will solve all personal problems and land us in a state of air-conditioned euphoria. Values that many people hold high today may go by the board, such as the affection older couples show for one another who have shared the same pains in life until they have grown but a single scar. It is also possible that a world of reduced family burdens might be one of shallow and fleeting erotic intrigues, based really on commercial interests.[11] Hollywood could conceivably be the ugly prototype of such a future world, especially in its earlier transitional phases. The most that might be claimed by any future apologist for such institutions, if they ever come to pass, is that they gave greater scope to the development of the creative aspects of the human personality than did the family, which had begun to damage rather than develop this personality under advancing industrialism. And the most that can be claimed for the arguments supporting this possibility is that they correspond to some important trends visible in the family itself as well as in the rest of society. Nevertheless, it would appear that the burden of proof falls on those who maintain that the family is a social institution whose fate will differ in its essentials from that which has befallen all the others.

NOTES

1. Ernest W. Burgess and Harvey J. Locke, *The Family* (2nd ed.; New York, 1953), p. vii. Though this work bears the earmarks of a college text, it is nevertheless authoritative. Burgess is one of the best known American students of the family.
2. Talcott Parsons, Robert F. Bales, et al., *The Family: Socialization and Interaction Process* (Glencoe, 1955), pp. 9–10, 16–19. In an earlier work, *The Social System* (Glencoe, 1951), p. 156, Parsons raises the possibility of the breakup of the family, mainly to indicate how improbable such an eventuality seems.
3. "Professional Ideology of Social Pathologists," *American Journal of Sociology*, vol. XLIX, No. 2 (September 1943), 165–180.
4. New York, 1929.
5. Compare George C. Homans, *The Human Group* (New York, 1950), pp. 444, 450.
6. The figures used in the accompanying table were adapted from the table in Paul C. Glick, *American Families* (New York, 1957), p. 104.
7. Compare Parsons, *The Family*, pp. 24–25.
8. "No culture places a value upon suffering as an end in itself; as a means to the ends of the society (punishment, discipline, etc.), yes; as a means to the ends of the individual (purification, mystical exaltation, etc.), yes; but of and for itself, never." A. L. Kroeber and Clyde Kluckhohn, "Culture: A Critical Review of Concepts and Definitions," *Papers of the Peabody Museum of American Archaeology and Ethnology*, vol. XLVII, No. 1 (1952), 177.
9. Ralph Linton, *The Study of Man* (New York, 1936), p. 246.
10. *Marriage and Morals*, p. 169. For Russell's qualifications see pp. 219–220.
11. For some suggestive counter arguments to this view, see Herbert Marcuse, *Eros and Civilization* (Boston, 1955), pp. 201–202.

PART IV

Epilogue

A Note on Theory and Familial Change

With the passage of time and the inestimable benefit of hindsight, one can readily see from the diverse conclusions contained in the foregoing selections that, even when the same datum is under inspection, considerable disagreement exists among social scientists regarding the causative factors and effects of change as they apply to the family. In the laboratory of time, many of the predictions presented in these selections will likely prove to be inaccurate. Perhaps, as with some of the predictions concerning the American family of the 1930's and 1940's, a few of these will appear as egregious in retrospect. Others, particularly those dealing with the structural properties of the family, have set forth predictions of such a general nature that it may be difficult to assess their plausibility. Some studies, in their prognostication of future alterations, are of an open-end character, lacking in the specification of a time interval for which their predictions hold. Still other predictions included here are of such a nature as to be correct merely by definition. Amid this diversity of theoretical deficiencies, however, many of these analyses of familial change clearly point up various probable alternative courses of change. Some even are clearly speculative, suggesting the range of possible alterations. And although speculation does not constitute theory, speculation often contributes to its inception.

The continuous effort to perceive orderly relationships in the constantly changing and sometimes chaotic situation of family life, as in many other areas of sociological concern, is frequently a complex and intricate scientific task. Neither the ability to predict nor the effort to control events is an easy endeavor. But with increasing emphasis on planned change, it is imperative that our future prognoses contain less sheer speculation and more fruitful predictions. To this end, it seems appropriate to offer here not a critique of previous studies but some constructive, if elementary, suggestions for future analyses of familial change. We wish to discuss: the application of a concrete referent in our predictions, the precise use of the concept "time," the recognition of reciprocity between units of change, and the propagation of less global statements of relationships. Each of these represents an important consideration in the development of the study of familial change beyond the descriptive level of analysis. In considering these conceptual refinements, it is hoped that a more intense interest will be taken in the development of theories of family change. In this way, our knowledge of change can become cumulative, more comprehensible, and thus meet two of the prime functions of theoretical inquiry: codification and the guidance of our attention to linkages among discrete generalizations.

Throughout these readings frequent reference has been made to "the family" and the "American family." In using these terms as the referents of predictions, the intent has been to generalize to the broad spectrum of families comprising American society. As such, the concepts are highly abstract, obviously ignoring many significant differences among families. Yet a voluminous body of research in sociology reports significant differences in family patterns between certain social classes. Established upper-class and blue-collar families, for instance, differ markedly with respect to their structural composition as well as to their ideology, life chances, marital roles, and style of life. Given these conditions, both external and internal sources of change may differ and may have quite dissimilar consequences in each of these types of families. The abstract quality of the concept "American family" also obscures the fact that, of the families in the United States, not all units meet the definition of a nuclear family, a large proportion of them, especially among lower-class groups, being matrifocal in structure. In view of the scientist's concern with predicting and controlling events and our knowledge of the major similarities and dissimilarities among families, the power of our predictions undoubtedly would be improved by specifying a more concrete and less encompassing referent in our study of change.

A similar comment can be made concerning the use of the term "American family," given the diverse ethnic, racial, and religious composition of the society. Each of these social distinctions has important ramifications for the belief systems, values, and behavior patterns of various families. The introduction of a change element is likely, therefore, to affect families in different ways, depending on their ethnic, racial, and religious heritage. For instance, economic change and alterations in the conditions of work such as automation are more likely to affect and have a more profound impact on the Negro family than on others, altering the Negro family's structure and functions to a greater extent. With the advent of widespread automation and the accompanying increased need for technical, managerial, and professional talent, the position of the Negro male in the family, especially in the working class, may be further weakened. Similarly, changes in sexual norms will have a differential effect on Catholic, Protestant, and Jewish families. The trend toward more permissive standards of premarital behavior is likely to be more readily adopted by the Protestant and Jewish groups. With their generally more liberal stand on social and religious issues (highly orthodox adherents excepted), these groups will perhaps see the long-range consequences of premarital intercourse as less serious.

The concept of time is an intrinsic property of any type of change. Without time, there is no past, present, or future. The converse, of course, is equally true, for without discernible alterations there would be no conception of time. Also true is the fact that time in itself seldom gives rise to change, contrary to most popular adages and notions of social change. Time, as Wilbert E. Moore points out, is primarily static and may constitute a source of alterations only insofar as we divide it into discrete units and attempt to regulate our social activities and behavior accordingly.[1] If, for example, a large amount of activity and behavior are to occur within a short period of time, this may be perceived as tension producing and subsequently may give rise to some change in the relationships occurring during that short period. Thus, as the number of years devoted to child bearing becomes shorter, the socialization process is intensified; this may then lead to the possible interpretation of child rearing as being more problematic and the current preparation for parenthood less adequate than formerly.

Time as a concept enters into the analysis of familial change in yet another way. Primarily its use (or more precisely, its disuse), raises a methodological question. Many of our studies of family change, as noted earlier, fail to specify a time interval in their predictions. They are, in this sense, open ended and are extremely difficult to assess in terms of their efficacy as predictions. Given a sufficient passage of time, many such forecasts may hold. Without the specification of an interval of time, in other words, our predictions of familial change lack useful predictive power. They can become self-fulfilling merely through the passage of time. Some predictions of the future, on the other hand, will not hold due to the lack of a specified time interval if our future observations are made at one time and not another. This simply means that for any prediction of change to be meaningful, a distinction must be made between short-term and long-term altera-tions. An estimate of future marriage rates, for instance, may be advanced with considerable precision when the short term is our focus. Any estimation of alterations in this rate over the long run may be hazardous, at best. What is even more crucial, however, is that unless a time interval is set forth in such an estimate, it not only will be inadequate from a methodological point of view but in many cases it will be wrong.

Not only is the precise use of the concept of time uncommon in our forecasts of future alterations but it is perhaps one of the most neglected subjects of change. In the process of dividing time into distinct and separate units, our perception of time acquires a quali-tative as well as a quantitative aspect. Thus, time is perceived as "passing" slowly in some instances and quite rapidly in others. The nature of this perception can have numerous consequences for the social activities taking place within a time unit and hence can influence the view one has of the alterations occurring during that interval. On some occasions, then, there exists a reciprocal relationship between the perceived tempo of time (which is essentially static) and the actual changes in social relationships. To illustrate: If the family perceives time as passing rapidly, external alterations of any kind are likely to be interpreted as being rather profound and radical due to the rapidity involved. Compensatory changes in familial relationships —reactions to external alterations—also are likely to occur swiftly, primarily as a result of the perceived tempo and qualitative interpreta-tion of time.

With the historical background of the study of change in mind, it is less than startling to note that until recently, most sociological analyses have treated alterations as being unidirectional. Most familial changes have been viewed as resulting from external forces without any reciprocal alterations in external conditions following from the altered family situation. In one sense, such a view has the decided flavor of nineteenth-century evolutionary theory which posited that changes occur in a single direction. Earlier evolutionary theory characteristically dealt with changes as representing an upward trend or an "improvement," although there were exceptions to this view. It was, essentially, the tool of optimists. Many sociologists who have postulated a single-directional trend in changing-family structure, on the other hand, have been pessimists, and the label of "evolutionist" is apt to rest uneasily upon their shoulders.

From another point of view, unidirectionality is less a theoretical stance and more a one-sided perspective on the interrelationships between variables. Positing the unidirectionality of change suggests a limited. analysis of a chain of reciprocal interchanges. Often, of course, this limitation is necessitated by the complexity of the phenomena. One example is the complexity of the relationship between work and family variables. As some of the selections reprinted here point out, the structuring of work can have a dramatic influence on socialization techniques and spousal relations. But tracing the relationship in this direction far from exhausts the intricacy of the relationship. Yet the attempt to unravel this complex relationship imposes serious limitations on the researcher. The danger here lies in the tendency to construe unidirectional analysis as deterministic and as an exercise in reductionism. Thus, a number of studies of familial alterations have been interpreted, sometimes unfairly, as espousing economic or technological determinism because of their emphasis on the affect of economic and technological innovations on the family.

More contemporary studies have partially corrected this somewhat myopic type of analysis. Several of the selections contained in this volume, as we have seen, deal specifically with the affect the family group may have on the structuring of our economic institutions. But still other studies concerning reciprocity between the family and other institutions of society are needed: Studies dealing with the interchanges between the family and religion, education, and the political institution. It is only with a more comprehensive view than presently employed that studies of social alterations will contribute significantly to the development of theories of change.

The structural–functional model, while containing a number of assumptions inimical to the analysis of change, potentially can contribute a great deal to this endeavor. As Norman W. Bell and Ezra F. Vogel have illustrated, this model explicitly indicates the mutual exchanges that occur between various societal institutions.[2] Conceptualized in this manner, the nuclear family is seen as being linked in a series of interchanges with the economy, polity, community, and value system. Each of these systems contributes goods, services, leadership, or support to the family. In turn, the family contributes its labor, assets, loyalty, and acceptance. Though the specific interchange may vary considerably from one social situation to the next, the important fact is that a two-way process exists, and it is assumed that some degree of reciprocity must occur for the society to maintain a semblance of equilibrium. At times, when reciprocity is either partial or nonexistent, change is highly probable. For any analysis of familial change that uses the structural–functional model, the problem therefore becomes one of identifying the units involved and specifying the sources of imbalance in the equilibrium between the social systems concerned.

This model, to be sure, does not exhaust the possible modes of analysis that may be applied to the subject of change. One of the principal difficulties in its use is its assumptions about equilibrium and the tendency for social systems to return to steady states, free of discordant elements. However, it does lead researchers to look for the mutual contributions between the family and other systems and to discount the unidirectionality of social alterations. Although only an elementary step is taken in adopting this approach to the study of family change, it is a step far beyond that taken by most studies.

Essentially, more concrete and less global propositional statements of the if–then kind are needed. Increased exactitude in these if–then statements, moreover, is highly desirable. In other words, we need to know a great deal more about the specific connections between less abstract variables. To understand fully the changes in family stability, for example, we must have more knowledge about the factors contributing to divorce. We need data to test such hypotheses as: If tolerance for frustration is high, then the probability of divorce is low; and, if couples interact frequently with previously divorced persons, then the likelihood of their divorcing is increased. The plea for developing this highly specific type of analysis should not be construed as an abandonment of the attempt to study the larger configurations of change. It is equally important that a total view of the family system not be lost. In some manner, the fragments must be put together if our comprehension of familial change itself is not to be limited. The point is that most analysts of change have put the cart before the horse, directing so much attention to the total con-figuration of alterations in the family that we have tended to be somewhat neglectful of the more concrete and specific relationships involved.

It should also be noted, however, that an overemphasis on the if–then approach may have equally grave consequences. Confining our analyses to this level, in the short term at least, is a necessary building block in the development of theoretical perspectives. In the long run, how-ever, the outer limits become rather apparent, for, basically, if–then propositions are hypothetical in nature, pointing to certain outcomes under carefully assumed conditions and contingencies. Thus, we can predict what the average size of nuclear families is likely to be twenty years hence if trends *abc* continue under conditions *xyz* and *rst*. But, within the confines of a scientific orientation, one cannot predict with a high degree of accuracy what family size will be after two decades. This latter type of prediction, which more appropriately should be referred to as a forecast, embodies certain hunches, guesswork, and intuition—the necessary components of long-range predictions that are ultimately crucial to the study of change.

It would appear, therefore, that in the endeavor to develop more precise theoretical frameworks of change, the adoption of both ap-proaches is advisable. In the behavioral scientist's concern with pre-diction and control, both the if–then approach and the element of forecasting tend to coalesce. In the sociologist's view of the future, neither can exist independently of the other without the risk of stagnation. Future events and future alterations as they pertain to the family can be stipulated with considerable accuracy only if both approaches are employed.

Theory building, in whatever substantive area, is never free of ob-stacles, particularly when social phenomena are involved. Insofar as theory construction concerns social change, the task becomes even more complex. Faced with numerous variables and several existing theoretical pitfalls, the theoretician and the student of change are confronted with one of the more vexing problems in the behavioral sciences. Our task in this collection has been of less magnitude, for we have attempted only to present some of the representative works dealing with familial change. While few of the readings contained in this book have overtly addressed themselves to the task of theory development, collectively they have done so, at least implicitly. To-gether, the analyses, regardless of their intent, illustrate some of the pertinent variables to be considered in any formalized theory and the range of logical and methodological problems that may be encountered in this endeavor. If this task has been adequately accomplished, then an essential though basic step has been taken in the evolution toward the development of heuristically sound theories of change.

NOTES

1. Wilbert E. Moore, *Man, Time, and Society* (New York: Wiley, 1963).
2. Norman W. Bell and Ezra F. Vogel (eds.), *A Modern Introduction to the Family* (New York: Free Press, 1960), pp. 1–33.

Selected Readings on the Family and Change

One of the principal tasks in compiling a collection of readings is selecting the articles and excerpts to be included. Due to the exigencies of book publishing, it is usually necessary that the contents be highly selective. Many works of interest, therefore, are excluded here. The following list contains some other analyses the interested student will wish to explore. The criteria used for inclusion here are somewhat more catholic. The list contains works dealing with the family in other cultures, articles of some historical interest, and a few analyses of specific aspects of various family systems. All, of course, deal with the family in a context of change.

Abu-Lughod, Janet, and Lucy Amin. "Egyptian Marriage Advertisements: Microcosm of a Changing Society," *Marriage and Family Living,* Vol. 21 (May 1961), pp. 127–136.

Aldous, Joan. "Urbanization, the Extended Family, and Kinship Ties in West Africa," *Social Forces,* Vol. 41 (October 1962), pp. 6–12.

Anshen, Ruth N. "The Family in Transition," in Ruth N. Anshen (ed.), *The Family: Its Function and Destiny.* New York: Harper, 1959, pp. 3–19.

Bardis, Panos D. "The Changing Family in Modern Greece," *Sociology and Social Research,* Vol. 40 (September–October, 1955), pp. 19–23.

Beck, D. F. "The Changing Moslem Family in the Middle East," *Marriage and Family Living,* Vol. 19 (November 1957), pp. 340–347.

Burgess, Ernest W. "The Family in a Changing Society," *American Journal of Sociology,* Vol. 53 (May 1948), pp. 417–422.

Calhoun, Arthur W. *A Social History of the American Family.* New York: Barnes and Noble, 1960. Three volumes.

Folsom, Joseph K. "Changing Values in Sex and Family Relations," *American Sociological Review,* Vol. 2 (October 1937), pp. 717–726.

Foote, Nelson N. "New Roles for Men and Women," *Marriage and Family Living,* Vol. 23 (November 1961), pp. 325–327.

Goode, William J. *World Revolution and Family Patterns.* New York: Free Press, 1963.

Hill, Reuben. "The American Family: Problem or Solution," *American Journal of Sociology,* Vol. 53 (September 1947), pp. 125–130.

Hsi-En Chen, Theodore, and Wen-Hui C. Chen. "Changing Attitudes Toward Parents in Communist China," *Sociology and Social Research,* Vol. 43 (January–February 1959), pp. 174–182.

Kuhn, Manford. "American Families Today: Development and Differentiation of Types," in Howard Becker and Reuben Hill (eds.), *Family, Marriage and Parenthood.* Boston: Heath, 1955. Chapter 5.

Levy, Marion J., Jr. *The Family Revolution in Modern China.* Cambridge, Mass.: Harvard University Press, 1949.

Litwak, Eugene, "Occupational Mobility and Extended Family Cohesion," *American Sociological Review,* Vol. 25 (February 1960), pp. 9–20.

Nimkoff, Meyer. "Changing Family Relationships of Older People in the United States During the Last Fifty Years," *The Gerontologist,* Vol. 1 (June 1961), pp. 92–97.

Nottingham, Elizabeth K. "Toward An Analysis of the Effects of Two World Wars on the Role and Status of Middle-Class Women in the English-Speaking World," *American Sociological Review,* Vol. 12 (December 1947), pp. 666–675.

Ogburn, William F., and Meyer Nimkoff. *Technology and the Changing Family.* Boston: Houghton Mifflin, 1955.

Omari, Peter. "Changing Attitudes of Students in West African Society toward Marriage and Family Relationships," *British Journal of Sociology,* Vol. 11 (September 1960), pp. 197–211.

Parsons, Talcott, and Robert F. Bales. *Family, Socialization, and Interaction Process.* New York: Free Press, 1955.

Rodman, Hyman. "The Changing American Family," in Hyman Rodman (ed.), *Marriage, Family and Society: A Reader.* New York: Random House, 1965, pp. 249–258.

Schermerhorn, Richard. "Family Carry-overs of Western Christendom," in Howard Becker and Reuben Hill (eds.), *Family, Marriage and Parenthood.* Boston: Heath, 1955. Chapter 4.

Schlesinger, Benjamin. "The Changing Patterns in the Hindu Joint Family System of India," *Marriage and Family Living,* Vol. 13 (May 1961), pp. 170–175.

Sjoberg, Gideon. "Familial Organization in the Preindustrial City," *Marriage and Family Living,* Vol. 18 (February 1956), pp. 30–36.

Spiro, Melford E. *Children of the Kibbutz.* Cambridge, Mass.: Harvard University Press, 1958.

Sussman, Marvin B. "The Isolated Nuclear Family: Fact or Fiction?" *Social Problems,* Vol. 6 (Spring 1959), pp. 333–340.

Talmon, Garber J. "Social Change and Family Structure," *International Social Science Journal,* Vol. 14 (1962), pp. 468–488.

Tambiah, S. J. "Secularization of Family Values in Ceylon," *American Sociological Review,* Vol. 22 (June 1957), pp. 292–299.

Theodorson, George A. "Change and Traditionalism in the American Family," *Journal of Social Research,* Vol. 1 (1960), pp. 17–28.

Vogel, Ezra F. "The Democratization of Family Relations in Japanese Urban Society," *Asian Society,* Vol. 1 (June 1961), pp. 18–24.

Willmott, Peter, and M. Young. *Family and Class in a London Suburb.* London: Routledge and Kegan Paul, 1960.

Wolfenstein, Martha. "Trends in Infant Care," *American Journal of Orthopsychiatry,* Vol. 33 (1953), pp. 120–130.

Yang, C. K. *The Chinese Family in the Communist Revolution.* Cambridge, Mass: Technology Press, Massachusetts Institute of Technology, 1959.

Young, Michael, and P. Willmott. *Family and Kinship in East London.* New York: Free Press, 1957.

Zimmerman, Carle C. *Family and Civilization.* New York: Harper, 1947.

Index

About the Author

John N. Edwards was born in Eldorado, Illinois, in 1938. He received his B.A. degree from Park College, in Missouri, and served as assistant professor at the University of Nebraska, where he received his M.A. (1962) and his Ph.D. (1965). His areas of specialization include sociology of the family and urban sociology. Professor Edwards is a fellow of the National Institute of Mental Health and has published in the *Journal of Health and Social Behavior, Sociological Inquiry, Journal of Marriage and the Family,* and *The American Sociologist.* He is currently on the faculty at the University of Kentucky.

A Note on the Type

The text of this book was set on the Linotype in a face called TIMES ROMAN, designed by Stanley Morison for The Times (London), and first introduced by that newspaper in 1932.

Among typographers and designers of the twentieth century, Stanley Morison was a strong forming influence, as typographical advisor to the English Monotype Corporation, as a director of two distinguished English publishing houses, and as a writer of sensibility, erudition, and keen practical sense.

Manufactured in The United States of America by The Colonial Press Inc., Clinton, Massachusetts. Typography by Mary Ahern.